Apache Server 2.0:
A Beginner's Guide

ABOUT THE AUTHOR

Kate Wrightson has been running Apache on a small network for several years, and has experience working with Linux and UNIX. She is also the co-author of *WordPerfect Suite 2000 for Linux: The Official Guide* and *Corel Linux Starter Kit: The Official Guide*.

Apache Server 2.0:
A Beginner's Guide

KATE **WRIGHTSON**

Osborne/**McGraw-Hill**
New York Chicago San Francisco
Lisbon London Madrid Mexico City Milan
New Delhi San Juan Seoul Singapore Sydney Toronto

Osborne/**McGraw-Hill**
2600 Tenth Street
Berkeley, California 94710
U.S.A.

To arrange bulk purchase discounts for sales promotions, premiums, or fund-raisers, please contact Osborne/**McGraw-Hill** at the above address. For information on translations or book distributors outside the U.S.A., please see the International Contact Information page immediately following the index of this book.

Apache Server 2.0: A Beginner's Guide

1234567890 CUS CUS 01987654321

ISBN 0-07-219183-X

Publisher
    Brandon A. Nordin
Vice President & Associate Publisher
    Scott Rogers
Senior Acquisitions Editor
    Jane Brownlow
Senior Project Editor
    Carolyn Welch
Acquisitions Coordinator
    Emma Acker
Technical Editor
    Jon Robertson
Copy Editor
    Marcia Baker

Proofreader
    Linda Medoff
Indexer
    Jack Lewis
Computer Designers
    Elizabeth Jang
    Tabitha M. Cagan
Illustrators
    Michael Mueller
    Lyssa Wald
Series Design
    Peter F. Hancik

This book was composed with Corel VENTURA™ Publisher.

For Joe

AT A GLANCE

CONTENTS

Part IV

Beyond the Basics: Advanced Apache Topics

Part V

Security and Apache

Part VI

Appendices

ACKNOWLEDGMENTS

As with any book, the author gets her name on the cover, but only does part of the work. This project has been no exception, with a full team working on all aspects of the volume you now hold in your hands. This was my third book with Osborne/McGraw-Hill and, once again, they proved themselves to be one of the most author-oriented publishers in the business. Working with OMH, and with the members of this team, is always a pleasure:

- ▼ Jane Brownlow acquired the project and set it in motion.
- ■ Emma Acker coordinated all of us and kept everything on track.
- ■ Carolyn Welch managed the project (and me) with the greatest of poise, efficiency, and good cheer.
- ■ Marcia Baker edited raw text into readable prose.
- ▲ The OMH production department designed a lively and visually striking book.

Lisa Theobald, who shepherded my first two Osborne books through the maze, left O/M-H shortly after this book was signed and started. Although she is greatly missed, I hope we will work together in the future.

I especially want to thank Jon Robertson, technical editor of this book. Jon is a long-time friend and took on this project at my request, despite his other duties and preferred free-time activities. I'm sure he never wants to talk to me about MacOS X again, let alone httpd.conf.

As always, I owe this book and my ongoing career to David Fugate and the whole Waterside Productions crew (especially Maureen Maloney, through whose good work we get our contracts and our checks). I'm always stunned when I hear of writers working without agents. Besides the obvious benefits, who else is guaranteed to answer plaintive e-mails and provide ongoing moral support?

My husband, Joe Merlino, was unfailingly supportive and helpful throughout the writing of this book, despite being wrapped up in his own project (*Perl Weekend Crash Course*, Hungry Minds, 2001—a great introduction to Perl, which you'll need after reading this book and becoming inspired to write your own Apache modules!). In addition to the two books we had in progress, we also bought a house 12 states away and managed to move and make emergency plumbing repairs, all while busily working on our laptops on a card table. My thanks to Joe and a promise that I'll finally get around to unpacking the kitchen and book boxes Real Soon Now.

Finally, my thanks to the community of hackers, BOFHs, and inquisitive programmers who build and perfect the software I make my living writing about. Whether you call it Free Software or Open Source—and regardless of the philosophical positions implied by each of those terms—it's a vibrant, curious, and dedicated bunch of folks who spend copious amounts of their time working on amazing projects. Apache is the gift of one such group and I'm grateful for their work, as I am for all the other free and open software I use every day.

INTRODUCTION

Everybody loves the Web. Many people think the Web *is* the Internet because it's the most widely advertised Internet service and the subject of much business experimentation over the past few years. Even though the Web is only one of several critical Internet services (along with e-mail, file transfer, and other useful technologies), it has certainly become a critical part of many people's daily lives and work. This is an amazing fact, but it's even more astonishing when you realize the Web is a new technology, developed and popularized within the last ten years!

While most people use the Web frequently and familiarly, far fewer are aware of the software that gets Web pages on to their monitors. Sure, everyone knows about Web browsers, but the servers that talk to the browsers and hand over the requested files are much more anonymous. However, without Web servers, no Web exists. A number of Web servers are available to the would-be Web administrator, from the complex and highly configured commercial servers sold as part of an e-commerce package to the most bare-bones and terse servers designed for test needs. Chapter 2, "Preparing for Apache," introduces some of these Web servers.

The two most popular Web servers, though, are Microsoft's Internet Information Server (IIS) and the Apache Web server. In fact, Apache is the most popular Web server in the world. It runs more than half the world's Web sites, and it performs well on rigorous benchmarking and performance tests. While IIS has the edge in some all-Microsoft networks, even the most hardcore Microsoft administrators often run Apache for their Web sites. To add to the popularity of the Apache server, you can download the software free. The source code is also openly available, meaning a constant and enthusiastic development community is building new features and functions for the server, and Apache is thoroughly tested in real-world situations and installations.

Obviously, this is a book about Apache, so you might expect me to be partial. Yes, I tend to think freely developed software has the edge on a lot of commercial software, but that's not the point with Apache. Apache is simply a better Web server than anything else out there. It's robust, streamlined, modular, responsive, and stable. That's the recipe for a darned good piece of software, which is precisely what Apache is. In this book, you find little preaching about Free Software or Open Source (though Chapter 1, "History and Background of Apache," contains an introduction to the topic, so you understand the community that created Apache). Instead, we explore one of the two most popular and successful freely developed programs and how it can work for you. My hope is learning more about Apache will dispel some of the myths you might believe about noncommercial software, and that you'll consider other such software for your system as well.

TIP: The other freely developed success is the Linux operating system. Both Apache and Linux come from dedicated and committed communities, which work on the projects as hobby and passion.

No matter the reason why you've chosen the Apache Web server—or the reason you chose this book—you can find something in it to challenge your skills and meet your needs. Apache is a great piece of software and I hope you share my enthusiasm for it after you finish this book. Please be aware, there are worlds beyond what's covered here. In particular, this book doesn't cover dynamic content served from databases, and it gives little room to module programming and advanced scripting. Other valuable books cover such topics. This book is an introduction and a guide to basic Apache administration, and I hope you continue to explore other topics once the basics are under your belt.

WHAT'S IN THE BOOK

This book is divided into six parts. The first three sections deal with the basic tasks involved in running Apache, while the last three introduce more extended topics and provide helpful information you can use as a resource. If you're completely new to Apache, start at the beginning and read the first two parts before you install the server, using the remaining parts to bolster your knowledge as you gain experience. If you're more experienced with Unix servers in general, you may choose to skip the first two sections (or use them as a reference) and move to the fourth and fifth sections to expand your knowledge about Web-related topics. All readers can use the appendices in Part VI as support for the rest of the book.

TIP: Two Tables of Contents at the beginning of the book. One is a chapter listing, while the second is expanded and contains the various subheadings of each chapter. Skim the expanded Table of Contents to learn more about the topics covered in each chapter and each part of the book.

Part I, Installing Apache, starts from the beginning, with an introduction to open software and to the Apache server itself. This part also includes practical information on preparing your machine for the Apache server, locating a recent copy of the software, and installing the server. Other chapters in this part introduce software that can help you run a network that includes more than one operating system, as well as introduce Apache's modular construction and the various modules that perform different functions for the server.

Part II, Configuring and Running Apache, is the next step after successfully installing the server. Part II contains extensive information about configuring the server to meet your particular needs, as well as help in testing your configuration and fixing any problems that might occur. Once the server is configured properly, you're ready to manage and operate the server to provide Web pages to your visitors. This part of the book concludes with an introduction to the ongoing world of Apache development, including numerous modules that provide extended features to the server.

Part III, Apache Administration, focuses on the basic tasks involved in being a Web administrator. Chapters on Apache logs, basic Unix disk management, and performance tuning can help you understand your server and site traffic, as well as keep your installation running as smoothly as possible. This part also contains a chapter on dealing with your user base and setting up appropriate user policies, plus a chapter on the HTML standard and why you should attempt to serve HTML code that's as standard-compliant as possible.

Part IV, Beyond the Basics: Advanced Apache Topics, moves to topics of interest to a Web administrator, but that aren't required to run the Apache server. This part begins with an explanation of the MIME standard and text types, including character sets, which you can serve on your site. In this part, you also find an introduction to CGI scripts, image maps, server-side includes, and cascading style sheets. These are all page design techniques, but those that require some attention from you as the site administrator. Here, you also learn how to host virtual domains from your regular site. This section of the book concludes with an introduction to e-commerce and its complications.

Part V, Security and Apache, concludes the main part of the book. Security is an integral consideration for any Web administrator. In this section, you learn about some basic security concerns and precautions, and what to do if your site is cracked. This section also contains an introduction to Secure Sockets Layer (SSL) technology, and explains how to set up firewalls and proxies to further secure your Web server.

The final part of this book, Part VI, contains five appendices for further information. Appendix A is a list of some helpful Internet resources for the Web administrator. Appendix B offers instruction for several popular Unix text editors, which you need when you configure Apache. Appendix C is a glossary, while Appendix D contains a list of commonly used Unix commands. Finally, Appendix E contains the text of Apache's configuration files.

WHO SHOULD READ THIS BOOK

No one "ideal reader" exists for this book. Yes, the material here is targeted at the beginning to the intermediate user of Apache, but enough information is contained in the book that almost anyone should be able to find it useful. The absolute beginner with both Unix and Apache can find help in working with a new operating system, as well as with the server software, while the more experienced administrator might find Part IV or V the most useful. Regardless of your level of experience, this book should be of help to you. That said, I did make some assumptions about you, the reader, as I wrote:

▼ You have more than an academic interest in running a Web server, whether you want to serve a personal noncommercial site from a home network or you're involved in administering an extensive and high-profile Web site at your workplace;

■ You have access to an always-on, high-speed Internet connection and a Pentium-level computer with sufficient RAM (or the equivalent Macintosh set-up);

■ You have, or are willing to install, a Unix variant as your operating system;

▲ You know, or are willing to learn, the rudiments of working on a Unix machine;

I also assume a majority of readers are working in a professional and technological job where Web administration is either part of your job description or something you might do in the near future. While there's certainly no reason why an individual cannot run a Web site—and, in fact, this is increasingly common—most sites on the Web are served by commercial entities and not by individuals.

NOTE: Although a vast number of personal pages and sites are on the Web, most of those pages aren't hosted by the individual who owns them. Instead, the pages are served by the individual's ISP, a third-party Web hosting service, or one of the free Web hosts, like Yahoo!Geocities or Angelfire. In that sense, the pages are hosted by a commercial entity and not by an individual.

Thus, I made an additional set of assumptions about readers who have a professional interest in running Apache:

▼ You manage computer resources for a nontechnical user base.

■ You have access to multiple machines on an internal network.

■ You serve (or plan to serve) a Web site that's critical to your company's work.

■ You might not have the ultimate authority over the files served from the site.

▲ You have root access to the machine that hosts the Web server.

Regardless of who you are or what you do, you can run a Web server. Special considerations will probably exist for your situation, no matter who you are, but the basic practices are the same in most scenarios. Every Web administrator should be concerned with security and with basic or advanced administrative topics. The difference between a personal site and a commercial site is simply a matter of degree and of ancillary software.

HOW TO USE THE BOOK

Books are easy to use. Just pick one up and start reading! In the case of technical books, though, some additional information can help before you get too deeply into the subject matter. As with most technical books, this one uses a certain set of conventions to indicate particular kinds of information:

A word in *italics* is a new or important word, which is usually defined within the next sentence. So, you might see a sentence like this: "Installing Apache on a Unix machine requires that you have *root access*. The root account is the administrative account under Unix, and has special privileges that normal user accounts don't have, such as installing and running server programs." Many of the italicized terms in this book are also found in Appendix C, the glossary.

URLs are shown in **boldface**. Be aware, though, many of the URLs in this book are fanciful and don't refer to real sites. They're used as examples. However, a number of URLs throughout the book point you to useful sites or extra information that can help you with running Apache.

Words or phrases in the Courier font are direct Unix commands, file or directory names, or full directory paths. Some Courier text is set off from the text paragraphs surrounding it, as in

```
Code is often shown in this format.
```

Lengthy text files or bits of code are usually set off like this.

Some text is printed inside a box with a shaded edge, which is called a *sidebar*. These sidebars contain information that adds to the chapter, but that didn't flow neatly with the main chapter text. A sidebar might explain a deeper technology topic or provide some background on a particular Apache function. You can also see special paragraphs in the text t labeled Tip, Note, or Caution:

TIP: A Tip is an extra bit of information that might interest you. Tips might contain links to more specialized Web pages, a piece of Unix or Apache history, or some other item that's interesting, though not critical to running Apache.

NOTE: A Note is something you should know before you begin working with the subject under discussion. Notes might be configuration details, additional commands, or other information to enhance your understanding of the topic.

CAUTION: Relatively few Cautions are in this book, but pay attention to the ones you find. A caution is a warning, whether about Apache itself, the Web, or some function on your Unix machine. Read the cautions carefully, so you can avoid the pitfalls they describe.

PART I

Installing Apache

CHAPTER 1

History and Background of Apache

Despite its dominance and importance today, the World Wide Web (WWW) is a relative newcomer to networked computing, having been developed only in the middle 1990s. Despite its late start, the Web has become the service synonymous with "Internet" to millions of users worldwide. Whether you've been around the Internet since the early days (and remember Gopher and other pre-Web services) or you arrived on the scene after the Web had become the most popular service for Internet users—running neck and neck with electronic mail—you know people want fast and reliable access to the millions of Web pages out there.

While you can't guarantee reliable service on the user's end, you can make sure your own pages are served rapidly and your Web presence is stable, whether you're running a small Web server out of your dining room or you're part of an administrative team operating a server that offers thousands of pages for millions of daily hits. The secret to a stable Web presence is choosing the right Web server for your site: the Apache Server. Over 60 percent of sites on the Web use Apache or one of its derivatives to power their pages. In this chapter, you learn why Web administrators choose Apache, as well as what makes it so powerful and unique.

WHAT IS APACHE?

At its most basic, the Apache Server is a standards-compliant Web server. This means the Apache Server supports the requirements of the HTTP 1.1 standard, a document that defines the method by which files encoded in Hypertext Markup Language (HTML) are moved across computer networks.

TIP: HTTP is an acronym for Hyper Text Transfer Protocol.

The term *server* means Apache responds to requests from other programs, but doesn't provide documents of its own volition. That is, when you open a Web browser—such as Netscape—and type **http://www.apache.org** into the text box and then press ENTER, your browser contacts the server at apache.org and requests the default page for that site. The server responds to the request with the file you want to see, which the browser then formats and displays. Figure 2-1 shows the basic process.

NOTE: These standards are maintained by the World Wide Web Consortium (W3C), a nonprofit group that works to develop standards for both HTTP and HTML. In Chapter 13, "Serving Compliant HTML," you learn more about working with standards and why they're critical to administrators and their sites.

Apache is more than a simple Web server, though. The true power behind the Apache Server lies in its modularity. The core of the server is actually quite small, serving as the central component of the program, but not providing a lot of extra functions. Those functions are added as *modules*, individual pieces of code that permit the server to handle a

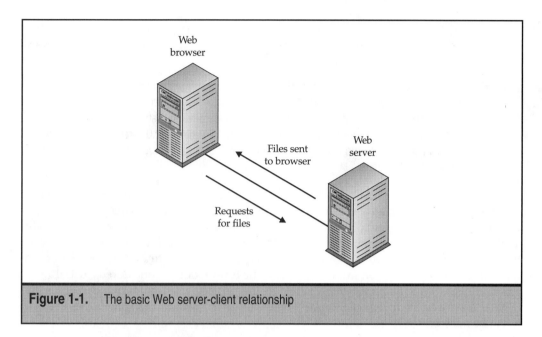

Figure 1-1.   The basic Web server-client relationship

particular type of request or file in the appropriate way. Chapter 5, "Apache Modules," covers the range of available modules, while Chapter 8, "Dealing with Innovation: mod_perl, A Case Study," explains one popular module in great detail. If you plan to run Apache in any serious way, you'll find its modularity means you only need to install the functions you plan to use—without wasting machine cycles on functions you don't need.

DEVELOPMENT AND HISTORY OF THE APACHE PROJECT

The Apache Server is the creation of a large group of programmers and developers who work together to build and strengthen Apache and its modules, as well as to incorporate new technologies into the server. The Apache project started in 1995 as an attempt to upgrade the original HTTP daemon (httpd) developed at the National Center for Supercomputing Applications by Rob McCool. Because McCool had taken a new job in 1994, nobody at NCSA had taken over the project, so httpd was languishing at a time when Web programming was starting to take off.

Web administrators were working on httpd on their own, and they began to share their patches and hacks with each other in an attempt to strengthen httpd without McCool's input. Soon, eight programmers announced the formation of the Apache Group, which would serve as a central node for httpd development. They took all the patches they could find and incorporated them into httpd code, releasing the first Apache server distribution in April 1995 as version 0.6.2. Testing and writing new code occupied the Apache group (including NCSA programmers) for the remainder of 1995, and after two more beta releases, Apache 1.0 was released in December 1995. Within a year, Apache was the most popular server being used on the Web. This popularity hasn't slowed, with Apache itself now serving 60 percent of Web sites and its derivatives adding another 3 or 4 percent to that total. Apache is currently in beta for version 2.0, with the most recent stable release being 1.3.

NOTE: This book is written using both Apache 2.0 and Apache 1.3. Since the 2.0 release is still under construction and is released only as beta software, those running Web sites that require reliability may need to stay with the current stable release (Apache 1.3) until the 2.0 version is released as stable. Significant differences from 1.3 are noted in this book, but some processes given here for 2.0 may not work on 1.3 installations.

At the end of 1999, the Apache developers took a somewhat unusual step. The server had become so popular, a more bureaucratic structure was needed to manage the project and its work. So, the Apache Software Foundation was established under United States law as a fully nonprofit organization. The foundation can receive donations, distribute funds to developers or other recipients, and manage the growth of Apache in an organized manner. Perhaps even more important, the foundation is considered a separate legal entity, apart from any people involved in the project. The foundation can enter into contracts, participate in legal action, and even sue or be sued, though one hopes that will never be necessary!

OPEN SOURCE SOFTWARE

Working with Apache without learning something about the Open Source or Free Software community is nearly impossible. Apache is often touted as one of the biggest successes to come out of this community, and the project has stayed faithful to its roots as the server has become more widely used. But what is Free Software, and why is it important?

At their most general, the terms *Free Software* and *Open Source* refer to software developed by volunteers and distributed with a license that's simultaneously restrictive and open. Free Software licenses usually require the user to contribute any changes made to the program back to the development community. They also require the full code base be distributed openly, holding nothing back as a "trade secret." Many programs released under such licenses, like Apache, are also distributed free of charge.

NOTE: Free Software doesn't always mean "no cost" software. The "free" refers to the way in which the code base, and improvements to the code base, must circulate among users and developers. People in the community use the phrase "free speech, not free beer" to indicate a difference exists between sharing without restraint and sharing without payment.

The Free Software movement is the brainchild of Richard Stallman, an MIT computer scientist who spent much of the 1970s decrying the rise of commercial software that hid its code from users and administrators. Without access to the code, Stallman knew administrators would have to rely on the software companies to fix bugs and produce upgrades.

These upgrades would be generic and not always useful for a particular administrator's needs. So, Stallman began working on projects that would be released freely to the computing community and has continued to do so for the last quarter-century. He also created a foundation, called the Free Software Foundation, which helps people write Free Software and get it distributed.

Many of Stallman's programs are now considered integral parts of a Unix system, which is ironic because his project name, GNU, stands for Gnu's Not Unix. Stallman wasn't the only person working on such programs, though. A robust international community of programmers, hackers, and students was building an amazing array of programs. The rise of the Internet and its growing availability to people outside the military and academic networks helped with this explosion of code. However, the catalyst for truly amazing growth came when a Finnish college student, Linus Torvalds, released the first version of a new operating system called *Linux*.

NOTE: You'll see Unix spelled both with the capital U and in all capital letters, as in UNIX. The latter is a registered trademark, while the former has become the general way to describe UNIX-based operating systems, which may or may not contain part of the code in the AT&T copyrighted UNIX. In this book, the Unix spelling is used.

Linux was a version of an older Unix-based operating system called Minix, but it was developed and released under a GNU-derived license. One major innovation was that Linux could run on a variety of hardware, a far cry from the days when individual computers arrived with their own unique operating systems. The wide distribution of Linux meant a large user base was available to work with new programs and to generate data that would work as independent of the hardware platform as possible. With a Free and flexible operating system now available, the community exploded . . . and business began to take note.

Unfortunately—or fortunately, depending on the side you take—Stallman's insistence on the term "Free Software" wasn't the best marketing tool. Businesses weren't comfortable with the concept of "free," thinking free code might be worth exactly what was paid for it. The programs were good and competitive, but the perception was a problem. Enter Eric Raymond, a programmer active in the Free Software community who identified this problem. In his landmark essay "The Cathedral and the Bazaar," Raymond suggested the term "open source" as a replacement. Open Source would carry the same connotations of open development and the distribution of source code, but would remove any financial or moral implications from the software's description. What term you use is up to you, but you should be aware of the shadings behind each description.

NOTE: If you're interested in learning more about this community, you can find out a lot by searching the Web and by reading the writings of both Stallman and Raymond. Raymond's book, *The Cathedral and the Bazaar* (O'Reilly & Associates, 2000), is a collection of his most important essays, which are also available on his Web site: **http://www.tuxedo.org/~esr/writings/**. You can learn more about Stallman's views by reading through the GNU site at **http://www.gnu.org**.

Why is this important to you, as an Apache administrator? Well, by choosing a freely developed Web server over a commercial server like Microsoft's Internet Information Server, you've decided to participate in the Free Software/Open Source community. That Apache is so widely used points to the quality that can be attained through open development, though the cost—free!—is what attracts a lot of people to the server. Picking Apache over IIS, however, may require some explaining to people who believe that brand name equals quality. Just tell them Apache is more robust, more widely used, and more responsive to user needs. Many 100 percent–Windows NT networks still run a single Unix computer to host Apache; it's that reliable and that good.

NOTE: While the Apache code itself is distributed free of charge, plenty of people out there are willing to work with you for a price. If you have special needs, you might want to purchase an Apache-based Web server, which has particular features or modules already integrated into the server. For example, you can buy one of several Apache-based servers that are already configured to host e-commerce scripts and software. While you can do this yourself, it's usually easier and more secure to purchase either an e-commerce service or a precompiled server. The beauty of Open Source software is that you can select the product that serves *your* needs, whether it's preconfigured or from scratch.

The Apache License

As with all software packages, Apache is distributed with a license. In keeping with its Open Source roots, the Apache license controls how the code may be distributed or altered. If you install the Apache server, you must abide by these requirements, because installing the package is an acknowledgment that you've read and agree with the entire license. The license is included with your Apache download as a text file. Here's its complete text:

The Apache Software License, Version 1.1

Copyright © 2000 The Apache Software Foundation. All rights reserved.

Redistribution and use in source and binary forms, with or without modification, are permitted provided that the following conditions are met:

1.   *Redistributions of source code must retain the above copyright notice, this list of conditions and the following disclaimer.*

2.   *Redistributions in binary form must reproduce the above copyright notice, this list of conditions and the following disclaimer in the documentation and/or other materials provided with the distribustion.*

3.   *The end-user documentation included with the redistribution, if any, must include the following acknowledgment:*

> *"This product includes software developed by the Apache Software Foundation (http://www.apache.org)."*
>
> *Alternately, this acknowledgment may appear in the software itself, if and wherever such third-part acknowledgments normally appear.*
>
> 4. *The names "Apache" and "Apache Software Foundation" must not be used to endorse or promote products derived from this software without prior written permission. For written permission, please contact apache@apache.org.*
>
> 5. *Products derived from this software may not be called "Apache", nor may "Apache" appear in their name, without prior written permission of the Apache Software Foundation.*
>
> *THIS SOFTWARE IS PROVIDED "AS IS" AND ANY EXPRESSED OR IMPLIED WARRANTIES, INCLUDING, BUT NOT LIMITED TO, THE IMPLIED WARRANTIES OF MERCHANTABILITY AND FITNESS FOR A PARTICULAR PURPOSE ARE DISCLAIMED. IN NO EVENT SHALL THE APACHE SOFTWARE FOUNDATION OR ITS CONTRIBUTORS BE LIABLE FOR ANY DIRECT, INDIRECT, INCIDENTAL, SPECIAL, EXEMPLARY, OR CONSEQUENTIAL DAMAGES (INCLUDING, BUT NOT LIMITED TO, PROCUREMENT OF SUBSTITUTE GOODS OR SERVICES; LOSS OF USE, DATA, OR PROFITS; OR BUSINESS INTERRUPTION) HOWEVER CAUSED AND ON ANY THEORY OF LIABILITY, WHETHER IN CONTRACT, STRICT LIABILITY, OR TORT (INCLUDING NEGLIGENCE OR OTHERWISE) ARISING IN ANY WAY OUT OF THE USE OF THIS SOFTWARE, EVEN IF ADVISED OF THE POSSIBILITY OF SUCH DAMAGE.*
>
> ==
>
> *This software consists of voluntary contributions made by many individuals on behalf of the Apache Software Foundation. For more information on the Apache Software Foundation, please see <http://www.apache.org/>.*
>
> *Portions of this software are based upon public domain software originally written at the National Center for Supercomputing Applications, University of Illinois, Urbana-Champaign.*

HOW APACHE WORKS

Think of Apache as a reference librarian. Every day, large numbers of people come to the desk and request information. Some of this information is restricted, some is unavailable, some is extremely complex, but all of it is controlled by the person behind the desk. This is how Apache works. Its name gives a clue to what it does: Apache is a *server*. What does it serve? Apache serves HTML-formatted files on request by an external party. When you type a URL into your Web browser, the browser generates a request that's sent to the Web server at that site. The server then locates the appropriate file and sends a copy to the browser, which formats it on-the-fly and displays it to you.

A smooth Web experience depends on several things: a well-configured Web browser, a relatively speedy and glitch-free Internet connection, and a responsive and well-maintained Web server. If the server is configured correctly, it provides a variety of files to the browser. Apache handles many file types beyond plain HTML; it can serve images, sounds, animations, and interactive scripts. It can also show complex and sophisticated images that serve as navigation tools, run securely enough to permit the use of credit cards for commercial transactions, and serve Web pages for a number of domains from one server. Throughout this book, you learn how Apache works with these file types and situations, and you find actual examples you can try on your own system should you want to duplicate that particular service.

FEATURES OF APACHE 2.0

Apache 2.0 is a significant upgrade from previous versions of the server. A number of changes are deep in the code that are primarily interesting to programmers, but a number of new features also make Apache more robust and useful in a wider variety of Web situations.

CAUTION: At press time, Apache 2.0 was available only in *beta* format. This means the current version, Apache 2.0.16, is a work in progress. Bugs might exist, or the server may behave oddly when a particular command is invoked. You use beta software at your own risk— though it's unlikely to harm your hardware irrevocably—and you should be prepared to send bug reports to the developers whenever you have a malfunction. If you don't like the idea of running test software, wait for the first official release of Apache (probably Apache 2.1) in the near future.

The biggest improvement in Apache 2.0 is in *scalability*. The developers have refined the way in which Apache generates processes, so it runs more neatly and efficiently. With this efficiency comes speed, as well as the capability to run larger installations without crashing from overload. Exploiting this development to its fullest requires that you run Apache 2.0 on a Unix platform, because Unix handles multiple processes and threads better than other operating systems.

TIP: See Chapter 2, "Preparing for Apache," for the other reasons why you should consider running Apache on a Unix system.

Other improvements in Apache 2.0 clean up unnecessary code from earlier versions, and repair commands that cause Apache to crash or to generate useless data. The changes are mostly directed at administration tasks and at the way in which Apache interprets HTTP.

> ***NOTE:***   By the time you read this, the available beta version may be a higher number than 2.0.16. In fact, it's likely. The Apache team moves quickly to release new minor versions of the server to address bugs and other inconsistencies that arise during the beta testing process. You don't need to reinstall with each new minor release; instead, keep an eye on versions with new numbers in the first two positions. Apache 2.1 will be a reason to upgrade; and, in the coming years, Apache 3.0 will probably have as many major changes as Apache 2.0 is currently implementing. If you're having a specific problem with the beta code, however, and you read at **http://www.apachenews.com** that the new minor release fixes that problem, go ahead and upgrade. It's okay to upgrade frequently if you need the bug fixes.

If you don't want to run beta software or you find 2.0 causes trouble on your particular network, whether because of operating system or configuration, you needn't go to the new version until a relatively stable and bugfree version has been released. You get most of the Web-serving power you need with Apache 1.3, the current stable release. Find it at the Apache Web site, **http://www.apache.org**. Note, some of the information in this book is 2.0 specific, though most of it should work on a 1.3 installation with some tinkering.

SUMMARY

Although the WWW is one of the newest services available over the Internet, demand for Web pages is vast and growing daily. The Apache Web server is the most popular program used to handle the flood of requests for Web pages and is used to host more than 60 percent of the world's Web sites. Apache is standards compliant and modular—two features that smooth the transmission of HTML files and make Apache more powerful for the kinds of files your site handles, while not wasting processor cycles on features you don't need.

Apache is the product of open development, a movement that focuses on flexibility and freedom of the code base for any particular project. Whether you refer to the movement as "Free Software" or "Open Source," the end product is robust and constantly under development by a cadre of volunteer programmers. Apache benefits from many hands and eyes who work to build the most stable and powerful Web server available. The current stable version is Apache 1.3, while Apache 2.0 is available as a beta release at press time. The 2.0 version includes code that streamlines the way Apache interacts with the operating system, as well as new functions and features that make it easier to administer and configure the server. Most of the information in this book should work with both 1.3 and 2.0; though where a difference occurs, 2.0 information is provided.

CHAPTER 2

Preparing for Apache

Ready to start working with the Apache Web Server? Then this chapter is your jumping-off point. Of course, you need to install the software and get it configured. Installation is covered in Chapter 3, "Installing Apache," and configuration in Chapter 6, "Configuring and Testing Apache." In this chapter, you learn where to find the latest Apache software, how to pick the proper version for your needs, how to set up the machine before you install, and how to deal with any previous Web servers that may still exist on that machine.

This chapter continues with a partisan appeal. Throughout this book, you see references to Apache running on a Unix machine. Information about Windows and MacOS will be there, but we strongly recommend you run your Web server on a Unix or Unix-derived operating system. This can give you the best opportunity to optimize your server security, operating speed, efficiency, and reliability. If you can't or won't install a Unix operating system, however, you won't lose out on Apache. Once installed and configured, Apache runs itself quite well on most operating system platforms.

Finally, you may wonder whether it's worthwhile to upgrade if you already have a version of Apache installed. Depending on the version number, you may not need to upgrade. Many new features are in the latest versions of Apache, however, so reviewing those new functions to see whether they'd fit your site is useful. If you do decide to upgrade your existing Apache installation, the final sections of this chapter walk you through the process.

LOCATING AND DOWNLOADING APACHE

Obviously, the first thing you need to do is to find a copy of the Apache software. If you recently purchased a computer book—especially one about Unix or a Unix-derived operating system—check the book's CD-ROM. Apache is a popular offering on book CD-ROMs, though you need to check the version before you decide whether to install from the CD-ROM. By far the most popular way to get Apache, though, is to download it directly from the Apache project's own servers.

TIP: Head to **http://www.apache.org** for the latest in downloads and other Apache news. You can also find documentation and news about a wide variety of Apache-related projects. Follow the links for Apache Server (several other software packages are available on the same site, so don't get confused). The downloads page, **http://www.apache.org/dists**, may direct you to choose a mirror site. Pick the one geographically closest to you so you get the cleanest and fastest download possible, lessening the chances that a corrupt file will break your installation.

Picking the Right Apache Version

When you get to the downloads section of apache.org, you can see at least two versions of Apache available for download. As with many Open Source software projects, Apache maintains two current versions at any given time. One version is the *stable* version, which is considered reliable for production environments that can't afford to go down unpredictably. The other version is the *beta* version, which contains newer code and is relatively untested compared to the stable version. At press time, Apache 1.3 was the stable version and Apache 2.0 was the beta version.

NOTE: While the beta version of Apache is never recommended for critical installations (e-commerce sites with multiple thousands of dollars in daily transactions, for example), it's not completely unreliable. Software is released in beta form so people will install it, use it in their regular situations, and report any bugs that may occur. You can probably use 2.0 without too much worry as long as you're not operating a site that requires high-level security or is the single point of failure for your company's success. Still, the possibility of a problem exists, leading to the following disclaimer.

CAUTION: If you have any concerns about an undocumented bug disrupting your Web presence or you're uncomfortable working with software still in the experimental stages, don't install Apache 2.0. Download and install Apache 1.3 (or whatever version is currently provided as the latest stable version). The new features and other advances in Apache 2.0 will be released as stable soon enough, so you can use them in the near future (as soon as 2.0 is certified stable). It's not worth risking your comfort level or skillset—or your data—on software you're not sure about running.

Downloading Apache

When you decide whether to download the stable or beta version of Apache, you can start getting the software. You have some choices at this point. What kind of file compression technology can you work with? Apache files are available in several different compression formats. Also, what sort of operating system are you running? You may need to download files designed specifically for your operating system because certain systems require certain kinds of code. Finally, if you're working with certain operating systems, you need to decide whether you want to use direct source code packages or packages already precompiled for your operating system.

File Compression Formats

If you're running a Unix-based operating system, check and see what uncompression utilities you have installed. Most systems have `tar` or `gzip` installed, and usually have both. Depending on what you have, download the appropriately compressed file for your installation. Those who have only `tar` installed should download files ending with the extension

```
*.tar.Z
```

while those who have both `tar` and `gzip` installed can either download the `*.tar.Z` files or ones with the extension

```
*.tar.gz
```

Files created with tar are simply large accretions consisting of multiple files, while files that were first `tarred` and then `gzipped` have also been compressed. This results in a slightly smaller file, which may download more rapidly on a slow connection.

NOTE: If you're running Windows, you need to download the self-extracting `*.exe` files rather than any files compressed with a Unix utility. You won't be able to uncompress those files cleanly. See the sidebar "Installing Apache on Windows" in Chapter 3, "Installing Apache," to learn more about working with these `*.exe` files and installing Apache on your Windows machine. If you're running MacOS X or MacOS X Server, you needn't download anything. Apache is available to you already in a format designed to integrate cleanly with your operating system.

Operating Systems

Should you want to download a version of Apache that has already been mildly configured to work with your particular operating system, you can find some of these packages on the **www.apache.org** site. The advantage of using the precompiled packages is they should take into account any quirks or necessary configurations for your system; however, they do have some drawbacks. The primary disadvantage of using precompiled binaries is the configuration is generic and some of the binaries don't let you modify them further on your own. If you want to make sure Apache does precisely what you want it to do—and doesn't do what you don't want—you should download the source code and go from there.

NOTE: Of course, those using operating systems that don't permit the use of source code, or that make using it somewhat difficult, need to download precompiled binary files for their particular situation.

If this is the first time you're installing Apache, and especially if it's your first time using Unix *and* installing Apache, you're in a unique situation. Using precompiled binary packages, if available for your platform, might be best for you, until you're more comfortable with your new operating system and with installing software. Also, you might want to use the precompiled binaries for your first installation of Apache, so you can determine how it works "straight out of the box" and how you want to configure it for your own needs before you reinstall with a source code version.

PREPARING THE WEB SERVER MACHINE

Once you make your choices about which packages you need, download the files. If you don't have a regular download destination, download the files into `/usr/tmp` on a Unix system. This directory never contains critical system files, so it's a good location for things you don't plan to store for long. Once the installation is complete and the files have self-installed into the correct locations in `/httpd` or `/apache`, you can delete everything in `/usr/tmp` with impunity.

NOTE: If you're using Windows instead, put the file wherever you want. For example, Windows 95 users usually store downloaded files in the My Download Files folder. The installation program automatically places all the program files into the correct location and you can delete the downloaded package when the installation is complete.

If at all possible, give your Web server its own machine on your network. This is the most secure way to handle the traffic to and from a Web server, which generates hundreds or thousands of insecure transmissions across your network daily. If you keep Apache on its own machine, you can control access from within your network as well as from outside. Keeping the files served by Apache on the same machine can also help you keep an eye on the total size of your Web presence and enables you to prune outdated pages, or those no longer requested or needed on the site. A dedicated Web server machine needs only an operating system, the Apache software, possibly your Web pages, and some basic Unix utilities:

▼ A text editor (see Appendix B, "Using a Unix Text Editor")

■ A compression/uncompression utility like `tar` and `gzip`

■ A text-based Web browser like `lynx`

▲ FTP software (and possibly an FTP server, depending on how you want your users to place their files on the machine)

CAUTION: If you choose to run an FTP server, select one that has routine security updates. Some FTP servers are easily cracked through known (and widely published) holes or flaws. Pick an FTP server that has a regularly updated Web site with a security section.

You can use your regular workstation to view the site through a graphical browser, such as Netscape, and you can put files on the machine with FTP, so you don't need an e-mail client on the server machine itself. The less software on the machine, the more room for Web files.

If you need to put Apache on a machine that has other uses as well, try to give Apache its own partition, so it can be treated as a separate entity. Placing Apache on the same partition as other software and data is a security risk, especially if you have a high-speed Internet connection that might be desirable to hackers or you have important data stored on the same partition. Keep that partition clean of other files and data. Apache will run better if it has room to work, and if its work environment is clean and neat.

System Requirements

You probably have a machine powerful enough to handle Apache. Most computers sold in the last few years are far more powerful than their users actually need. However, if you've thrown Apache on an old pizza-box 486 you have lying around, in response to the advice in the previous section to keep Apache on a separate machine, you might need to check your set up and see if you have adequate resources for the server.

CAUTION: Remember, "adequate resources" means different things, depending on the kind of site you want to run. A bare-bones site with plain-text pages and possibly a few small images can run on a slower and smaller machine. But, when you start adding complicated images or image maps, applets, JavaScript programs, or CGI scripts, your system requirements will skyrocket. Scale your site to your resources. If you don't have a fast machine, don't offer files or programs that take up a lot of overhead. Your pages will take forever to load on the viewer's screen, and you may lose a visitor to a faster and better-managed site.

So, what does it take to run Apache? The server itself can function on as little as 8MB of RAM on a Unix system, with at least 6MB of free hard disk space. You probably have that in your system right now, even if you don't have a multigigabyte hard drive (and why not? they're quite cheap). That's really only enough to make the server go, though. Running Apache on that small a system means it takes a while to answer requests for files, and you can't keep many files on 6MB. In fact, that 6MB of hard disk is just enough to hold Apache itself, so you'd need to add extra room for the actual files you plan to serve.

Practically speaking, as with any software, the more RAM and disk space you have, the better. RAM has been quite inexpensive in recent years, so you can probably upgrade your machine to 128MB for under $150 (if you're running an Intel-type machine and it uses a standard RAM module). Apache runs happily on 128MB, though people serving a large amount of dynamic content, including JavaScript and CGI, cannot have enough RAM and should put in as much as they can spare. As for disk space, a drive that's a gigabyte or larger will be sufficient (multigigabyte drives have plummeted in price recently). A 10GB drive should keep you happily Web serving for a few years if you're not a large corporation with many files. If you are, you have a good idea of your data storage needs already.

No matter how big your drive, though, you need to keep an eye on the logs generated by Apache. In Chapter 9, "Logs," you learn about the various log files Apache creates for you. These logs can grow quite large, especially if you get a lot of hits every day. It's not out of the question for the logs to grow larger than the total amount of data in your Web site if you don't review and clean them regularly. If you let the logs grow and grow, your spacious hard drive might not be sufficient after all.

IDENTIFYING AND REMOVING PRIOR SERVERS

Should you pull older versions of Apache or other Web servers off your machine before you install the version you're going to work with? This is a matter of some discussion. In general, you needn't remove earlier versions of Apache. In fact, you may be able to upgrade that installation without having to remove the older one and installing the new one cleanly. See the section "Upgrading from Earlier Versions of Apache," later in this chapter, to learn how to determine what version you have installed, and see if you can upgrade it in place or if you're better off uninstalling and putting in fresh new Apache files.

TIP: If you have an Apache version already installed that's earlier than the most recent (not the current) stable release, you may save some time by removing it. Apache releases change a lot between stable versions and installing a new version onto a clean disk might actually be faster. This is especially the case when the upgrade has a completely new version number, as in upgrading from 1.3 to 2.0. If you do choose to remove an older server, save the configuration file (kept at `/etc/apache/httpd.conf` for versions 1.3 and older). You may want to take some of those settings and transfer them to the new configuration file.

If you have another Web server running on the machine where you want to install Apache, however, the safest thing to do is to delete it. Yes, this is the conservative approach, but it eliminates the chance that another program will respond to a browser request for files. If you haven't configured that other server properly, this could cause problems.

CAUTION: Make a habit of running only one server of any given kind: one mail server, one news server, one Web server, and so on. For the average administrator, tracking one of each type of server is work enough. Running more than one may be an invitation to a hack.

Other Web Servers

Many people are surprised to hear Web servers other than Apache and Microsoft's Internet Information Server (IIS) exist. Indeed, other servers do exist, though Apache has the majority of the market and IIS takes the second share. Many of these smaller servers have specific strengths or serve particular administrative needs. If you want to see what your alternatives to Apache might be, here are some of the most popular:

▼   **boa**   A server that's been under development since 1991, boa serves multiple requests without forking processes (unlike Apache). This offers a faster response time, though Apache scales better for large Web sites. **http://www.boa.org**

■   **fhttpd**   This server attempts to bridge the gap between FTP servers and Web servers. fhttpd is especially useful for sites that serve as many downloadable files as they do Web pages. **http://www.fhttpd.org**

■   **kHTTPd**   If you run Linux, try this server, which is kernel-based and, thus, can run only on Linux distributions. Because of the stability of the kernel, kHTTPd is quite sturdy and fast. **http://www.fenrus.demon.nl**

▲   **WN**   This server has many of the same features as Apache, but runs on a much smaller segment of the drive. The user base is quite small, though, so there isn't a community as large as Apache's to work on bugfixes, and to develop modules and other ancillary programs. **http://hopf.math.nwu.edu**

In addition, the Jigsaw Web server is worthy of mention. The product of a development team at the World Wide Web Consortium (W3C), *Jigsaw* is a server that meets every component of the Hypertext Transfer Protocol (HTTP), also maintained by the W3C. Jigsaw is written in Java and is intended primarily for programmers who need a server that only serves compliant code, as a test environment.

USING APACHE WITH UNIX

Throughout this book, I recommend and encourage you to install and administer Apache on a machine running some form of Unix, whether it be a "true Unix" like AIX or SCO, or one of the Unix-derived operating systems like FreeBSD, Linux, or Sun's Solaris. Even if you're running a network on which no other Unix or Unix-based machines exist, it's still a good idea to put your Web server on a separate machine running one of these operating systems.

Why? It's simple: Unix and its derivatives are reliable and straightforward operating systems you can trust. If you use one of the newer Unix derivatives, like Linux, you'll be able to work with all the code on the machine; some commercial Unices aren't as free with the codebase as the Open Source operating systems. Still, working with Unix gives you access to an immense range of administrative possibilities, some of which simply aren't possible on a machine running another form of proprietary software.

Another Unix advantage is uptime. Unix machines routinely run for months without needing to be rebooted, and any problems that crop up are usually fixable from the command line without having to restart the machine, even when adding new hardware. That's not always the case with Windows or MacOS. You can run a Unix system on a relatively bare-bones machine because you needn't have advanced graphics capabilities to run a graphical user interface. This means the overall cost may be less, especially when you factor in the cost of the operating system itself, which is an especially good deal if you choose Linux or FreeBSD, both of which are free of charge if you download them from the Web.

TIP: If you're interested in adding a Unix machine to a network that uses other types of operating systems, you'll be creating a *heterogeneous network*. Before you get going on the new addition, read Chapter 4, "Running a Heterogeneous Network." New software packages vastly simplify the process of integrating different operating systems, and they're easy to configure and administer.

You may wonder if this recommendation is a not particularly well-disguised method of Windows-bashing or Mac-bashing. It isn't. I routinely use both Windows and Linux, often at the same time, and I spent many years working in a Mac-centric department. Advantages exist to Windows and MacOS for the individual user, just as advantages exist to

If You Can't Use Unix . . .

Some readers may be unable to adopt the Unix suggestion on their own sites or networks. Perhaps you work in an environment where only one operating system is permitted or you have a supervisor who won't let you work with operating systems that don't come with consultants and service contracts. (You can buy contracts and consulting for any operating system, though the cost does detract from part of the point in using FreeBSD or Linux.) Regardless of the reason, you may be wondering whether you can run Apache confidently without a Unix server machine.

Yes, you can. This may require more of your time for upkeep, though a well-run machine of any operating system is better than a badly run Unix machine. Just be aware you'll need to do some extra work in configuring your system. You might have to install from precompiled binaries, for example, or you might find you need to use complicated workaround for some modules. People run Apache on a huge variety of operating systems, though, so you won't be alone no matter what operating system you choose. MacOS X even integrates Apache directly into its server software! However, if you do have the opportunity to build a heterogeneous network, give it a try. You might be surprised at how efficient you and your data become.

Although this book is targeted primarily at Unix users, some information for MacOS and Windows administrators is also included. And, you can find support from other non-Unix administrators through the Internet (see Appendix A, "Internet Resources," for a list of USENET newsgroups that target various operating systems). You needn't give up Apache if you can't—or won't—run Unix.

Unix and its derivatives for the administrator. In the case of Apache, where you may be responsible for hundreds or thousands of files that flow to hundreds or thousands of requests per minute, it's critical for you to select an operating system in which you can be confident and place your trust. Benchmarking tests show Unix can handle vast amounts of traffic, most likely powers of magnitude above what you'll be handling.

Which Unix?

Okay, so you've convinced yourself to give a Unix Web server a try. Now, the big question: which Unix to use? Hundreds are available, from insanely expensive Unices written for large-scale mainframe installations to bare-bones, low-cost Unices that run on old Intel 386 pizza box computers. If you've thought about Unix before, but have been baffled by the array, you're not alone. It's truly confusing, and—to make matters worse—each individual Unix claims to be the best at some facet of administration or operation. What's a novice Unix admin to do?

Some folks just close their eyes and point, while others go with something their friends recommend. Still others pick the nicest box off the shelf at Best Buy, yet other sets of people choose based on the distribution's logo or mascot. The truth of the matter is this: you can sift out a lot of Unices early in the game and narrow it down to two or three choices without too much effort.

> **TIP:** Regardless of the Unix you choose, a comprehensive reference is a must-have. Even the most jaded Unix administrators refer to guidebooks as they work with this vast and complex operating system. For obvious reasons, I'm partial to *Mastering Unix*, by Kate Wrightson and Joe Merlino (Sybex, 2001). In that book, we covered Linux, BSD, and Solaris in detail; however, the material is applicable to any Unix. Plus, Apache's on the CD!

Large-Scale Commercial Unices

Unless you work for a major corporation with money to burn—and even then, in some cases—you won't be looking at the high-end commercial Unix market. This market includes operating systems like AIX, SCO Unix, HP-UX, and IRIX. These distributions are written to mesh perfectly with particular hardware. For example, IRIX runs on Silicon Graphics machines, which are insanely expensive and usually found only in academic research laboratories or high-end development labs. You, the average person, cannot afford an SGI machine and an IRIX license. Your company may be unable to buy you specialized hardware and software just to run a Web server, either.

If you work for a big company that already has high-end hardware installed somewhere in the networking department, however, you may run across these flavors of Unix, especially if your workplace relied on massive mainframes not so long ago (or still does). In that case, even if you're running a smaller Windows NT or MacOS network in your own department, it may make sense to ask for a small corner of the big Unix machines where you can plunk your server and its files. Be sure the mainframe administrators are willing to take on the system overhead of all those connections from the Internet and your local intranet. At the very least, you should be able to get some Unix tutoring within the company, even if you can't wangle some free server space.

Small-Scale Commercial Unices

Much more affordable are the small-scale commercial Unices, the best known of which is Sun's Solaris operating system. This is an ambiguous category, as it can also be argued that versions of Free Unix-based operating systems (like Linux and BSD), which are marketed for a cost, are also "commercial Unices." However, the term is used here to describe Unix versions that aren't Free Software. Rather, they have some proprietary code or they're simply not available free.

> **NOTE:** Solaris is technically "free of cost," though you have to pay to get it. When you send in a check to Sun, you're buying the CD-ROMs and some documentation, though Sun says you're not paying for the operating system itself. It's a fine distinction and most people think of Solaris as a commercial Unix anyway.

Smaller companies and some individuals can afford these Unices. There's an attraction in getting your operating system from a known company like Sun; and Solaris is certainly an industry standard for workstations, whether they're Sun's own Sparc line or other generic hardware. The disadvantage is this: Sun has made some idiosyncratic changes to Solaris, so it works differently from other Unices in some critical ways. Solaris is a good operating system Just be sure you get Solaris-specific documentation and binary packages should you choose it.

Another good choice in this range is BSD/OS, which is the current name for the commercial form of Berkeley Systems Division Unix, formerly known as BSDI. BSD is one of the oldest forms of Unix and has a wide range of adherents who like its structure and security features. BSD/OS is being marketed as part of a wider Internet service–oriented software array, which includes packet and IP management tools, among other interesting utilities.

TIP: Find out more about Solaris at **http://www.sun.com/solaris** and more about BSD/OS at **http://www.bsdi.com**.

Free Unices

These days, most people who are interested in trying Unix or its derivative operating systems make their first forays with one of the Free Software operating systems developed as a Unix-type program. The two most popular of these Free Unices are Linux and FreeBSD. As with many Free Software programs, you can choose to obtain these operating systems free of charge or you can pay for them. Getting them free usually means you need to download the latest versions from an appropriate Web site, though you can also get various distributions sent to you for the cost of the CD-ROMs and postage. If you want a bit more interaction with the company providing your operating system, you can buy some Linux distributions off the shelf at computer stores—most notably, the Red Hat distribution—or you can order versions from various vendors who might also offer customer support or other extras, such as printed documentation rather than electronic.

There's no reason to get involved in a Linux-FreeBSD flame war in an Apache book, and no reason to get involved in one at any time. Both operating systems have adherents and detractors, both run equally well, and both provide a stable and strong platform for your Apache needs. Linux has the slight edge right now (early 2001) in terms of software being released to fit the platform and commercial support, but the FreeBSD community is vocal and active, and keeps a wide variety of programs flowing to users.

TIP: If you're working in a commercial situation and want to use a Free Software Unix, you'll probably have better luck with a Linux distribution right now. Several companies are willing to sell Linux systems and support contracts in the manner that large companies are used to buying their software: with a sales representative and a written contract. Those having a problem selling Linux to their superiors often have better luck once a more traditional marketing pattern is used.

> ## Your First Unix: A Suggestion
>
> If you're completely new to Unix and have no determined preferences for the operating system you want to use, I suggest Linux as a first venture. It's free to download, so you won't lay out too much cash. Many books and Web pages are out there to help you work through it, so you won't be working in a vacuum. Depending on the distribution you choose, software installation is easy and often automated, so you can keep your machine upgraded and efficient. The two distributions considered most accessible to new users are Debian and Red Hat.

TIP: Find Debian at **http://www.debian.org**, and Red Hat at **http://www.redhat.com**.

UPGRADING FROM EARLIER VERSIONS OF APACHE

Those readers who already have Apache or another Web server installed on their machines may wonder whether it's time to upgrade. While the decision whether to upgrade is a personal one, your final choice might be swayed by the various functions now available in the 2.0 release or by all the work you've put into configuring a 1.* version for your particular Web site—especially because 1.* modules won't work on a 2.0 installation without extra work.

The first step, of course, is determining whether you have a Web server running. If you just inherited a new machine or you know something is running, but you don't know what, take a few minutes to check and see what's already installed. You can install a new version alongside the existing server or wipe it off and install the new one in its place. In the following paragraphs, you learn how to disable previous servers and get some help deciding whether you should upgrade to a beta version of Apache or stay with a stable release.

NOTE: Upgrading to a new major release as soon as it comes out is always tempting. Apache 2.0 is no exception, especially because so much has changed with the new major version. However, waiting until a 2.* stable release exists before you upgrade might be prudent. Only you can determine whether it's safe to risk your Web site on beta software, which is unstable by definition.

IDENTIFYING PREVIOUS APACHE INSTALLATIONS

You probably know if you're running Apache already. If you're running a Web site, you are running a Web server and, chances are, it's Apache. You might not know which version of Apache you're running, however, especially if you weren't around when it was installed. Check the version by issuing the command

```
httpd -v
```

at the command prompt. The current version prints to the screen. Ideally, you're running a 1.3.* or later version because that's the current stable release.

If you're not sure whether a Web server is running on your machine, issue the command

```
ps ax | grep httpd
```

at the command prompt. The flags on this particular command force ps to search for all running processes, not only your own, and look for processes that match the httpd server's name. If any other Web servers are running on your machine, the processes associated with the server prints to the screen. You can kill the process with the command

```
kill -9 processnumber
```

where *processnumber* is the number associated with that process in the ps output.

If you have a Web server already installed on your machine, you need to do some work to ensure it doesn't respond to browser requests or load automatically on boot up. Several files need to be edited to remove reference to the currently installed server. The installation process, when you install the new version of Apache, reedits these files with reference to the new server.

▼ Configure the files in /etc/rc.d/init.d, where the *d* in rc.d is a number representing the particular run level being configured. These files contain the triggers for software automatically loaded at boot (on a Linux system). Open each init.d file in a text editor and remove any lines referring to httpd.

■ Configure /etc/inetd.conf, the file that handles traffic across networks, including the Internet. Open that file in a text editor and remove any lines beginning with httpd.

▲ Configure /etc/services, the file that defines all services run by the operating system. Open that file in a text editor and remove any lines beginning with httpd.

Removing Other Servers

One of the more-frequently argued topics in Unix administration is whether you should remove old software when installing newer versions or different programs. The answer depends partially on the kind of administrator you are and partially on the software itself. In addition, disk space is always a primary concern.

If you're the sort of administrator who likes to run a clean and streamlined machine, knowing where every piece of software is stored and keeping total control over the disk, you certainly want to remove the old server before you install a new version of Apache. If, on the other hand, you're the sort of administrator who doesn't care what your disk looks like as long as everything on it runs, then you may want to leave the old server there after removing any references to it from system scripts. I tend to err on the side of cleanliness.

Although I'm not an absolute stickler for disk neatness, I prefer to have only one copy of a particular server at any given time. You may differ, and as long as the older server isn't responding to browser requests, there's no reason why you absolutely must remove it.

If you decide to keep the old server around, you may want to make an exception for versions that predate the current version. That is, if the current version is 1.3.*, you should consider deleting copies of Apache with a 0.* version number. In this scenario, when 2.* becomes the stable version, you would delete copies with the version number 1.* A more careful approach to this method would be to delete copies older than the second-most recent stable version. If 1.3 is the current stable version and 1.2 was the previous stable version, then remove everything with numbers up to, but not including, 1.2.

Removing Old Software

Removing old software depends on how you installed it. If you're running a Unix variant that uses a package management tool and you installed the software with that tool, you should be able to uninstall it with the same program. Using a package management tool for software removal is a good way to ensure all the associated files are deleted, especially if they don't appear at first glance to be part of the installation.

If you installed from source code, you need to look through your root directories. Look first for a directory called /httpd or /apache. This should be in the root account's home directory. If the directory isn't there, you may need to search around until you find it. Apache 1.3 installs into the /usr directory, so look there for /usr/apache or /usr/local/apache as well. (Let's hope whoever installed the software put it in a logical place and not buried in some directory with an odd name like /blort—another argument for consistent and clear naming structures!)

Once you find the correct directory, you need to remove everything in it. You can use the rm command, but be careful. Indiscriminate use of rm can destroy files you needed and there's no way to get back files that have been removed with this command. Move into any of the subdirectories and issue the command ls to see what files are contained there. Then, issue the command

```
rm *
```

at the prompt. Depending on how your system is configured, you may be asked to confirm each file's deletion. If you don't have confirmation autoconfigured, issue the command

```
rm -i
```

which turns on delete confirmation. Once all the files are deleted, issue the command ls -la to see if any hidden files exist. Delete the hidden files with the command

```
rm filename
```

and then move up one directory and remove the subdirectory with the command

```
rmdir directoryname
```

Repeat until all files and subdirectories have been deleted.

NOTE: Yes, this is a slow and repetitive way to delete files, but it's the safest way to remove data from the disk. If you want to do it more quickly, however, change to the top directory in the Apache tree (either /httpd or /apache, depending on your installation). Issue the command rm -r. This command deletes all subdirectories and the files they contain. If you want to do this with confirmation, issue the command as rm -ir.

SHOULD YOU UPGRADE?

At times, it's better to work with an older version of software than to upgrade. One of the main reasons to hold off on an upgrade is when you have the latest stable version installed, but you're thinking about upgrading to the current beta release. Installing beta Apache should pose no problems for most Web administrators; but, if your company relies on Web traffic for any significant portion of its business, think twice before putting your trust in beta software. Stable releases are reliable and much less likely to fail spectacularly.

You should also hold off on upgrading, at least until you have time to think about programming issues, if you're running an older version of Apache that's been heavily configured to your particular situation. For example, you may have written or commissioned Apache modules for specific uses that were written to the Apache 1.3 API (Application Programming Interface, or programmer's guidelines). Modules written to the 1.3 API won't work under Apache 2.0, so if you want to continue using those modules, you shouldn't upgrade at this point. Perhaps waiting until a 2.0 version is certified as stable and getting the modules rewritten to the 2.0 API would be a better use of your time than upgrading right now.

In general, if you're happy with the way Apache is working for you right now, and you're running it on a Unix-based operating system that doesn't routinely receive a heavy load of hits, you may not need to upgrade. Heavy users can probably appreciate the newly streamlined way in which Apache 2.0 handles multiple modules and non-Unix users certainly can enjoy the tighter integration with their native APIs. Certainly, non-Unix users should upgrade as soon as practical for their situation. The non-Unix ports of Apache are quite clunky and prone to error because of the way the ports were made. Now that the APIs for those operating systems are available to Apache programmers and the 2.0 version is written in the native API for each platform, Apache should run well on all platforms: Unix and non-Unix alike.

Of course, if you're the sort of person who only runs the latest and best software, go ahead and install 2.0. It's reliable, if not completely stable, and you get the added benefit of working with bleeding edge software (one step ahead of the leading edge, of course). 2.0 will be a stable release soon enough for the rest of us.

SUMMARY

To begin working with Apache, you need to obtain the software. Although it's found on the CD-ROMs included with many computer books, you can always get the latest stable and beta versions of the server from **http://www.apache.org**. Select compressed source code packages, which should work with any platform that permits the use of code and compilers, or choose precompiled binary packages designed to work with your particular operating system. Download the files onto the machine that will host the Apache server, preferably a machine dedicated solely to the Web server or a partition devoted only to Apache on a multiple-use machine.

If at all possible, run Apache on a machine that uses a Unix or Unix-derived operating system, such as Linux or FreeBSD. Using Unix means you have more control over the server, as well as an enhanced range of security and configuration options. Even networks otherwise composed of machines running a single operating system can integrate a single Unix server machine and run just as cleanly.

Not every administrator needs to run the latest version of Apache. For many sites, running beta software is dangerous because it isn't certified as stable and might crash without warning. Keeping the latest stable version installed is enough of an upgrade for critical sites without adding in the uncertainty of lightly tested software. For those administrators who have configured their current versions of Apache heavily, the decision to upgrade must be made in light of the fact that modules written for Apache 1.* won't work on Apache 2.*. For all other administrators, the decision comes down to individual comfort with experimental software. Many amazing features certainly are in the new major version, but a stable 2.* release will be available soon enough that you needn't sacrifice reliability for new possibilities.

CHAPTER 3

Installing Apache

Once you download the appropriate software and decide how to prepare your server machine, you're ready to install Apache. You can install the server in two ways: from precompiled binary packages and from source code. The precompiled binary packages are already partially configured for particular operating systems and can save a lot of time for harried administrators. You can't adapt these binaries as closely to your particular needs as you can with an installation from source code, however. Code, on the other hand, can be tricky to work with if you don't have much experience with it, and it can be intimidating. Each administrator must find the appropriate method for installing Apache that balances skill and capability with flexibility and power.

In this chapter, you learn how to install both binary packages and source code packages for the Apache Server. The advantages and disadvantages of each type are described in their respective sections, and the installation process is laid out step by step. As with many programs available today, the installation process for Apache is fairly straightforward and requires your input only at a few points. The most important thing to remember when installing Apache for the first time is to pay attention to where the files are being placed on your hard drive and to note any error messages that print to the screen.

NOTE: If you get an error message during installation, you'll probably need to abort the installation and fix the problem before starting again.

INSTALLING APACHE FROM BINARIES

For many Apache administrators, the availability of precompiled binaries is a boon. These files have already been configured and are ready to be installed on particular operating systems without much further work on the administrator's part. Binaries are available for many popular Unix-based operating systems, as well as for non-Unix operating systems like Windows or MacOS X. In some cases, the precompiled binaries are the best way to install Apache, because on some operating systems, this is far easier than dealing directly with source code downloads.

NOTE: At press time, precompiled binaries for non-Unix systems were still available only for Apache 1.3. You may be able to find source code packages for the beta 2.0 release, however, and precompiled binaries will be available as soon as a volunteer creates them.

If you're new to Apache, using a precompiled binary for your first installation may be a good introduction to the software. You can decide later whether you need the extra control over Apache that source code can offer or whether the default configuration in the precompiled packages is sufficient for your needs. Precompiled binary downloads of Apache are currently available for these operating systems, among others:

▼ AIX, HP-UX, IRIX, and Ultrix: high-end commercial Unices

■ BSD and its derivatives: FreeBSD, NetBSD, and OpenBSD

- Linux and all its distributions
- MacOS X
- Sun operating systems: Solaris, SunOS
- ▲ Windows: Windows 95/98 and Windows NT

These platforms form the vast majority of operating systems in use on the Internet. Using an operating system that's fairly popular is a good move, especially if you plan to get involved with Apache development or merely want to seek help from more experienced Apache hands. Operating systems have unique quirks and if you're working on a rare platform, finding someone who can help you might be hard.

NOTE: If you're using another operating system that can't function with any of the platforms previously listed, you might be able to find a precompiled binary for your particular system, but you'll probably have better luck working directly with source code. See, "Installing Apache from Source Code," later in this chapter, for more information.

Identifying Appropriate Binary Packages

Finding the platform-specific binary packages on the Apache Web site is easy. Navigate to the downloads page, **http://www.apache.org/dist/**. As you move around the file listings on this site (or on a mirror site nearer to you) and select the Apache version you want to download, avoid downloading files with the `*.tar.Z` or `*.tar.gz` extensions. These are source code files and not the binaries you need. The binaries are kept in individual subdirectories named for the operating system.

When you locate the appropriate packages for your operating system, download them onto your hard drive, as described in Chapter 2, "Preparing for Apache." You probably only need to download one compressed file (be sure you have an uncompression utility that can handle the format in which the Apache files were compressed). Unix users should have `tar` and `gzip`, while Windows users will download self-extracting files. MacOS X users will download a `.tar.gz` file like that provided for Unix.

"My Platform Isn't Here . . ."

If you searched in vain through the binaries available on the Apache Web site, but you can't find a precompiled package for your operating system, don't worry. You can probably install directly from source code. Using precompiled binaries isn't a requirement for installing Apache and you won't have to give up endless hours to configuration.

Some administrators have succeeded in using precompiled binaries for an operating system similar—though not identical—to the one they're running. For example, if you're running a BSD variant, but you can't find a package for your particular flavor of BSD, try another BSD. It may work well enough for your initial needs.

Note, this isn't always a successful gambit. The idiosyncrasies of operating systems may be enough to keep you from installing another platform's binary, let alone configuring it to work efficiently.

Certainly, if you're trying to install Apache from a CD-ROM, you may have trouble with precompiled binaries. When installing from a CD-ROM that came with a magazine or book, it's best to go with the source code version. Some of these freebie CD-ROMs offer precompiled binaries, but don't mention what operating system they're compiled for! Installing an unlabeled binary package is an exercise in frustration. You always get the cleanest and latest software by downloading it directly from Apache at **http://www.apache.org**.

Uncompressing and Extracting Binaries

You might not need to uncompress precompiled binary packages, depending on your operating system. Those administrators who use package management tools (described in "Installing Binaries," the next section of this chapter) use the files just as downloaded. Windows and MacOS users will have self-extracting files, so no uncompression is necessary. MacOS X requires the use of tar and gzip, the Unix uncompression utilities.

If you need to uncompress files, however, use the utility appropriate for your system and the Apache package you downloaded. Once the files are uncompressed, look for files named README and INSTALL. You'll learn the particulars of that Apache package and what you need to do to install it on your system. Read any text files included with your distribution before you begin work.

Installing Binaries

If you're using an operating system that encourages the use of precompiled binary files, you'll probably install these packages with a package management tool. These *package management tools* are usually graphical interfaces that automate software installation, leaving the administrator little to do during the install process other than answer a few questions. You're most likely to be using a package management tool if you're using Solaris or a Linux distribution (or MacOS X), though other Unices and variants have embraced the management concept wholeheartedly because it removes one of the main frustrations for administrators.

TIP: The newest generations of package management tools offer more than just software installation. They can alert you when new versions of your programs are released, and some even download and install new software automatically. Others have a wide array of functions that help you configure your installations even more than the program's developers intended. Or, they build useful databases of all your installed software, so you can see what's already there in a single screen.

Those readers with package management software on their machines should consult the documentation for their particular tool. In general, these tools are invoked either at the command line or through a graphical interface. The graphical interface is becoming increasingly popular and may offer additional functions. Simply issue the command your package management tool needs, including the name of the Apache package you downloaded, and the tool does the rest.

> **NOTE:** If your package management tool has a verbose output feature, use it. Watching what the tool is doing as it installs your software is helpful, especially if a hitch occurs and you have to stop the installation. Likewise, if the tool generates a log, be sure to review the log afterward to see if you need to fix anything by hand.

There's not much more to it than that! The combination of precompiled binary packages and package management software (or self-extracting packages) is designed to make software installation as simple and timesaving as possible. The less an administrator interferes in the software installation process, the less likely human error will cause the installation to fail. While using the precompiled binaries and their generic configuration isn't the best solution for every Apache administrator, this is certainly a good way to get a basic Web server up and running with the least investment of time and effort.

Installing Apache on Windows

Yes, it's possible to install Apache directly onto a Windows machine. You can even download source code to do it, as long as you have an appropriate compiler already installed. Working with source code under Windows is a tricky proposition, however. If you're not already a whiz with Windows-based C++ programming, stick to the precompiled binaries. Note, depending on when you obtained your Apache files, you may have either an *.exe file or an MSI package installer file. This sidebar contains instructions for both types of file.

You can get the *.exe files for Windows from **http://www.apache.org**, as with all other Apache downloads.

NOTE: Be sure to download all relevant files! In the past, Windows packages haven't contained user documentation, so be sure to get both the binary package and the documentation package. You do need to have the documentation, and it doesn't take up much space. Be sure to install it in the same location as Apache, so you can get to the documentation files quickly when they're needed.

As with other Windows software, to start the installation, all you need to do is run the file you downloaded. Go to the directory where you put the downloaded *.exe and double-click the file, or call it up with the Run utility found in the Start menu. The file opens itself and launches a graphical installation window. Accept the conditions of the license to continue with the installation, and then accept the default location (`C:\Program Files\ Apache`). The installer prompts you to choose a type of installation; go ahead and select Typical. The Custom installation doesn't do anything significantly different from Typical.

When the installer has finished, you're prompted to click a Finish button to close the installation process. All the files should be in their correct locations. You can use Windows Explorer or the desktop icons to view the contents of the Apache folder.

If you have the newer downloads with the *msi extension, which are MSI package installer files, you need to use a different procedure. Windows Me and Windows 2000 users already have the MSI package manager installed by default. All other Windows versions need to have it installed. Obtain the MSIEXEC file from **http://www.apache.org/dist/httpd/binaries/win32**, being sure to get the right package for your Windows version. Open the folder to which you downloaded the MSIEXEC file and double-click it. The package manager then self-extracts and installs.

Once MSI has installed, it reboots the machine. When the machine restarts, open the folder to which you downloaded the Apache `*.msi` file, and double-click it. You're then prompted to accept the license terms and to provide an e-mail address for the server to use with error or warning messages. Click the Complete button and accept the default file location, `C:\Program Files\Apache Group\`. The installer then installs Apache in that location. When the installation has ended, click the Finish button. You can use Windows Explorer or the desktop icons to view the Apache folder and its contents.

Only Windows Me and Windows 2000 have MSI support on the operating system by default, so Windows NT 4.0, Windows 95, and Windows 98 users must first install MSIEXEC, available also on **http://www.apache.org/dist/httpd/binaries/win32**. Packages for several versions of Windows and Windows NT are on the page. You must download the one appropriate to your version of Windows, as well as Apache as an `*.msi` package file. Double-click the instmsi icon, or call it up with the Run utility found in the Start menu. After it has installed and rebooted your system, double-click the Apache package you downloaded. Accept the conditions of the license as before. Enter the domain and name of your server, as well as an address for the server to mail when it has problems, and then click Complete (which has replaced typical) and accept the default location (`C:\Program Files\Apache Group\`).

Troubleshooting Binary Installations

Trouble with binary package installations usually occurs during installation. If the installation crashes or fails to complete installation successfully, look for a log file or other message generated during the installation. The problem might be as simple as a missing flag or other parameter, or you may have gotten a corrupted file during download. If the problem described in the error message is something you can fix, do so and try reinstalling the package.

If a second attempt at installation fails as well, delete the package you downloaded and get another one. You may want to download from a different mirror site, if a second mirror is still reasonably close to you. Sometimes files can get corrupted during the download process, causing installation to fail, and getting a clean copy can often fix the problem.

NOTE: In the rare event that redownloading and reinstalling doesn't work, you might need to work directly from source code. See the following section, "Installing Apache from Source Code," to learn how to work with these files.

Other installation problems may not crop up until you begin configuring the system. Remember, the precompiled Apache binaries aren't as flexible as the source code—so if one of the configurations is causing you trouble, it might not be easily fixed unless you turn to the source code distribution instead. In general, the precompiled packages should work as long as you have a reasonably standard installation of your operating system. If you've done a lot of unique configuration or you're running nonstandard patches, expect to spend some time working with your installation. Such sites are better off installing from source code anyway.

INSTALLING APACHE FROM SOURCE CODE

While the precompiled binary packages described in the previous section, "Installing Apache from Binaries," are certainly useful, the real power of Apache is available only when you choose to install the server directly from the source code itself. Installing from source code requires a bit more work on your part, but you're rewarded with greater flexibility and the power to configure your particular installation in exactly the right way. Precompiled binaries sacrifice some configurability to convenience.

Working with source code can seem intimidating at first. It removes the comforting middleman of the graphical installation interface and requires you to work directly with both the code and the operating system. What you gain from this process, however, is a much better understanding of how the software interacts with the operating system. You also gain the opportunity to configure individual aspects of the server, changes that might not be possible with the generic configuration of the precompiled binary packages.

NOTE: The directions in this chapter are for those using Unix or Unix-based operating systems. Those using other operating systems should see the sidebar "Source Code and Non-Unix Systems" in this chapter to learn how to use source packages on their own machines.

CAUTION: You must install Apache when you're using root or have otherwise assumed superuser capabilities. You cannot install Apache in a regular user account and expect it to work. If you don't have superuser privileges on this machine, you must obtain them before proceeding with the installation.

What Is Source Code?

What exactly is this mysterious source code, anyway? *Source code* is essentially the code as it was written by the programmer. It is the set of instructions written to direct the operating system's behavior. Unix source code is usually written in the C or C++ programming languages, though some new languages—like Java—are beginning to appear in recent code.

Although C and C++ are common languages, you cannot directly run code written in those languages on your machine. Rather, you need to *compile* the code into a format readable by your operating system before it can be used. Unix systems should have at least one compiler installed, and most Unix-based operating systems include a compiler as part of the default installation. The compile process changes the code from programming language into machine-readable binary code. Thus, the binary packages described in the previous chapter have already been compiled and can simply be run as executable files on the server machine.

Getting the Right Code

Getting the right code to install Apache is easy. As with the binary packages, your best bet is to go to the Apache Web site and download the latest packages. If this is the first time you've worked with source code, download the latest stable release for your initial installation. You can install the beta release when you're more confident about your installation and configuration abilities.

TIP: Several different packages of the source code are available at **http://www.apache.org**. See Chapter 2, "Preparing for Apache," to learn what the different extensions mean and what sort of uncompression software you need to pull the files apart.

Download the files into an appropriate directory on your system. The best place to keep downloaded files is in /tmp. By its very name, the /tmp directory shows it's a place for transient files. During installation, you tell Apache where the downloaded file should go permanently; but when the install is completed, you can clean out /tmp without worrying.

Source Code and Non-Unix Systems

If you aren't running a Unix-based operating system, you can still work with source code, but you need to purchase a third-party commercial compiler to do so. For example, Windows administrators often choose the Borland C++ compiler. Note that some compilers are fussy about the kind of code they'll work with. You may need to obtain a second compiler to work with files written in C, not C++.

A good habit is to download all files into one consistent directory. If you put files in different places when you download them, keeping track of what software is where is difficult, and keeping your disk clear of extraneous data is hard. You can also use the /usr/tmp directory. The point is to designate a part of your directory system as the place where temporary files are stored.

Identifying Source Code Packages

Apache files are named in a consistent manner. You can tell simply by looking at the filename which version you have downloaded and how it was compressed. The filename always begins with the word apache, and is then followed by the version number and an extension showing the file type. So, the filename

```
apache_1.3.12.tar.gz
```

shows the version contained in this package is Apache 1.3.12, and the file has been compressed with both the tar and gzip utilities.

TIP: You may also find packages labeled httpd_version.number instead of apache. The Apache server is a form of the httpd server, a generic term for any server that works with the Hypertext Transfer Protocol.

If you keep more than one uncompiled version of Apache on your hard drive (perhaps you're running a public site with the stable release and building a prototype site with the beta release), don't change the filenames. Filenames are the easiest way to figure out what you're working with. If you change the name for any reason, you may make distinguishing one uncompiled package from another difficult. The only way to tell what version you have is to unpack it and check.

Uncompressing and Extracting Source Code

Now that you've downloaded the appropriate version of Apache in uncompiled source code and placed it in the /tmp directory, you're ready to start the installation process. When working with source code, the first step is to uncompress the files. This can be a rather impressive process, as a single file magically mushrooms into dozens upon dozens of individual files. Apache is no different. When you uncompress the source code package, it automatically creates a complete directory structure, sorting all those files into their appropriate locations for compilation.

To unpack the source code package, move into the /tmp directory. At the command prompt, issue the command

```
tar xvfz filename
```

substituting the actual name of the Apache package you downloaded for the wildcard filename. The tar xvfz filename command unpacks the compressed file, expanding all the individual files to their full sizes. This particular version of the `tar` command puts `tar` into *verbose* mode, so you see a list of all the files scroll up your screen as the archive uncompresses. Many files are in the Apache tarballs, so don't expect to be able to read each individual filename as it goes past.

> **TIP:**   The term *tarball* is used to refer to file archives compressed with the `tar` program.

Once the filenames have stopped scrolling and you're returned to a command prompt, issue the command `ls`. This prints the contents of the current directory, showing you filenames and directories. Note, unpacking the source code package created a new subdirectory with a name similar to that of the file you unpacked. Change into that directory with the command

```
cd directoryname
```

and issue another `ls` command. In this directory, you see a number of subdirectories, as well as several files with single-word names written in capital letters. Of particular concern at this point are the README and INSTALL files. Open each file with the commands

```
more README
```

and

```
more INSTALL
```

You may want to print these files or keep them open in a separate terminal window while you work.

> **CAUTION:**   If any direction in those files is different from information you get in this book or in other sources, **always follow the directions in the files that accompany the software**.

In general, whenever you install files from source code, stop and read any files that have urgent names. README and INSTALL are typical names for such files. These files contain critical information about installing the software. For example, sometimes things change for a particular version after the accompanying documentation has been written—or perhaps no documentation exists. If you don't read the README file, you won't know about special steps you might have to take to get the package to install properly.

Apache usually installs normally, so the README and INSTALL files shouldn't hold any major surprises. Those files are the last chance the developers have to communicate with you before you install, however, so checking them out first is always a good idea. You can also move into the `docs` subdirectory and see what sort of documentation is contained with this package, though much of it is man pages and other material accessible from within Apache once it's installed. (*Man pages* are documentation files installed by default on most Unix systems. You can access the pages by issuing the command man *command* at the system prompt, where *command* is the program or command you want to learn about.)

> *TIP:* Apache documentation is quite good. In the world of Free Software, documentation is some-times the forgotten child, and many popular programs have little or no usable documentation. Apache is the shining exception, with files that are both comprehensive and readable.

Installing from Source Code

When the package has been successfully unpacked, you're ready to begin installing. Most software installed from source code can be added using a simple procedure, and Apache falls into that category. Much of the installation work is done automatically, but you must issue three separate commands in the proper order to move the process along. The process is divided into three steps:

▼ **Configuration**   In this step, you run a small script that checks your system hardware and software. The script also checks for essential system files that are required for the proper function of the software you're installing.

■ **Building**   Once the configuration of your system has been noted, you can compile the software. As mentioned previously, compilation is the process of changing code from the programming language into a machine-readable executable binary file.

▲ **Installation**   Finally, once the code has been compiled, it can be installed as an actual program on the hard drive. When installation is finished, the program can be run like any other program, configured, and managed with commands at the system prompt or through a menu system.

If you've installed Unix software before, you already know how to install Apache. If this is your first time installing Unix software, you learn a set of skills that are transferable to almost any other Unix program you might want to install later.

Compiling Apache 1.3

Once you read the README and INSTALL files, look for files named `Configuration` and `configuration.tmpl`. This is a template file that sets up the structure for another file used in the compilation process. If you don't already have a file named `Configuration`, copy the `configuration.tmpl` file to a new file called `Configuration`, using the command

```
cp configuration.tmpl Configuration
```

Open the Configuration file with your preferred text editor (see Appendix B, "Using a Unix Text Editor," for more information). The main function of the Configuration file is to alert the installer to which modules you want to install. Apache is a modular program. You select which features should be included in the installation by choosing which modules to include or delete at installation.

NOTE: The modules contained in the Configuration file by default are the basic set of modules Apache 1.3 needs to function correctly. Don't remove modules unless you are well aware of what you're doing and how you'll handle those functions in the absence of the module. See Chapter 5, "Apache Modules," for more information.

For your first installation of Apache 1.3, don't amend the Configuration file. Simply look it over, noting the various kinds of information contained within the file. Four general categories of commands are in this file:

▼ **Makefile** Commands that affect how the Makefile (used in the next step of installation) is configured

■ **Rules** Commands that tell the installer what system rules you want Apache to obey

▲ **Modules** Commands that define which modules should be added to this installation of Apache and how they should be configured

Pay special attention to the lines in the Rules section of the file. If any commands here call for settings you don't have configured on this system, edit the file so it reflects your actual setup. Save the file and close the editor. You are now ready to proceed with configuration.

To run the configuration script, simply issue the command Configure at a system prompt. The script then starts, and you see several lines of output. Depending on your machine setup, you may or may not see all the following lines (don't worry if you don't see all the lines beginning with +):

```
% Configure
Using 'Configuration' as config file
   + configured for <name> platform
   + setting C compiler to <name>
   + setting C compiler optimization-level to <level>
   + Adding selected modules
   + doing sanity check on compiler and options
Creating Makefile in support
Creating Makefile in main
Creating Makefile in os/unix
Creating Makefile in modules/standard
```

The configuration script has checked your particular setup and noted those settings in the various Makefiles it created. A *Makefile* is a file generated by configuration scripts in the standard Unix installation process. It contains individual settings for your system and tells the actual installer how to handle your unique configuration during installation.

Makefiles also contain any error messages generated during the configuration script's work. A good idea is always to scan the Makefiles before proceeding further. Look over the general Makefile by issuing the command

```
more Makefile
```

at the system prompt. If you're also installing the support functions (recommended), change directories to the support directory and read the Makefile there as well.

Compiling Apache 2.0

After reading the README and INSTALL files (and any other files with important-sounding names), you can proceed to compiling the program. Apache 2.0 has changed to a more traditional compilation process, unlike the method used for Apache 1.3.* and earlier. To install Apache 2.0, follow the steps described in the remainder of this section.

In the directory where you chose to install Apache, issue the command

```
./configure
```

at the system prompt. A series of messages then scroll past on the screen, probably too fast to read. Don't worry too much about missing a message, as these are simply reports from the installer. If the configuration process runs without trouble, the last line should read "Created Makefile," "Makefile successfully created," or some similar phrase.

When you see a successful Makefile message and the command prompt has returned, issue the command

```
make
```

at the prompt. This command begins the compile process, converting the downloaded source code into machine-executable binary code. The make process may take a while, depending on your system configuration and the directions contained in the Makefile. You see another list of messages scroll by; keep an eye on these if possible. Errors will stop the make process. If you get an error, resolve the problem before trying again.

When the make process finishes and the system prompt has returned, issue the command

```
make install
```

This is the final step of the installation process and this actually installs the Apache Server on your machine.

When you're ready to do a more complicated installation, you can configure Apache before compiling it. In the directory where you chose to install Apache, issue the command

```
./configure -help | more
```

This command displays the four areas in which you can configure the initial Apache installation:

▼ **Configuration**   Commands to the configuration program that don't affect how Apache is installed.

■ **Directory and Filenames**   The locations for required software libraries and other directories. You should need this category only if files are stored on your machine in nonstandard locations.

■ **Host type**   The kind of machine on which Apache is being installed. This is usually determined by the install program when it builds the Makefile, so you probably won't need to make changes here.

▲ **Features and Packages**   The primary part of the configuration for most users, these commands enable various Apache features and modules.

Building Apache

Once you run the configure script, check the Makefile, and fix any errors reported there, you're ready to build the code. Unix administrators usually use the term *build* to refer to the process of compiling the code. This is a simple process, which requires only one piece of input from you.

To compile the configured source code, issue the command

```
make
```

at the system prompt. The make program takes the data from the Makefiles generated in the previous step. Then, it compiles the Apache source code into a machine-readable binary file, which takes into account the settings and options on your system that are selected in the Configuration file.

NOTE: To build the code, the make program runs the original source code through a compiler. You need to have the gcc compiler installed on your system for Apache to compile correctly. If you don't have gcc, you can't build the code. You can get gcc at any Unix software archive or directly from the GNU project at **http://www.gnu.org**.

Installing Apache

When the compiler finishes and you return to the command prompt, it's time for the actual installation. The make process has generated a single executable binary file called httpd, which has been placed in the /src directory of your Apache files. Change to that directory.

TIP: People installing the precompiled binary packages described in the previous chapter begin working with Apache at this point. From here on, the method of installation is basically the same unless a package management tool is used to install the precompiled package.

Because Apache installs into the directory from which httpd is run, you need to decide where to install it. Up to this point, you've been working in the /tmp directory (or in whichever directory you downloaded the code into). Go back to the root directory and create a new directory called apache with the command

mkdir apache

Move back to the /tmp/httpd/src or /tmp/apache/src directory and issue the command

mv httpd ../../apache

This command moves the executable httpd binary into the new apache directory. You can now run the file and let it create a full set of directories in the appropriate place.

Change back to the new apache directory and issue the command

make install

at the system prompt. This command runs the httpd binary and installs the Apache server onto your hard disk. The installation procedure doesn't take long, though the actual time used depends on your processor speed and amount of RAM. When the system prompt returns, Apache is installed.

Browse through the new subdirectories to see what's there. You'll have a set of documentation files in the /doc subdirectory and the /conf directory will contain a set of configuration files.

TIP: The configuration files are covered in detail in Chapter 6, "Configuring and Testing Apache." You can see the full text of these files in Appendix E, "Apache Configuration Files."

You can save some time when invoking the server if you put its directory into your PATH environment variable. Not putting it in PATH means you must use the full directory name, such as /apache/httpd, when you start the server. You probably won't be starting the server that frequently, however, so this is a judgment call. Consult a Unix reference if you don't know how to edit your environment variables.

NOTE: If you plan to compile the support programs—a good idea—change into the support directory at this time and issue the command make at the system prompt. This installs all the various support software automatically.

The last installation step is simply housework. Go back to the /tmp directory and clean out any files that remain from the download or installation process. Some administrators like to save the downloaded tarball in an archive directory, so they have ready access to the code they've installed. If you like that idea, move the downloaded file to the archive directory (often /usr/src). Otherwise, delete it with the rest of the files. All the files necessary for Apache's functioning have been placed in their proper locations by the installer, and none of them should be in /tmp.

NOTE: If you haven't set the system time correctly, do so now. Apache and its log functions rely on correct system time, as do many other programs on your machine.

Troubleshooting Source Code Installations

If the installation fails at any point, first read through the Makefile or other log file generated by the particular process you're using. Error messages are usually sent to logs during Unix installation instead of being printed to the screen. Also, make sure you have a current and functioning compiler on your system. If you aren't sure, reinstall gcc from code (you can use this same basic process) before installing Apache.

TIP: If the process fails and you can't figure out why, try cleaning out every file already generated, either from the unpacking or the installation. Then, download a fresh copy of the source code and start again. The file may have been slightly corrupted during the download.

Another likely source of error appears if you edit any of the configuration files before proceeding to the next step. If you made changes to Configuration, such as deleting particular modules or changing Rules settings, try reinstalling with a default Configuration file to see if that solves the problem. The syntax of Configuration is quite specific. Also, when you read the Makefiles after running the configuration script, never make changes. The Makefile needs to be in the same state when it's used during build. If problems occur in the Makefile, go back to the configuration step and start over rather than editing the Makefile. Advanced administrators can edit Makefiles carefully, but it's not something for the neophyte or inattentive person to do.

A third common source of installation errors lies in the software already installed on your machine. If you don't have the appropriate *software libraries* (data the compiler uses to build the code) installed, the build or installation may fail. Check the Makefile to see whether a particular library is causing the failure. You may need to obtain a particular library from a software archive or reinstall your compiler.

SUMMARY

The fastest and easiest way to install Apache is by downloading and installing precompiled binary packages designed for your particular operating system. Such packages are available for a wide variety of platforms, including most of the Unices and Unix variants, as well as the personal operating systems like Windows and MacOS X. These packages take into account any idiosyncrasies of the operating system for which they're designed and also offer a generic Apache configuration, which is sufficient for many smaller or general Web sites. To install a precompiled binary package, you'll probably use a package management tool that's part of your operating system. Whether this is run from the command line or has a graphical interface, such a tool handles most of the installation work automatically, requiring little input from you during the process. If you have trouble during installation, check any error messages or logs for suggestions, or download another copy of the binary package and reinstall. If the problem persists, consider installing Apache directly from source code instead.

Apache is the most flexible and configurable when it's installed from source code, code that's basically the programmers' output. With source code, you can decide which modules to use and make sure Apache is configured to work with your particular hardware setup. Download source code packages from the Apache Web site, being sure to get files compressed with utilities you have installed on your system. Installing source code packages is a three-part process. First, edit a configuration file and run the configuration script included in the Apache download. This script determines your hardware configuration and creates a series of Makefile documents to assist the compiler in the next step. After configuring, build the code. This second step involves a compiler, which changes the programmers' output into machine-readable binary code. Third, and finally, install the program onto the hard drive. Once you install the software, you can begin to configure it for your particular needs.

CHAPTER 4

Running a Heterogeneous Network

Unless you run a very small network indeed, you probably have machines connected to your network that run different operating systems. In some cases, these differing systems are merely different Unix variants, such as Linux and FreeBSD. In other cases, especially those in a commercial setting, the different systems might include a Unix variant or two, a Windows version, and possibly some Macintoshes. Whether you have only two operating systems on your network or many more than that, you're running a *heterogeneous network*.

TIP: People who have only one operating system across the network have *homogeneous networks* instead. This is often the case for home networks or in small commercial installations.

While heterogeneous networks are common because different operating systems do different tasks well, the administrative side can be complicated. Some of these operating systems don't communicate well and others don't communicate at all. The administrator's task is to get these different systems talking to each other and to make the overall network run as smoothly as possible, no matter what operating system a particular user is logged into.

Luckily, software programs are available to do exactly those things. In this chapter, you learn about two of these programs: Samba, designed to connect Windows and Unix machines, and netatalk, designed to connect Macintoshes and Unix machines. These programs are simple to configure and use, and have made heterogeneous networks a lot less complicated for thousands of administrators. This chapter covers installation and configuration of Samba and netatalk, as well as more general information about building and maintaining heterogeneous networks. The issues relevant to administrators who run multiple Unix variants are also addressed.

Heterogeneous networks are the answer for many administrators with a number of users. The different skills and job requirements within your user base will probably require you to install several operating systems, so each user can work with the software required for his or her job. For example, the graphics department probably needs Quark Xpress on Macs, while the finance department wants Peachtree Accounting on Windows, and the administrators want Perl and C++ on Unix. You can meet all these needs—and run your Apache server on a Unix variant as well—if you use the right software to build the network.

SAMBA FOR WINDOWS USERS

The program most widely used to connect Windows and Unix machines is called *Samba*. Samba takes the Session Message Block (SMB) protocol, which Windows uses to move data, and converts it to a native Unix protocol, because Unix cannot understand data written in SMB. Samba is a suite of programs that takes different sorts of SMB data and converts them to Unix-recognizable formats. If you're working with Windows NT, Samba can even force your Unix servers to emulate NT servers, so there's as little loss of data as possible.

You may already have Samba installed on your Unix variant because it's included more frequently with some versions of Unix. However, check for newer versions at the Samba project's home site, **http://www.samba.org**. Run the newest version of Samba that you can handle to get the latest features and security patches. Install the software on your Unix machine in the same way you install other packages (see Chapter 3, "Installing Apache," for information about installing both precompiled binary packages and source code packages).

NOTE: Only basic Samba configuration is covered in this book. If you're interested in learning more about the program, get a copy of *Using Samba* (Robert Ecksten and David Collier-Brown (O'Reilly, 1999). Although this book isn't written by members of the Samba team, the developers have adopted it as the official documentation for the program.

Configuring Samba

Once Samba is installed, it must be configured. The main Samba configuration happens in the /etc/samba/smb.conf file. Open this file in your favorite text editor and look at it. Most smb.conf files are quite short, though all must have at least the [global] entry to define the network settings.

TIP: The location of the Samba configuration file can vary depending on the method you used to install the package. Some installations, such as the Linux RPM package format, place the file in the /etc directory; while installing on Red Hat (and others) from the source places the file in /usr/local/samba/lib.

Windows Apache administrators need to remember that each directory you want to share with Windows machines on the network must also have its own entry. In the case of a Web server, you probably want to include entries for each directory where users might place files. Note, the Samba configuration file uses the semicolon (;) instead of the hashmark (#) to denote comments, lines that won't be treated as code by the computer. A basic smb.conf file looks like this:

```
[global]
    workgroup = WEBDESIGN
    server string = designfiles
    encrypt passwords = Yes
    update encrypted = Yes
    log file = /var/log/samba/log
    max log size = 60
    socket options = TCP_NODELAY SO_RCVBUF=8192 SO_SNDUP=8192
    dns proxy = no
```

With this global configuration, the name of the network is defined as WEBDESIGN in the Windows machines' Network Neighborhood folder. Use anything you like as the network name, but try to keep it obvious so your users can find the correct folder and file. The server string variable defines the text that appears under the icon in the WEBDESIGN folder. The log file location defines where Samba logs are to be written and the log size variable defines the maximum number of lines in the file at any time. The socket options variable determines how data is to be sent across this network, while the dns proxy variable denotes whether this server (the Samba server) is going to be a local DNS proxy server.

To define an individual directory that's going to be made available to every Windows machine on the network, you must add a separate entry. Having separate entries for each directory means you can choose to share only certain directories, such as the public HTML directories, with your user base. This is especially helpful if your users all have Windows desktop machines and you want to control which directories they can use on the Unix machines. The individual directory entries take this format:

```
[directoryname]
    comment = text to go under icon
        path = directory path
        guest ok = yes
        writable = yes
        printable = no
        public = yes
```

The path variable should contain the actual directory path on the Unix machine. The value of guest ok determines whether users must log in with their actual password and user name or whether you allow anyone on the network to access the directory. The writable and printable variables set file permissions. If you want users to see data in the directory, but to not change anything, set writable to no. If you set writable to no, however, nobody else can add data or files to that directory.

When you finish configuring Samba, save the file and exit the editor. Start Samba by issuing the command

```
/etc/init.d/samba start
```

at the command prompt. (If you already had Samba running before you configured it, issue the command /etc/init.d/samba restart instead.) You can see the Windows machines attached to the network from the Unix machine, but you won't be able to see the Unix machines from the Windows machines yet. This is because each Windows machine must be individually configured to recognize the new network.

NOTE: On systems that use System V init methods, a good idea is to place an entry for Samba into /etc/init.d, the file that defines the programs that automatically start when the system boots up. Learn more about /etc/init.d and other init styles in Chapter 7, "Managing the Apache Server."

On each Windows95 machine attached to the network, open the Control Panel and select the Network icon. Select one of the TCP/IP components, click the Properties button of the Network box, and make sure you have your network's gateway and DNS numbers entered correctly. Next, click the Identification tab and enter the Windows machine's name and the network name in the appropriate text boxes. The Unix machine needs machine names for each of the Windows machines, so it can sort out the data flow correctly.

CAUTION: Use the same network name you defined in the `[global]` entry of your Samba configuration or you won't be able to see the Unix machines across the network.

Click the Apply button to set changes, or simply click OK to save and exit the Network box. Open the Network Neighborhood icon on the desktop to see if the Unix machines have appeared. If not, reboot the Windows machine and check again. Rebooting usually gets them to show up.

NETATALK FOR MACINTOSH USERS

Just as Samba translates the Windows SMB format into a protocol that Unix machines can understand, the `netatalk` program translates the Macintosh AppleTalk protocol into a Unix-understandable data protocol. As with Samba, once you install and configure `netatalk`, Macintosh users on your network can see and use any Unix directories you made available to them. `netatalk` has run successfully on a wide range of Unices, especially FreeBSD, because it has `netatalk` support directly integrated into the kernel. Regardless of the Unix variant you installed, you should be able to install `netatalk`.

TIP: If you run into trouble while you're installing or running `netatalk`, consult the `netatalk` Web site. A number of helpful files are there, including a useful HOWTO file and a number of bug notes related to various Unix variants. You can probably fix your problem after you visit the site.

Get the latest version of `netatalk` from the Web at **http://www.umich.edu/~rsug/netatalk/**. Like Apache, the `netatalk` team usually has both a stable and a beta version of the program available for download. Pick the stable version—unless file sharing isn't a primary need for your network, and you have the time to chase down bugs and report them. Once you download the appropriate `netatalk` packages, install the software on your Unix machine using the techniques described in Chapter 3, "Installing Apache."

NOTE: Linux users should download `netatalk` 1.3.3 or higher because those versions contain explicit Linux support. FreeBSD users should be running FreeBSD 2.2 or higher, which has `netatalk` support integrated into the kernel. If you're running Solaris, you need `netatalk` 1.4b2 or higher, especially if you want to print. `netatalk` supports the native Sun print format only in version 1.4 and higher. If you don't plan to print, earlier versions of `netatalk` may work for you.

Configuring netatalk

Once you install `netatalk`, it's time to configure. Unlike Samba, `netatalk` requires quite a bit of configuration and uses five different configuration files to set its parameters. The five files you need are found in the `/etc/netatalk/conf` directory after installation. Don't edit these files directly! Instead, copy them to the `/usr/local/atalk/etc` directory.

NOTE: `netatalk` installs to the `/usr/local/atalk` directory by default. If `netatalk` didn't do so when you installed it, open the Makefile and check the DESTDIR variable. Change it to `/usr/local/atalk` and install again.

To move the five files, issue the following commands at the system prompt (the prompt returns after each `cp` command is completed):

```
cp /etc/netatalk/conf/atalkd.conf /usr/local/atalkd/atalkd.conf
cp /etc/netatalk/conf/apfd.conf /usr/local/atalkd/apfd.conf
cp /etc/netatalk/conf/AppleVolumes.default /usr/local/atalkd/AppleVolumes.conf
cp /etc/netatalk/conf/AppleVolumes.system /usr/local/atalkd/AppleVolumes.system
cp /etc/netatalk/conf/config /usr/local/atalkd/config
```

atalkd.conf

The `atalkd.conf` file is short and easy to use. It sets the parameters used for the Macintoshes' network interfaces when they connect to the Unix machine for files. Because `netatalk`'s daemon, called `atalkd`, has strong auto-detection capabilities, you don't need to change anything in this file. If you're the type of administrator who installs fallbacks wherever possible, though, you can simply add an entry for `eth0` (on Linux or FreeBSD and similar variants) or `le0` (on Solaris and other Sun-like Unices). Here's a complete `atalkd.conf` file with an `eth0` entry for a Linux machine:

```
#
#  Format of lines in this file:
#
#      interface [ -seed ] [ -phase ] [ 1 | 2 ] [ -addr net.node ]
#      [ -net first[-last] ] [ -zone ZoneName ]  . . .
#
#  -seed only works if you have multi-interfaces. Any missing arguments
#  are automatically configured from the network. Note: lines can't actually
#  be split, tho it's a good idea.
#
#  Some examples:
#
#  The simplest case is no atalkd.conf. This works on most platforms
#  (notably not Solaris), since atalkd can discover the local
#  interfaces on the machine.
#
#  Very slightly more complicated:
```

```
#
#     le0
# or
#     eth0
# for Solaris/SunOS or Linux.
#
# A much more complicated example:
#
#     le0 -phase 1
#     le1 -seed -phase 2 -addr 66.6 -net 66-67 -zone "No Parking"
#
# This turns on transition routing between the le0 and le1 interfaces
# on a Sun. It also causes atalkd to fail if other routers disagree
# about its configuration of le1.
#
eth0
```

apfd.conf

The `apfd.conf` file manages password access from remote Macintoshes on your network. Because passwords are a major source of security failure, as described in Chapter 20, "Basic Security Concerns," `netatalk` uses a password-security concept called shadow passwords.

TIP: *Shadow passwording* means your users' passwords aren't actually stored in the `/etc/passwd` file, but are automatically encrypted (again, because `/etc/passwd` also encrypts) and stored elsewhere, usually in `/etc/shadow`.

Using shadow passwords with `netatalk` enhances the secure transfer of data, because this is one more safeguard against unauthorized access of your Unix server.

NOTE: If you want to enable shadow passwords, you must configure the Makefile to include shadow password support before you install the `netatalk` software. After you run the configuration step of installation, locate the file `/etc/afpd/Makefile` and open it in a text editor. Find the entry beginning with `CFLAGS:`, and just before the hashmark in that line, add the phrase `~DSHADOWPW`. Save the file, exit the editor, and proceed with installation.

Like the `atalkd.conf` file, `apfd.conf` is well commented and straightforward. The following is a sample `apfd.conf` file that shows several sample entries and the correct syntax for these entries. You needn't use shadow passwords with `netatalk`, but if you think they're an appropriate security measure for your system, you can use the `apfd.conf` comments to build a configuration file to meet your network's needs.

```
#
# Format of lines in this file:
#
#    server [ -tcp ] [ -ddp ] [ -guest ] [ -loginmesg message ] . . .
```

```
#
# To specify a line with the default server name, use a "-" as the
# server name.
#
# There are a whole plethora of options available. Here they are
# for your edification:
#
#    toggles [-no<option> turns that option off; -<option> turns it on:
#        transports: tcp, ddp, transall
#        debug: nodebug (can only turn off debug)
#        auth: cleartxt, afskrb, krbiv, guest, randnum, rand2num
#            authall (doesn't include randnum/rand2num)
#        passwd: savepassword, setpassword
#        user volumes: uservolfirst, nouservol (don't look for
#            ~/.AppleVolumes)
#
#    options w/ argumrnts (-<option> <argument>):
#        defaultvol, systemvol, loginmesg, guestname address (binds
#        a server to a specific address)
#        port (has to be specified if more than one tcp server is
#            to be served)
#        ticklevel (sets the tickle interval in seconds)
#        uampath, nlspath
#
# Order of precedence:
#    options in afpd.conf > command-line options > built-in options
#
# Some examples:
#
#    The simplest case is not to have an apfd.conf.
#
#    4 servers w/ names server1-3 and one w/ the hostname. Servers 1-3
#    get routed to different ports with server 3 being bound specifically
#    to address 192.168.1.3
#        -
#        server1 -port 12000
#        server2 -port 12001
#        server3 -port 12002 -address 192.168.1.3
#
#    a dedicated guest server, a user server, and a special ddp-only server:
#        "Guest Volume" -nocleartxt -loginmesg "Welcome Guest!"
#        "User Volume" -noguest -port 12000
#        "special" -notcp -defaultvol <path> -systemvol <path>
#
```

AppleVolumes.default

When one of your regular users logs into the network using netatalk, the AppleVolumes.default file is called into play. This file determines how a given user can use the volumes and file types on the network. If your users want to override your general settings defined in this file, they can create individual AppleVolumes files in their user accounts, but most users won't do so, preferring to rely on the system defaults. Therefore, a good idea is to review the AppleVolumes.default file, even if you don't change anything, so you know how network connections and file transfers are managed.

The most basic AppleVolumes.default file contains only the tilde character, or ~. This character sets the user's home directory as the default for any logins from a known user. If you want to make more configurations, use the comments to help you construct entries. The following shows a sample AppleVolumes.default file.

```
#  This file looks empty when viewed with "vi". In fact, there is one '~'
#  so users with no AppleVolumes file in their home directory get their
#  home directory by default.
#
#volume format:
#path [name ] [casefold=x] [codepage=y] [options=z,l,j] [access=a,@b,c,d]
#    [dbpath=path] [password=p]
#
#casefold options:
#tolower      -> lowercases names in both directions
#toupper      -> uppercases names in both directions
#xlatelower  -> client sees lowercase, server sees upper
#xlateupper  -> client sees uppercase, server sees lower
#
# access format:
# user1,@group,user2  -> restricts volume to listed users and groups
#
# miscellaneous options:
# prodos         -> make compatible with appleII clients
# crlf           -> enable crlf translation for TEXT files
# noadouble      -> don't create .AppleDouble unless a resource fork needs
#      to be created
#
# codepage=filename     -> load filename from nls directory
# dbpath=path           -> store the database stuff in the named path
# password=password     -> set a volume password (eight characters max)
#
#
~ Home
```

AppleVolumes.system

Of all the configuration files used with `netatalk`, the `AppleVolumes.system` file is the most lengthy and complex. Luckily, you'll probably never need to touch the file and can exist quite happily with the default file provided when you install the `netatalk` program. The `AppleVolumes.system` file maps the disk volumes to pathnames so files can be distributed accurately across the network, regardless of how they're defined on their home operating system.

CAUTION: The language and syntax in this file is extremely specific. Be careful if you do edit the file. A mistake will cause the volume in question to return an "Unknown Document" file every time it's accessed.

In this sample from an `AppleVolumes.system` file, you can see the file defines precise file types. Each entry contains the file extension used by a particular file type, the type itself, and the program on the Macintosh that opens or runs the file as necessary.

```
# Last updated July 8, 1999
#
#Use at your own risk. No guarantees express or implied.
#
# Try to use MacPerl script 'ICDumpSuffixMap' included in /usr/doc
# to download file mapping list from your Internet Config Preference.
#

.text/plain    "TEXT"    "ttxt"    ASCII Text        SimpleText
.mf            "TEXT"    "*MF"     Metafont          Metafont
.sty           "TEXT"    "*TEX"    TeX Style         TeXtures
.psd           "BBPS"    "8BIM"    PhotoShop         PhotoShop
.pxr           "PXR"     "8BIM"    Pixar Image       PhotoShop
.sea           "APPL"    "????"    Self-Extracting Archive
.apd           "TEXT"    "ALD3"    Aldus             PageMaker
.pm3           "ALB3"    "ALD3"    PageMaker 3       PageMaker
```

The file covers multiple pages and contains entries for every possible file type that may come across your network. If you use unique file types in your work, check the `AppleVolumes.system` file to see whether an entry already exists for that type. If not, add one so your users can work with these files on your network.

config

Finally, the `config` file is the standard configuration file for `netatalk` itself. As with most of the other configuration files, the `config` file is short and basic. Each entry turns a particular `netatalk` module on or off. The file also sets the name of the server as seen over AppleTalk and defines the number of clients that can be connected to the Unix machine over `netatalk` at any given time. The following shows a sample `config` file with basic settings.

```
# AppleTalk configuration
# Change this to increase the maximum number of clients that can connect:
AFPD_MAX_CLIENTS=10
# Change this to set the machine's atalk name:
# ATALK_NAME='echo $(HOSTNAME) | cut -d. fl'
ATALK_NAME=webdesignserver
# Set which daemons to run:
PAPD_RUN=no
AFPD_RUN=yes
# Control whether the daemons are started in background
ATALK_BGROUND=yes
```

When you finish editing all the configuration files, you can start `netatalk`. Issue the command

```
/etc/init.d/netatalk start
```

at the command prompt to boot the server. If the Macintoshes on the network were already attached to the network before you booted the server, you should be able to see them from the Unix machine now. (If they don't, issue the command /etc/init.d/netatalk restart to reboot the server. One reboot usually brings them up.)

NOTE: FreeBSD and BSD-like users will probably be done at this point because `netatalk` runs almost perfectly on BSD Unices. Linux users may have to consult the Linux `netatalk` HOWTO document, written by Anders Brownworth, which can be found at **http://www.thehamptons.com/ anders/netatalk**. Solaris users need to read the `README.SOLARIS` file packaged with the `netatalk` downloads.

WHEN YOU RUN MULTIPLE FLAVORS OF UNIX

While this may seem like the easiest option for a heterogeneous network, running several different Unix variants brings its own complications. Certainly, it's simpler to move between machines that use basically the same command language, but subtle differences exist between Unices that can throw a wrench into your network. The solution is the Network File System (NFS).

NFS makes moving files and other data across a multiple-Unix network simple, regardless of the individual quirks of each Unix variant connected to the network. With NFS, you can mount directories either locally or remotely. That is, you can be at machine 1 and pull up a directory on machine 3, use it as if it were a local directory, and then unmount it when you finish. You can even use NFS to run automatic processes remotely, such as a mail notification program or some administrative programs and scripts.

If you've done much reading about Unix or have participated in discussions about administering Unix systems, you may have seen warnings about NFS as a security risk. Yes, NFS has some security problems. No alternative exists, however, for efficient and transparent file sharing across a multiple-Unix network, so we must live with NFS and its risks. The best way to deal with the NFS holes is to beef up your external security and to keep a good eye on your internal traffic and users.

NOTE: Don't install NFS on the main partition of your main server machine. Put it somewhere else, perhaps even on its own machine. With that simple precaution, you can lock down the server if one of its well-known security flaws is exploited.

You probably have NFS already because it's included with almost all Unix distributions, regardless of variant. In fact, NFS probably was installed when you first created your Unix machine. Go to the /etc/init.d directory, and look for a script called nfs-server. If you find it, then you have an active NFS server already installed on your machine. If you installed your Unix variant some time ago and have never worked with NFS, however, you may need to upgrade. You can get a recent copy of NFS from any reliable Unix software archive.

TIP: When installing NFS, you might as well get and install the Network Information System (NIS). NIS is a database that contains a variety of administrative data, like passwords or the /etc/hosts file (defining the machines that can connect to your server through NFS or other networking programs). You don't have to run NIS, but it does cut down on the administrative slogging that's part of network management.

Install NFS using either the precompiled binary or the source code method covered in Chapter 3, "Installing Apache." You need to install the main NFS server on the server machine (but not on the main partition, as previously noted) and an individual NFS client on each Unix machine that attaches to the network. You can find NFS clients at the same archive where you downloaded the server packages.

You needn't do much configuration to NFS itself. You should modify your bootup scripts, however, so NFS is started automatically when the server reboots. Learn how to do this in Chapter 7, "Managing the Apache Server." Note, the nfsd daemon must be running on the server machine and the mountd daemon running on the client machine for an NFS connection to succeed. Thus, you should add mountd to the boot scripts on each of the client machines, so it also runs automatically there, in case the client machines need to be rebooted at any time.

Using NFS

To use directories remotely across the network, you must edit the /etc/exports file on the server machine and approve each directory for export. Note, you must be logged in as root or have assumed superuser powers in some other manner to edit /etc/exports. Assume your network has a planetary name theme and the server machine is called sol.

If you want to export the /var/logs directory from sol to the client machine jupi-ter, you'd add this line to /etc/exports:

```
/var/logs             jupiter
```

Save the file and exit your text editor. Then, issue the command exportfs at the system prompt. This command runs the /etc/exports file through NFS and makes all the di-rectories listed in the file available to the named client machines.

NOTE: Your /etc/exports file may get quite long, depending on how many client machines you have attached to the network. Keep an eye on /etc/exports and clean out no longer needed entries. This cuts down on possible security weaknesses.

Next, on the client machine jupiter, create an empty directory as a mount point for the remote directory. You can do this by issuing the command mkdir /network to build a directory called network, which can be used to mount any remote directories. This is easier than creating a local directory for each remote directory you might use on that cli-ent machine. Then, issue the command

```
mount -t nfs sol:/var/logs /network
```

The NFS client on jupiter accesses the NFS server on sol, obtains the /var/logs di-rectory, and mounts it on the /network directory on jupiter. If jupiter hadn't been listed in /etc/exports as an allowed remote client, the connection would have failed. When you finish with the directory, you can use the umount command on the client ma-chine to unmount the remote directory.

NFS and Apache

One NFS trick used by many Web administrators involves the HTML and other files served by Apache to external browser requests. On your Apache machine, the direc-tory /htdocs usually contains the files that appear on your site. If you make /htdocs an empty directory, you can use it as a mount point. Instead of keeping your documents on the Web server machine (which may take up a lot of disk space), you can put them on the main NFS server and mount the directory remotely.

With this method, you can manage your disk space separately from the Web server. This is also somewhat of an internal security precaution, because you needn't give your users write permissions on the actual Apache server, and you can set up inter-nal firewalls so the NFS server only serves Web files to your Web server through an entry in /etc/exports. The downside is that Web requests are answered more slowly than they would have been with the files directly on the Apache machine, but you do gain a great deal of flexibility in managing your data.

SUMMARY

Most administrators run networks composed of machines running different operating systems. Whether the network is built of different Unices, or also includes Windows or Macintosh computers, it can be difficult—or impossible—to trade files and data between the machines without some software tools for file management and protocol translation. Luckily, several software programs are available to make administrating a heterogeneous network an easy and straightforward task.

Administrators of Unix-Windows networks use the Samba program to translate data from the native Unix protocol into SMB, the Windows Session Message Block protocol. With Samba, Unix machines can be part of the Windows Network Neighborhood, and Windows machines can be seen on the Unix network as well. Macintosh administrators use the netatalk program to accomplish the same goal, but netatalk translates between Unix data and the AppleTalk protocol used by Macs. Finally, administrators who run different kinds of Unix can share directories and files with the Network File System (NFS). Although NFS has some well-known security holes, it is the best solution for sharing files across a Unix network.

CHAPTER 5

Apache Modules

One of the major benefits of working with Apache is that its various features are modular. That is, you can choose which features you want to have in your Apache server and which you don't, and then install the appropriate modules accordingly. This capability gives you a great deal of flexibility in installing Apache. For example, if you run multiple Web sites on multiple servers, you might not want all the sites to have the same configuration. One site might be far more complex than another, or one might need a limited set of features for security reasons. You can set up each site with its own Apache server and its own set of modules.

Any single browser request to an Apache server might require the services of multiple modules. The kind of file requested, the browser used by the requester, the directories where the file is stored, and many other basic pieces of information about a particular request each prompt an individual module into action to serve the browser request. The modules included in a default Apache installation take care of the vast majority of requests, but you can install many other modules that confront particular situations or needs.

TIP: Find the latest Apache modules at **http://modules.apache.org**. Users contribute their own modules to this database, which you can search by keyword. You can also find documentation and other useful information.

So, what's a module? At its most basic, a *module* is a self-contained software program or routine that performs a particular function. Modules are an intrinsic part of the Apache experience. When the Apache developers completely rewrote the main part of the server for release 0.8.* (still in beta at that time), they pulled out much of the material in the program and placed it into individual modules. This means the core of the program is small and takes up relatively little server overhead, so it runs faster and more accurately. The more unused modules you remove from your installation, the better Apache runs.

In this chapter, you learn more about how the modules work as part of the Apache server, and what modules are installed by default in Apache 1.3.* and Apache 2.0. Finding new modules, whether Apache distributed or third party, and installing them is something almost every Apache administrator must do. Finally, you learn more about writing and testing your own Apache modules, and how to share them with the Apache community.

NOTE: If you plan to write your own modules, knowing the programming language Perl and understanding how regular expressions work can be immensely helpful. You need to know either Perl or C to write usable modules.

HOW APACHE MODULES WORK

As you previously read, almost everything in Apache is modular. Except for the functions directly related to executing HTTP in a standard way and the manner in which

Apache deals with errors, almost all other functions of the server are embedded in individual modules, which can be installed or deleted as necessary. Many of the modules must be initialized in a particular order because they require functions included in previous modules. This can be an irritating "feature," especially when you get the order wrong on installation and can't get the server to run, but this is one of the costs you pay to get the flexibility inherent in a modular system.

Understanding how Apache modules work is understanding how Apache itself works. When you run the server, as described in Chapter 7, "Managing the Apache Server," the initial Apache routine begins. This first step initializes the program, and then grabs some memory and CPU cycles to fill. Then, as Apache works through its boot-up steps, it checks the various configuration files created during the installation process. These files provide the list of modules to be used and the order in which they should be initialized.

As Apache boots, the main server process runs as root (the same account you log into when you assume superuser powers on your machine). As the modules initialize and spawn processes, though, these child processes usually have few privileges. When the child processes need to do something in response to a call or request, the appropriate module decides whether to handle the request.

NOTE: Be sure you double check the order in which your modules initialize, as listed in the configuration files used during install and boot up. Modules not only initialize in sequential order, they run in sequential order. That is, if a module is called by a browser request, but needs the output of a previous module to operate, that previous module must have initialized before the called module. If the previous module isn't there or if it initializes after the called module, the request will fail. It may take several go-throughs to get your module table exact and correct. The server will fail until you get it right, so some impetus exists for you to complete the testing.

THE DEFAULT MODULES

When you download the software to install the Apache Web server, you also download a set of modules that are the most commonly used features. Some of these modules install by default when you install the server, while others simply remain in your Apache directories until you decide to use them. Regardless of whether they install, these are the modules the Apache development team thinks are the most important ones to have.

NOTE: With the basic installation described in Part I, relatively few modules install. This is why reinstalling Apache is a good idea once you determine how it works and how you want it to run on your machines. You may need to reinstall it several times until you have the right blend of modules to handle the files you serve from your site.

In this section of the chapter, you learn about the modules included with the Apache software. The list is different for Apache 1.3.* and Apache 2.0.* because the way in which modules are handled by the core program was changed with the 2.0 release. The names of many of the modules are identical, but you must use 2.0 modules with 2.0 installations, so they'll work properly. The biggest difference between 1.3 modules and 2.0 modules is that the 2.0 server has five multiprocessing modules, which handle certain core functions more efficiently. 1.3 modules, and the other noncore 2.0 modules, reserve one function to each individual module to amplify the flexibility of the server.

NOTE: If you want to use 1.3 modules in an Apache 2.0 installation, see whether a 2.0 version is already released. If you wrote your own 1.3 modules or you had them programmed for your site, check the Apache 2.0 module API to see what needs to be done for the modules to be usable under Apache 2.0.

Default Modules in Apache 1.3.*

Forty-four modules are included in the Apache 1.3.* software download. They cover a wide range of functions, from the basic core software that makes up Apache to features like cookies, authentication, and various responses based on browser or file types. Some of these modules are no longer current, but are included (and installed) to make Apache 1.3.* work according to the HTTP standard. You needn't install all these modules, but you'll probably want to change the limited set of modules included in the default Configuration file (see Chapter 3, "Installing Apache") once you master the basic server administration concepts. The following is a list of the modules included in Apache 1.3.* download packages, as well as a brief description of their function and other important information.

Core

The *Core* module contains the basic functions that make the Apache server operate. You must run the Core module even if you run no other modules (a highly unlikely case, however). This module handles the basic interaction between the server and the operating system, as well as the way in which browsers interact with the server and request files. Even if you edit the Core module to change some variables, don't delete any of the functions contained in the module. If you do, your Apache installation will probably cease to function.

mod_access

The *mod_access* module defines who can obtain files on your site. You can set different levels of access for different kinds of files and different types of users, based on IP address, originating host name, or several other filters. If a request has multiple filter triggers, you can use this module to determine which filters override others.

mod_actions

If you plan to run CGI scripts on your server, you need the *mod_actions* module. This module ties CGI functions to file type, so a designated file type is always treated by the server as a CGI script. You can also use this module to trigger CGI when an external browser uses a certain URL format to request a file.

mod_alias

When you need to serve pages that aren't in your main Apache Web directory, the *mod_alias* module enables you to define other parts of the directory structure as part of the Web site. This is especially useful if you need to move files around on your disk or partitions while you're doing system housekeeping. You can also use mod_alias to redirect requests from the requested URL to the appropriate URL, with several options for how the redirect is handled.

mod_asis

The *mod_asis* module returns files to a requesting browser without adding an extra layer of Apache headers. Rather, the file is returned with its own HTTP headers. This is useful when you don't want the additional system overhead of CGI scripts or other extra server work, and when the files you serve already contain appropriate headers, so the browser can parse the file correctly.

mod_auth

Not the most secure form of authentication, the *mod_auth* module uses plain text files to store passwords and group information used to authenticate requests for files from your site. If you're at all concerned about security, consider using the mod_auth_digest or mod_auth_dbm modules instead, which offer stronger protection for passwords than a plain text file can provide.

mod_auth_anon

The *mod_auth_anon* module replicates a traditional FTP login method on your Web server. On most FTP sites, you can log in as anonymous and send your e-mail address as a password. This module enables you to set up the same kind of anonymous access for files on your site. You can control the variables of the module to define log locations and other access options.

mod_auth_db

Those using Berkeley Unix-based operating systems (FreeBSD, NetBSD, and OpenBSD are the most popular) should use the *mod_auth_db* module instead of the mod_auth_dbm module described in the following. The database file structure under Berkeley Unix requires a different file format than that generated by the mod_auth_dbm module.

NOTE: You need to have the software libraries for DM 1.85 or 1.86 installed to use the mod_auth_db module.

mod_auth_dbm

As opposed to the *mod_auth* module, the mod_auth_dbm module places password and group information into database files using the DBM file format. This is more secure than putting that information in plain text files. You can determine the level of authentication needed on your site by editing the module variables. Although the database files aren't encrypted, they're better than plain text files.

> **CAUTION:** Don't leave the database files in your main Apache directory. Store them elsewhere, so they aren't accessible from your Web site.

mod_auth_digest

The *mod_auth_digest* module is experimental and isn't recommended for sites with security concerns or that need to run stable software. This module authenticates browser requests using the MD5 Digest Authentication method, which is supported by only a few browsers. Microsoft's Internet Explorer 5.0 is the primary browser that supports MD5 authentication. If you know your site is only accessed by browsers that support MD5, you can give this module a try. Otherwise, continue to use mod_digest, discussed shortly, until sufficient support exists for the MD5 technology across browsers.

mod_autoindex

The *mod_autoindex* module provides an attractive format and structure for directory listings retrieved by browsers. You can select icons to represent different file formats, which makes finding files on your system easier for those looking for something specific. If you enable the FancyIndexing variable in this module, users of your site can sort the files in a given directory by a number of parameters, including date, size, name, and file type.

mod_browser

The *mod_browser* module was used in Apache 1.2.* and earlier. It was used to set environment variables for a requesting browser. This module has been superseded by the mod_setenvif module and shouldn't be installed unless you must run a 1.2.* Apache installation.

mod_cern_meta

If your Web designers add metaheaders to files served from your site, you'll want to enable the *mod_cern_meta* module, which allows metainformation to be sent along with other regular HTTP headers. Multiple ways exist for dealing with metainformation, but the CERN method is widespread and accepted by a number of browsers. Metainformation is most frequently used by search engines to index sites, but it can be used for a number of site identification reasons.

mod_cgi

The *mod_cgi* module is the basic module needed to serve CGI scripts on your site. This module identifies CGI files as scripts when they're requested by an external browser and runs the script on your server. The output of the script is then sent to the requesting browser as a page.

> **NOTE:**   Be sure to enable the error log variable in this module. If you're having trouble with CGI on your site, the mod_cgi error log is a good place to start tracking the problem.

mod_cookies

User tracking for Netscape browsers was handled by the *mod_cookies* module in Apache versions prior to Apache 1.2. With the release of Apache 1.2, the mod_usertrack module replaced mod_cookies. The mod_cookies module shouldn't be installed; the mod_usertrack module, discussed later in this chapter, should be used instead.

mod_digest

The *mod_digest* module enables administrators to authenticate requesting browsers with the MD5 protocol. However, advances have been made in both MD5 and Apache modules since mod_digest was released. If you plan to use MD5 authentication, install the mod_auth_digest module instead because it uses a later version of the MD5 standard. The mod_auth_digest module is only a beta release, however, so you might want to stick with mod_digest if you must use MD5 authentication, but cannot afford to run experimental software.

> **NOTE:**   Not all browsers support MD5 authentication, so you should have an idea of the kinds of browsers that visit your site before you decide to implement this form.

mod_dir

The *mod_dir* module is extremely helpful to users, especially to those who don't understand the requirements of a properly phrased URL. (This includes most people on the Web, including many Web professionals.) The mod_dir module parses URLs sent without a trailing slash. The *trailing slash* defines the directory to be searched for the requested file, usually index.html. The file that's served is defined by the DirectoryIndex variable of this module.

mod_dld

Another obsolete module still included in the Apache 1.3.* downloads, the *mod_dld* module, was intended to streamline the administration process by loading modules at restart

or bootup, instead of requiring a reinstall to add a new module. In Apache versions 1.3.*
and later, use the *mod_so* module instead.

mod_env

The *mod_env* module is used for CGI files and those incorporating server-side includes
(SSIs). This module changes environment variables before those scripts or includes are
run on the server, so the output is appropriately formatted and parsed. It's usually used
to set the directory path for particular software libraries needed for given scripts.

mod_example

The *mod_example* module is exactly what its name implies: a working example used to il-
lustrate the Apache API for Apache 1.3 modules. You needn't bother with this module
unless you're interested in writing your own Apache modules. If you are interested, see
the "Writing Your Own Modules" sidebar, later in this chapter.

mod_expires

The *mod_expires* module is used to determine the length of time a given file should remain
in a requesting browser's cache. If you don't want users to keep outdated versions of your
pages in their cache, especially if the data on your site changes rapidly, you can use the
mod_expires module to force early deletion of your files. The user's browser is then
forced to get a new copy directly from your site each time the page is requested, instead of
using the previously cached version.

mod_headers

The *mod_headers* module is used to customize the HTTP headers on each file served from
your site. If you want to send additional information to requesting browsers, use this
module to define that information. Common uses of the mod_headers module include
adding a timestamp to outgoing files or showing the length of time it took to fulfill the request. The mod_headers module must be edited carefully because it processes information in a predetermined order from the largest set to the smallest.

mod_imap

If you serve image maps on your site as navigational aids, you must have the *mod_imap*
module enabled. This module streamlines the image-mapping method and allows large
graphical files to be used without an overly heavy strain on the Web server. Even if you
don't offer graphical navigation on your main site, some of your users may want to use
this tool on their own pages, so keep the module enabled. (Note, this module applies
only to image maps you serve from your site, not image maps on other sites viewed by
your users.)

mod_include

Those administrators who serve files with SSI need to have the *mod_include* module enabled. This module passes files from your site through a filter before passing the resulting output to the requesting browser. The filter enables the various settings made with the includes, such as formatting or attaching other files.

> **TIP:**   Server-side includes are covered in Chapter 17, "Using Apache to Save Time—SSI and CSS."

mod_info

The *mod_info* module produces a useful administrative tool. It generates a snapshot file showing the status of your entire server configuration at the time of boot up. You can view the file at the URL **http://www.your.site/server-info** by default, but you can configure a different URL when you configure the module. Be sure to set authentication so this page isn't world-viewable. Having this information freely available on the Web is somewhat of a security risk.

mod_isapi

The *mod_isapi* module is used by those who run Windows Apache. It enables an Apache server to serve ISAPI extensions, used by Microsoft Web creation products like FrontPage. Microsoft has written unique extensions to the HTTP standard, so these extensions aren't normally served by HTTP-compliant Web servers. With the mod_isapi module, you can offer pages written with ISAPI functions from a non-Microsoft server.

> **NOTE:**   The Apache development team didn't write the mod_isapi module. It's provided as a courtesy to Microsoft Web administrators, but the team cannot answer questions about the module. Contact the authors listed in the module if you need help with ISAPI functions on your Apache server.

mod_log_agent

Some modules in Apache 1.3.* are included merely because they help other forms of HTTPd work seamlessly with Apache. The *mod_log_agent* module is one of these modules. It enabled the administrator to set the locations of log files that would record information about requests coming into the server. Use the mod_log_config module instead.

mod_log_common

Early versions of Apache used multiple modules to control the logging of information about browser requests. The *mod_log_common* module created a log of all requests to the Apache server. Its function has been absorbed into the mod_log_config module, so use this module instead.

mod_log_config

The *mod_log_config* module supersedes the three log modules from earlier versions of Apache: mod_log_agent, mod_log_common, and mod_log_referer. You can use mod_log_config to determine the kind of user information logged on your site. You cannot control error logs from this module (this is handled in the core Apache configuration described in Chapter 6, "Configuring and Testing Apache"). However, you can record a wide variety of information about your site visitors with the different options in the mod_log_config module.

mod_log_referer

As with the mod_log_agent and mod_log_common modules, the *mod_log_referer* module is an earlier component of the user information logging modules. This module was responsible for logging the sites from which browsers made requests to your site (the *referring site*). Its function is now part of mod_log_config.

mod_mime

The *mod_mime* module determines the file types of various requested files on your system and associates those files with appropriate handler programs to serve them properly to requesting browsers. You can define file types, handlers, and other functions with the module's variables. mod_mime works with character sets, encoding structures, and various content types.

mod_mime_magic

Use the *mod_mime_magic* module in conjunction with mod_mime, not on its own. This module parses the first few bits of data in a requested file to see what the file type is. This is useful in cases where the file type isn't indicated by the filename extension. mod_mime_magic uses a configuration file called MimeMagicFile to decipher the data. Don't change the syntax in this file or the module won't work correctly.

NOTE: This module must be installed before mod_mime in your configuration files, so file type identification will work correctly.

mod_mmap_static

The *mod_mmap_static* module is an experimental module and shouldn't be used on installations that need to remain stable. Use this module at your risk. The mod_mmap_static module places certain defined pages into memory at bootup, rather than requiring the server to pull those pages into memory each time they're requested. Be careful about using this module because it can lead to broken sites. This function has been taken over by the mod_file_cache module in Apache 2.0.

mod_negotiation

The *mod_negotiation* module is used when a browser requests a file that doesn't exist or that exists in several forms on your site. The module scans the information the browser provides about itself and determines which file is most appropriate to be returned to the requester. If you have files with identical content that vary in character set or language type, mod_negotiation is the module that determines the file actually sent, based on the requesting browser's characteristics.

mod_proxy

The *mod_proxy* module is a complicated and powerful module, which builds a proxy for all HTTP services, as well as FTP and SSL (Secure Sockets Layer) connections. You can also build in support for other kinds of proxies. With mod_proxy, you can permit access from certain IP numbers and not others, force the FTP mode from binary to ASCII on given files, and configure many other options to make the proxy most effective for your site. You can also integrate the Apache proxy with a systemwide SOCKS proxy to make everything even more secure.

TIP: Learn more about proxies in Chapter 23, "Firewalls and Proxies."

mod_rewrite

The *mod_rewrite* module is a deeply complicated module that contains a programming engine that rewrites URLs on-the-fly. URLs can be rewritten based on a number of variables defined in mod_rewrite, HTTP headers, time stamp, and other unique bits of data. URL rewriting is beyond the scope of this book; but, if you're interested, consult the mod_rewrite documentation for a comprehensive introduction to the module and several examples of the engine in operation.

TIP: Find the mod_rewrite documentation at **http://httpd.apache.org/docs-2.0/mod/mod_rewrite.html**.

mod_setenvif

The *mod_setenvif* module defines environment variables on-the-fly for any given browser request to your server. The environment variables may change based on browser identification, file requested, or other data contained in the request itself. This module is most commonly used to serve different versions of a file based on the browser being used. For example, if you have two versions of a given page, one that uses Microsoft ISAPI extensions and one that doesn't, mod_setenvif serves the ISAPI page to Internet Explorer requests and the non-ISAPI page to Netscape requests.

TIP: mod_setenvif uses *regular expressions*, a programming construct found in most Unix-friendly programming languages like C and C++. Understanding regular expressions is always a good idea if you're going to spend much time around Unix.

mod_so

For Windows Apache administrators, the *mod_so* module is part of your default module installation. Unix administrators may compile it as an extension module if desired. mod_so enables you to add new modules at bootup or to restart instead of compiling them into a new installation. Note, this can be a tricky process and works better under Windows than under Unix. This is a good way to test out new modules before you decide to reinstall, though.

mod_speling

The *mod_speling* module has two main functions. The first function allows Apache to ignore capitalization in filenames and browser requests. Without mod_speling, users must request files with the same capitalization as the filename uses on your system. This can be tricky if you don't tell users the capitalization structure used on your site. With mod_speling, a user can request the file with the appropriate spelling, but needn't worry about capitalizing anything properly. You can also use mod_speling to override any one given misspelling of a filename on your site, though this function is less useful than the capitalization option.

mod_status

Check the current status of your Web server with the *mod_status* module, which generates a Web page (like mod_info) that gives you a current snapshot of your server and what it's doing. You see information about data being served, number of processes, and other useful data. Find this page at **http://www.your.site/server-status**. Note, as a basic security precaution, you should change the authentication file so random viewers can't see what your site is doing.

mod_userdir

The *mod_userdir* module is used to define the subdirectory in each user's home directory where Web pages are stored. When a request comes in for a page hosted by one of your users, with the URL form **http://www.your.site/~delilah/filename**, Apache checks in `delilah`'s user directory for the subdirectory defined in mod_userdir, and then locates the requested file in that subdirectory. The default is `public_html`. If you change this value, be sure to tell your users, so they can place their Web files in the appropriate location.

mod_unique_id

For those administrators who need or want to give each request to the server a unique identifier, the *mod_unique_id* module does so. You may need unique identifiers for performance tracking or for extremely strict security policies. This module enables you to reset numbering for a new batch of random numbers or to define the size of the tag. The module's authors guarantee that each identifying tag will be unique among a given set of requests.

mod_usertrack

The *mod_usertrack* module enables you to track the behavior of those who visit your site. This module uses *cookies,* a technology that places tiny identifying data bits in requesting browsers, so the browser can be recognized when it visits your site again at a later time. You can set logs to track user visits with this module and you can configure it so users with cookies from your site can bypass authentication.

> **TIP:** Chapter 11, "Performance Tuning," contains more information about cookies and user tracking in general.

mod_vhost_alias

The *mod_vhost_alias* module works with virtual hosts to serve dynamically generated pages for any number of virtual sites hosted on your Apache server. This module identifies the correct virtual host from the IP number or host name used in the browser request and serves the appropriate pages to the requesting browser. For anyone serving virtual hosts on Apache, this module saves a ton of time in site configuration and administration.

> **NOTE:** If you want to see the most recent version of the default modules list for Apache 1.3, consult **http://httpd.apache.org/docs/mod/index.html**. You can see documentation for each module there, as well as see the modules arranged by function, rather than alphabetically.

Default Modules in Apache 2.0

If you compare the list of default modules for Apache 1.3.* and the list in this section, you'll notice a couple of major differences. The 2.0 version handles modules quite differently than previous versions of the server, which can lead to problems or confusion if you don't understand the difference between the two. Under 2.0, five core modules can process multiple actions at one time, and forty other modules are included with the default package. Some of these other modules are installed as part of the base 2.0 package, and some are extensions. Some experimental modules are also included in the 2.0 download.

Table 5-1 shows the different types of modules included with the download. Whether or not you choose to run most of the 40 secondary modules, you must always run the appropriate core modules for Apache to work properly.

Module Status	Module Name
Base	mod_access
	mod_actions
	mod_alias
	mod_asis
	mod_auth
	mod_autoindex
	mod_cgi
	mod_cgid
	mod_dir
	mod_env
	mod_imap
	mod_include
	mod_isapi
	mod_log_config
	mod_mime
	mod_negotiation
	mod_setenvif
	mod_so (Windows only)
	mod_status
	mod_userdir
Extension	mod_auth_anon
	mod_auth_db
	mod_auth_dbm
	mod_cern_meta
	mod_dav
	mod_example
	mod_expires

Table 5-1. Apache 2.0 Modules Included in Download

Module Status	Module Name
	mod_file_cache
	mod_headers
	mod_info
	mod_mime_magic
	mod_rewrite
	mod_so (Unix only)
	mod_speling
	mod_unique_id
	mod_usertrack
	mod_vhost_alias
Experimental	mod_auth_digest
	mod_charset_lite
	mod_ext_filter

Table 5-1.   Apache 2.0 Modules Included in Download *(continued)*

NOTE: Even though many of these modules carry the same names as Apache 1.3.* modules, you cannot substitute modules from earlier versions under 2.0. The names remain the same because external functions and third-party software call for those particular module names, but the way in which the modules function is completely different. Reinstall all your modules when you upgrade your Apache installation.

Core Modules

The five Core modules of Apache 2.0 handle the basic functions that make up the server itself. These are *multiprocessing* modules, meaning each one handles multiple inputs and outputs at the same time. Apache 2.0 relies on threading to handle requests, meaning the Core modules spawn child processes (as in Apache 1.3), but then also spawn threads within those processes to handle requests. In contrast, Apache 1.3 uses an individual server process for each request. The threading makes Apache 2.0 faster and more efficient.

Core   This is the "big daddy" of Apache modules. If you don't include the Core module in your Apache installation, Apache won't work—Core handles all the main functions of the server. Over 50 individual functions are controlled by Core, ranging from simple host name lookups to more complicated XML and virtual host features. You can edit the parameters of many of these features, though most people don't need to do anything but accept the defaults.

CAUTION: Don't edit the Core module to remove any of the functions. Apache expects all of these functions to be available at all times, which is why they're in the Core module and not in individual modules.

mpm_threaded_module The *mpm_threaded_module* is the multiprocessing module for Unix and Unix-variant operating systems. If you're running something that looks like Unix, whether it's BSD, Linux, or something else, you'll choose the mpm_threaded_module to handle multiple processes. This module manages the number of processes spawned by Apache to handle incoming requests. In the Apache configuration process, described in Chapter 6, "Configuring and Testing Apache," several of the variables in the apache.conf file set the parameters used by this module to control the number of processes that exist at any given time.

NOTE: The relevant variables are MinSpareThreads, MaxSpareThreads, MaxClients, ThreadsPer Child, and MaxRequestsPerChild.

mpm_winnt Unlike the Unix method of handling multiple processes, the Windows NT module *mpm_winnt* uses a single process. This process then spawns one child process, which then spawns as many individual threads as are necessary to handle incoming requests. Don't attempt to run this module on Unix machines or to run mpm_threaded_module on Windows machines. The ways in which Unix and Windows handle system calls and processes are completely different and the attempt will fail.

perchild Just as the mpm modules create processes or threads in response to server load, the *perchild* module manages the individual threads. The perchild module can assign each thread a different kind of user identification, which permits some processes to be run with higher privileges and some with lower. This is a good security precaution in that many Apache processes don't need to have a lot of privileges, but can run quietly at a low level without requiring write or execute permission on other files.

NOTE: The perchild module is managed by the configuration variables NumServers, MinSpare Threads, MaxSpareThreads, MaxThreadsPerChild, and MaxRequestsPerChild.

prefork The *prefork* module, though an Apache 2.0 module, sets up a server that works like Apache 1.3. Why would you need this? Perhaps you have to serve clients that aren't designed to handle Apache 2.0. Or, you have some custom software that requires the nonthreaded manner in which Apache 1.3.* operates, but you want the other advantages of the 2.0 server. The prefork module maintains a certain number of idle server processes that respond to external requests, but doesn't spawn threads within each of those processes.

Other Modules

Although these aren't the core modules, the other modules included with the Apache download serve many critical needs for the Apache administrator. You'll probably never need to install all these modules and your needs may change as your site changes. However, becoming familiar with what's available in the world of Apache modules is good, even if you don't plan to install most of them.

> **TIP:**   Review your modules regularly and check to see what's new in the module database at **modules.apache.org**.

mod_access   Use the *mod_access* module to determine who can access various files on your Web site. You can set access privileges based on the requester's host name, IP address, or particular environment variable. If you already have password protection enabled for particular files, mod_access won't conflict with that protection. You must define the Satisfy directive in this module, however, so Apache will know whether the password restrictions or the mod_access restrictions should take precedence. The mod_access options are Allow, Deny, or Order, based on the parameters defined in the module. Allow and Deny are self-explanatory; Order tells the module the order in which the parameters should be checked. For example, if you Allow requests from a certain host name, but Deny from a given IP, the Order variable determines which variable is checked first.

mod_actions   The *mod_actions* module is used in conjunction with CGI scripts and it only does two things. First, the mod_actions module permits CGI scripts to run whenever a particular file type is requested by a browser. Second, it permits CGI scripts to run when an external browser uses a particular method to request a file. Both of these options make CGI run faster on your site and also enable you to set a particular file type (often *.cgi) as a trigger for the cgi-script function.

mod_alias   You might not always want to place all the files you serve on the site into the main Web directory. With the *mod_alias* module, you can build various aliases that map URLs to different paths through the file system. This gives you greater flexibility in allocating disk space for Web files, while allowing external users to use a familiar URL for making requests. The mod_alias module also handles redirects, in which a no-longer-current URL is sent automatically to a new URL. You can define the redirect so it either happens automatically, with a delay time (so the user can read a message about the new URL), or it doesn't happen automatically. This is a useful module to include.

mod_asis   One quick way to handle certain requests is to return files that contain their own HTTP headers, sending information back to the browser without forcing the use of CGI scripts. If the file contains its own HTTP headers, Apache won't add a large number of additional headers, thus the "as is" component of the module's name, *mod_asis*. You can use these files to redirect the browser to a different file or location. This is a basic function that's useful if your site does anything more than serve plain text and image files, and if you don't like to program your own scripts.

mod_auth   The *mod_auth* module implements the authentication functions of HTTP, using plain text password files to look up users and see whether they can be granted access to given files. This can also be used to work with user groups. This module is somewhat outdated. You can do better with the mod_auth_dbm and mod_auth_digest modules described shortly.

mod_auth_anon   If you've ever used an FTP site and logged in as anonymous, sending your e-mail address as a password, you're familiar with the kind of authentication offered by the mod_auth_anon module. This is a good way to share files if you want to have your users actually log in, while people from other systems can use the anonymous/e-mail address ID/password pairing to get access to the files. You can set the module's parameters to look at the text string sent as a password to see whether it matches the form of an e-mail address (with an @ in the middle and at least one dot toward the end), and have all the e-mails sent as passwords logged to a file.

mod_auth_db   If you use a Berkeley Unix-based variant, such as FreeBSD, NetBSD, or OpenBSD, you need to use this authentication module—the *mod_auth_db* module—instead of the mod_auth_dbm module described next. Berkeley Unices use a particular library for their database files (you need the library for DB 1.85 or 1.86).

mod_auth_dbm   Instead of using the mod_auth module, which places passwords or group information into plain text files, use the *mod_auth_dbm* module instead. This places sensitive information into database files (DBM type), which isn't stored as plain text. It is not encrypted, but anything is better than plain text. Various parameters in this module should be set to the level of authentication you want on your site.

CAUTION: Don't keep this file in with your Apache files. You need to put it somewhere where it can't be downloaded.

mod_auth_digest   The *mod_auth_digest* module is a beta module, which is under development. If you have any concerns about security or using experimental software on your Web server, use the mod_digest module described earlier instead. Don't run both mod_auth_digest and mod_digest at the same time or Apache will crash.

CAUTION: Don't use this module if you're running a large site with multiple types of browsers making requests. If a non-MD5 browser accesses your site and you have mod_auth_digest enabled, you won't be able to authenticate that request.

For those interested in using beta modules, the mod_auth_digest module incorporates the MD5 Digest Authentication method, which is more secure than other forms of Web authentication. Unfortunately, relatively few browsers support MD5, so sticking with mod_digest is best unless you know only MD5 browsers will be accessing your site.

NOTE: Internet Explorer 5.0 is the only major browser to incorporate MD5 technology at this time.

mod_autoindex   The *mod_autoindex* module is a handy tool that allows automatic directory indexing. If you serve a lot of directory pages, rather than graphically designed pages, mod_autoindex can sort the files in the directory for you. Most people who use mod_autoindex enable the icons and FancyIndexing capabilities, to make the automatically generated index more attractive and easy to understand. Icons differentiate the file types in the directory, while FancyIndexing sorts the files by various parameters: size, alphabetical, date, and so forth.

mod_cern_meta   The *mod_cern_meta* module allows Apache to attach CERN-style metafiles to outgoing Web documents. *Metafiles* contain additional information about the document, including subject tags and other identifying data. The CERN method is one of the most widely used ways to deal with metafile data, though other ways exist to handle it (and other modules are available if you prefer not to use CERN-style metaheaders).

TIP: *Metaheaders* are often used by search engines to catalog sites. If you've ever run a Web search for a celebrity or a popular athlete, you might have received returns that include a wide range of inappropriate or unrelated sites. Some site operators stick the names of many famous people or topics into metaheaders, so their sites always pop up on Web searches. Annoying, but it works.

mod_cgi   If you're going to serve CGI scripts on your site, you need to have the *mod_cgi* module. This module identifies files as scripts when a request is made and runs the script on the server. The output of the script is then returned to the requesting browser. Check the variables of this module and alter them if necessary to fit your particular site's needs. Be sure the log for CGI errors is enabled so, if you have troubles with your scripts, you can see where the errors begin.

NOTE: If you're running the multiprocess threaded module previously described in the "Core Modules" section, don't run mod_cgi. Instead, install the mod_cgid module described next. mod_cgid is designed to work with multiple threads, while mod_cgi isn't.

mod_cgid   For those administrators running the mpm_threaded_module (part of the Apache 2.0 core module set) on a Unix machine, the *mod_cgid* module is required for CGI scripts. Users won't be able to tell the difference, but the mod_cgid module handles spawned threads through an external daemon, which makes CGI run much more cleanly with the upgraded core modules.

mod_charset_lite   The *mod_charset_lite* module is experimental and beta. Its intention is to enable on-the-fly translation between character sets. This module is currently being developed as part of Russian Apache, but, eventually, it should be usable for all sorts of character sets. Because character sets are notoriously disorganized and nonstandardized, however, this module will take some time to develop properly.

CAUTION: mod_charset_lite is beta software. Don't use it on a site that must remain stable and operative. If you want to serve files in different character sets, encode that data in the file, rather than relying on mod_charset_lite.

mod_dav   If your designers want to work remotely on the server, investigate the WebDAV project. WebDAV is an acronym for Web-based Distributed Authoring and Versioning, and is a tool that enables users to work on files and directories located on a remote Web server. If you're interested in enabling WebDAV for your users, you need to install and configure the *mod_dav* module.

TIP: Learn more about WebDAV at its Web site, **http://www.webdav.org**.

mod_dir   One of the basic modules on which users have come to rely, the *mod_dir* module redirects URLs that are requested without a trailing slash. That is, if you ask your browser to get the page **http://www.foo.com/bar,** mod_dir at FOO's site will know you're actually requesting **http://www.foo.com/bar/**. (All directories require a trailing slash, which identifies them as directories.) What's served when this URL is located depends on the settings of mod_dir: this can be either a file identified in the DirectoryIndex variable or a listing generated by the server (following the settings made in mod_autoindex if you're using it).

mod_env   For those administrators serving CGI scripts and SSIs, the *mod_env* module modifies the environment sent to those scripts when invoked. This module provides various environment variables that may affect the way in which the scripts are run and may alter the output if they aren't present. mod_env is often used to set variables like the paths of required software libraries.

mod_example   The *mod_example* module is a working module, but it isn't required for regular Web serving. Rather, it's a sample of a module written according to the Apache module API. If you're not writing your own modules, you needn't install or worry about mod_example. If you're interested in writing your own modules, see the "Writing Your Own Modules" sidebar at the end of this chapter and take a good look at mod_example.

mod_expires   If you want to control what happens to your pages once they're requested and sent to a remote browser, investigate the *mod_expires* module. This module enables you to use the Expires HTTP header, which determines when the document should disappear from the remote site. Depending on the remote browser's cache, the file may remain in cache for some time after it's initially requested. With an Expires header, you can determine how long the file should remain in cache after it's requested and the browser will be forced to obtain a new copy if the viewer wants to see the page again.

mod_ext_filter   The *mod_ext_filter* module is experimental and shouldn't be used on any site that cannot risk using untested software. This module is designed to pass files from your site through an external filter, designated in the module, before sending the resulting output to the requesting browser. mod_ext_filter isn't written to the Apache module API, however, so it's quite slow. Install it if you're interested, but be forewarned it could slow your response time and crash Apache because it's still in beta.

mod_file_cache   The *mod_file_cache* module can be quite helpful, but it can also create huge problems for your server. This module stores certain frequently requested pages in a separate cache, reducing the time Apache has to spend on starting a process and answering the request. Separate methods exist for building the cache, depending on the operating system you're using. If you select the wrong method, the file won't be cached, but you'll incur additional system overhead. Use mod_file_cache if you have certain files that take up a large part of your total request pool, but be extremely careful when you edit the module, lest you crash your site.

> **NOTE:**   mod_file_cache only works on static pages, those that don't change and have permanent individual URLs. You cannot use mod_file_cache to speed up dynamically served pages or pages generated from CGI scripts or SSIs.

mod_headers   If, for some reason, you want to customize the HTTP headers sent as part of each browser request and server response, you can do so with the *mod_headers* module. This module can be used to send additional information to the browser, to attach a timestamp to each request, or for other useful information. Be sure you place the header modifications in the correct order because this module processes information sequentially from the largest (main server) to the smallest (individual files) data set.

mod_imap   The *mod_imap* module enables you to serve image maps as navigational aids on your site. Because many Web designers like to use image maps rather than, or in addition to, textual navigation links, this is an important module. mod_imap is designed to streamline earlier image mapping methods that relied on CGI scripts and individual configuration files. With mod_imap, you can serve image maps with less strain on the server and faster response to your requesting browsers.

> **TIP:**   Learn more about image maps in Chapter 16, "Image Maps."

mod_include   The *mod_include* module is used with SSIs. It enables files from your server to be passed through a filter before the resulting output is sent to the requesting browser. This filter sets various variables defined by the SSI settings, such as visual settings or other environment variables. If you plan to use SSI to speed up browser request time and cut down on server overhead, you must have this module installed.

TIP: Learn more about SSIs in Chapter 17, "Using Apache to Save Time—SSI and CSS."

mod_info   The *mod_info* module compiles a snapshot of your entire Apache server configuration at the time of bootup. It lists all installed modules and any directives you added to the configuration files. If you have this module installed, the snapshot will be visible at the URL **http://www.your.site/server-info**. Note, unless you configure authentication on that file so only certain people may access it, anyone in the world will be able to see your server configuration. This may or may not be a good thing for you. Generally, this isn't the best security precaution, though.

mod_isapi   For those administering Apache on a Windows server machine, the *mod_isapi* module allows Apache to use ISAPI extensions. These extensions are those used by Microsoft's Web server, the Internet Information Server (IIS). If you're serving files written using Microsoft's unique extensions to the HTTP standard (such as pages written with the FrontPage authoring program), you need to enable this module for those extensions to be usable.

NOTE: The Apache development team provides the ISAPI module as a courtesy. This module is written by third parties using Microsoft's API. The Apache team can't help you, so contact the authors named in the module if you have trouble.

mod_log_config   The *mod_log_config* module determines how information is logged by the server. As you've seen throughout this book already and you'll see in future chapters, Apache's logs are one of the most critical sources of information about the server. While the error logs are controlled elsewhere, the logs controlled by mod_log_config can give you a good idea of the pages requested most frequently on your site. You have the option to configure custom logs that record specific information you want or you can use some standard configurations that are described in the module itself.

TIP: Learn how to set mod_log_config's options in Chapter 9, "Logs."

mod_mime   The *mod_mime* module does a lot of important work with file types. It can determine the actual type of a file from the extension on the filename or from information in the metaheaders. Once the file type is determined, that information can be either sent to the requesting browser or used to pull up a handler to deal with the file before it's displayed. (*Handlers* are programs designed to work with particular file types, so they can be displayed properly.) The mod_mime module can work with character sets, various encoding structures (like MIME), handlers, languages, or other content types.

TIP: Learn more about MIME in Chapter 14, "MIME and Other Encoding."

mod_mime_magic   The *mod_mime_magic* module is used as a backup to mod_mime and isn't usually used on its own. Instead of using the meta and other header data to determine a file's type, the mod_mime_magic module actually looks at the first bits of data in the file to see what type of file it is. This module uses a file named MimeMagicFile, which has a particular syntax, to define the various data structures it's likely to encounter.

NOTE: If you use mod_mime_magic, place it before mod_mime in your configuration files, so mod_mime runs properly and executes before mod_mime_magic.

mod_negotiation   The *mod_negotiation* module comes into play when a browser requests a particular document, which either doesn't exist or that exists in several forms. mod_negotiation considers the information the browser has sent about itself, and sends the form most appropriate to the browser or tries to find the best match on the site. This module is used most frequently for encodings that may not be readable on all browsers or when a browser has particular variables already set, such as language or document type.

mod_proxy   The *mod_proxy* module may, in some cases, be listed in your Apache 2.0 download, but it hasn't been upgraded to Apache 2.0. You can build it yourself by getting the module code from the Apache Web site, but it's no longer distributed as part of the 2.0 package.

mod_rewrite   If you're ready to delve into the real guts of Apache modules, the *mod_rewrite* module is a good place to start. This module is actually an engine that rewrites URLs on-the-fly, whether to other URLs or to filenames. This is an advanced mechanism and the documentation for the module runs to nearly 30 pages, with examples and flowcharts galore. You can use this module to rewrite URLs based on time stamp, various variables, HTTP headers, and other bits of data in the browser request. URL rewriting is a topic beyond the scope of this book but, if you're interested, check out the mod_rewrite documentation for more information. You can find it at **http://httpd.apache.org/docs-2.0/ mod/mod_rewrite.html**.

mod_setenvif   The *mod_setenvif* module allows Apache to set environment variables on-the-fly, depending on the various attributes of the incoming browser request. One of the most common uses for this module is to serve different pages or environments, depending on the browser being used to make the request. For example, a page using Microsoft ISAPI extensions wouldn't be served to a Netscape browser request. mod_setenvif uses regular expressions, a type of programming construct common to languages like C and C++. If you're running a Unix-based operating system, knowing about regular expressions is a good idea.

mod_so   If you're running Windows Apache, mod_so is part of your regular modules. If you're running Unix Apache, it's an extension. The *mod_so* module addresses one of the frequent complaints about Apache: to get a new module, you need to recompile. With mod_so, this isn't necessarily the case. This module enables you to load certain modules at boot or restart without having to compile them into the server and reinstall Apache. This is an easier process under Windows than under Unix, and it's somewhat tricky in both cases. This does make trying out a new module easier if you're unsure whther you want it compiled directly into your installation, however, and it's worth a try.

NOTE: If you want to try out mod_so, read the documentation carefully and follow it explicitly. You can read more about this module at **http://httpd.apache.org/docs-2.0/mod/mod_so.html**.

mod_speling   The *mod_speling* module is a nice way to be helpful to your site's visitors. You can use mod_speling to ignore capitalization in URL requests. For example, if your products page is named Products.html, you can use mod_speling so requests for **products.html** and **Products.html** are both honored. You can also use mod_speling to accept the most common spelling mistake on your site, but you're allowed only one spelling error. The module is quite limited in the sort of spelling errors that are fixable, though. It won't work on user names, which is one of the most common causes of Page Not Found errors.

mod_status   The *mod_status* module generates a Web page that tells you how your server is doing. This module provides information on the number of active processes, how much data has been served, server uptime, CPU use, and other interesting and useful data. Use a browser to open the URL **http://www.your.site/server-status** to see the report. Be sure to set authentication for this file if you don't want random users viewing your site statistics. If you're using a browser that supports the Refresh feature, you can use the URL **http://www.your.site/server-status?refresh=N**, where *N* equals the number of seconds at which you want the report to rebuild.

mod_userdir   You need the *mod_userdir* module if you permit your users to host Web pages in their home directories. This module sets the default location for Web files in directories outside the main Web document tree. The default setting is public_html; that is, if Apache receives a browser request for the URL **http://www.your.site/~margie/filename**, it automatically looks in `margie`'s home directory for a subdirectory called `public_html`, and for the filename file in that subdirectory. If you want your users to use a different directory for their personal Web files, you must change the setting in mod_userdir to reflect that new location.

mod_unique_id   The *mod_unique_id* module provides a unique identifying tag for each browser request. These tags are guaranteed to be unique among all requests in a given set of requests. While this isn't something most administrators would find useful or necessary, it can be helpful in certain situations. If you need to identify each request as a unique entity, whether for performance tracking or for other reasons, you can use this module to do so. Note, you must reset the module occasionally to generate a new set of random numbers.

mod_usertrack   The technology in the *mod_usertrack* module is more familiarly known as cookies. In fact, under versions earlier than Apache 1.3.*, this module was known as mod_cookies. Cookies are small bits of data that track user behavior on your site. Cookies are useful on both ends, enabling users to bypass identification processes once logged in and allowing administrators to track site use. Under Apache 2.0, cookies have been streamlined and the new module is far easier to use, with a lot more options for your log files.

TIP: See Chapter 11, "Performance Tuning," for more information about mod_usertrack and about cookies in general.

mod_vhost_alias   If you're interested in running virtual hosts on your site, you want to run the *mod_vhost_alias* module. This module enables you to serve dynamically generated pages for a virtual host. It uses the IP address or the hostname in the browser request to find and serve the appropriate pages from the server. This cuts down on a lot of site configuration and makes serving more pages for more virtual hosts easier on a single Apache installation.

NOTE: To see the most recent version of this list or to see the modules sorted by function, visit **http://httpd.apache.org/docs-2.0/mod/**. You can also get full documentation for each module at that site.

LOCATING MODULES NOT INCLUDED WITH BASIC PACKAGES

While you can do a great deal with the modules already included in the Apache download package, many more modules are available beyond those. Depending on how you want your Apache server to respond to requests and the kind of data you serve, you might want to explore the other modules contributed back to the Apache community. These modules range from the nearly essential, like the mod_perl module, to the extremely specific or arcane modules designed for one highly specific system and need.

TIP: Learn more about mod_perl in Chapter 8, "Dealing with Apache Innovation (mod_perl: A Case Study)."

The first—and best—place to check for Apache modules is **http://modules.apache.org**. Not only does this database include updated versions of the various standard modules previously described, but it accepts contributions from Apache users and programmers who aren't part of the central development team. If you decide to write your own modules, you can send them in to the database, so other people can use them as well. Many, many modules are in the database and more are added each week. Search for an appropriate module by keyword, which might be the module function, a part of the name, or another related character string.

If you don't find the module you want at the module database, you can search elsewhere on the Web or in archives that aren't controlled by the Apache development team. Be aware, though, not all modules are created equal. A module submitted to the Apache database is likely to be written in conformation with the Apache API (programming rules) and isn't intended to do malicious damage. While modules not submitted to the Web aren't necessarily harmful or badly written, you do get an extra layer of protection when you download something from the Apache site. In practice, most people who write Apache modules and want to share them submit to the Apache database anyway. If you find a good one on the Web that isn't on the Apache site, encourage the programmer to submit it. Modules in the database get the best distribution and use, including feedback for future versions and bug reports.

TIP: If you want to get the latest news about new Apache modules, sign up for the Apache mailing list devoted to module development announcements. You can sign up via the Apache Web site, at **http://modules.apache.org/subscribe**. This list *isn't* the place for help questions or other basic information, however. This is a fairly low-traffic list that only permits posts from the moderators. You can usually find Apache module help in the documentation or on newsgroups, such as `comp.infosystems.www.servers.unix`.

INSTALLING MODULES

To install a new module, you have to reinstall Apache. This is annoying, but if you think about the structure of the server, this makes a great deal of sense. Remember, when you began your installation, you told Apache which modules to include. (More likely, if it was your first Apache installation, you accepted the default configuration, which included the central set of modules required for most standard Web sites.) If you want to add other modules, you need to reconfigure the installation and reinstall, alerting the Apache installer to add those modules while the server is building.

NOTE: If you installed from preconfigured binaries, you might not have had the option to configure your modules. In general, when you begin working with modules beyond those specified in the default configuration, working directly with source code is best. Even some binary packages for Unix variants make it difficult to configure modules. If you have the source code opportunity on your operating system, use it.

Refer to Chapter 3, "Installing Apache," to refresh your memory of the source code installation procedure. Note, for Apache 1.3.* versions, you can edit the Configuration file directly to show which modules should be included. Follow the file's syntax exactly, so the installation won't abort and the modules install correctly. Under Apache 2.0, you're prompted during the configuration process to select the modules you want to install.

Once you edit the appropriate configuration files, finish the installation procedure as directed for your particular version of the Apache server. When the server finishes installing, you might need to reboot your machine, depending on the operating system you're using. The server then makes the new modules available and you can begin to serve the type of data, or answer the kind of requests, the new module makes possible.

TIP: If you're installing new modules, take the time to remove any modules you don't use. The fewer modules you have installed, the faster the server runs and the more efficiently your CPU cycles are allocated.

Writing Your Own Modules

If you have some programming skills and are interested in configuring Apache to serve your site's needs as closely as possible, you might want to investigate writing your own Apache modules. Many administrators find writing and testing a module is faster than tinkering with an existing module, trying to get it to do what's needed. Certainly, many of the Apache modules available in the database at **modules.apache.org** were contributed by members of the Apache community and you can share your modules with other Apache administrators as well.

To write Apache modules, you need to know how to program in C, C++, or Perl. You also need to know how to read an API and how to use the API's instructions as you build your code. The Apache module API has several components, including rules on how modules should access and use system memory, how output should be logged, how the module should clean up after itself, and how the module must be configured. Finally, you should be prepared to spend time debugging your module, especially if you plan to share the module with other Apache administrators.

Programming new Apache modules is beyond the scope of this book. If the idea intrigues you, consult a more advanced Apache reference for a detailed description of the Apache API and helpful hints on constructing a usable and solid module. One such book is *Administering Apache*, by Mark Allan Arnold, Clint Miller, James Sheetz, and Jeff D. Almeida (Osborne/McGraw-Hill, 2000), which has a lengthy chapter entitled "Programming the Apache Server."

SUMMARY

The core of the Apache server is quite small. Most of Apache's functions are handled by modules, individual software routines that provide one particular feature for the server. A wide range of Apache modules is available to the administrator. Quite a few of these modules are contained in the software packages you downloaded to install the Apache server. Some of these modules install by default, while you must intentionally compile others into the server by reinstalling.

Apache modules range from basic functions to more esoteric caching and authentication routines. You can use modules to serve different forms of a given file, based on the browsers your users employ, or to limit access to particular files. If a person wants to do something with the Web, an Apache module probably exists to enable it. If no such module exists, however, one can be written. To write a new module, simply follow the Apache API, or programming standards, using a common programming language. Once the module is finished and debugged, it can be submitted to the modules database at the Apache Web site, so other Apache users can share your work.

PART II

Configuring and Running Apache

CHAPTER 6

Configuring and Testing Apache

Now that you've installed Apache successfully, you need to configure it before it can run on your system. The configuration process enables you to set the various Apache parameters to meet the needs of your own network and requires you to insert particular data about your network and site. This is so the server can respond appropriately to the various requests made from other machines.

Apache configuration takes time, but it's not particularly complicated. The process focuses on one particular file, `httpd-std.conf`, which is found in the `/usr/local/apache2/conf` directory in Apache 2.0, and as `httpd.conf` in `/etc/apache` in Apache 1.3.

NOTE: Depending on your Unix variant, Apache may have used the term `httpd` instead of `apache` when building its directories. If you can't locate the `/etc/apache` directory, look for `/etc/httpd` instead. No practical difference exists between the two, but you need to make the substitution, if necessary, whenever you read a filename in this book.

The `httpd-std.conf` file is extremely long. In Appendix E, "Apache Configuration Files," where all the Apache configuration files for Apache 2.0 are listed, `httpd-std.conf` takes up nearly 30 pages! Luckily, it's also one of the better-written configuration files for Unix programs. Many comments from the developers are included, as well as many good instructions on how best to edit the file for your needs.

TIP: A *comment* is exactly that: it's a message from the file's author to you. You can tell a comment from other data because lines with comments are always started with the # character, which is called a *hashmark* in Unix parlance. The hashmark indicates that particular line isn't part of the code to the operating system and it shouldn't be executed as part of the program. Hashmarks can appear anywhere in a line; whatever data follows the hashmark is simply ignored as the program runs.

In this chapter, you learn how `httpd-std.conf` is constructed and how to edit it for your particular situation. We begin with the Unix configuration because this is the most common way to run Apache, and then look at the Windows configuration. The Windows configuration file is similar to the Unix file, but the information you provide is quite different. Before you begin the work in this chapter, write down the following information and keep it close by:

▼   Your domain name

■   The full machine name of the Web server

■   The full machine names of any other machines on the network

■   Internet Protocol (IP) numbers for your domain and all machines on the network

■   The way you want your users' Web files to be managed

▲   Any virtual host information you need (see Chapter 18, "Virtual Domain Hosting")

TIP: You'll be editing the configuration files with a text editor. If you've never worked with a text editor under Unix before, consult Appendix B, "Using a Unix Text Editor," for some hints and assistance. Practice on a different file before you dive into the Apache configuration files if you're new to text editors.

THE APACHE CONFIGURATION FILES

Three files are in the `/usr/local/apache2/conf` subdirectory: `httpd-std.conf`, `httpd-win.conf`, and `highperformance-std.conf`. The `httpd-std` file is for Unix, while the `httpd-win` file is for Windows installations. You also see files for more advanced Apache configuration, such as `magic` and `mime.types`, but you can ignore those for now. The `*.conf` files are the ones that need to be edited for any Apache installation.

NOTE: You can use `httpd-std.conf` to configure a Windows installation of Apache, but it will be a real pain. Use the file already edited for Windows and save some time. You won't be able to use `highperformance-std.conf` directly on a Windows box, though. Read through the file and adapt its solutions to your own network.

The `highperformance-std` file is a sample designed to show you one way of optimizing Apache for fast response and smooth operation. This isn't necessarily the best solution for everyone, but it's a good place to start. See Chapter 11, "Performance Tuning," for more information on this file and on getting your Apache installation to run as efficiently as possible.

Read through the appropriate file for your system before you begin to edit it. If you don't like reading files on the screen, flip to Appendix E, "Apache Configuration Files." In this appendix, you can find the complete text of these three files (taken from the Apache 2.0 distribution). You might want to make notes in the margin before you begin editing. Check off your notes while you work, so you don't forget any one piece of information that may keep Apache from working.

As the configuration files note, both the `httpd-std` and the `httpd-win` files are divided into three parts:

▼ How Apache works as a running server process or "global environment" settings

■ Configuration of your main Apache server (and basic virtual host information)

▲ Configuration of any virtual hosts you might be running

This chapter covers the first two parts of the configuration file in detail. The third part, dealing with virtual host configuration, is discussed in Chapter 18, "Virtual Domain Hosting."

CONFIGURING APACHE FOR UNIX

To configure Apache on a Unix variant, open the file `/usr/local/apache2/conf/httpd-std.conf` in your favorite text editor. (If your system uses `httpd` instead of apache, open the file /etc/httpd/docs/conf/httpd-std.conf instead.) For the first few times you configure Apache, printing the file or using the version printed in Appendix E could be helpful. Highlight or flag the sections you want to edit first, if you like.

NOTE: At the very least, during your first experience with httpd-std.conf, mark the sections you've already dealt with. The file looks much the same no matter where you are because most of the lines are commented out with the hashmark character. Skipping important code blocks is easy if you're not paying close attention.

The remainder of this section contains code blocks from the httpd-std.conf file and the suggested configuration for each. The blocks appear in the same order as they appear in the file itself, so you should be able to follow along with ease. Note, some of these blocks are mandatory configurations, while others are simply suggested. You need to insert the information called for at the beginning of this chapter in various places, so you can save time if you jot down the answers to the bulleted items on page 4 before you begin.

```
# Do NOT simply read the instructions in here without understanding
# what they do. They're here only as hints or reminders. If you are unsure
# consult the online docs. You have been warned.
```

This warning isn't merely for show. Printed documentation doesn't change as rapidly as the code itself can change. If anything in your version of the httpd-std.conf file looks different from what is printed here, check http://www.apache.org to see if updated information is on the site.

NOTE: This is especially important when using beta software. Things change quickly when software is undergoing beta testing, so changes might exist in the various configuration files that can't be forecast at press time. Check the documents on the Apache Web site if you're having trouble or if your configuration file looks different.

```
# Configuration and logfile names: If the filenames you specify for many
# of the server's control files begin with "/" (or "drive:/" for Win32), the
# server will use that explicit path. If the filenames do *not* begin
# with "/", the value of ServerRoot is prepended — so "logs/foo.log"
# with ServerRoot set to "/usr/local/apache" will be interpreted by the
# server as "/usr/local/apache/logs/foo.log".
```

You define the ServerRoot variable in the next step of configuration. Using ServerRoot as part of your configuration saves time and keystrokes because you need not specify a complete file path for each file Apache uses or may create. Note, if you want to call a file outside the Apache root directory, you need to specify the full path. Thus, if you want logs to go to /var/log/apache instead of /usr/local/apache as shown in the previous example, but ServerRoot is defined as /usr/local/apache, you need to spell out the full /var/log/apache path—regardless of what's already defined in your operating system PATH variable.

```
# ServerRoot: The top of the directory tree under which the server's
# configuration, error, and log files are kept.
#
# NOTE!  If you intend to place this on an NFS (or otherwise network)
# mounted filesystem then please read the LockFile documentation
# (available at
<URL:http://www.apache.org/docs/mod/core.html#lockfile>);
# you will save yourself a lot of trouble.
#
# Do NOT add a slash at the end of the directory path.
#
ServerRoot "@@ServerRoot@@"
```

Here is the entry for `ServerRoot`. Setting this variable with the Apache root directory as its value is easier. So, if Apache created its root directory as `/etc/apache` during
installation, use that as the value. If Apache created `/etc/httpd` instead, use that value.
The entry should be on a line by itself without a hashmark, replacing the sample entry,
but it must retain the quotes in the sample:

```
ServerRoot "/usr/local/apache2"
```

The LockFile warning is addressed in the next entry.

NOTE: You probably needn't change this value unless you want to put ServerRoot into a nonstandard directory. When Apache installs, it usually sets the correct value in this variable, depending on the
directory into which it was installed.

```
# The LockFile directive sets the path to the lockfile used when Apache
# is compiled with either USE_FCNTL_SERIALIZED_ACCEPT or
# USE_FLOCK_SERIALIZED_ACCEPT. This directive should normally be left at
# its default value. The main reason for changing it is if the logs
# directory is NFS mounted, since the lockfile MUST BE STORED ON A LOCAL
# DISK. The PID of the main server process is automatically appended to
# the filename.
#
#LockFile logs/accept.lock
```

You can simply uncomment the sample entry by removing the hashmark. If Apache
crashes, you won't be able to restart it because the crash will have generated a lockfile.
The *lockfile,* as its name implies, locks Apache so you won't have more than one Apache
server running at once. To remove the lockfile and allow Apache to be rebooted, simply
remove the file designated in this entry. In this case, `/etc/httpd/logs/accept.lock`
(if `/etc/httpd` was the value of the `ServerRoot` variable in the previous entry).

CAUTION: If you're running Apache across a network that uses the NFS system to mount remote directories locally (see Chapter 4, "Running a Heterogeneous Network"), be particularly careful with this entry. You *must* place the lockfile on the same machine or partition where the Apache server itself is running. Never place the lockfile on a remotely mounted directory. If Apache crashes and the lockfile is physically on another machine, you might have to rebuild the entire network.

```
# PidFile: The file in which the server should record its process
# identification number when it starts.
#
PidFile logs/httpd.pid
```

Leave this entry as is. The process ID number is important for some internal Apache processes. You can always learn the PID for Apache by issuing the command ps x at the system prompt if you're logged in with superuser powers or by issuing the command ps -ax if you're logged into your user account.

```
# ScoreBoardFile: File used to store internal server process information.
# Not all architectures require this. But if yours does (you'll know because
# this file will be created when you run Apache) then you *must* ensure that
# no two invocations of Apache share the same scoreboard file.
#
<IfModule !perchild.c>
ScoreBoardFile logs/apache_runtime_status
</IfModule>
```

As the comment makes clear, you may not need to this entry. Check to see whether you do need it by starting Apache. When the server has booted up, check your directory listings to see whether the apache_runtime_status file exists in the /etc/{apache|httpd} /logs directory.

TIP: The {option|option} expression is a convenient shorthand taken from Unix programming languages. The curly brackets enclose all possible options for that particular space, which are separated with the *pipe*, or vertical bar, character.

If the file doesn't exist, you can comment out this entry by placing hashmarks at the beginning of each of the three lines. If the file does exist, however, leave this entry alone. The IfModule will run in the background and handle the process information required by Apache on your particular hardware.

```
# Timeout: The number of seconds before receives and sends time out.
#
Timeout 300
```

If you read a busy Web site on a regular basis, you've probably been subject to this variable. The Timeout variable determines how long an individual request can wait to be answered before it's rejected. Three hundred seconds equals five minutes, which is quite long. If you set this to be shorter, however, you run the risk of increasing total requests—and, thus, traffic load on the server—because people may try to reload the page more frequently.

```
# KeepAlive: Whether or not to allow persistent connections (more than
# one request per connection). Set to "Off" to deactivate.
#
KeepAlive On
```

Leave this variable set to On unless you're trying to regulate use of your site. This variable doesn't cause a great deal of system load and it can speed things along for those viewing your site. You can determine how persistent any given connection can be with the next variable.

```
# MaxKeepAliveRequests: The maximum number of requests to allow
# during a persistent connection. Set to 0 to allow an unlimited amount.
# We recommend you leave this number high, for maximum performance.
#
MaxKeepAliveRequests 100
```

If you permit persistent connections, you should limit the number of requests any given connection is allowed to make to the server. For those who run sites with low traffic (under 500 hits a day, for example, which is quite quiet), this variable can be set to a low number: perhaps 20 or 30. The higher you set this variable, the easier it is for multiple users to access your files in a timely manner. The default of 100 is fine.

```
# KeepAliveTimeout: Number of seconds to wait for the next request from the
# same client on the same connection.
#
KeepAliveTimeout 15
```

No matter how low you set the MaxKeepAliveRequests variable, you should set some sort of limits on persistent connections. The default of 15 seconds for the KeepAliveTimeout variable is a good one. If someone is skimming your site, trying to drill down to a particular page or set of files, it's considered friendly to keep that connection alive and responding rapidly. If someone waits more than 15 seconds to move to another page or file on your site, however, this is probably because that person is reading or viewing something that could take some time to complete (or he isn't paying attention to the screen at that moment). You can safely terminate that connection. The next request from that person's browser opens a new connection, which is subject to the persistent connection parameters anew.

```
## Server-Pool Size Regulation (MPM specific)
```

The various configurations in this block of code (deleted, but visible in Appendix E) help Apache handle the various server processes required to answer multiple requests for multiple files. Apache handles these processes dynamically, that is, the number of processes running at any given time is determined by the number of active requests at the same time. To configure the server pool size, or number of processes, you need to set five separate parameters:

▼   `MinSpareServers` The minimum number of idle processes waiting to answer a browser request

■   `MaxSpareServers` The most idle processes waiting at any given time

■   `StartServers` The number of processes started at boot up

■   `MaxClients` The total number of processes that can run at any time

▲   `MaxRequestsPerChild` The number of requests that any one process can answer before exiting

On bootup, Apache starts the number of processes specified in `StartServers`. Apache regularly checks the number of idle processes waiting for a browser request. If that number is lower than `MinSpareServers`, new processes are spawned. If it's higher than `MaxSpareServers`, some of the idle processes are ended. Apache never runs more processes than the value of `MaxClients`. Finally, each of the processes can only answer as many requests as are determined by `MaxRequestsPerChild` before it dies. This setting prevents some issues of memory leak caused by particular libraries or platforms (especially under Apache 1.3 and on Solaris).

Set these variables to your desired levels or leave the defaults. You should probably run your site with the default values for a while to see whether these values are sufficient for your needs. You can always reconfigure Apache later if you need more or fewer processes.

TIP: You see several occurrences of this IfModule segment. The server uses these iterations to determine how multiple threads are to be handled. Apache then adjusts its internal operations accordingly to make the best use of the allotted machine resources.

```
# Listen: Allows you to bind Apache to specific IP addresses and/or
# ports, in addition to the default. See also the <VirtualHost>
# directive.
#
#Listen 3000
#Listen 12.34.56.78:80
```

Uncomment these lines only if you want Apache to answer browser requests on ports or IP numbers other than those you use for your primary domain name. Assume you run the site **prettygardenflowers.com**, a site for people who like to look at pictures of lovely gardens and the flowers in them. You also own the domains **prettynasturtiums.com**, **prettyroses.com**, and **prettylilacs.com**, however, each with its own IP number. If you enter those IP numbers as values for Listen, Apache serves the main **prettygardenflowers.com** page each time it receives a request for one of the other three domains you also own.

> **TIP:** This is done more flexibly with virtual hosting, but if you don't want to go to that trouble—or if you're basically parking the other three domains and don't plan to do individual work on each site—you can use Listen to save time.

```
#
# BindAddress: You can support virtual hosts with this option. This directive
# is used to tell the server which IP address to listen to. It can either
# contain "*", an IP address, or a fully qualified Internet domain name.
# See also the <VirtualHost> and Listen directives.
#
#BindAddress *
```

If you plan to use virtual hosts, as described in Chapter 18, "Virtual Domain Hosting," you can use the BindAddress variable to define the IP addresses to be monitored by Apache. The values for BindAddress can be * (no value), a numeric IP address, or a qualified and registered domain name. As with other settings in this file, be sure any IP address or domain name you use here is registered with the appropriate authorities and you have permission to use it.

```
# Dynamic Shared Object (DSO) Support
#
# To be able to use the functionality of a module which was built as a DSO you
# have to place corresponding 'LoadModule' lines at this location so the
# directives contained in it are actually available _before_ they are used.
# Please read the file README.DSO in the Apache 1.3 distribution for more
# details about the DSO mechanism and run 'httpd -l' for the list of already
# built-in (statically linked and thus always available) modules in your httpd
# binary.
#
# Note: The order is which modules are loaded is important.  Don't change
# the order below without expert advice.
#
# Example:
# LoadModule foo_module modules/mod_foo.so
```

In Apache 2.0, modules are the primary way to add new functions to the basic Apache server. When you work with modules, you must tell Apache which modules you're running before you start using them. Then Apache can determine how to work with each module before it's called. Modules must be installed in a particular order. In the Apache 1.3 `httpd.conf` file, the default modules are listed explicitly. In Apache 2.0's `httpd-std.conf` file, modules aren't listed explicitly, so you must be careful when adding new modules.

NOTE: To learn more about modules and Apache, see Chapter 5, "Apache Modules."

Modules are the last section of global configuration. The configuration files now move to the details of the individual Apache server being set up.

```
# If your ServerType directive (set earlier in the 'Global Environment'
# section) is set to "inetd", the next few directives don't have any
# effect since their settings are defined by the inetd configuration.
# Skip ahead to the ServerAdmin directive.
```

This direction is an artifact from the Apache 1.3 configuration file because no ServerType variable is in the Apache 2.0 configuration.

```
# Port: The port to which the standalone server listens. For
# ports < 1023, you will need httpd to be run as root initially.
#
Port @@Port@@
```

Web browsers send their requests to port 80 by default. If you choose another port, you must publicize it along with your URL, so people know to use it. A URL that includes a particular port is written like this: **http://www.domainname.com:xxxx**, where the **:xxxx** component is the actual port you want requests sent to. So, set this entry to

```
Port 80
```

TIP: Want to preview and test your site before making it public? Set the port value to something unusual and release the new port number only to those who are working on the site. Remember to change it back to port 80 when you're done or nobody else will be able to see your site.

```
# If you wish httpd to run as a different user or group, you must run
# httpd as root initially and it will switch.
#
# User/Group: The name (or #number) of the user/group to run httpd as.
#  . On SCO (ODT 3) use "User nouser" and "Group nogroup".
#  . On HPUX you may not be able to use shared memory as nobody, and the
#    suggested workaround is to create a user www and use that user.
#  NOTE that some kernels refuse to setgid(Group) or semctl(IPC_SET)
#  when the value of (unsigned)Group is above 60000;
#  don't use Group #-1 on these systems!
#
User nobody
Group #-1
```

Unless you're using one of the operating systems cited in the previous code block, leave this entry as is. A good security idea is to run as few processes as possible directly from the root account. Be sure to create the user nobody before you run Apache.

```
# ServerAdmin: Your address, where problems with the server should be
# e-mailed. This address appears on some server-generated pages, such
# as error documents.
#
ServerAdmin you@your.address
```

Change the value of ServerAdmin to your e-mail address or to another address you defined as the Web administrator. The server uses this address to mail you critical administrative messages, and it is also printed on some automatically served pages, such as the "404—Page Not Found" error page, so you may get mail from site visitors as well. If you don't want your personal address splashed across the site, consider creating a neutral address like web-admin@your.site. The added advantage is that you can transfer Web duties and e-mail to another person without having to separate your personal mail first.

```
# ServerName allows you to set a host name which is sent back to clients for
# your server if it's different than the one the program would get (i.e., use
# "www" instead of the host's real name).
#
# Note: You cannot just invent host names and hope they work. The name you
# define here must be a valid DNS name for your host. If you don't understand
# this, ask your network administrator. If your host doesn't have a registered DNS
# name, enter its IP address here. You will have to access it by its address
# (e.g., http://123.45.67.89/) anyway, and this will make redirections work in a
# sensible way.
#
#ServerName new.host.name
```

If you change no other entries in this file, *you must change this entry*. Replace the placeholder new.host.name with the actual domain name of your site and remove the hashmark at the beginning of the line. If you don't do this, Apache won't work. Period.

NOTE: If you want to run Apache on a single machine to test something, you can change this value to localhost. Apache only responds to requests from the same machine on which the server is running, however—it doesn't even respond to requests from other machines on the same network. You shouldn't use the localhost variable for anything other than time-limited testing.

```
# DocumentRoot: The directory out of which you will serve your
# documents. By default, all requests are taken from this directory, but
# symbolic links and aliases may be used to point to other locations.
#
DocumentRoot "@@ServerRoot@@/htdocs"
```

You needn't change this entry unless you want to change the directory where Apache searches for pages. Where you keep your Web files is a personal decision. I like to keep them in the `/var/www` directory, but that's a longtime habit drawn from a desire to keep Web files in a unique location apart from other documents and data.

NOTE: Whatever you set as `DocumentRoot` will be what Apache considers as its public root directory. Anyone using a browser to contact your Apache server can only get to files in that directory and its subdirectories. This is a security mechanism that prevents people from nosing around your directory structure and using Apache to crack your system.

The next blocks of code (deleted here, but visible in Appendix E) construct the framework for what files are available to browser requests and who may have access to particular files. You might want to limit certain files to browsers from your local network, for example.

```
# UserDir: The name of the directory which is appended onto a user's home
# directory if a ~user request is received.
#
UserDir public_html
```

Leave this as is. Tell your users to issue the command

```
mkdir public_html
```

in their home directories. They should place all files destined for the Web into the `public_html` directory. Then, when a browser requests a URL like **http://www. your.site/~username/filename.html**, Apache knows in which directory the named file can be found.

```
# Control access to UserDir directories.  The following is an example
# for a site where these directories are restricted to read-only.
#
#<Directory /home/*/public_html>
#    AllowOverride FileInfo AuthConfig Limit
#    Options MultiViews Indexes SymLinksIfOwnerMatch IncludesNoExec
#    <Limit GET POST OPTIONS PROPFIND>
#        Order allow,deny
#        Allow from all
#    </Limit>
#    <LimitExcept GET POST OPTIONS PROPFIND>
#        Order deny,allow
#        Deny from all
#    </LimitExcept>
#</Directory>
```

Next, uncomment the previous section beginning with "<Directory" and ending with </Directory>. This section defines what files will be made available to requests for documents in individual users' public_html home directories. This default setting permits browsers to request any documents or files contained in users' public_html directories.

> **NOTE:**   Control what your users offer with your system wide policies. See Chapter 16, "Dealing with Users," for some suggestions.

```
# DirectoryIndex: Name of the file or files to use as a pre-written HTML
# directory index.  Separate multiple entries with spaces.
#
DirectoryIndex index.html
```

This setting determines what file will be sent if a browser simply sends a request for the root URL. Setting the value of this variable as index.html is standard and few people even know they're requesting the page set by this variable if they only request the URL **http://www.your.site**. You can change this to whatever you want as your initial page and you need to do so if you're generating pages dynamically, as with ASP.

```
# AccessFileName: The name of the file to look for in each directory
# for access control information.
#
AccessFileName .htaccess

#
# The following lines prevent .htaccess files from being viewed by
# Web clients. Since .htaccess files often contain authorization
# information, access is disallowed for security reasons. Comment
# these lines out if you want Web visitors to see the contents of
# .htaccess files. If you change the AccessFileName directive above,
# be sure to make the corresponding changes here.
#
# Also, folks tend to use names such as .htpasswd for password
# files, so this will protect those as well.
#
<Files ~ "^\.ht">
    Order allow,deny
    Deny from all
</Files>
```

Leave these sections as they are. It's not a good idea to make the contents of your .ht* files publicly viewable because they may contain sensitive data written in cleartext (not encrypted as most password or authorization files usually are).

```
# CacheNegotiatedDocs: By default, Apache sends "Pragma: no-cache" with each
# document that was negotiated on the basis of content. This asks proxy
# servers not to cache the document. Uncommenting the following line disables
# this behavior, and proxies will be allowed to cache the documents.
#
#CacheNegotiatedDocs
```

Leave this setting as is. If a particular file has been sent only after negotiation between Apache and the requesting browser, this is probably something you don't want lying around on the other person's machine. The easiest way to safeguard such files is to make them noncacheable.

```
# UseCanonicalName: (new for 1.3)  With this setting turned on, whenever
# Apache needs to construct a self-referencing URL (a URL that refers back
# to the server the response is coming from) it will use ServerName and
# Port to form a "canonical" name. With this setting off, Apache will
# use the hostname:port that the client supplied, when possible. This
# also affects SERVER_NAME and SERVER_PORT in CGI scripts.
#
UseCanonicalName On
```

At first glance, this setting may seem redundant. With the rise of virtual hosts and other network capabilities, however, it can actually be quite important. Assume you host a virtual domain, fabulousfrenchfries.org, for a friend. Your friend has configured his operating system to reflect that domain name. But your friend doesn't connect to the Internet through your machine. Instead, he uses his Verizon DSL account to get online. When he connects to your Apache server and requests a page, Apache sees two things: first, his browser announces he's connecting from fabulousfrenchfries.org; second, the ServerName variable for that connection indicates a Verizon DSL machine and port. If, for some reason, Apache needs to build a URL for your friend, it will use the information about the machine he's actually connecting from, not the machine he claims to be on at the time.

```
# TypesConfig describes where the mime.types file (or equivalent) is
# to be found.
#
TypesConfig conf/mime.types


#
# DefaultType is the default MIME type the server will use for a document
# if it cannot otherwise determine one, such as from filename extensions.
# If your server contains mostly text or HTML documents, "text/plain" is
# a good value.  If most of your content is binary, such as applications
# or images, you may want to use "application/octet-stream" instead to
# keep browsers from trying to display binary files as though they are
# text.
#
DefaultType text/plain


#
# The mod_mime_magic module allows the server to use various hints from the
# contents of the file itself to determine its type. The MIMEMagicFile
# directive tells the module where the hint definitions are located.
# mod_mime_magic is not part of the default server (you have to add
# it yourself with a LoadModule [see the DSO paragraph in the 'Global
# Environment' section], or recompile the server and include mod_mime_magic
```

```
# as part of the configuration), so it's enclosed in an <IfModule> container.
# This means that the MIMEMagicFile directive will only be processed if the
# module is part of the server.
#
<IfModule mod_mime_magic.c>
    MIMEMagicFile conf/magic
</IfModule>
```

These code blocks define the various file types that will be processed as MIME files. Learn more about MIME and how Apache handles it in Chapter 14, "MIME and Other Encoding." In this chapter, you find more information about how to edit these blocks in the configuration file.

```
# HostnameLookups: Log the names of clients or just their IP addresses
# e.g., www.apache.org (on) or 204.62.129.132 (off).
# The default is off because it'd be overall better for the net if people
# had to knowingly turn this feature on, since enabling it means that
# each client request will result in AT LEAST one lookup request to the
# nameserver.
#
HostnameLookups Off
```

Despite the preachy tone of the comment for this setting, the Apache developers are right. You can get by just fine with a log containing only the IP addresses of those browsers that have requested data from your site. If you're curious about the actual domain name associated with any of those IP numbers, you can always use the nslookup utility or some other nameserver client.

```
# ErrorLog: The location of the error log file.
# If you do not specify an ErrorLog directive within a <VirtualHost>
# container, error messages relating to that virtual host will be
# logged here. If you *do* define an error logfile for a <VirtualHost>
# container, that host's errors will be logged there and not here.
#
ErrorLog logs/error_log
```

It doesn't matter where you put your logs, as long as it's consistent. The easiest way to ensure consistency is to accept the default settings for log locations. Note that the directory specified in ServerRoot is prepended to the directory path given above.

```
# LogLevel: Control the number of messages logged to the error_log
# Possible values include: debug, info, notice, warn, error, crit,
# alert, emerg.
#
LogLevel warn
```

If you have disk space concerns or you simply hate reading long log files, you can define the level of messages sent to the error_log log. If you select the debug level, you get all messages Apache generates. If you select emerg, you get only emergency warnings. The best choice is somewhere in the early middle: either notice or warn. This way, you get messages that can help you run Apache more efficiently, but you won't be bombarded with purely informative messages.

CAUTION: Setting the level of messages means absolutely nothing if you don't read the logs routinely. See Chapter 9, "Logs," to learn more about what the Apache logs contain and how to use the information in them.

```
# The following directives define some format nicknames for use with
# a CustomLog directive (see below).
#
LogFormat "%h %l %u %t \"%r\" %>s %b \"%{Referer}i\" \"%{User-Agent}i\"" combined
LogFormat "%h %l %u %t \"%r\" %>s %b" common
LogFormat "%{Referer}i -> %U" referer
LogFormat "%{User-agent}i" agent
```

Leave this section as is. It defines the format used in various Apache logs. If you change any of this information, the logs might not work correctly.

```
# The location and format of the access logfile (Common Logfile Format).
# If you do not define any access logfiles within a <VirtualHost>
# container, they will be logged here. Contrariwise, if you *do*
# define per-<VirtualHost> access logfiles, transactions will be
# logged therein and *not* in this file.
#
CustomLog logs/access_log common
```

The access_log contains a list of IP numbers, indicating the origin of all requests made to Apache for data stored on your site. This list can get quite long—especially if you have a busy site—so be sure to clean it out or archive it regularly.

```
# If you would like to have agent and referrer logfiles, uncomment the
# following directives.
#
#CustomLog logs/referer_log referer
#CustomLog logs/agent_log agent
```

The referer_log (the misspelling is accurate for Apache) contains a list of pages. These are the pages from which a request was made for one of your pages. That is, if someone is on a directory site like Yahoo! and clicks a link for your site, the Yahoo! page shows up as the referrer. Most of your referrers will be pages or files on your own site.

The agent_log tracks the browsers used to access your site, if the browser made that information available to the server. This is particularly useful if your Web designers are using HTML extensions that are more reliable with one browser than another. The FrontPage extensions developed by Microsoft are the dominant example.

NOTE: Nonstandard extensions don't meet the HTML standard. See Chapter 13, "Serving Compliant HTML," for more information about the HTML standard and why following it is a good idea.

```
# If you prefer a single logfile with access, agent, and referrer information
# (Combined Logfile Format) you can use the following directive.
#
#CustomLog logs/access_log combined
```

Some administrators prefer a lengthy log file that contains all the data written to the previously described individual log files. If this describes you, comment out all the previous log information (except for the LogFormat section) and uncomment the line that appears above it. Note, tracking important information or data trends in a combined logfile might be more difficult. You also still get the error_log as a separate document.

```
# Optionally add a line containing the server version and virtual host
# name to server-generated pages (error documents, FTP directory listings,
# mod_status and mod_info output etc., but not CGI generated documents).
# Set to "EMail" to also include a mailto: link to the ServerAdmin.
# Set to one of:  On | Off | Email
#
ServerSignature On
```

This is a nice feature to provide. If Apache generates a page on-the-fly, it can print a message showing the current version and hostname. You can also have Apache attach the e-mail address previously defined as the ServerAdmin variable. Set this either to On or Email, unless you have compelling reasons to hide this information.

```
# Aliases: Add here as many aliases as you need (with no limit). The format is
# Alias fakename realname
#
# Note that if you include a trailing / on fakename then the server will
# require it to be present in the URL. So "/icons" isn't aliased in this
# example, only "/icons/"..
#
Alias /icons/ "@@ServerRoot@@/icons/"

<Directory "@@ServerRoot@@/icons">
    Options Indexes MultiView
    AllowOverride None
    Order allow,deny
    Allow from all
</Directory>
```

Set aliases, using the syntax explained in the configuration file, for any directories that will be called on a regular basis as people use your site.

```
# ScriptAlias: This controls which directories contain server scripts.
# ScriptAliases are essentially the same as Aliases, except that
# documents in the realname directory are treated as applications and
# run by the server when requested rather than as documents sent to the client.
# The same rules about trailing "/" apply to ScriptAlias directives as to
# Alias.
#
```

```
ScriptAlias /cgi-bin/ "@@ServerRoot@@/cgi-bin/"

<IfModule mod_cgid.c>
#
# Additional to mod_cgid.c settings, mod_cgid has Scriptsock <path>
# for setting UNIX socket for communicating with cgid.
#
#Scriptsock              logs/cgisock
</IfModule>


#
# "@@ServerRoot@@/cgi-bin" should be changed to whatever your ScriptAliased
# CGI directory exists, if you have that configured.
#
<Directory "@@ServerRoot@@/cgi-bin">
    AllowOverride None
    Options None
    Order allow,deny
    Allow from all
</Directory>
```

As with the directory aliases, if you're using CGI scripts on your site, you should edit these entries to ensure Apache sends requests to the proper directory. Leave the data between the <IfModule> brackets as is.

```
# Redirect allows you to tell clients about documents which used to exist in
# your server's namespace, but do not anymore. This allows you to tell the
# clients where to look for the relocated document.
# Format: Redirect old-URI new-URL
```

Redirect is another nice touch. If you've moved pages that get significant traffic (check your logs), you can set up a redirect to bounce requests for those pages to their new location. Using Redirect makes the transition automatic. If you don't want to send people away without giving them the option to go or to stay, You can also put up a new page at the old location with a clickable link to the new page.

```
# FancyIndexing is whether you want fancy directory indexing or standard.
# VersionSort is whether files containing version numbers should be
# compared in the natural way, so that 'apache-1.3.9.tar' is placed before
# 'apache-1.3.12.tar'.
IndexOptions FancyIndexing VersionSort
```

If a browser requests a directory without specifying a filename, but no index.html file is in that directory, Apache serves a directory listing instead. Use the default here; the difference between fancy indexing and standard indexing is slight. *Fancy indexing* shows icons for various file types, where *standard indexing* doesn't. A minimal effect is on server load to use fancy indexing.

```
# AddIcon* directives tell the server which icon to show for different
# files or filename extensions. These are only displayed for
# FancyIndexed directories.
```

This entry contains a list of image files (deleted here, but visible in Appendix E) and defines which image is shown for which file type in a FancyIndexed directory listing. Accept the default as generated by Apache unless you have specific images you'd rather use instead.

The next few code blocks (deleted here, but visible in Appendix E) contain further options for FancyIndexed directory listings. If you want to use any of them, remove the hashmark at the start of the line to uncomment the particular entry you want to use.

```
# AddEncoding allows you to have certain browsers (Mosaic/X 2.1+) uncompress
# information on the fly. Note: Not all browsers support this.
# Despite the name similarity, the following Add* directives have nothing
# to do with the FancyIndexing customization directives above.
#
AddEncoding x-compress Z
AddEncoding x-gzip gz tgz
```

Although this entry refers to only a portion of the total browser market, go ahead and leave these lines active. Netscape and Mosaic browsers newer than version 2.1 (most currently installed versions of these browsers) can handle certain data types without having to download the files first. Configuring Apache to support this option is a courtesy to these browsers.

```
# DefaultLanguage and AddLanguage allows you to specify the language of
# a document. You can then use content negotiation to give a browser a
# file in a language the user can understand.
```

In general, you needn't worry about language settings unless you serve multiple versions of the same document in different languages. If this is the case, make sure each document is marked with the correct language tag, and then set a default language for all other files. Any file without a specific language tag is sent in the default language.

If every page on your site is in the same language, don't bother with this function. In addition, pay attention to the Apache comments: "It is generally better to not mark a page as being a certain language than marking it with the wrong language!" Table 6-1 shows some of the language tags used in Apache. Those who are familiar with the RFCs for language codes may note some differences. Work is underway to make the Apache language tags RFC compliant.

Language	Tag
Danish	da
Dutch	nl
English	en
Estonian	et
French	fr
German	de
Greek	el
Italian	it
Norwegian	no
Korean	kr
Portuguese	pt
Russian	ru
Spanish	Es
Swedish	Sv

Table 6-1. Apache Language Tags

TIP: An RFC is a Request for Comments, the way in which Internet standards are announced.

If you want to add language support to your Apache installation, consult the complete text of `httpd-std.conf` in Appendix E and follow the directions in the text.

```
# Specify a default charset for all pages sent out. This is
# always a good idea and opens the door for future internationalisation
# of your web site, should you ever want it. Specifying it as
# a default does little harm; as the standard dictates that a page
# is in iso-8859-1 (latin1) unless specified otherwise i.e. you
# are merely stating the obvious. There are also some security
# reasons in browsers, related to javascript and URL parsing
# which encourage you to always set a default char set.
#
AddDefaultCharset  ISO-8859-1
```

As the developers note, no reason exists to set a default character set for your site. If it's a site on which all the pages are written in English, the default character set is sufficient. If you're serving pages that use another character set, substitute the correct ISO number in this entry. More information on character sets follows this code block (deleted here, but visible in Appendix E).

```
# AddType allows you to tweak mime.types without actually editing it, or to
# make certain files to be certain types.
#
# For example, the PHP3 module (not part of the Apache distribution - see
# http://www.php.net) will typically use:
#
#AddType application/x-httpd-php3 .php3
#AddType application/x-httpd-php3-source .phps

AddType application/x-tar .tgz
```

This section, and the AddHandler section that follows, are used primarily with files designed to be generated dynamically. You can also use them to define new extensions for particular file types, however. For example, if you have a number of file archives compressed with gzip on your system, but you want them to download as Windows *.zip files, you can set an entry in AddType to perform that extension change. Note, you're not actually changing the file type, but merely helping that particular file type masquerade as something else.

```
# AddHandler allows you to map certain file extensions to "handlers",
# actions unrelated to filetype. These can be either built into the server
# or added with the Action command (see below)
#
# If you want to use server side includes, or CGI outside
# ScriptAliased directories, uncomment the following lines.
#
# To use CGI scripts:
#
#AddHandler cgi-script .cgi

#
# To use server-parsed HTML files
#
#<FilesMatch "\.shtml(\..+)?$">
#    SetOutputFilter INCLUDES
#</FilesMatch>

#
# Uncomment the following line to enable Apache's send-asis HTTP file
# feature
#
```

```
#AddHandler send-as-is asis

#
# If you wish to use server-parsed imagemap files, use
#
#AddHandler imap-file map

#
# To enable type maps, you might want to use
#
#AddHandler type-map var
```

Uncomment the appropriate lines for the file types and handlers you want to use. If you want to use one that isn't here, the handler should provide some documentation to help you make the correct AddHandler entry.

```
# Action lets you define media types that will execute a script whenever
# a matching file is called. This eliminates the need for repeated URL
# pathnames for oft-used CGI file processors.
# Format: Action media/type /cgi-script/location
# Format: Action handler-name /cgi-script/location
```

If you rely on CGI scripts heavily on your site, set an Action entry for each file type and handler that calls a particular script. Using Action entries cuts down on the load when the scripts are called.

```
# MetaDir: specifies the name of the directory in which Apache can find
# meta information files. These files contain additional HTTP headers
# to include when sending the document
#
#MetaDir .web

#
# MetaSuffix: specifies the file name suffix for the file containing the
# meta information.
#
#MetaSuffix .meta
```

You needn't use metaheaders. In fact, they're most frequently used by porn sites these days, which stuff the metaheaders full of currently popular names and topics. (That's why porn sites often pop up in a search engine when you're looking for something benign like Sailor Moon fan art.) If you want to enable metainformation to be sent with your pages, though, uncomment these two entries.

```
# Customizable error response (Apache style)
#  these come in three flavors
#
```

```
#     1) plain text
#ErrorDocument 500 "The server made a boo boo."
#
#     2) local redirects
#ErrorDocument 404 /missing.html
#  to redirect to local URL /missing.html
#ErrorDocument 404 "/cgi-bin/missing_handlder.pl"
#    i.e. any string which starts with a '/' and has
#    no spaces.
#  N.B.: You can redirect to a script or a document using server-side-includes.
#
#     3) external redirects
#ErrorDocument 402 http://some.other_server.com/subscription_info.html
#    i.e. any string which is a valid  URL.
#  N.B.: Many of the environment variables associated with the original
#  request will *not* be available to such a script.
#
#     4) borderline case
#ErrorDocument 402 "http://some.other_server.com/info.html is the place to look"
#     treated as case '1' as it has spaces and thus is not a valid URL
```

You should select one of these options, which determines how Apache responds to a request for a page that doesn't exist on your site. The most common response is #2, which generates a "404—Page Not Found" page on the requester's browser.

```
# The following directives modify normal HTTP response behavior.
# The first directive disables keepalive for Netscape 2.x and browsers that
# spoof it. There are known problems with these browser implementations.
# The second directive is for Microsoft Internet Explorer 4.0b2
# which has a broken HTTP/1.1 implementation and does not properly
# support keepalive when it is used on 301 or 302 (redirect) responses.
#
BrowserMatch "Mozilla/2" nokeepalive
BrowserMatch "MSIE 4\.0b2;" nokeepalive downgrade-1.0 force-response-1.0
```

Leave these entries as is. They fix known broken behavior for both Netscape and Internet Explorer. People using these browsers may experience trouble at your site if you comment out these entries.

```
# The following directive disables HTTP/1.1 responses to browsers which
# are in violation of the HTTP/1.0 spec by not being able to grok a
# basic 1.1 response.
#
BrowserMatch "RealPlayer 4\.0" force-response-1.0
BrowserMatch "Java/1\.0" force-response-1.0
BrowserMatch "JDK/1\.0" force-response-1.0
```

As with the previous setting, leave these three entries alone. They also fix broken browser behavior. As you can see, several problems are inherent in the decision to ignore known standards when developing software.

```
# Allow server status reports, with the URL of http://servername/server-status
# Change the ".your_domain.com" to match your domain to enable.
#
#<Location /server-status>
#    SetHandler server-status
#    Order deny,allow
#    Deny from all
#    Allow from .your_domain.com
#</Location>
```

This useful tool is best restricted to requests from your domain only. To activate it, remove the hashmarks for the lines <Location> to </Location> and change the entry .your_domain.com to your actual domain name.

```
# Allow remote server configuration reports, with the URL of
#  http://servername/server-info (requires that mod_info.c be loaded).
# Change the ".your_domain.com" to match your domain to enable.
#
#<Location /server-info>
#    SetHandler server-info
#    Order deny,allow
#    Deny from all
#    Allow from .your_domain.com
#</Location>
```

As with the previous setting, uncomment the settings if you want to use this tool and change the domain entry to reflect your actual domain name.

```
# There have been reports of people trying to abuse an old bug from pre-1.1
# days. This bug involved a CGI script distributed as a part of Apache.
# By uncommenting these lines you can redirect these attacks to a logging
# script on phf.apache.org. Or, you can record them yourself, using the script
# support/phf_abuse_log.cgi.
#
#<Location /cgi-bin/phf*>
#    Deny from all
#    ErrorDocument 403 http://phf.apache.org/phf_abuse_log.cgi
#</Location
```

Uncomment these lines. It's unclear how frequent this particular bug exploit is these days, but you can use this setting to help Apache track attempts.

```
# Proxy Server directives. Uncomment the following lines to
# enable the proxy server:
#
```

```
#<IfModule mod_proxy.c>
#ProxyRequests On
#
#<Directory proxy:*>
#    Order deny,allow
#    Deny from all
#    Allow from .your_domain.com
#</Directory>
```

If you're running a proxy server on your network, enable this entry and change the sample domain name to your actual domain.

```
# Enable/disable the handling of HTTP/1.1 "Via:" headers.
# ("Full" adds the server version; "Block" removes all outgoing Via: headers)
# Set to one of: Off | On | Full | Block
#
#ProxyVia On
```

Uncomment this entry to enable the use of Via: headers, which are part of the HTTP standard. While these aren't frequently used, they should be configured. If you're concerned about sending your proxy location information on outgoing requests from your network, select the Block setting.

```
# To enable the cache as well, edit and uncomment the following lines:
# (no cacheing without CacheRoot)
#
#CacheRoot "@@ServerRoot@@/proxy"
#CacheSize 5
#CacheGcInterval 4
#CacheMaxExpire 24
#CacheLastModifiedFactor 0.1
#CacheDefaultExpire 1
#NoCache a_domain.com another_domain.edu joes.garage_sale.com
```

You can set cache details for the proxy server, including any domain names you want to block from caching files originating on your network. You must set the CacheRoot entry if you want to enable the cache. If you uncomment all the other lines, but not CacheRoot, the cache won't work properly.

NOTE: As previously noted, the third section of the `httpd-std.conf` file configures virtual hosts. You can see this section of the file in Appendix E and learn how to edit it in Chapter 18, "Virtual Domain Hosting."

Save the file in your text editor and exit the editor. You can now start Apache and have your new configurations take effect. Skip the next section of this chapter and move to the section "The apachectl Utility" to learn how to test your configuration.

CONFIGURING APACHE FOR WINDOWS

The `httpd-win.conf` file contained with the Apache 2.0 beta at press time is similar to the Apache 1.3 Windows configuration file. If you're installing Apache 2.0 beta on a Windows network, check to see whether recent documentation for a truly 2.0 version of the `httpd-win.conf` file is on the Apache Web site before you begin to work with the file.

Most of the settings in the Unix and Windows versions of the Apache configuration files are the same. Thus, I eliminated any sections of the Windows file already discussed in the Unix section and for which the values or settings are the same.

CAUTION: Read the Unix section, as well as this section, if you're configuring a Windows installation of Apache. You won't get information on critical elements of the configuration file if you only read this section.

To work with this file on a Windows installation of Apache, open the `httpd-win.conf` file in a text editor like Notepad or Wordpad. You needn't open it in a word processor like Word but, if you must, make sure you save the file as Text Only with no end-of-line characters. The extraneous characters most word processors add invisibly might cause Apache to fail when it tries to read the configuration file and cannot understand those characters.

```
# NOTE: Where filenames are specified, you must use forward slashes
# instead of backslashes (e.g., "c:/apache" instead of "c:\apache").
# If a drive letter is omitted, the drive on which Apache.exe is located
# will be used by default. It is recommended that you always supply
# an explicit drive letter in absolute paths, however, to avoid
# confusion.
```

Establish the habit of providing full pathnames when working with Unix-based software on Windows platforms. You can rely on ServerRoot for subdirectories, but be aware Apache might not always handle implied paths in the way you intended.

```
# Apache on Win32 always creates one child process to handle requests. If it
# dies, another child process is created automatically. Within the child
# process multiple threads handle incoming requests. The next two
# directives control the behaviour of the threads and processes.
```

As with the Unix version, Apache requires you to define the parameters of the server pool. Windows Apache uses an internal threading to handle multiple incoming requests, however, where Unix Apache spawns new processes as required to meet the parameters. Thus, on Windows, you needn't set the MinSpareServers and MaxSpareServers parameters.

```
# MaxRequestsPerChild: the number of requests each child process is
# allowed to process before the child dies.  The child will exit so
# as to avoid problems after prolonged use when Apache (and maybe the
# libraries it uses) leak memory or other resources. On most systems, this
# isn't really needed, but a few (such as Solaris) do have notable leaks
```

```
# in the libraries. For Win32, set this value to zero (unlimited)
# unless advised otherwise.
#
MaxRequestsPerChild 0


#
# Number of concurrent threads (i.e., requests) the server will allow.
# Set this value according to the responsiveness of the server (more
# requests active at once means they're all handled more slowly) and
# the amount of system resources you'll allow the server to consume.
#
ThreadsPerChild 250
```

For initial Apache installations on Windows, accept these default settings. You can change them later if you notice significant system load or if you feel you can accept more connections than are currently permitted.

```
# ServerName allows you to set a host name which is sent back to clients for
# your server if it's different than the one the program would get (i.e., use
# "www" instead of the host's real name).
#
# 127.0.0.1 is the TCP/IP local loop-back address. Your machine
# always knows itself by this address. If you machine is connected to
# a network, you should change this to be your machine's name
#
# Note: You cannot just invent host names and hope they work. The name you
# define here must be a valid DNS name for your host. If you don't understand
# this, ask your network administrator.
# If your host doesn't have a registered DNS name, enter its IP address here
# You will have to access it by its address (e.g., http://123.45.67.89/)
# anyway, and this will make redirections work in a sensible way.
#
#ServerName @@ServerName@@
```

As noted in the Unix section, you *must* change this entry to reflect your actual domain name or Apache won't run. You can use IP address or domain name, but you must enter something.

```
# UserDir: The name of the directory which is appended onto a user's home
# directory if a ~user request is received.
#
# Under Win32, we do not currently try to determine the home directory of
# a Windows login, so a format such as that below needs to be used.  See
# the UserDir documentation for details.
UserDir "@@ServerRoot@@/users/"
```

As long as you set ServerRoot, you can leave this as is. Windows handles user directories differently than Unix. Under Windows, user profiles exist, but there isn't an analog to the absolute user space designated under Unix.

NOTE: As noted at the start of this chapter, the third section of the `httpd-win.conf` file configures virtual hosts. You can see this section of the file in Appendix E, and learn how to edit it in Chapter 18, "Virtual Domain Hosting."

Save the file in your text editor, and then exit the editor. You can now start Apache and have your new configurations take effect. First, though, go to the next section of this chapter, "The apachectl Utility," to test your configuration and fix any resulting problems.

THE APACHECT1 UTILITY

Before you begin to serve pages on your Web site, you need to test the installation and see whether the server has been configured correctly. First, open a Web browser and enter the URL **http://localhost/**. The browser should pull up a default page with the title "It Worked!" If you don't see any results in the browser window, check the settings in apache.conf and make sure you entered all the appropriate identification for your server and your network.

Once you test the installation by looking at **http://localhost/** and receive a page in return, you're ready to use the `apachectl` utility to test your configuration further. `apachectl` is a tool included with the Apache server and installed by default. This is kept in the `/bin` subdirectory of your main Apache directory—so if `/usr/local/apache2` is your default directory, `apachectl` would be found in `/usr/local/apache2/bin/apachectl`. Change to that directory and issue the command

```
./apachectl configtest
```

at the system prompt. The utility then runs quietly as it checks through your configurations for any errors. If no errors occur, you see the line

```
Syntax OK
```

print to the screen.

If errors are in the configuration, `apachectl` prints an error message to the screen. The message describes the problem and often gives the specific filename and line number that contains the error. With this information, you can go back to the configuration file and fix the problem. After you make the proper changes, run the configtest again. Repeat until you receive the "System OK" message from `apachectl`.

TIP: The `apachectl` utility has far more options than simply testing your configuration. In Chapter 7, "Managing the Apache Server," you learn many other ways to use `apachectl` with your installation.

SUMMARY

Installing the Apache server is only the first step. Once the server is successfully installed, it must be configured. Apache is configured by editing a lengthy file called `httpd.conf` under Apache 1.3 and `httpd-std.conf` under Apache 2.0. The equivalent file for Apache 2.0 on Windows is called `httpd-win.conf`. The file should be edited using a text editor like the ones described in Appendix E.

When working with the configuration file, you'll change some entries to reflect the individual facts about your Web setup, such as domain name and file system structure. Other entries are fine in their default form. You may need to uncomment some entries or make them active, by removing the # character from the beginning of a line. Other entries that you don't want to affect your Apache installation may be commented out by placing the hashmark at the start of that line. Any commented-out line won't run when the server boots up.

Once you finish editing the configuration files, use the `apachectl` utility to check your work. The utility scans all the configuration files and looks for errors. If none are found, it reports a "System OK" message. If errors exist, `apachectl` describes the error and provides the precise location of the mistake. You can then fix the problem and run the `apachectl` configuration test again to ensure the installation is error-free.

CHAPTER 7

Managing the Apache Server

Now that you've installed and configured the Apache Web server, following the instructions given in previous chapters, you're ready to get your Web site up and running. Running Apache is simple; you've done most of the work already. Apache tends to run cleanly and quietly, requiring little intervention from its administrator. As long as you keep an eye on the logs the server generates, you probably won't have to do much directly with the server until you're ready to upgrade or add new features.

Running the server itself isn't the only job of an Apache administrator, though. You also need to maintain the site's files in an appropriate and understandable manner. A site that's easy to navigate is a site that gets return visitors. If your visitors find it impossible to get where they want to go or to locate the files they want, they probably won't be back. Maintaining your site also involves adding new content and deleting old files. If you're responsible for the site, but not for dealing with the content, you need to work out a system for adding the content that's workable for everyone involved: you, the Web designers, and the Web content team.

TIP: If other people are responsible for the site content and design, find out how much they know about Apache. An understanding of how the Web server operates can lead to better design and site navigation. In return, you might learn more about the arts of Web design and the ins and outs of content production.

In this chapter, you learn about all these tasks. We begin with the basic administrative tasks: starting, stopping, and restarting the server. You learn the difference between rebooting and restarting, and when one method is better than the other. You also learn how to configure your operating system so Apache starts automatically when the machine is rebooted. Although this might not happen often, making Apache part of the reboot process takes one less thing away from your reboot To Do list. Finally, you learn about managing the site itself. Site navigation and adding new content are critical concepts that often get pushed to the back of an administrator's mind, especially if the administrator isn't responsible for the site's content.

CONTROLLING APACHE WITH DIRECT COMMANDS

You control the actions of the Apache server in three ways: with a direct command, with the `apachectl` utility, and as part of the bootup process. In this section, you learn the direct commands used to manage the server. Of the three, using direct commands is the slowest and least common, but it's useful to know how to use these commands in an emergency or if your other methods are unavailable.

As with most Unix programs, you can start the Apache server from any location on the machine. If you're already in the Apache directory, you can issue the command directly. If you're somewhere else in the file system, you can issue a command that includes the full directory path of the program you're invoking.

> **TIP:**   If you want to start a program without issuing the full directory path and without changing to the program's home directory, edit the PATH environment variable in your user shell. Your shell environment can use the directories listed in PATH as arguments, so you only need to issue the actual command. See a comprehensive Unix guide to learn how to edit shell environment variables.

Starting the Apache Server

To start the Apache Server, you must know the full directory path to the server. If you don't remember where this is, issue the command

```
where httpd
```

at the system prompt. The directory path then prints to the screen.

> **TIP:**   Usually, the `httpd` server (the actual Apache daemon) is stored in the `/usr/sbin` directory, but this may be different on your system or with your Apache installation. Use the appropriate directory path for your machine whenever you control Apache with direct commands.

Once you know the actual directory path for the server, you can issue the command

```
/usr/sbin/httpd
```

(or whatever the actual path is) at any system prompt to invoke the server, as long as you're logged in as root or have otherwise assumed superuser powers.

When Apache starts, it checks for its configuration files in the location you specified at installation. The default for Apache 1.3.* is /apache/conf, while under 2.0, it's /apache/docs. If you want to store your configuration files in another location, then you need to reinstall Apache and specify the new location to start the server without specifying the actual location. However, if you don't want to reinstall, or you've moved the configuration files temporarily for some reason (or you want to start the server with a test set of files stored in a different directory), you can issue the command

```
/usr/sbin/httpd -f /new/configuration/location/apache.conf
```

substituting whatever the actual directory paths are on your system for both `httpd` and the configuration files.

> **NOTE:**   You need to use this long command every time you start Apache by hand if you haven't reinstalled and informed Apache where the configuration files are stored. After a few times of issuing this command, you aren't saving any time over reinstalling.

Stopping the Apache Server

If you're managing Apache without the apachectl utility described in the following, the only real way to stop the server is with brute force. On a Unix system, that brute force is the kill command. kill comes in a number of strengths, and can be used both to stop and to restart Apache (and other programs). To stop a program, you need to use the strongest kill command, which sends the TERM signal to the shell. TERM is short for "terminate," which is exactly what the command does.

Before you can issue the kill command to stop the server, you need to know the unique process identification number (PID) assigned to the server process. Every process that runs on a Unix machine has a unique identifier that can be used to manage or administer the process. You can learn the PID of the httpd server process in two ways: issue the ps command at the shell prompt and pick the httpd PID out of the resulting table or consult a file Apache creates each time it's booted.

The httpd.pid file is something Apache automatically creates as soon as the httpd process starts and gets a PID. The file is stored with the Apache logs, usually in the file /apache/logs/httpd.pid. The file contains the identification number for the main httpd process. Although other child processes also appear in a ps table, you only need to kill the main process. The other processes die as well. All you must do to learn that process number, then, is to issue the command

```
more /apache/logs/httpd.pid
```

(or whatever the actual path for the file is. Use the where command shown in the previous section) at a shell prompt. The contents of the file then print to the screen.

Once you know the process identification number, you can kill the process. Simply issue the command

```
kill -9 process-identification-number
```

at the system prompt. You can also issue the command as

```
kill -TERM process-identification-number
```

if you prefer letters over numbers in identifying kill levels. The kill program ends the process. When the system prompt returns to your screen, the httpd process is dead. You must start the server again before any Web pages can be served on your site.

Restarting the Apache Server

Sometimes you don't need to kill the server: stopping, and then starting the server again can be a hassle. If you want to stop and start the server just because you edited a configuration file or made some other small change, you can avoid some of the work by restarting the server instead. To restart the server, use the same commands described in the previous section to stop the server. Instead of using the kill -9 or TERM signal, however, issue the command with the HUP signal. HUP is used to stop a given process and immediately restart the program.

Reboot vs. Restart

Whenever possible, restart your server instead of rebooting the entire machine. Restarting the server accomplishes much the same result: configuration files are re-read, connections are restored, and the server begins again cleanly. When you reboot the machine, however, everything on the machine must be shut down and the power cycled. This is common behavior for Windows users (less so for Macintosh users), but it isn't at all common for Unix users. A Unix machine can run happily for weeks or months on end without ever needing to be rebooted. If a service is giving you trouble, fix the service. Don't reboot the machine for one problem. If you use the `apachectl` utility described in the next section of the chapter, you can choose between two restart methods. Both work fine in getting Apache back to regular condition. Even big changes to the operating system itself rarely require complete reboots on a Unix machine, so Apache changes are much less likely to need reboots themselves. As your machine runs longer and longer, your uptime will become a source of pride and you'll find yourself scrambling to avoid reboots just to reach that next magical milestone.

To restart the Apache server, as with stopping it, you need to know the PID for the `httpd` server process. Identify the PID using the methods described in the previous section. Once you have the PID, issue the command

```
kill -1 process-identification-number
```

or use the command

```
kill -HUP process-identification-number
```

if you find letters easier to remember than numbers. Once the `kill -HUP` command is issued, the `httpd` process restarts. Restarting forces the server to read the configuration files anew, so any changes you made are taken into account at this time.

USING `apachectl`

While there's nothing wrong with using the commands described in the previous section to manage your Web server, another option exists. Why not use the `apachectl` utility? `apachectl` is a front-end to the server itself; a *front-end* is an interface designed to make using a particular program easier. Some front-ends are graphical, while others, like `apachectl`, are simply text commands. However, using `apachectl` means server commands will always be issued correctly.

`apachectl` is installed when you install the server. If you followed the installation and configuration process described in previous chapters, you might have used `apachectl` already to test your Apache configuration and the edits you made to the various configuration files. You can use `apachectl` many other ways, though, and you might find this is an efficient way to manage the server.

To start the server with `apachectl`, simply issue the command

```
apachectl start
```

at the command prompt. Likewise, to stop the server, issue the command

```
apachectl stop
```

Starting and stopping are basic functions, but `apachectl` can do more than that. One of the more useful functions is restarting. You can choose from two methods. The simple restart flag restarts Apache, killing all open connections to the server. If you don't want to be so drastic to your visitors, though, you can use the graceful flag, which restarts the server without disconnecting anyone currently using your site. Table 7-1 contains the various Apache options. All options are issued using the syntax

```
apachectl option
```

Some of the `apachectl` options require you to have the mod_status module installed and configured. mod_status is usually installed as part of the default module set, but make sure you configure it correctly before you use `apachectl` to generate status

Option	Function
configtest	Checks the syntax of all server configuration files.
fullstatus	If mod_status is enabled, this command generates a status report at the URL defined in the configuration files for the module.
graceful	Restarts the Apache server without killing current connections.
help	Displays `apachectl` help file.
restart	Restarts the Apache server, checking the configuration files. Current connections are killed.
start	Starts the Apache server. If the server is already running, you see an error message.
status	Prints a brief status report that omits the requests currently being served. mod_status must be enabled.
stop	Stops the Apache server.

Table 7-1. Options for the `apachectl` Utility

reports. You should also set permissions on the mod_status report pages, so random visitors can't see what your system is doing at any given point.

> **NOTE:**   To issue `apachectl` commands from anywhere on the system, you must place the path to the utility in your shell as part of the PATH environment variable.

STARTING APACHE AUTOMATICALLY AT SYSTEM BOOT

If you can manage Apache with simple commands, and the `apachectl` utility makes running the server even easier, why introduce a third method? Well, even though `apachectl` makes server management simple, it still requires you to issue the commands. You must still remember to restart the server after rebooting the machine, when you probably have dozens of other things on your mind. Instead of relying on your memory, why not streamline the process even more and have your operating system deal with Apache for you?

When your computer boots up, part of the boot process involves reading and executing a number of initialization (`init`) scripts. These `init` scripts contain directions to the operating system that invoke various programs, and set different parameters and variables, so the system runs the programs you want in the manner you prefer. You can use these `init` scripts to control Apache as well as all the other programs you run on that machine. To add Apache to your system's init scripts, you need a good understanding of how your particular operating system initializes and how to edit the appropriate files.

> **NOTE:**   Two major initialization methods are used under Unix. The System V method applies to Unices derived from the old AT&T System V Unix: Linux, Sun Unices, and some other commercial Unix variants. The BSD method applies (obviously) to Unices derived from Berkeley Systems Unix: BSD itself, FreeBSD, OpenBSD, and others. Some commercial Unices are also derived from BSD. MacOS X and MacOS X Server are BSD-derived and use the BSD method for initialization.

The System V Unix `init` Method

The System V Unix initialization method depends on a program called `init`. The `init` program is one of the first things that starts running when a System V machine is powered on. `init` is a critical process because it's the process that starts all other processes and programs on the machine. If your `init` program isn't working correctly, the system won't boot. You can use `init` to save yourself a lot of administrative tedium because `init` can start particular arrays of programs and services in response to specific commands.

These arrays of services are defined by the runlevel you select. *Runlevels* are a System V concept: the different runlevels are numbered and each runlevel represents a different mode of operation. Traditionally, seven runlevels are numbered 0 through 6. Runlevel 0 is designated as the shutdown level, while runlevel 6 is the reboot level. Runlevel 1 is generally designated as a single-user mode level, usually used for system repairs as a bare-bones installation. Runlevels 2 through 5 are available to be configured for different kinds of program arrays. For example, the following /etc/inittab file identifies these runlevels for Red Hat Linux installations:

```
# Default runlevel. The runlevels used by RHS are:
#   0 - halt (Do NOT set initdefault to this)
#   1 - Single user mode
#   2 - Multiuser, without NFS (The same as 3, if you do not
#       have networking
#   3 - Full multiuser mode
#   4 - unused
#   5 - X11
#   6 - reboot (Do NOT set initdefault to this)
```

CAUTION: The developers of your particular System V variant may have already configured individual runlevels for specific purposes. Consult your system documentation or the /etc/inittab file to see whether you have preconfigured runlevels and whether they can be edited.

When you boot up a System V Unix variant, the init process consults the /etc/inittab file to learn system configuration settings. This file defines the various runlevels and the processes that run at each level. The default /etc/inittab file for a Red Hat Linux system is printed in the following. This is a fairly standard version of /etc/inittab, outlining the runlevels and starting various getty programs.

TIP: gettys are the programs that listen for external connections, such as logins. If you don't run gettys, you can't get into your machine.

```
# inittab    This file describes how the INIT process
# should set up the system in a certain run-level.
#
# Author:       Miquel van Smoorenburg,
# <miquels@drinkel.nl.mugnet.org>
# Modified for RHS Linux by Marc Ewing and Donnie Barnes


# Default runlevel. The runlevels used by RHS are:
#   0 - halt (Do NOT set initdefault to this)
#   1 - Single user mode
#   2 - Multiuser, without NFS (The same as 3, if you do not
#       have networking
#   3 - Full multiuser mode
```

```
#    4 - unused
#    5 - X11
#    6 - reboot (Do NOT set initdefault to this)
#

id:5:initdefault:

# System initialization.
si::sysinit:/etc/rc.d/rc.sysinit

l0:0:wait:/etc/rc.d/rc 0
l1:1:wait:/etc/rc.d/rc 1
l2:2:wait:/etc/rc.d/rc 2
l3:3:wait:/etc/rc.d/rc 3
l4:4:wait:/etc/rc.d/rc 4
l5:5:wait:/etc/rc.d/rc 5
l6:6:wait:/etc/rc.d/rc 6


# Things to run in every runlevel.
ud::once:/sbin/update


# Trap CTRL-ALT-DELETE
ca::ctrlaltdel:/sbin/shutdown -t3 -r now


# When our UPS tells us power has failed, assume we have
# a few minutes of power left. Schedule a shutdown for
# minutes from now. This does, of course, assume you have
# powerd installed and your UPS connected and working
# correctly.
pf::powerfail:/sbin/shutdown -f -h +2 "Power Failure; System Shutting
Down"


# If power was restored before the shutdown kicked in, cancel it.
pr:12345:powerokwait:/sbin/shutdown -c "Power Restored; Shutdown
Cancelled"



# Run gettys in standard runlevels
1:2345:respawn:/sbin/mingetty tty1
2:2345:respawn:/sbin/mingetty tty2
3:2345:respawn:/sbin/mingetty tty3
4:2345:respawn:/sbin/mingetty tty4
```

```
5:2345:respawn:/sbin/mingetty tty5
6:2345:respawn:/sbin/mingetty tty6

# Run xdm in runlevel 5
# xdm is now a separate service
x:5:respawn:/etc/X11/prefdm -nodaemon
```

Note, this file contains operating system instructions for a UPS device (Uninterruptable Power Supply), because Red Hat Linux has specific power-management tools that work with UPSes in a power failure.

The majority of this `/etc/inittab` file is fairly straightforward. It defines the scripts associated with each runlevel. These scripts execute various commands, such as mounting particular file systems or starting certain programs. Each runlevel has its own script. Under Red Hat, as in this sample file, the scripts are kept in the directory named `/etc/rc.d/rc*.d`, where * is the number of the particular runlevel associated with the scripts in the directory. Thus, the directory for runlevel 2 would be `/etc/rc.d/rc2.d`.

NOTE: Different System V variants keep these scripts in different locations. Start looking under the `/etc` directory and search for a series of directories using the `rc` naming convention.

If you move into one of these directories and issue the `ls` command, you see the list of scripts kept there and which are executed when that particular runlevel is called. You might see an output like this:

K10xnptd	K55routed	S10network	S25netfs
S45pcmcia	S80sendmail	S90vmware	K20nfs
K83ypbind	S11portmap	S30syslog	S50inet
S85gpm	S90xfs	K20rstatd	S50inet
K14nfslock	S35identd	S55sshd	S90cdwrite
S99linuxconf	K20usersd	S05kudzu	S16apmd
S40atd	S60lpd	S90fonttastic	S99local
K20rwhod	S09net-setup	S20random	S40crond
S75keytable	S90mysql		

The entries that begin with *S* are scripts that start services when this runlevel is invoked. The entries that begin with *K* are scripts that halt services. The number after the *S* or the *K* is a numeric ranking. Entries with lower numbers are started or stopped earlier than those with higher numbers. You can edit what happens in a particular runlevel by changing the scripts contained in its associated directory.

NOTE: These scripts are actually symbolic links to files stored elsewhere on the system. If you add a new script, don't actually place the script itself in the directory. Just create a symbolic link to the actual script location.

On most System V Unix variants, you can change between runlevels without rebooting the system. Simply issue the command

```
init X
```

where *X* is the runlevel to which you want to change. For example, if you're currently in runlevel 5 and you want to change to runlevel 3, you would issue the command

```
init 3
```

The functions associated with the previous runlevel stop and the associated scripts of the new runlevels power up the appropriate processes and programs.

The BSD Unix `init` Method

Although the BSD Unix `init` method is different from the method used by System V Unices, the general principles are the same. Where System V Unices use the `/etc/inittab` and `/etc/rc.d/rc.sysinit` files to control initialization, BSD Unices use the `/etc/rc` and `/etc/rc.conf` files to accomplish the same functions. BSD Unices don't use the runlevel concept, however. Instead, they use one single mode of operation in which starting or stopping services must be done individually. While this means much less configuration must be done to your initialization scripts, it can be more time-consuming if you run a lot of services.

NOTE: This isn't to say that System V Unices are superior to BSD Unices. Both are outstanding versions of Unix. If you prefer to administer your services in "suites" depending on the runlevel you choose to load, however, a System V Unix is more to your taste. If you'd rather have control over each individual service and don't always want to run the same arrays of services at any given time, a BSD Unix may be the right choice for you.

The `/etc/rc` file is used to define all the configuration variables and parameters used by the machine. `/etc/rc` files vary wildly from installation to installation; so if you're running a BSD Unix, a good idea is to look at your own `/etc/rc` file and see what's already configured. You'll likely see information about both hardware and software, as well as operating system instructions. The `/etc/rc.conf` file, meanwhile, contains most of your system variables. If you need to change basic settings on your system, you'll probably do so in `/etc/rc.conf`. As with `/etc/rc`, the contents of `/etc/rc.conf` change from system to system, so you should look at the file as it's constructed on your own machine.

NOTE: Commands that start individual services at bootup are kept in the `/etc/rc.local` file, which is called by `/etc/rc` when the machine starts. Add services like Apache to `/etc/rc.local`, instead of adding them to `/etc/rc` directly or placing them in `/etc/rc.conf`.

Apache and `inet`

The `inet` program is a great way to manage services that respond to external requests. `inet` is a program that receives incoming requests, identifies them, and routes the requests to the appropriate server. You can run a number of services under the `inet` umbrella and manage all those services without having to deal with each one individually. Because Apache is such a server, doesn't it sound like a good idea to place it under `inet` and let `inet` deal with incoming Web requests?

Unfortunately, this isn't the best solution. While `inet` works wonders with particular kinds of data service, like FTP servers, it doesn't do so well with the Web. In fact, Apache recommends the server not be run under `inet`. `inet` won't break `httpd`, the Apache daemon, but that's not the main reason to avoid running `inet` and Apache together. Instead, this is an issue of time and system load. Where a regular Apache server takes X amount of time to respond to an incoming request, using `inet` adds additional time in which `inet` identifies the request, identifies Apache as the appropriate service, and routes the request. In addition, `inet` takes up extra CPU cycles that would be free if the request went directly to `inet`.

Certainly, a role exists for `inet` on most Unix machines that offer services across the Internet. You can use `inet` to manage FTP, `rlogin`, and Telnet (though the security risks of those programs may not be acceptable); nameserver functions; SSH; and other useful programs. Just keep Apache out of your `inet` configuration and you should be fine.

DEFINING THE FILE SYSTEM

One of the most annoying things on the Web is a site that has abysmal navigation. You've probably visited one of these sites and found yourself completely lost within the various pages and files without a way back to higher levels or different information. While the actual navigation through a site is controlled by the HTML used to code the visual appearance of the site, you can do a lot to assist navigation by how you set up and define your file system at the start of your work with Apache.

As you begin to define the organization of your site, think about how you want visitors to use the material you present. Do you want them to download files, such as drivers or new software? Do you want them to watch streaming media clips? Do you want them to read static text pages, to take interactive quizzes, or to play games? Do you want them to upload their own files to your site to be archived and shared with others or to be evaluated by someone at your end of the connection? You have to know why people are visiting your site to know the best way to organize the data you present.

NOTE: You might think you know how people are going to use your site, but you might be wrong. If you haven't brought the first version of the site online yet, you might be surprised when you see how people actually use your files. Things you and your site designers might consider important may be virtually ignored, while visitors drill deep into the site in search of specific information. For example, if a company that makes network cards doesn't put a link to driver downloads on the `index.html` of their site, visitors will search out drivers wherever they're located. You might need to change your site architecture as you begin to understand what visitors want from your Web presence.

Once you and your team have determined how to organize and present your data to visitors, you need to build the site to reflect that organization. Use the same concepts for your Web site that you do on the entire system: directories for main topics and nesting subdirectories for increasingly narrow divisions of that topic. For example, if you run a site that helps kids with their math homework, you might have a set of directories that looks like this:

```
/math/geometry/proofs/cubes
/math/algebra/equations/quadratic
/math/division/long/decimals
```

and so on. Each of those directories would probably contain an `index.html` file that provides more navigation help to visitors. Try to keep your directories organized logically. The logic you use doesn't matter as much as being consistent with whatever plan you choose. The set of directories on your math homework site might be equally logical like this:

```
/math/kindergarten/counting
/math/kindergarten/counting
/math/highschool/algebra/advanced
/math/college/calculus/differential-equations
```

Information architecture is a growing field, and rightly so. Efficient planning of Web file systems takes a variety of things into account, including user psychology, vocabulary, jargon, the goals of the company, the products or information being provided, time, and mouse clicks. If you or your company are getting frustrated because visitors aren't using your site in the way you intended or because you don't like the layout of the site, consider bringing in an information architect to review your organization and make some suggestions.

TIP: Some extremely good books on Web architecture are available at your friendly neighborhood bookstore. One of the best is *Web Navigation: Designing the User Experience,* by Jennifer Fleming (O'Reilly & Associates, 1998). Although three years is eons in Web time, Fleming's examples and theories are still useful today.

Adding Content to the Site

It's not much of a Web site if it doesn't have any content! As soon as you've set up your site and have Apache working properly, you can start adding content. The first thing you need to do is to replace the default `index.html` file provided by Apache. If you don't replace this file, your visitors will see an Apache-generated page that says nothing specific about your site.

NOTE: If for no other reason, replace this page so Apache won't get queries about your site. One of their Frequently Asked Questions concerns sites that show this page. Visitors might wonder if Apache has taken over your site.

Even if you don't have your beautifully designed site ready to go, put some kind of identifying document into your site as the `index.html` file. This alerts visitors that you've started running and the site will be available soon.

Various ways of managing site content exist. The method you choose depends on the security level you want to maintain, the number of people who'll be adding content, and how many users you have in general. Your own job description will also probably affect your choice because you only have so much available time to spend on content each day once you take all your other tasks into account.

If you run a site with many users, where each one wants to maintain individual Web presences, make sure each places their Web files into the correct subdirectory in their home directories (see Chapter 6, "Configuring and Testing Apache," for the appropriate configuration). If you work with a small number of people who add content, you can create a user group for them and construct group permissions so they have access to the server. If you have extreme security concerns or a rigid site content policy, you might need to add each new file yourself or delegate that task to a trusted person. Most Web administrators hit a happy medium somewhere around the level of creating user groups, with particular areas on the site getting more attention than others. Just be sure you know who has permission to add content to your main site and who doesn't.

Even though the architecture of your site may not be your responsibility, it's still your site and you're the one who has to administer it. Make it easy on yourself by grouping like with like. For example, keep all image files in an, `images` directory. You'll know where they are and it's easy to find the appropriate file when you need to change or delete the file. Because all images will have the same URL, except for the actual filename, this can also make it easier for visitors or your own Web team to view image files in a browser. Images take up the most space of any Web file type, and keeping them in a separate directory also means you can control the disk space used by images or, if necessary, you can move the image directory to a different place.

CAUTION: Any CGI scripts you serve from your Web site *must* be kept in the `cgi-bin` subdirectory under your main Apache directory. If scripts are placed elsewhere, they won't execute properly and you might introduce a security hole. See Chapter 15, "CGI—The Common Gateway Interface," for more information about running CGI scripts from your site.

You should have the authority to enforce some policies about the architecture of your site. What seems like a good idea to a committee may not be workable in practice, or it might slow down the user experience. If a proposed plan could make running your machine harder or place an unnecessary load on the system while far-flung files are found and served, then point this out before you change anything. Again, settling on a basic site architecture before you begin building the site and designing the pages is best. It's always easier to get it right the first time, especially if your site features a lot of fancy graphical navigation tools like image maps, which can be a real bear to re-create when the site's architecture changes.

NOTE: If you do have to change the entire directory structure of the site after it's already been available on the Web for some time, try to provide redirects for the most frequently visited pages on your site. See Chapter 5, "Apache Modules," to learn more about the individual modules that will automatically redirect browser requests to the correct pages once the module has been enabled and configured.

SUMMARY

Once you install Apache successfully and configure it appropriately for your site, there's relatively little work left for you to do. Apache runs independently most of the time, requiring little from you. Apache responds to several basic commands, such as Stop, Start, and Restart. You can either issue these commands directly from the system prompt or you can use the front-end utility `apachectl`. The `apachectl` utility offers some additional features, such as a choice between two restart methods and a feature that checks your configuration files to see if they're formatted correctly.

While using shell commands or `apachectl` is a great way to manage the server, you might also want to add Apache to the bootup files on your machine, so Apache automatically restarts when the machine's power cycles and the system reboots. The method used to start Apache automatically depends on whether you're running a System V Unix variant or a BSD Unix variant. While these methods are similar, they aren't identical, and you must use the appropriate form for your operating system.

Running a Web site isn't only about Apache. While you might have little or no input into the design and coding of the site's files and documents, you do have some say in how the site is organized because that architecture determines how your file system is defined. Try to keep like files together, such as CGI scripts or image files. This decreases the load on the server and on your system, as well as making it easy to manage individual data types without searching across the server for each file of that kind.

CHAPTER 8

Dealing with Innovation (mod_perl: A Case Study)

W hat sort of administrator are you? Are you the kind of person who wants to get the network "just so," with the precisely perfect blend of software and hardware, all configured to meet the exact needs of your user base and your visitors? Or, are you the sort of person who scours the Internet and print media for the latest innovation, whether it's tested or not, to boost the performance and speed of your system and knock the socks off your fellow administrators? No matter what kind of administrator you are, you need to deal with innovation in software at some point. The difference lies in when you adopt a new program or technique: the adventurous probably install it in beta format (and some in alpha, the truly experimental code), while the more cautious wait for a stable release or some other official imprimatur of reliability.

Innovation is especially important when you're working with Free or Open Source software. Because the development community for these programs is open and loose, individual programmers or small teams are constantly working on myriad patches, add-ons, upgrades, and new features for their favorite software. Some of these items make it into a formal release, but many more are released on the Web by being uploaded to software archives, shared over e-mail or USENET, or simply placed on the author's own Web site. Compare this to the more traditional business model for closed-source software, where innovations and advances are programmed by company employees following a general outline of new features provided by the marketing and managerial staff. New releases for traditional software are infrequent, and few "extras" are available on the Web (mostly because the commercial software companies don't release their programming standards, so it's hard to write something to mesh with the main program).

NOTE: Just as you can benefit from the work of other Apache enthusiasts, you can share your own work with the community as well. If you develop a CGI or Perl script that makes your administrative life easier, for example, consider uploading it to a software archive, so others can try your program. A real boost comes from "giving something back." Plus, this is a great way to develop your programming skills, as well as improve your ability to think innovatively about your network and the software that runs on it.

Apache is no exception to the Open Source innovation craze. Much of Apache itself was written by small groups or individual developers, especially the modules. New Apache-related code appears all the time on the Web, whether in archives or in the various Apache mailing lists and newsgroups. Much of this new code is exciting and reasonably innovative, creating new functions or streamlining old ones. Of course, some clinkers are out there, too, but that's to be expected when you have a large volunteer base programming for their favorite software. The trick is figuring out what's worthwhile and what isn't.

So, what's a bemused administrator to do? I assume you fall somewhere between the mild extremes posed in the first paragraph of this chapter. Furthermore, I assume the true extremes aren't even reading this book: the truly conservative administrators are probably still running the "big iron" servers of the '70s and early '80s, while the experimentalists have moved way beyond Apache and are probably running some sort of nanotech

Web server that fits inside the lenses of trendy eyeglasses. What the average Web administrator needs is software that fixes known problems, answers unmet needs, and works with a minimum of fuss and error, much like Apache itself.

In this chapter, you learn about Apache innovation in general. We cover the various sites where you can find new software to download and the Apache-related media to alert you to new administrative tricks that don't require anything but time. This chapter includes a lengthy table describing the various modules available through Apache's module registry and spends some time with one particular module, mod_perl. The *mod_perl module* is one of the most interesting things to come out of the Apache community in recent years, and it's been adopted widely by sites looking to boost efficiency and provide faster service. To narrow the topic even more, you then learn about a particular software program designed to run with Apache and mod_perl; this code is scalable and runs on sites that handle nearly a million hits a day. Finally, you learn more about the security risks that come with adopting new technology and how to counter or lessen their danger to your network.

WHEN TO USE A NEW IDEA

While finding new code or administrative tricks can be fairly easy—especially if you keep an eye on Apache news and the latest postings to Apache software archives—a bigger question exists. At what point should you adopt a new technology? Certainly, you can wait until the new method is absorbed into the regular Apache distribution. At that point, the module or technique is already commonplace and probably the standard way of handling that particular function anyway. Waiting until something is included in Apache packages may be a long time to sit around, though. Even popular modules like mod_perl aren't yet included in regular Apache releases, and mod_perl is vastly successful.

On the other hand, you probably don't want to jump on every new idea that's floated across mailing lists or newsgroups. Running alpha releases is even more dangerous than running beta software. *Alpha software* hasn't had any bugs taken out of it at all, except maybe bugs that prevent the software from actually running. Even *beta software* is risky for a company or a group that relies on its Web site for income or public exposure. If you're running a Web server on the side and you like to figure out things, adopting alpha software may be a fun way for you to learn more about Web programming and to keep your site on the "bleeding edge" of Web technology. For most of us, though, beta is experimental enough.

As with almost everything else, the middle ground is the best solution. Keep up on the latest Apache news and take time to surf the archives on a regular basis. If you read industry newsletters or online Web-related media, like *Apache Week* (**http://www.apacheweek.com**), you'll know what's new and exciting. Learn more about the things that interest you. Perhaps you want to subscribe to a new module's mailing list when the software is released in beta format. Let the experimentalists find the truly traumatic bugs and write patches, and then you can install a second beta version later that has improved code.

As you read later in this chapter, one of the biggest concerns with new software isn't that it will break your machine or cause trouble on the network, but that it might contain security holes that nobody—certainly not the programmer—is aware of. Savvy crackers love to find weaknesses in new software, especially if the program is so useful that it's rapidly adopted. One good reason to hang back and follow the mailing lists or news stories about a particular new piece of code is that, if security risks are discovered, you can wait until patches are released or the code itself is updated to remove some of the risk. How much risk you want to take with your installation depends on the kind of traffic you get on your site and how important the site is. Basic security concerns affect everyone, though, whether you're running an e-commerce site with millions of hits a day or a dinky little server that hosts a site proclaiming your love for the New Kids on the Block ten years after they broke up.

TIP: If you have the resources, why not set up a second server machine to test new software? You can build a nice little Apache box from an outdated Pentium machine and an old monitor. Use this as a test server where you can install beta, or even alpha, software and thoroughly test the new code before you add it to your main server. You don't even have to connect the test machine to the Internet full-time. In fact, it's probably better if you don't, simply to keep things more secure.

FINDING NEW MODULES AND SHORTCUTS

When you decide to get some new software for your Apache machine, it's time to go hunting. New Apache software can be found in a number of places on the Internet, whether it's on the Web itself, a USENET newsgroup, an e-mail list, or in a file archive.

TIP: Appendix A, "Internet Resources," contains a list of sites, newsgroups, and mailing lists that are excellent places to search. Some of the most popular locations are discussed in this chapter, but also look through the additional sites listed in Appendix A. You might find something truly unique that hasn't yet made it to the mainstream sites.

Some sites are more official than others, though "official" doesn't mean a great deal in the Apache world. The only truly official things are those included in the Apache download, such as the modules listed in Chapter 5, "Apache Modules." Other modules, even those provided in the archive on the Apache modules Web site (as the following describes), might be useful and nearly essential, but they aren't part of the official download. So, don't be worried that something you want to use isn't stamped with an official seal. Just do your research and know enough about the software in question before you download and install it on a production Web server.

Apache's Modules Registry

Because modularity is such a critical feature of the Apache Web server, most new Apache innovations are released as modules. If you're looking for new modules, the best place to start is **http://modules.apache.org**. This is the home of the Apache modules database, and, though it's located on the official Apache site, anyone is welcome to contribute modules to the registry. You can find all sorts of patches and unique modules here, for almost anything you can think of. If you think a module you got as part of the Apache download isn't working properly, you can also get a second copy of "official" modules here. Just re-install the module and try again.

The modules database is searchable by keyword. If you're looking for authentication modules, for example, the keyword "authentication" brings up over 50 modules. Not all of these are explicitly authentication modules, of course, but all the modules on the list have some authentication feature.

TIP: To view the entire database, click the Search button without entering a keyword. Everything on the site will be displayed in the resulting output.

Table 8-1 contains a list of modules currently found in the Apache module registry. Note, this list may change because of new modules being added or older ones being removed, but the table should give you a good idea of the various ways in which people are adapting Apache for their particular site needs. Certainly, the registry is the first place you should look if you're hoping to find new software that can enhance your current Apache installation, add new functions, or fix known problems.

Module	Function
ADML Language	A server-side scripting language that incorporates support for mySQL databases
All4Chinese	Encoding Chinese character sets on-the-fly
Apache DSSI	Extensions for server-side includes that are dynamic function calls
Apache Intrusion Detection Module	A real-time test of incoming requests checking for attempts to break into the server
ApacheSSL	SSL extensions
Apache::ASP	Embedded support for Active Server Pages
Authentification (for both NIS and WindowsNT methods)	Password authentication using existing user account names
auth_ip	Authentication by requesting browser's IP address

Table 8-1.   Modules in the Apache Module Registry

Module	Function
auth_ldap	Authentication module using LDAP technology
auth_oracle_module	Authentication with Oracle8 mechanism
auth_script	Authentication passed to an external script
AxKit	Toolkit for XML files
Bandwidth Management	Manage bandwidth through connection limits
BOA Scripting Engine	Scripting language with extensive database functions
bwshare	Manage bandwidth by requesting IP address
C/C++ Interpreter Module	Embeds a C/C++ compiler into Apache
CGI SUGId	Defines group and user IDs for CGI scripts
ChangeGroup PL/SQL Server Pages	Parses database server pages and serves them
Chatbox	Enables Chatbox support
Chili!Soft ASP	Enables ASP support on Apache
Chroot Security Patch	Allows httpd to run under chroot instead of root
Cold Flame	Enables ColdFusion support under Apache
ColdFusion Module	Enables access to ColdFusion server process
CommProc Messaging System	Enables dynamic content service
Connection Limitation	Manages bandwidth by limiting connections by host
Cookie Authentication	Authentication through cookies—various modules based on MySQL, existing files, and mSQL
Covalent Antivirus	Enables virus scan support in Apache
Covalent Intrusion Detector	Detects altered site content and alerts administrator
Covalent NetTruss	Streamlines the site creation process
Covalent Raven SSL	Enables SSL and TLS support for site security
Covalent SNMP Conductor	Enables SNMP support
Csacek	Encoding Czech and Cyrillic character sets
CyPay Module	Enables real-time e-commerce financial transactions

Table 8-1.   Modules in the Apache Module Registry *(continued)*

Module	Function
DCE Authentication	Enables DFS access and secure authentication
Decentralized Permanence Control System	Enables CVS and RCS support for document maintenance
dir_log	Enables logging on a directory-by-directory basis
dir_patch	Suppresses HTML headers for directory listings
Disallow ID	Controls access to files based on user ID or group ID
Distributed Permanence Control	Enables CVS and RCS support for document maintenance (see Decentralized version)
Dynamic Virtual Hosting	Enables virtual hosting based on directory listing
Enhydra Director	Enables support for the Enhydra server
External Authentication	Authentication based on user-provided scripts
External Authentication (/etc/passwd)	Authentication based on Unix `/etc/passwd` file
FastCGI	Maintains open CGI connections to improve response
FTP Conversions	Converts FTP directory listings to HTML format
GIF Counter	Stable support for GIF files being served
heitml	Enables a database extension to HTML
Hotwired mod_include	Extension for mod_include to support Hotwired
HTML::Embperl	Supports embedded Perl in HTML pages
Hyper Text Compiler	Enables server parsing of HTML documents
iHTML Application Server	Enables additional HTML extensions and functions
Indexer	Enables a configurable directory listing
inst_auth_module	Authentication by password
iProtect (mod_iprot)	Enables additional password security measures
Java Wrapper	Enables CGI execution of Java applications
Kerberos Authentication	Enables Kerberos security methods

Table 8-1.   Modules in the Apache Module Registry *(continued)*

Module	Function
LDAP Authentication	Authentication by LDAP
Log Data Scrambler	Experimental module that scrambles log data for security reasons
Midgard	Enables PHP support in Apache
mod_auth_anv	Authentication extensions
Mod_Fusion	Enables ColdFusion support
MOD-SNMP	Enables SNMP agent to report server status
mod-throttle	Manages bandwidth for individual users
modxslt	Enables XSLT support
mod_accessCookie	Configures access based on cookies
mod_access_identd	Enables access based on identd
mod_access_rbl	Enables access based on DNS information
mod_access_referer	Enables access based on HTTP header information
mod_allowdev	Manages file access
mod_aolserver	Enables AOL emulator
mod_auth2	Enables multiple NCSA-method password files
mod_authz_ldap	Authentication based on LDAP and certificates
mod_auth_ldap	Authentication based on LDAP
mod_auth_mysql	Authentication based on MySQL
mod_auth_nds	Authentication based on NDS
mod_auth_notes	Authentication based on Lotus Notes
mod_auth_ns.c	Authentication based on UIUC Nameserver
mod_auth_nt_module	Authentication based on WindowsNT
mod_auth_ntdom	Authentication based on WindowsNT module
mod_auth_ora7	Authentication based on Oracle7
mod_auth_ora8	Authentication based on Oracle8
mod_auth_oracle/ win32	Authentication based on Win32-Oracle
mod_auth_pgsql	Authentication based on PostgreSQL
mod_auth_radius	Authentication based on RADIUS
mod_auth_rdbm	Authentication based on networked DBM

Table 8-1.   Modules in the Apache Module Registry *(continued)*

Module	Function
mod_auth_rom	Authentication for ROM-style MUD gaming
mod_auth_samba	Authentication based on Samba
mod_auth_shadow	Authentication based on `/etc/shadow` file
mod_auth_smb	Authentication based on SMB
mod_auth_sys	Authentication based on system accounts
mod_auth_sysIRIX65	Authentication based on IRIX 6.*
mod_auth_tacacs	Authentication based on TACACS+
mod_auth_tds	Authentication based on TDS (MSSQL)
mod_auth_tkt	Authentication based on MD5 tickets
mod_auth_tkt_revisited	Authentication based on MD5 tickets (improved)
mod_auth_udp	Authentication based on UDP packets
mod_auth_yard	Authentication based on YARD
mod_auth_vp.c	Authentication based on NIS/Yellow Pages
mod_babble	Enables response of a predetermined size
mod_backhand	Load-balancing mechanism
mod_bakery	Enables encrypted cookies
mod_bandwidth	Bandwidth management for virtual hosts
mod_become	Defines setuid/setguid for each HTTP request
mod_beza	Character set conversion tools
mod_blob_pg95	Maps URIs to Postgres95 objects
mod_bol	Authentication based on BOL
mod_bunzip2	Decompresses bunzip-encoded documents on-the-fly
mod_cbroker	Enables CORBA gateway
mod_cgisock	Enables CGI at socket level
mod_cgi_debug	Debug support for CGI
mod_color	Enables color syntax designation
mod_corba	Enables module API through CORBA
mod_cplusplus	Enables a C/C+ wrapper
mod_cpp	Tools for C++ Apache module programming
mod_cscript	Support for embedded C code in HTML

Table 8-1.   Modules in the Apache Module Registry *(continued)*

Module	Function
mod_cvs	Enables CVS file updates
mod_cwa	Enables dynamic content from ZIP files
mod_dav	Enables WebDAV extensions
mod_dlopen	Enables dynamic content from ELF files
mod_dns	Manages domain resolution in real time
mod_dtcl	Enables Tcl support
mod_ecgi	Enables embedded CGI
mod_fcache	Supports MIME caching
mod_filename	On-the-fly translation of URIs to filenames
mod_filter	Enables modules to pass output through filters
mod_fjord.c	Enables a Java processor
mod_fontxlate	Character set management tools
mod_format	HTML formatting of C, C++, and Java code
mod_frontpage	Enables Microsoft FrontPage extensions
mod_gd	Enables a TrueType image generator
mod_gunzip	Enables support for gunzipped files
mod_gzip	Enables support for on-the-fly compression
mod_haskell	Enables an embedded Haskell language interpreter
mod_hosts_access	Enables use of the hosts_allow and hosts_deny files existing on the server
mod_index_rss	Enables RSS directories on-the-fly
mod_ip_forwarding	Enables IP forwarding support for use with proxies
mod_javascript	Enables JavaScript support
mod_jserv	Enables support for Java servlets
mod_layout	Adds header and footer support to pages in a variety of languages and formats
mod_ldap	Conflates two earlier LDAP authentication modules
mod_ldap.c	Authentication through LDAP
mod_LDAPauth	Authentication through LDAP
mod_limitipconn	Manages bandwidth by IP number

Table 8-1. Modules in the Apache Module Registry *(continued)*

Module	Function
mod_litbook	Enables document referencing tools
mod_lock.c	Enables selective file locking
mod_log_spread	Extension for mod_log_config module
mod_loopback	Debugging tools
mod_macro	Enables extended macro support
mod_mmap_static	Enables MMAP lists of files for faster response
mod_mocrify	Streamlines HTML on-the-fly
mod_mp3	Enables audio streaming of MP3 files
mod_mva	Authentication through MySQL
mod_mylog	Streams logs to a MySQL database
mod_neoinclude.c	Enables Tcl scripting extension
mod_ntlm	Authentication through NTLM
mod_odbc.auth	Authentication through ODBC
mod_ora_plsql	Enables direct serving of Oracle SQL files
mod_owa_module	Updated support for OWS PL/SQL files
mod_pagescript.cc	Enables SSI extensions
mod_perl	Enables an embedded Perl interpreter
mod_plsql	Enables Oracle file support
mod_pointer	Enables domain name mapping to other files
mod_prolog	Enables an embedded Prolog interpreter
mod_proxy_add_forward	Enables extended proxy forward headers
mod_proxy_add_uri	Enables extended proxy headers
mod_put	Adds a handler for specified HTTP headers
mod_pweb	Enables additional virtual host tools
mod_python	Enables Python support
mod_raah	Enables remote authentication
mod_random	Random URL generator
mod_redundancy	Sets a master/slave mechanism in case of server failure
mod_relocate	Enables log location requests for external locations

Table 8-1.   Modules in the Apache Module Registry *(continued)*

Module	Function
mod_repository	File management mechanism
mod_roaming	Enables Netscape Roaming Access support
mod_root	Enables support for server-side scripting in C++
mod_rvps	Enables RVP/S instant messaging module
mod_scgi	Enables SSI directives in CGI output
mod_sequester	Enables access control for documents on site
mod_session	Additional session management tools
mod_sm	Authentication through SiteMinder
mod_snake	Support for embedded Python
mod_sqlinclude	Enables additional MySQL support
mod_ssl	Enables SSL support
mod_tcl*	Enables Tcl support (similar to mod_perl)
mod_test	Support for authentication testing
mod_text	Enables some text to HTML conversion
mod_text2html	Advanced text to HTML conversion
mod_throttle/3.1.2	Manage bandwidth for virtual hosts
mod_throttle_access	Manage bandwidth on per-resource basis
mod_ticket	Enables digital tickets
mod_tproxt	Enables transparent HTTP proxies
mod_tracker	Advanced user tracking tools
mod_trailer	Enables additional HTML trailers to files
mod_trigger	Enables conditional triggers for each request
mod_usertild	Enables requests for user directories without ~
mod_usertrack	Manages SetCookie HTTP headers
mod_usertrack_proxy pass_front	Paired with previous module
mod_v2h	Enables virtual hosting from MySQL database
mod_verify	Various verification tools
mod_video	Enables support for frame-grabber hardware
mod_view	Enables users to view individual sections of text file

Table 8-1.   Modules in the Apache Module Registry *(continued)*

Module	Function
mod_virgule	Enables Advogato.org support
mod_wap_status	Monitors status of a Wireless Access Protocol server
mod_watch	Tracks data flow through server per request
mod_weborb	Enables CORBA objects for CGI scripts
mod_websh	Enables Tcl extensions
mod_xmlrpc	Enables XMLRPC extensions
mod_z_auth	Authentication based on NIS
Moto	Enables support for Moto programming language
mSQL Authentication	Authentication based on mSQL
MultiWeb	Support for character set conversions
NDS Authentication	Authentication based on NDS
NeoWebScript	Enables server-side includes based on Tcl
OpenASP	Enables Open Source version of ASP
PAM Authentication	Authentication based on PAM
parselog	Enables a Perl-based log parser
Patch for SunOS 4.1.*	Enables Apache compilation on SunOS 4.1 servers
PHP	Enables PHP support
PHP/FI	Enables PHP support with RDBMS
Postgres95 Authentication	Authentication based on Postgres95
PostgreSQL Authentication	Authentication based on PostgreSQL
PSX Scripting	Enables PSX macro language
PvApache	Enables embedded Python interpreter
Query String for SSI Variables	Parses a query string for certain defined variables
RADIUS Authentication	Authentication based on RADIUS
RADpage	Enables advanced application development tools
Realm and MD5 Digest Authentication	Authentication based on MD5 and Realm

Table 8-1. Modules in the Apache Module Registry *(continued)*

Module	Function
Rewriting/Mapping of Local URIs	On-the-fly rewriting of URIs
ROOT	Enables support for embedded C/C++ code
Russian Apache	Translates to Russian character set on-the-fly
Russian Charset	Support for Russian character sets
SecurID Authentication	Authentication based on ACE/Server tokens
Simplified PostgreSQL Authentication	Authentication based on postgreSQL
SOLID Database Authentication	Authentication based on SOLID
SpiderCache Server Side Caching	Enables SpiderCache tools
SSI for ISO-2022-JP	Enables SSI for Japanese character set
Stripper	On-the-fly graphic file optimization
System Authentication	Authentication based on .htaccess
TalentSoft WebPlus	Development toolset for Web+
ThunderWAP	Enables Wireless Access Protocol functions
UniversalChat	Enables chat functions
User/Domain Access Control	Authentication based on user/domain matching
UserPath	Mapping based on user-supplied URLs
var_patch	Enables character set negotiation
VelociGen for Perl	Enables commercial Perl processor
VelociGen for Tcl	Enables commercial Tcl processor
VITRAGE	On-the-fly HTML cleaning
Web+Shop	Commercial shopping cart module
WebCounter	Access tracking and page counter module
Whitebeam	Enables XML design environment
WhizBanner	Adds banner to CGI script before serving output
zmod_module	Enables logs for VDZ accounting software

Table 8-1. Modules in the Apache Module Registry *(continued)*

THE MOD_PERL MODULE

The mod_perl module is one of the most popular Apache modules in the past year or two. mod_perl embeds a Perl interpreter directly into Apache. This means when a script written in Perl is called as part of a browser request, Apache can parse the script immediately and send the result to the requesting browser. Without mod_perl, Apache would have to invoke a completely different program elsewhere on the machine, send the script to be parsed, receive the output, and then send it off. By using mod_perl, a Web administrator can streamline the entire process and make using Perl as simple as possible. Because Perl is easy to work with anyway and the majority of CGI scripts are now written in that language, having an embedded interpreter makes a significant difference in the response time of an Apache process.

mod_perl not only enables Perl CGI scripts to run better, it also allows Perl to be used in server-side includes and in any other Apache application where different chunks of code are parsed by the server. Because of mod_perl, even more Perl-based applications and scripts are being developed for Apache. This is truly a mutually beneficial scenario, where both the Apache and Perl development communities can work together to create code that benefits everyone who uses the Web.

CAUTION: Because the underlying code mechanisms changed so dramatically between Apache 1.3 and Apache 2.0, those running Apache 2.0 might not be able to get mod_perl working properly. The module developers are working to fix these new problems and a revised mod_perl should be available for the 2.0 release at about the same time Apache 2.0 is released as stable. Those running Apache 1.3.* won't have any trouble with the module.

Unless you're a Perl hacker already, you'll probably find the inner workings of the module less than interesting. (If you're already a Perl person, you know enough to go off and write your own Perl-Apache code.) As long as you have an up-to-date version of Perl installed on your machine, a working installation of Apache, and some time to spare, you can install mod_perl successfully.

TIP: Learn more about installing Perl by reading Chapter 15, "CGI—The Common Gateway Interface."

Installing mod_perl

Be sure you don't install mod_perl like you would install other Apache modules. Download the module from the Apache registry, as described earlier in this chapter. Unpack the file and read the INSTALL files contained in the download. You can read them either with a text editor or by issuing the command

```
perldoc INSTALL
```

Those files can tell you everything you need to do to get mod_perl working properly on your site. You need to pick a "recipe" that matches your needs and resources, and then follow the instructions in that recipe. The Makefile mod_perl generates can do everything that needs to be done. Any additional work you do could cause the whole installation to fail, and then you'd have to start over from point one.

Working with compilers and interpreters is, in general, a tricky business. Everything needs to be in the perfect place, so scripts and programs parse properly and the output is formatted correctly for its ultimate purpose. Follow the mod_perl directions and you'll be on your way to using this module to speed the various executable programs served on your Web site.

Once mod_perl is installed and working properly, you need to configure Apache to recognize the module. Although the Apache configuration files should automatically update when you install the module, open the appropriate configuration file for your version of Apache in your preferred text editor. Search the document for the line

```
AddModule mod_perl.c
```

which should be near the other modules listed in the configuration file. If the line isn't there, add it. (You might need to reinstall mod_perl anyway. Simply adding the line might not be enough to fix whatever problem could have occurred during installation.)

To ensure mod_perl only activates when there is Perl to be interpreted, you should enable a handler for the module. Enabling a handler means Apache won't hang when it gets a script that isn't written in Perl, or a file that isn't a script at all, and it won't throw out error messages instead of serving the file. To enable a handler for mod_perl, search the configuration file for any lines beginning with <IfModule>.

TIP: Because several IfModule configurations are in the default file, look for the IfModule handler associated with the mod_mime_magic module.

Below that section, enter a new section of code like this (assuming /perl-bin is the appropriate directory on your machine):

NOTE: This section of code should appear automatically after the module has been installed, but if it doesn't, you need to add it by hand.

```
<IfModule mod_perl.c>
    <Location /perl-bin>
        SetHandler perl-script
        PerlHandler Apache::Registry
    </Location>
</IfModule>
```

Save the configuration file and exit the text editor. You need to restart Apache, so the new settings take effect. To restart the server without breaking any existing connections, issue the command

```
apachectl graceful
```

at the command prompt. If nobody is connected, you can use the `apachectl graceful` command or you can simply issue the command as

```
apachectl restart
```

Using mod_perl with Existing CGI Scripts

One of the main reasons to install mod_perl is to streamline the execution of Perl-based CGI scripts. As you might remember if you have already read Chapter 15, "CGI—The Common Gateway Interface," CGI scripts must be passed through a Perl interpreter before the output can be sent to the requesting browser. If you don't have mod_perl enabled, Apache must invoke a Perl interpreter located elsewhere on the machine, wait for it to start, pass the script through the interpreter, close the interpreter, and send the output in answer to the request. This can take some time, depending on the speed of your processor and the length of the script. Enabling mod_perl means a Perl interpreter is configured right into the server, so Apache can parse Perl scripts much more quickly.

You can't start using mod_perl and expect all your scripts to work right out of the box, however. Most of them will probably do fine because the Apache::Registry and Apache::Perl-Run functions mimic a native CGI environment and can pass most Perl CGI without a problem. A few scripts on your machine, though, might need reconfiguration or some judicious editing before the scripts run properly through the mod_perl module.

CAUTION: Once you compile mod_perl and have it running properly, be careful with any Perl scripts you didn't write yourself. Because mod_perl embeds a Perl interpreter directly into Apache, which, in turn, runs as root, an unscrupulous programmer could hide a back door into your system deep within a Perl script. Know what you're running before you run it under mod_perl.

To make any necessary adjustments to your Perl CGI scripts, you need to have some understanding of Perl in general. Don't make any changes to the scripts unless you're sure of what you're editing; Perl is a concise-enough language that an inadvertent error can make the script stop running. The biggest things to check for are that each Perl CGI script includes a `use strict` statement and that Perl warnings are enabled. These precautions can help if problems occur and it'll be easier to debug anything that appears as an issue. As previously noted, chances are good that your script will run fine. If it doesn't, consider finding—or writing—another script to replace the one you're using. CGI scripts are short enough that writing a new one is sometimes less strenuous than amending an old one.

> **TIP:**   To make your Perl CGI scripts whiz through mod_perl and out to requesting browsers, consider rewriting them to call mod_perl explicitly or even as mod_perl modules themselves. You needn't do this before using the scripts, and you're certainly not required to do it. Some administrators are speed demons, though, and this is a good way to boost the efficiency of your site. Learn more about writing scripts for mod_perl from the definitive resource, *Writing Apache Modules with Perl and C: The Apache API and mod_perl*, by Lincoln Stein and Doug McEachern (O'Reilly & Associates, 1999).

mod_perl may seem like a strange module to star in a chapter about innovation, but it's one of the most useful modules you can compile into Apache (after the default modules, of course). With mod_perl, you can rewrite whatever you like on your Web site as a Perl script and have it parse quickly; and accurately. mod_perl speeds up CGI; is a great way to push Apache's boundaries, and also can hone your scripting skills, which can be put to great use elsewhere on your machine. While mod_perl isn't as "sexy" as some of the other modules you might find in the Apache module registry, you'll probably end up using mod_perl on a frequent and regular basis—and isn't that what innovation is all about?

SECURITY VERSUS INNOVATION

Of course, you need to think about security every time you add new software or functions to your machine. When you're dealing with the cutting edge, though, security takes on an additional facet. Sometimes programmers are so excited by a new technique or a particularly dazzling bit of code, they release the patch or module without thoroughly testing it for any security risks it might bring to your site. While this is understandable, it can be dangerous for your Apache installation if you unknowingly install software that causes additional risk.

One example of a security risk from an innovative new piece of code is described in the previous mod_perl section. Should you stop running mod_perl because it embeds Perl into the Apache server, which, in turn, runs as root, on the chance that someone will write a script exploiting that hole? No, of course not. The benefits of mod_perl are so great, they outweigh knee-jerk security reactions. What you do need to do, though, is to check your scripts, rewrite ones you're not sure about, and keep a close eye on Apache while it's running. You should take these security precautions anyway; it's not mod_perl's fault in any way, except it happens to be the container for the risk.

The safe way to deal with innovation is to hang back a bit. Don't be the first adopter of a new program or patch. Let the true experimenters get it first, test it out, and find the gaping holes. When a revised version is released, you can snap it up, knowing the biggest problems are gone. Just be sure to watch for additional patches or newer releases, so you can incorporate new functions or improved security. You needn't stop installing new software, but you might have to revise your risk tolerance in light of the kind of Web sites you serve. If you're hosting e-commerce sites that turn thousands of hits a day and are a major source of revenue for their owners, you'll probably need to be a little more risk-averse than if you're hosting fan sites for teen television starlets.

SUMMARY

No matter what kind of Apache administrator you are, you probably want to experiment with more Apache functions than those found in the basic download packages. Additional functions can make your server work with a variety of data formats, including those of various commercial programs. Because Apache is an Open Source project, the development community is free to work on projects of personal interest, instead of only those ideas that bring profit. A number of places exist to find innovative additions and patches for Apache, but the best place to start is the Apache Module Registry. In this registry, you can find hundreds of useful and unusual modules that enable you to configure your server to suit your precise needs and desires.

One of the most useful modules not included with the basic download is mod_perl. This module embeds a Perl interpreter directly into the server, allowing Apache to parse Perl CGI and other Perl scripts quickly and efficiently. You can use most of your existing Perl CGI scripts with mod_perl, but you might have to edit some to make more efficient use of the module. As with any new software, including mod_perl and scripts that use it, be aware of the potential security risks involved. As long as you're aware of potential problems, you'll be more attuned to any breaches that might happen.

PART III

Apache Administration

CHAPTER 9

Logs

In the first eight chapters of this book, you learned how to install, configure, and manage the Apache Web server. Apache is quite a simple program and, once it's up and running properly, there isn't a great deal to do. Don't expect to laze around making paper-clip chains, though, because tasks still need to be accomplished and data needs to be reviewed, no matter how easily the server runs on your site. Luckily, Apache has several automatic functions that provide assistance to administrators, as well as giving them a significant amount of data concerning the site and its operation.

Apache offers a lot of help to its administrators through the various log files it generates. These logs can tell you a great deal about your Web site. You can learn many different things about the people who visit your site, and you can track and identify any errors that might interfere with Apache (or be serious enough to crash Apache itself). You can even set logs for each of the virtual sites you might host, tracking the same information, which you can share with the owners of the sites or with other interested parties. To make this even better, many Apache modules also generate their own logs. You shouldn't have any shortage of reading material when you're at your Web administration job (or when you're logged in late at night).

Once you find the various logs generated by Apache and its modules, you need to know how the logged information is structured, so you can read the files and get the most from the data. Each file is organized slightly differently, but they're all reasonably easy to understand. Once you figure out how to read the data, you can use the logs to keep an eye on your system. Throughout this book, you find repeated reminders to check the logs; knowing your logs is the best way to know your installation. If you know what "normal" looks like on your server, then you're better equipped to recognize "abnormal" when it appears. You'll be able to pick unusual errors out of the error log or recognize strange patterns in the access log. You'll also have a better idea of the normal traffic to your site, so you can spot new trends or unexpected spikes that might lead to changes in the way you organize or present your files.

In this chapter, you learn the basics of Apache logs. We begin with the logs themselves: what they do, where they are, and how to read them. You learn more about the mod_log_config module and how it's used to shape the information that's logged, and about the various log settings in Apache configuration files. The chapter concludes with some log tricks that can help you get the most out of your installation.

APACHE LOGS

Two kinds of Apache logs exist. The first kind is a true *log,* that is, the server writes a particular type of information to a designated file, adding subsequent records each time the information reappears. For example, the log file access_log gets a new entry each time a new browser request is received by the server. These log files are plain-text files. You can read them with Unix commands like less and more, or you can open them in a text editor and read them there. You can even pass the logs through additional programs to parse the data and get more useful reports.

NOTE: The second kind of log isn't really a log, but more of a status report. In Chapter 5, "Apache Modules," you learned about the mod_info module. This module configures certain HTML documents on your site, which you can view with a regular browser. These documents contain up-to-date status reports on your server. You can see the number of connections, the uptime, and an array of useful information about the server itself. While these are immensely helpful documents and can tell you a great deal, they aren't technically logs. Consult the mod_info section of Chapter 5 to learn more about these reports, where to view them, and what information they contain.

While status reports are certainly critical for effective server administration, the data contained in log files is important for different reasons. Status reports contain information about what's happening *right now.* You can't tell what happened three hours ago or what the server load was like yesterday. Logs, however, are historical documents. Until you refresh the log file, as described later in this chapter, you have a complete list of entries concerning whatever the log subject is, whether this be server accesses, errors, or other useful information. Apache logs are constructed using the Common Log Format (CLF), a generally accepted standard that enables administrators to read logs from multiple programs, andyou can expect all the logs to be in roughly the same format. (If you have to learn a new format for each log, the job of log surveillance becomes distinctly less pleasant and, thus, less likely to be done.)

Log locations are configured through the regular Apache configuration file, `httpd.conf`. In the "Configuring Logs" section of this chapter, you learn how to edit these files so your logs are kept in a logical location. You also learn how to enable optional logs that can track information beyond error and accesses, though `error_log` and `access_log` are the only default log files. The error log is probably the most important of the log files because it records messages from the server about anything that goes wrong. You can set the level of warnings you want to receive, so the file doesn't become too large to work with. The access log contains a record for each browser request, which is a wonderful way to learn who is visiting your site and how often.

FINDING THE LOGS

Apache logs, by default and convention, are kept in the /logs subdirectory of your main Apache directory. If you change into that directory immediately after installing Apache and before running the server while connected to the Internet, you won't see any logs. The logs are created automatically as soon as the first piece of logged information appears on the server. That is, `access_log` won't be created until the first connection is made to the server. Likewise, `error_log` won't be created until the first error—of the minimum level specified in the configuration file—is recognized by the server.

If you want to place log files in a different location, please think twice. If you keep your logs together, it's far more likely you'll read all of them on a regular basis. Having to hunt through your file system for random log files decreases the likelihood you'll peruse the logs and take action based on the information they contain.

NOTE: The exception to this suggestion is logs for virtual hosts, sites you host on your machine without actually granting them their own hardware. When you configure a virtual host, you create a special container for that site's configurations in `httpd.conf`. Logs for virtual hosts should be enabled within the host's configuration container. Having separate logs for virtual hosts is best, so their traffic and errors aren't jumbled together with the data for your main server.

HOW TO READ LOGS

Reading logs configured in the CLF is simple. Each entry follows a standard syntax and, once you're used to this, it's easy to skim the logs and still retain the most important information. Log entries in `access_log` take the syntax

```
host    ident    authuser    date    request    status    bytes
```

Each of these items contains a specific type of information. In entries where not all the elements are present, a hyphen replaces the missing element. Table 9-1 shows these elements and their meanings.

Entries in `error_log` take a slightly different form. `error_log` entries also have a regular syntax, but the data in the entries may be much longer than entries in `access_log`. Error entries take the syntax

```
date    priority    host    error
```

where each element has a specific meaning:

- ▼ `date`—the date of the logged error
- ■ `priority`—the danger level of the error
- ■ `host`—the IP number of the browser that made the request triggering the error
- ▲ `error`—a text message describing the problem

For example, Apache might record an error entry that looks like this:

```
[Mon May 12 09:15:12 2001] [error] [client 192.168.0.1] unable to
process CGI script guestbook.cgi
```

Depending on the kind of error reported, the text messages can be lengthy or cryptic. You get a better sense of what different levels of error look like as you get more experience reading the `error_log` file.

CONFIGURING LOGS

Whether or not you use the mod_log_config module to configure additional options for your logs, you must make some basic configurations in the server itself before logs work

Element	Data Represented
host	The IP address of the requesting browser (if configured, the full domain name appears instead)
ident	If identity checking is enabled, the value of the IdentityCheck directive
authuser	If authentication is enabled, the valid user name of the person making the request
date	The date and time of the browser request, in the format day/month/year:hour:minute:second zone
request	The actual request from the client browser, enclosed in quotation marks
status	The HTTP status code returned by Apache to the client
bytes	The size of the file returned to the client browser, not including the various HTTP headers

Table 9-1.   Elements in an access_log Entry

properly. You might have already made these changes when you configured the server, as described in Chapter 6, "Configuring and Testing Apache," but it's always good to recheck and make sure you're sending the logs to the correct locations.

NOTE: You can find this section about a third of the way into the configuration file.

Open the appropriate configuration file for your version of Apache in your favorite text editor. (See Appendix B, "Using a Unix Text Editor," if you need help in selecting or using such a program.) Move down through the file until you locate the section that contains most of the log configurations.

NOTE: You might see configurations that refer to the /logs subdirectory earlier and later in the file than the section reprinted here. While you can also check those sections and get a better understanding of what is kept in the /logs directory, the main configurations are those described here.

```
# ErrorLog: The location of the error log file.
# If you do not specify an ErrorLog directive within a <VirtualHost>
# container, error messages relating to that virtual host will be
# logged here.  If you *do* define an error logfile for a <VirtualHost>
```

```
# container, that host's errors will be logged there and not here.
#
ErrorLog logs/error_log
```

As described in the first part of this chapter, `error_log` is one of the basic logs Apache generates. By default, it's kept in the `/logs` subdirectory with this basic name. You don't need to change anything here, but, if you do change something, remember what you did. Changing both the location and the name at the same time might be confusing enough that you lose the log in the depths of your machine.

```
#
# LogLevel: Control the number of messages logged to the error_log
# Possible values include: debug, info, notice, warn, error, crit,
# alert, emerg.
#
LogLevel warn
```

Select the level of messages that makes you the most comfortable. You have several options here, described in Table 9-2. If you're unsure what you should select here, opt for warn. Lower levels may generate too many log entries, while higher levels may not give you enough information to know your server well. You can always change this level later if you're unhappy with the resulting data.

```
#
# The following directives define some format nicknames for use with
# a CustomLog directive (see below).
#
LogFormat "%h %l %u %t \"%r\" %>s %b \"%{Referer}i\" \"%{User-Agent}i\"" combined
LogFormat "%h %l %u %t \"%r\" %>s %b" common
LogFormat "%{Referer}i -> %U" referer
LogFormat "%{User-agent}i" agent
```

You can leave these settings alone. They're used to define variables in a custom log. Custom logs can be used to track two important facts about your visitors: the site they were visiting immediately before accessing your site and the kind of browser they're using. Tracking referrers give you a good idea of who's linking to your site or how people are learning about your pages. Knowing what browser your visitors prefer could change the way in which you code your pages or the features you offer.

```
#
# The location and format of the access logfile (Common Logfile Format).
# If you do not define any access logfiles within a <VirtualHost>
# container, they will be logged here.  Contrariwise, if you *do*
# define per-<VirtualHost> access logfiles, transactions will be
# logged therein and *not* in this file.
#
CustomLog logs/access_log common
```

As with the `error_log` file, you should always enable the `access_log`. Access logs tell you who has visited your site. You can use this data to learn more about your visitors or to understand the ebbs and flows of your bandwidth. Select the CLF unless you have good reason to do otherwise. In general, letting logs do their work without requiring a lot of format changes is a good idea.

Level	Resulting Data
emerg	Errors that render Apache unable to operate. If an emergency error happens while the server is running, this is usually the result of a dysfunctional child process. Such drastic errors are far more likely to occur at bootup.
alert	Errors that cause a child process to die, but don't stop the main server process.
crit	Errors that might stop Apache from answering certain types of browser requests because a certain subroutine has been damaged. Critical errors sometimes result in the server crashing.
error	The median level of error. Errors that result from a failure to answer a browser request, perhaps because of bad CGI or malformed URLs.
warn	Errors that don't cause a problem in Apache's operation, but that generate a warning saying you need to undertake a particular administrative task soon.
notice	Errors that might occur at bootup or shutdown. These are usually minor problems, which might simply require a reboot.
info	Not actually errors. Messages that note when child processes are spawned, andwhen browsers disconnect before getting their requested data, and alerts that the server is nearing its configured server and child process capacity.
debug	Informational messages only. Debug messages are logged when the server performs any action, including system calls or opening a particular file. Use only for debugging purposes, as the sheer number of messages can quickly overwhelm the useful data in `error_log`.

Table 9-2. Warning Levels for the Apache Error Log

NOTE: People who host virtual sites need to place access log files within those virtual host directory containers. If you forget to do so, you'll have virtual host accesses mixed in with access data for your regular site. This can be both confusing and misleading when you review the file.

```
#
# If you would like to have agent and referrer logfiles, uncomment the
# following directives.
#
#CustomLog logs/referer_log referer
#CustomLog logs/agent_log agent
```

This is where you can use the variables defined a few steps ago. When you're just beginning to work with Apache, it's fun to enable these logs and see where your hits are coming from and what browser people are using. As you get more comfortable with the server, these logs remain useful. You can track the sites that link to you or sites that generate a lot of traffic for you, even if no link exists (perhaps your site is mentioned in a news story). You can also tailor your site's HTML coding to the browser that most of your visitors use. If you want to use these specialized log files, uncomment the lines to enable them.

CAUTION: Don't go overboard with browser customization. If you code exclusively for one, visitors who use other browsers might be unable to view your site at all. This is particularly a problem with sites that have been tailored to Microsoft's Internet Explorer. Sometimes these sites won't show up at all on Netscape.

```
#
# If you prefer a single logfile with access, agent, and referrer information
# (Combined Logfile Format) you can use the following directive.
#
#CustomLog logs/access_log combined
```

While many people like to have separate logs for different kinds of log data, you might not share that view. You can comment out the lines for access_log, referer_log, and agent_log, and then uncomment this line instead. You then get a log that has all three types of data combined in one file. Once you figure out how to read it, you might find you check your logs more often because you only have to look at one file.

When you finish making the configurations for your logs, save the configuration file and exit the text editor. You need to restart the Apache server to take advantage of your new configuration. As described in Chapter 7, "Managing the Apache Server," the best way to restart your server is to issue the command

```
apachectl graceful
```

at the command prompt. This command forces Apache to restart, checking the newly edited configuration files, but it won't bump any existing connections off your site. If you know nobody is connected or you don't care if they're bumped, you can issue the command

```
apachectl restart
```

instead. No functional difference exists between the two commands.

THE MOD_LOG_CONFIG MODULE

When you're ready to move beyond the basic logs—`error_log` and `access_log`—it's time to begin working with the mod_log_config module. This module is designed to provide much more flexible logging, where you can track individual bits of data about your visitors or amass a great deal of information in one or several log files. The format that mod_log_config uses is highly customizable. This format even offers conditional logging, where a piece of data is only added to the log if that browser request meets certain parameters.

TIP: To learn more about modules in general and how to enable particular modules in your Apache installation, see Chapter 5, "Apache Modules."

mod_log_config uses four main directives. With these directives, you can set up amazingly precise log files or you can simply track standard HTTP header information, such as cookies. Enter the appropriate directives into the directory containers in `httpd.conf`. If you want to have these logs apply to all requests on your site, place the directives into the main directory container. If you want them to apply to particular directories, place them in the appropriate directory containers.

CAUTION: If you want to log information about virtual hosts you enabled on your system, you must place these directives in the appropriate virtual host container. If you place the directives in your general directory containers, the information is mixed together with data about your site. I repeat this caution several times throughout this chapter, but it's important enough to stand repetition.

The mod_log_config directives are explained in Table 9-3. If you're interested in programming your own custom logs, consult the mod_log_config documentation at **http://www.apache.org/docs/mod/mod_log_config.html**. You can also find good documentation for this advanced log technique in *Administering Apache,* by Mark Allan Arnold, Clint Miller, James Schultz, and Jeff D. Almeida (Osborne/McGraw-Hill, 2000), a solid intermediate/advanced look at Apache.

Directive	Function
CookieLog	Defines the file that logs cookies, as required by the mod_cookies module. Because mod_cookies is deprecated and mod_usertrack is now the preferred method for tracking cookies, this directive remains in mod_log_config for historical compatibility.
CustomLog	Defines the various parameters of a custom log. Use this directive to define the log format and any conditional parameters that might be requested. This directive is also used to determine what information, such as the value of a particular HTTP header, will be logged.
LogFormat	Defines the format of the access_log file. If you change access_log from the CLF, you can give the new format a nickname with this directive. The nickname works like a variable, so you can use the same format with other custom logs.
TransferLog	Directs the server to move a particular log to another location or to pipe the log input through a specified Apache or Unix command.

Table 9-3.   Directives for the mod_log_config Module

USEFUL LOG TRICKS

Although the logs themselves are the most useful data Apache can generate for you, a few tricks can streamline the way in which you work with your logs. The server includes several programs that shave time off your total list of administrative tasks. You can also combine these programs with some performance-tuning ideas to get the most out of your server.

TIP: Learn more about tuning your Apache server for maximum speed and efficiency in Chapter 11, "Performance Tuning."

Resetting Log Files

Log files can get extremely big. The general rule of thumb for access_log, for example, is that it grows by 1MB for every 10,000 browser requests. If you run a reasonably popular site with some complicated HTML, ten thousand browser requests isn't a particularly high threshold. Unfortunately, you can't simply delete the log files and expect Apache to start over from scratch. For programming reasons, Apache takes the same amount of space the original log file occupied, fills it with empty characters, and then starts the new log. You don't save any disk space by deleting or moving the logs.

So, what can you do if you don't want to read through multiple megabytes of outdated logged information every time you want to read the logs? Luckily, there's a trick. You must first move the existing log file (even though I just told you not to). The trick comes in then issuing a signal that tells Apache to reopen the files. Apache then starts a new log file from scratch, and you have the data from the old file to peruse at your leisure.

Two commands are involved in resetting your log files correctly. First, move into your logs subdirectory and issue this command at the command prompt:

```
mv access_log access_log.old
```

You now have no access_log file. Then, issue the command

```
kill -1 'cat httpd.pid'
```

This command issues the HUP signal to Apache, using the process identification number stored in the httpd.pid log file. As noted in Chapter 7, "Managing the Apache Server," Apache's PID is automatically stored in httpd.pid each time the server is started. Apache then reopens the log files and begins from line 1.

NOTE: When you finish reviewing the log file access_log.old, you can delete it. Apache doesn't mind if you delete the log file once another log has begun.

rotatelogs

The rotatelogs program is an Apache feature that automates the creation of a new log at a specified time. If you like to restart logs cleanly every day or every few hours, depending on your site traffic, you might find rotatelogs helpful. It uses Apache's capability to pipe log files to a new location without changing the essential configurations of the server. rotatelogs is best used in conjunction with Unix programs designed to automate routine administrative tasks, such as cron. You can save a lot of time with a well-edited crontab file (cron's configuration document), and I recommend learning more about this command to save yourself time and drudgery.

NOTE: If you plan to use rotatelogs as part of your general system automation with the cron command, be sure to add a command that copies the existing log to another location on the drive before the rotatelogs command restarts the log. If you don't copy the existing log, the data will be erased and you won't be able to review it later.

Open your `httpd.conf` file in a text editor and locate the log configuration section. Add a line like this:

```
TransferLog "|rotatelogs /log/directory/path/access_log 86400"
```

Save the file and exit. This command identifies the location of the `access_log` file and sets a rotation of 24 hours. (You can set any amount of time you like, but it must be defined in seconds.)

logresolve

In Chapter 11, "Performance Tuning," you learn that one way to slow down your Apache installation is to require Apache to resolve every IP number that accesses the server before logging the connection. Because looking up IP numbers requires calls to the DNS server, a completely different server from Apache itself, resolving IPs can take up a significant amount of server resources and cause your server to respond sluggishly. To counteract this drag, I suggest you change Apache's configuration so only IP numbers are logged in your `access_log` file.

Doing this doesn't mean you must be resigned to scanning line after line of IP numbers when you review `access_log`, though. You can use the `logresolve` program to turn those IP numbers back into resolved domain names, which should make reading the log much easier. Only a rare system administrator can read a list of IP numbers not in her own domain and still know where those machines are located, especially with the explosion of domains and individual sites on the Internet today.

`logresolve` is a program included with the Apache server. You simply need to issue the command, specifying the file you want to work with, and the program does the rest of the work. Note, `logresolve` might take some time to generate its final output because it needs to contact the DNS server at least once for each individual IP number. `logresolve` takes the syntax

```
logresolve [ -s filename ] [ -c ] < access_log > access_log.new
```

The [-s filename] and [-c] components are optional, so the minimal `logresolve` command would be

```
logresolve < access_log > access_log.new
```

This command takes the current version of `access_log`, resolves all IP numbers, and pipes the output to a file called `access_log.new` in the same directory. Note, you should be in the logs directory to issue this command. Table 9-4 shows the two options for `logresolve`.

Option	Function
-s *filename*	Specifies a new file in which logresolve records statistics about its work.
-c	Specifies that logresolve should perform additional DNS checks to verify the validity of the IP numbers in access_log. logresolve resolves the logged IP numbers, and then reverse-resolves the domain names back to the IP numbers. If the logged IP number and the resolved IP number don't match, you may have an IP-spoofing security problem.

Table 9-4.   Options for the logresolve Program

Multiple Log Files

As described earlier in the chapter, the mod_log_config module permits a wider range of log features than is possible with a plain Apache installation. One of the features mod_log_config contributes is the capability to configure multiple log files beyond the default access_log and error_log files. In fact, when you edited httpd.conf to place logs in the correct locations, options for multiple log files were already in the default configuration file.

You can create two different kinds of log files with mod_log_config. You can set up new logs that use the CLF or you can set up logs to record unique information that isn't usually part of a log. In the default configuration file, access_log is configured as a CLF log:

```
#
# The location and format of the access logfile (Common Logfile Format).
# If you do not define any access logfiles within a <VirtualHost>
# container, they will be logged here.  Contrariwise, if you *do*
# define per-<VirtualHost> access logfiles, transactions will be
# logged therein and *not* in this file.
#
CustomLog logs/access_log common
```

However, the two optional log files shown in the default configuration are both set up as customized logs using formats defined as variables earlier in the file:

```
LogFormat "%h %l %u %t \"%r\" %>s %b \"%{Referer}i\" \"%{User-Agent}i\"" combined
LogFormat "%h %l %u %t \"%r\" %>s %b" common
```

```
LogFormat "%{Referer}i -> %U" referer
LogFormat "%{User-agent}i" agent
```

This section defines the variables and the following section sets up the special logs:

```
#CustomLog logs/referer_log referer
#CustomLog logs/agent_log agent
```

NOTE: The variables used in creating a custom log must be defined before they can be used to create a new log. Therefore, the variable settings must be placed earlier in the configuration file than the CustomLog commands.

If you want to create additional logs—perhaps to track the various browser preferences used by your visitors, such as language preference—you can do so. Simply define the variable so it captures the data in the appropriate HTTP header and create a new log with the CustomLog command that uses your new variable. A wide range of data can be included in HTTP headers, so you should be able to build variables to trap the precise information you want in a log file. You can then use the data to tune your Web site so it suits the needs of your regular visitors as closely as possible.

NOTE: Keep your custom logs in the regular /logs subdirectory of the main Apache directory. This way, you'll be more likely to read them and review the data they contain on a regular basis.

SUMMARY

Once Apache is installed, you can monitor its performance by reading the automatically generated log files. These logs note errors in the server, as well as the origin of each request made for files on your site. Logs are structured in a manner known as the Common Log Format (CLF), which makes understanding the entries and the information they contain easy. The default Apache logs are error_log and access_log. You can configure error_log so it gives you messages of varying importance, from the critical to the mundane. The access_log reports data taken from the HTTP headers of each incoming browser request.

If you want to define customized logs, which can track any information that can be contained in an HTTP header, you must do so with the mod_log_config module. This module is easy to work with and is compiled into Apache with the default installation. mod_log_config offers a variety of possible log formats, including conditional logging where you can set parameters that must be met before an item is logged. Be aware, though, the more information you ask Apache to track, the bigger your log files will be. Some useful tricks exist for keeping your log files at a manageable level, which means you'll be more likely to read and use them as an administrative aid.

CHAPTER 10

Disk Management

Disk management is one of the basic administration skills. To manage a computer or network successfully, you should know how to move files from one location to another, how to copy or archive data, and how to track your users and their disk use. If you have administered other sorts of systems in the past, you have some disk management skills already. Unix administrators have the choice of using either text-mode commands or graphical user interfaces. In this chapter and throughout the book, we rely on the text-mode commands because you might not always have a GUI available. If you're accustomed to a graphical interface, whether under Unix or not, a good idea is to learn at least the rudiments of text-mode disk management as an emergency fallback.

If you're in charge of a single Web server, you have less to worry about than the administrator of multiple machines and services. Disk space allocation is one of the core jobs of any administrator because a finite amount of disk space is available for all the things your users expect from the system and the things they want to store or create on the disk themselves. Certainly, you should keep an eye on the amount of space each user occupies and also keep the space open needed by administrative tasks and programs. In addition, you should be aware of the security issues inherent in disk management, such as file and directory permissions. In this chapter, we review the basic tools for these tasks and other issues of Unix disk management and for managing files destined for your Web site.

FILE SYSTEM MANAGEMENT

As you read elsewhere in this book, Unix represents everything as a file. Whether program, data, document, or any other item, each is considered a file and can be treated with file commands. These files are maintained in a directory system, just like the directory systems on almost every other kind of operating system. Each file, regardless of the directory in which it's stored, has a unique *pathname* or *filepath* that describes its precise location. You've seen a number of these pathnames already in this book, such as `/usr/local` or `/var/logs/apache`.

While you're probably already familiar with directory-based systems, unless you've had minimal exposure to computing in general, the way in which Unix structures its system may be less familiar. Unix uses somewhat cryptic notations for each of its main directories. At the top of the Unix file system is the / directory, which contains all other directories on the drive or partition. A number of subdirectories are in the / directory, including these:

▼ `/dev` Contains entries representing physical drives and partitions

■ `/usr` Contains files pertaining to the machine's user base and their individual accounts

■ `/var` Contains log and spool files

■ `/bin` Contains system commands

■ `/sbin` Contains administrative programs and commands

▲ `/etc` Contains configuration files

DISK PARTITIONS

One common way to handle disk drives under Unix is to create a number of *disk partitions,* which are disk segments defined in the operating system. Although all are residents on one single hard disk, each partition is treated as a separate disk or drive. You may see other terms used to refer to disk segments, like *volume* or *slice,* but they all mean the same thing: a segment of the hard disk that's treated as an individual unit by the operating system. Although this isn't a common practice among Windows and Macintosh administrators, almost all operating systems permit the creation of partitions, though it may be a difficult and not particularly useful process under some.

Unix administrators usually create partitions to separate administrative and system files from user files. By placing user files on a separate partition, you can restrict the files to which users have access. This is important both from a security viewpoint—restricting access to important programs and files—and from the practical point of restricting the amount of disk space your users can take up as a group. If you have a user who collects large files or who programs frequently (but isn't very good at it, creating massive output files), you'll be glad you parked user files on a separate partition, rather than letting them squeeze out your critical administrative data.

Certainly, a good habit is to place servers, like Apache, on their own partitions. This is both a security measure and a simple organizational aid. If someone breaks into your Apache partition, there's really nowhere else for them to go. Plus, you can restrict access to the partition, so regular users can't write to the disk or cause other problems just by looking around or trying new things. Servers that might be overwhelmed by an unusual amount of traffic, such as a mail server, should be on their own partitions as well, in case the traffic causes the entire system to slow down or crash.

NOTE: If you make the partition too small for the data on it, you might run into a problem. You may be unable to use the `mv` command to move directories from one partition to another (though you can use it to move directories on a single partition). If this happens, you'll have to compress and archive the data, usually with the `tar` and `gzip` commands, and move it with FTP or another file transfer method.

The process of partitioning a disk differs from Unix variant to variant. Under Linux, for example, you'd probably partition with the `cfdisk` program, which actually edits the partition table, though some Linux variants use other tools. The *partition table* controls how the space on the disk is divided and allocated. Under FreeBSD and the BSD variants, you'd use the `sysinstall` program to create new *disk slices.* Under Solaris and the SunOS-type variants, you must use the native Solaris formatting utility. Solaris is slightly trickier than other Unices because its `format` program creates a unique partition from all the free disk space on the drive. When a new volume is created, that unique partition must be made smaller to permit the new volume. See the documentation or a good user book for your particular Unix variant to determine the tools you need to make partitions on your disk.

Mounting Partitions and Drives Automatically

In Chapter 4, "Running a Heterogeneous Network," we covered the Network File System (NFS). NFS enables you to mount a remote directory in an empty directory on your local machine and to use those files as if they were located directly on your local hard disk. The directories you mount with NFS don't always have to be on a remote machine in a different physical location, however, You can use NFS to mount directories from different partitions on the same hard drive as well.

If you have several remote directories you mount regularly on a local machine, you can use a handy shortcut to ensure those directories are mounted automatically each time the local machine is rebooted. This shortcut is the /etc/fstab file. /etc/fstab is a feature of both BSD variants and Linux, and is edited automatically each time you add a new partition or hardware to reflect the various devices attached to the machine. (The equivalent file under Solaris is /etc/vfstab.) Plus, you can use the entries in /etc/fstab to determine how frequently each directory is going to be backed up and other routine administrative tasks.

Note, if the remote machine isn't running, /etc/fstab continues to try to mount any remote directories on that machine. This can make booting the local machine tedious and time-consuming. Be sure the remote machine is operating before you reboot any local machine that has remote directories in /etc/fstab.

CAUTION: Before beginning to make partitions, you should be aware that partitioning effectively destroys the data on the hard drive in most cases. Try to partition a new disk or one that has recently been wiped and reformatted. If you need to partition a disk that already has data on it, BACK UP YOUR FILES BEFORE YOU BEGIN PARTITIONING. It's always safest to assume, when working directly with the disk, you're going to lose all the data already on the disk.

MOVING CONTENT

Whether you move data for your users or they move their own, the same commands are used. Under all operating systems, files can be moved, copied, renamed, or deleted. If you have an operating system installed that uses a graphical user interface, like Windows, you can do most of these tasks with the mouse by dragging files into new folders, into a trashcan or other deletion location, and by right-clicking to get additional file management options. Depending on the Unix variant you installed and whether it permits the use of a graphical file manager, you might also be able to handle most content administration with mouse moves.

TIP: If you want to run a graphical user interface with your Unix system, check to see whether one is already included. For example, Solaris runs graphically most of the time. For the more text-oriented Unix variants, like Linux or the BSD variants, you can install an integrated desktop program or a window manager to make things more familiar. I recommend using an integrated desktop like Gnome, KDE, or Ximian (a version of Gnome). These desktops offer a wide array of helpful tools and programs, and allow drag-and-drop, mousing, and other interactions familiar to those coming from Windows or the Macintosh. You can find them at any Unix file archive, or at their home sites: **http://www.gnome.org**, **http://www.kde.org**, or **http://www.ximian.com**.

Depending on the file permissions you placed on the various files on your system, your users can go back and forth between different directories to work with their documents and programs. If you want to limit access on your Apache server machine, consider creating a single directory for Web files and mounting it remotely on the various user machines. (See Chapter 4, "Running a Heterogeneous Network," for more information on remote mounting and file sharing.) Whether you have this directory mounted remotely or you have it on the same machine and partition as your user files, remember to set permissions so people who should have access can write to the directory (edit and add new files) and those who shouldn't can only read the files that are there.

TIP: Make the permissions easier to manage by creating a user group that contains all the people who should have write access to the Web file directory. See Chapter 12, "Dealing with Users," for more about user groups and how to create them.

Moving and Renaming Files

Moving files under Unix is done with the mv command. You can also rename files with this command because the operating system interprets a command to move a file as a command to rename it to a file with the new pathname. That is, if you issue the command

```
mv /usr/local/filename1.txt /usr/local/filename2.txt
```

the operating system takes the contents of filename1.txt and puts that data into the file filename2.txt. If filename2.txt doesn't already exist, it's created as part of this command.

CAUTION: If filename2.txt already does exist and has content, the content is erased as the data from filename1.txt is moved into the existing file. Don't rename files to existing files unless you intend to replace the content of the existing file.

You can move files within the same directory without giving the full pathname, as in the command

```
mv photo.html picture.html
```

This command simply changes the name of the `photo.html` file to `picture.html`, but the copied file remains in the directory where you were when you issued the command. If you want to move files between directories, you must issue the full pathname, as in

```
mv /var/logs/apache/accesslog /usr/barney/logs/apache12-2-01.log
```

This command both moves a file from the `/var/logs/apache` directory to user `barney`'s home directory and renames that file in the subdirectory of `barney`'s logs.

NOTE: When you move a file, the initial file no longer exists. That is, in the previous example, a file will no longer be located at `/var/logs/apache/accesslog` once the command has executed. If you want to retain the original file as well as create a new file elsewhere on the disk, you need to use the copy command described in the next section.

Copying Files

To create new copies of files without destroying the original file, use the `cp` command. You can copy files from any location to any other location, as long as the original file's permissions and the destination directory's permissions are set to enable you to do so.

TIP: Note that, if you are logged in as root, you can do anything you want. File and directory permissions don't apply to the root account.

To copy a file to another file in the same directory, issue the command

```
cp filename1.txt filename2.txt
```

If you then issue the `ls` command to see a directory listing, you'll see both `filename1.txt` and `filename2.txt` in the output. Note, as with `mv`, if you copy a file to an existing file, the data in the existing file is then overwritten by the copied file. Don't copy files to existing files unless you're willing to lose the data in the existing file.

TIP: If you're worried about losing data or you want copies of log files, using the `cp` command instead of `mv` is best. This way, the program that writes to that particular logfile won't find it missing, which could cause problems with the program's operation. Use `mv` only when you don't mind that the original file will disappear.

To copy a file from one directory to another, you must supply the full pathname of both the original and the destination file. If you issue the command

```
cp /var/logs/apache/accesslog /usr/barney/logs/apache12-2-01.log
```

the `accesslog` file is then copied, with the new name `apache12-2-01.log`, to user barney's logs subdirectory. Unlike the previous example with `mv`, however, the `accesslog` file remains unchanged in the `/var/logs/apache` directory.

NOTE: If you use `cp`, check the new file after it's been copied to be sure the file's permissions are set properly. See "File Permissions," later in this chapter for more information on permissions.

DISK QUOTAS

If you have a large number of users on your system, you might want to limit the amount of disk space each user can occupy. You can do this in two ways: you can institute a quota you enforce or you can institute a quota enforced by software. The latter is by far the easier task, but some systems are small enough that a manual check and appropriate reminders can keep everyone within their quota.

To manage quotas, no matter the method, you must determine the appropriate disk allotment for each user. In general, your users should have at least 5 megabytes of space. This contains their user files, mail, and other required system files and optional user files. If you have users who generate large amounts of data, they probably need more space. 25 megabytes is a large amount that's acceptable for most users, unless they're archiving and storing large amounts of material. Of course, the disk quota depends on both the size of your user base and the size of your hard drive, or the partition where user files are kept.

TIP: You can always expand a given user's disk space at a later time. Many administrators require an application from the user, in which the reason for needing more space is stated. You can make the expansion temporary or permanent. Having consistent policies for quota expansion is best, as it is with any policy issue where a large user base exists.

Managing quotas manually requires you to remember to check account sizes on a regular basis. Many administrators of small systems simply check the total disk use once a week or so, and then send out a reminder to delete unused files if the disk is too full. Others use various Unix commands to check the size of each user's account and send messages if the user is taking up too much space. While this is certainly a valid way to handle user disk use, it can become tedious or too easily forgotten.

A much better way to handle quotas, if you need them, is with the Unix program `quota`. The `quota` program lets you define both a soft quota and a hard quota for the users on your system. The *soft quota* is the maximum space a user can occupy, but quota permits users to exceed the soft quota for a predetermined grace period during which the user gets messages about exceeding quota. The *hard quota* is the bottom line: the user cannot use more space than that defined in the hard quota. Hard quotas can only be used in conjunction with a grace period and a soft quota, under the theory that people should get a chance to clean out their accounts and old mail before their access to disk space is blocked.

You can find the quota program in many Unix file archives. If you're running Linux, consult the Linux quota HOWTO file at **http://www.linuxdoc.org/HOWTO/mini/ Quota-5.html**. Users of other Unix variants might also find this HOWTO useful, though its comments about kernel integration are specific to Linux. Once you set up the quotas for your users, they can check their disk use by issuing the command

```
quota -v
```

at the system prompt. The output shows the disk space used, the limit, time left to clean out a file (if the soft quota was exceeded), and other useful data.

NOTE: You can only set quota limits on one file system at a time. If you need to set quotas for different drives or partitions, you must install and configure quota separately on each one. You can have different quotas for the same users on different file systems, if necessary.

FILE AND DIRECTORY PERMISSIONS

Just as each piece of data on the drive is represented as a file, each of those files has an encoded label that determines the permissions that apply to the file. *File permissions* under Unix determine who owns a particular file and what can be done to the file by the owner, members of the owner's user group, or global users. If the file is a document, the permissions determine who can read or edit the file. If it's an executable program, the permissions define who can run the file and who can't.

File Ownership

Each Unix file has an owner. Usually, the owner of the file is the person who created it—like a text file—or the person who downloaded it—like some file from the Web or an FTP site. Once the file is installed, however, if it's a program, the individual program files are probably owned by the program itself and not by the person who downloaded or installed it. You can determine who owns a file by issuing the ls -l command at a system prompt. The output shows all the files in your current directory and their owners, as well as size and a creation time stamp. Here's sample output from ls -l:

```
[kate@maguro backupfiles]$ ls -l
total 145
-rw-rw-r-    1 kate    kate    11558 Apr 12   08:14   accesslog
-rw-rw-r-    1 kate    kate    18419 May 3    11:12   notes.txt
-rw-rw-r-    1 kate    kate    16655 Nov 1    07:53   ch01.doc
-rw-rw-r-    1 kate    kate    20608 Nov 1    08:11   fig0103.tif
-rw-rw-r-    1 kate    kate    20468 Nov 15   14:33   mailbackup
-rw-rw-r-    1 kate    kate     9517 Jan 28   21:19   .newsrc.old
```

The third column of this output shows the file's owner, while the last column shows the file's name. Thus, user `kate` (me) owns every file in this directory. Every file in this directory is also owned by my user group, called `kate`.

TIP: In Chapter 12, "Dealing with Users," the *user group* concept is introduced. Under Linux, the operating system on my home network, each new account created gets both a user account and a group with the same user name. Groups are important parts of file permissions because you can set group permissions, as well as individual or global permissions.

Although the initial owner of a given file is usually the person who created it, file ownership is transferable. To change the owner of a file, you must be logged in either as root or as the current file owner. Then, issue this command at a system prompt:

```
chown user filename
```

Substitute the new owner's user name for *user* and the file's full name for *filename*. The new owner then has the capability to set file permissions for that file. Only the file's owner or the root account can set file permissions.

File Permissions

In the first column of the `ls -l` output shown previously, you can see an arcane string of dashes and letters. This sequence identifies the permissions attached to each of these files. The character string is always ten characters long, with each space in the string representing a particular type of permission. Three variables can be used in a permission string:

- ▼ r Read permission. The file may be read, but not edited or executed, if it's an executable file.
- ■ w Write permission. The file may be read and edited, but not executed, if it's an executable file.
- ▲ x Execute permission. The file may be read, edited, and executed if it's an executable file.

The first character in the permission string is always an indication of the file type. Six possible characters can be used in this position, shown in Table 10-1. The remaining nine characters define the file permissions for the three possible user types: user (the file's owner), group (any group to which the owner belongs), and global (everyone who can see the file).

TIP: If the file has global permissions set and is contained in a directory with global permissions, then the file can be seen across networks. This is how the Web works: files available on the Web are kept in globally accessible directories, and the files have globally accessible permissions.

Character	File Type
-	Regular file
b	Block device (disk drives, partitions, and other such devices)
c	Character device (input devices like keyboards, pen tablets, or modems)
d	Directory
l	Link (any file that merely redirects to another file)
p	Pipe (a programming tool)

Table 10-1.   Initial Characters for File Permission Strings

To see how these permissions work, take the example

```
-rw-rw-r-
```

from the `ls -l` output shown earlier in this section. The initial dash shows this is an ordinary file with no special function. The first `rw-` component shows the owner (`kate`) has both read and write permissions on the file; thus, I can both read and edit the file. The second `rw-` component shows the owner's group (also `kate`) has read-and-write permissions on the file. If the system administrator adds anyone to the group `kate`, as shown in Chapter 12, those users would also have read-and-write access to the file. Finally, the last component is `r-`. This shows that any global users or those who are neither the owner nor in the owner's group, only have read access to this file.

If you want to change the permissions on any file for which you're the owner (or if you assumed superuser powers), you can do so with the `chmod` command. `chmod` uses a fairly straightforward syntax, though you do need to memorize the various components to issue the command correctly. `chmod`'s syntax is

```
chmod [class(es)] [+ or -] [permissions] [filename]
```

The class possibilities are u (file's owner, or *user*), g (group), and a (all users, or global). As previously shown, the permissions are *r*, *w*, or *x*. You can grant a permission with the plus (+) sign or revoke one with the minus (–) sign.

Thus, if you want to change file permissions on a Web file you created about alpacas, granting read-and-write access to all global users, you would issue the command

```
chmod a+rw alpaca.html
```

If someone then played a joke on you and changed the page so it contained information about llamas and vicunas, but didn't have any alpaca information, you could revoke the write privileges with the command

```
chmod a-w alpaca.html
```

TIP: Giving write privileges to the global user community is almost never a good idea if you care about the content in the file.

SUMMARY

One of the major components of administering a system or machine is managing the files stored there. Unix treats every data unit as a file, whether it's a program, document, image file, or some other form of data. These files are stored in a directory system similar to the ones used in other operating systems. Under Unix, the top directory is called / and a number of subdirectories with specific functions are contained within the / directory. Even though most Unix variants now permit the use of a graphical file manager, which makes the directory system visual, learning text-based commands is good in case a graphical interface isn't available to you.

If you require multiple functions from your hard drive, you might want to consider partitioning the drive. To partition a drive is to separate the full drive into smaller parts with a software command. The operating system then views each partition as a separate drive. This can be useful both for file management and for security. If you have many users, you might want to set disk quotas on one or more of your drives and partitions. You can administer quotas either manually or with the Unix program quota. The files your users create can be moved, renamed, or copied with basic Unix commands. Only the file's owner or the root account can work with files, however, either to move them or to change the file's permissions.

CHAPTER 11

Performance Tuning

When you've had your first Apache installation running for a while, you may begin to wonder whether there's a more efficient way to manage the server. Certainly, many people use a straight-from-the-box Apache installation without any trouble at all; but others try constantly to shave every bit of extraneous code from the server to improve response and stress on the server. Think of the basic Apache installation as being a reliable, roomy, and user-friendly, four-door sedan, maybe a Honda Civic or a Ford Taurus. Millions of people drive Civics and Tauruses without ever wanting more.

A segment of the population is always dissatisfied with plain old sedans, though, just like many administrators want to streamline their Apache installation. These streamlined servers are the Porsches and Maseratis of the Web server world. They run faster and leaner, providing rapid response time and imposing as little load on the server as possible. Even if you're not a Porsche person, you could benefit from souping up your Apache installation a bit. You can see rewards, no matter how small the changes.

NOTE: Don't feel you must run a performance-tweaked server. It's a subject of concern mostly to people who run high-traffic sites or who have underpowered machines running the servers. Even if you aren't interested in getting the fat out of your Apache installation, though, read through the chapter to see the kinds of things that might be slowing you down. Whether you tinker with your server setup now or later, at least you can have a good understanding of what could be changed and what should be left alone.

In this chapter, you learn more about Apache performance tuning. You learn why tuning is a good idea for most Apache administrators and what the trade-offs are with a slimmer server. You review a suggested high-performance version of `httpd-std.conf` and look at other ways to adapt your configuration files and module array. You look at your own site to see whether specific things can be streamlined on your own server and learn more about load balancing across your system as a whole. Finally, you learn the truth about cookies and how tracking your users can improve site performance (and when tracking your users is a bad idea).

WHY TUNE?

Most administrators don't need to tune their systems for high performance. The standard Apache installation is completely functional for a wide variety of uses and you should be able to adapt your configuration to meet your needs, regardless of the kind of traffic you host. In some situations, though, tuning your server is a good idea. Whether this is because of the kind of traffic you have, the kind of machine you're working with, or the kind of administrator you are, performance tuning is a subject you should at least become familiar with, even if you decide not to implement any of its aspects.

Performance tuning encompasses a number of factors. Often, Apache isn't having the problems. Perhaps your operating system is having difficulty dealing with the number of spawned processes, your operating system doesn't handle TCP load well, or you're experiencing some trouble with the various pieces of hardware and other software installed on your network. The kinds of problems that arise from your operating system vary from

OS to OS. For example, some Solaris installations experience significant lag, while some BSD systems suffer memory-allocation problems. You might need to work on your kernel—for kernel-accessible operating systems—or make some system-level changes to let Apache run better. Learn more about specific operating systems and ways to tune Apache on those platforms at **http://www.apache.org/docs-2.0/platform/perf.html**.

CAUTION: Make absolutely sure you've applied the latest TCP/IP patches for your Unix variant, especially if you're running a commercial Unix or one that was initially installed on your system earlier than the mid-1990s. The way Apache works—and the way most Web traffic works—can crash your operating system if you don't have upgraded TCP capabilities. People running recent versions of Linux and FreeBSD are safe in this regard, but everyone else should check their patches.

So, who should tune? Sites that host a vast amount of traffic should consider tuning their server to deal more efficiently with the flood of requests Apache handles. What counts as vast? Check your *hits*, or browser requests. If you're getting more than a hit per second, you should look into streamlining your installation. A hit per second is about the most an untuned Apache installation should be expected to handle. Sites that get fewer hits than one per second are okay with the regular Apache configuration. If you still want to tune your installation, you'll do fine with minimal run-time changes, such as those suggested in the next section. You probably won't need to address Apache's interface with your operating system until you pass the one-per-second hit threshold.

According to Apache, most sites on the Web require less than 10Mb of outgoing bandwidth. That's quite a lot, so the likelihood you're one of those sites is pretty good. For those who are serving more than that, you'll probably need to consider other measures, as well as cleaning up your Apache server and its configuration. Remember, if you're serving files that require more from the server, like CGI or other executable programs, you need more machine power to handle the same amount of outgoing data than if the files were merely static text.

One thing to consider, before you even begin to work with the server, is whether you have enough power at your disposal. A lot of performance issues can be resolved handily by adding more RAM to the Web server machine. RAM is cheap these days and it's a lot easier to add RAM than to fight with configuration files. You might also consider the speed of your Internet connection. If you're trying to serve a popular Web site on a relatively pokey line, you can probably speed up your responses (and keep your visitors happier) if you upgrade your connection. Granted, RAM is a lot cheaper than upgrading to a partial T1 line. This all depends on the kind of files you serve and the sort of traffic you get on a daily basis.

TIP: One of the simplest ways to address a hardware-based performance issue is to move the Apache Server to its own machine. Those who installed Apache to a machine already in use—whether on the main drive or on a separate partition—may see significant progress both with Apache and with the other programs on the machine once Apache has moved and has a place of its own. If you have the ability to add another machine just for Apache, do it. It makes good performance sense, as well as being an excellent security precaution.

STREAMLINING YOUR APACHE INSTALLATION

Whether or not you have the resources to upgrade your physical Web server and its connection to the Internet, you can do a lot with the Apache software itself. The Apache default installation is reasonably fast all by itself and should be able to handle the traffic for most Web sites. You can make some changes in your configuration files to address certain areas you've noticed as problems, but you needn't throw Apache out the window or give it a severe trim for it to work even better for you.

One sample configuration for a streamlined Apache installation is already contained in your Apache installation. In the same directory in which your `httpd-std.conf` file is stored, you can find the `highperformance.conf` file.

TIP: Under Apache 2.0, these documents are stored in the `/docs` subdirectory of your main Apache directory. Under previous versions, you can find your configuration files in the `/conf` directory, but you won't find a copy of `highperformance.conf` because this is only included in Apache 2.0 distributions.

The `highperformance.conf` file is an example, not the canonical way to streamline Apache. It offers some good tips, though, and shows you what's needed in a configuration file and what isn't. Read through the file, printed in the following, to see what a truly minimal and speedy Apache setup can look like. The comments interspersed with the file indicate useful shortcuts for the average Apache administrator and point out the tricks often known only to those with particular speed requirements.

NOTE: The authors acknowledge that `highperformance.conf` is a short file. It's short because they've deleted sections from `httpd-std.conf` instead of using the hashmark character to comment them out. Usually, commenting out unused sections is best rather than deleting them, but a bit of system loading is involved in ignoring the commented lines. If you do delete sections from your own configuration files, make a copy of the unchanged file first. That way, if you delete something and realize you need it back later, you can copy the relevant section from the original file.

```
# Ha, you're reading this config file looking for the easy way out!
# "how do I make my apache server go really really fast??"
# Well you could start by reading the htdocs/manual/misc/perf-tuning.html
# page.  But, we'll give you a head start.
#
# This config file is small, it is probably not what you'd expect on a
# full featured internet webserver with multiple users.  But it's
# probably a good starting point for any folks interested in testing
# performance.
#
# To run this config you'll need to use something like:
#     httpd -f @@ServerRoot@@/conf/highperformance.conf
```

Generally, a good idea is to keep your test scripts separate from your regular `httpd-std.conf` or `httpd.conf` file. If something goes wrong with the test script, you can always revert to the default configuration file. You can force Apache to start with a configuration script not defined as the default by using the previous command: where the script says `@@ServerRoot@@`, replace this with the actual path of your Apache directories. It should be the same as the value of the `ServerRoot` variable you supplied when you configured the server.

```
Port 80
ServerRoot @@ServerRoot@@
DocumentRoot @@ServerRoot@@/htdocs

User  nobody
# If you're not on Linux, you'll probably need to change Group
Group nobody
```

These variables are the same as in the default `httpd-std.conf` file. Provide the appropriate values for the `ServerRoot` and `DocumentRoot` variables.

```
<IfModule prefork.c>
MaxClients        8
StartServers      5
MinSpareServers   5
MaxSpareServers 10
</IfModule>

<IfModule threaded.c>
MaxClients        8
StartServers      3
MinSpareThreads   5
MaxSpareThreads 10
ThreadsPerChild 25
</IfModule>
# Assume no memory leaks at all
MaxRequestsPerChild 0
```

Note that these values are basically the same as those in the default configuration file. These are reasonable settings for a fairly popular Web site. You won't have too many spare processes sitting around, but you can respond within a reasonable time period to each incoming request. Depending on your operating system, though, you might need to adjust these settings to deal with the particular needs of your OS. Some handle large numbers of threads better than others.

```
# it's always nice to know the server has started
ErrorLog logs/error_log
```

```
# Some benchmarks require logging, which is a good requirement.  Uncomment
# this if you need logging.
#TransferLog logs/access_log
```

Logs are good, so make sure both options are enabled. Note, however, the act of logging does consume some time and system resources. The benefits of the logs far outweigh the cost, though. Those running a high-performance script as a test case should definitely turn on the logging, just to see what happens and what kind of data is recorded.

TIP: In general, log at the beginning to decide whether the logged information is useful to you. If it isn't useful, you can always turn the logs off. If you never start logging a particular kind of data, however, you won't know whether you find it helpful.

```
<Directory />
    # The server can be made to avoid following symbolic links,
    # to make security simpler. However, this takes extra CPU time,
    # so we will just let it follow symlinks.
    Options FollowSymLinks
```

Symbolic links aren't that big of a problem and they can sure speed up your administrative time. (A *symbolic link* is a file that isn't actually a file. It's a link to a real file or document, but the operating system and various programs treat the symbolic link as if it were an actual document.) You'll probably experience more grief in recoding to avoid symbolic links than you will if you simply let the server use them.

```
    # Don't check for .htaccess files in each directory - they slow
    # things down
    AllowOverride None
```

Apache normally looks for a file named .htaccess in each of its subdirectories. This file is used to determine who has access to the files in that directory and who doesn't, overriding any larger permissions set with Apache access modules. If you're happy with your server-wide settings, leave this set at None.

```
    # If this was a real internet server you'd probably want to
    # uncomment these:
    #order deny,allow
    #deny from all
</Directory>

# If this was a real internet server you'd probably want to uncomment this:
#<Directory "@@ServerRoot@@/htdocs">
#    order allow,deny
#    allow from all
#</Directory>
```

These settings determine the priority in which Apache checks identification on browser requests. If deny comes first, then Apache denies every request unless the browser shows the appropriate identification. If allow comes first, then Apache answers every request unless the browser shows some specified identification that causes the server to reject the request.

```
# OK that's enough hints.  Read the documentation if you want more.
```

As I warned you, the sample file is pretty basic. The thing to take from this file is you can run an Apache server with minimal configuration. You probably don't want one as bare bones as this, but you can do quite well with a short set of choices.

You can do quite a bit to your Apache configuration in the name of performance tuning. The most useful configurations, though, are those that reduce server load or reduce the time spent processing an individual request. If you make some simple changes that address these issues, you'll notice a significant speed increase in the server's response time, and you'll probably also notice a more efficient use of the machine resources. Comb through the `httpd-std.conf` file and look for any items you configured for redundancy purposes. If you're trying to go fast, double-checking every step and enabling backups isn't the way to go. Treat each request as quickly as possible, so it can be dealt with and then filed away.

NOTE: Because this is an introductory book, the only suggestions contained here are those that affect Apache while it's running. To get more information on maximizing Apache's interaction with your operating system at the time of compilation and bootup, see the Apache Performance Notes document at **http://www.apache.org/docs/misc/perf-tuning.html**.

Performance Tuning Suggestions

The tuning suggestions offered in `highperformance.conf` are the best place to start. They address some of the main areas where Apache is redundant or simply moves slowly. Even if you don't want to run `highperformance.conf` as your server configuration file, take a few tips from it to edit your `httpd-std.conf` file and make it more efficient.

NOTE: Apache says the main goal of the Apache Web server is, first, to be accurate, and then to be fast. Although Apache is extremely fast anyway, there are elements of the default configuration that stress the accuracy at the expense of speed. Those are the elements you strip away when you tune the server.

Symbolic Links

You might have Apache set to check symbolic links before they're followed. This, in theory, is a good idea. Checking symbolic links adds a bit of security and it's a touch of redundancy that usually doesn't affect system performance. If you use a lot of symbolic links and you get reasonably high traffic to your site, however, these links could be generating a small, but significant, system load.

The reason for this load is that Apache doesn't differentiate, when checking symbolic links, between the file actually requested and everything else in the file's path. That is, if you received a request for the file **http://www.your.site/sales/toys/lincolnlogs/index.html**, Apache would run the lstat(2) command on each of these directories:

```
/www
/www/sales
/www/sales/toys
/www/sales/toys/lincolnlogs
/www/sales/toys/lincolnlogs/index.html
```

Every one of those lstat(2) commands is an individual call to the operating system, generating an individual process and all the related system load.

Turning off symbolic link checking is a common start when performance tuning Apache. A suggested setting for your configuration files is shown in highperformance.conf:

```
<Directory />
    # The server can be made to avoid following symbolic links,
    # to make security simpler. However, this takes extra CPU time,
    # so we will just let it follow symlinks.
    Options FollowSymLinks
```

Check in your configuration to see whether you have this option already or you enabled the SymLinksIfOwnerMatch option instead. Note, if you don't have the FollowSymLinks option explicitly included, Apache checks symbolic links. You need to enable this setting deliberately.

Hostnames

Aren't hostnames convenient? Imagine the difference between an access log containing strings of IP numbers and an access log containing a list of hostnames. You can actually read the hostnames, getting a better idea of your visitors' originating sites and saving yourself all the muss and fuss of looking up the IP numbers to get the hostname for each. Heck, everyone uses hostnames to describe their sites, to trade favorites, and in almost every other conversation that touches on the Internet. Yes, hostnames are marvelous things. Unfortunately, they aren't a streamlined Apache's best friend. Those logs filled with domain names should be kept for slower sites or even as a fond memory because DNS lookups take an amazing amount of Apache's time.

In the earliest versions of Apache (before 1.3), DNS lookup was the default. For every request, Apache would contact the local DNS server and resolve the hostname from the sending IP number. The IP had to resolve before the request could be answered. Sounds good? Think about it for a minute. Assume you run a site that receives 40 hits a minute. For each of those 40 requests, Apache would have to connect to an external server, make a request, wait for an answer, close the connection to the DNS server, and only then begin to process the actual Web request. That's slow—and imagine what would happen if the DNS server was down or being balky for some reason!

Beginning with Apache 1.3, the DNS lookup requirement was still found in the configuration files, but was turned off by default. This doesn't solve the DNS problem completely, but it does make things a bit easier. The problem with post-1.3 Apaches now lies in access configurations. If you decide to limit access to certain files on your site, so only people from specified domains can get to the data, using the mod_access module, you can set limits on each file. The primary options are `Allow from domain` and `Deny from domain`, though mod_access does offer additional features.

> **TIP:**   See Chapter 5, "Apache Modules," to learn more about mod_access and other access authorization modules.

If you use these Allow and Deny options, Apache has to consult the DNS server twice: once to resolve the hostname and once to resolve the hostname back to an IP number. This double-check is done to prevent *hostname spoofing,* where someone configures their machine and browser to pretend to be from a site other than their actual originating site. This is usually done to disguise illicit entry into files requiring authorization, so the double-check is a good idea even though it slows down Apache's response.

The fastest way to deal with authorization and DNS resolution is to ignore it. Learn to live with IP numbers in your logs and don't enable mod_access restrictions on a large number of your files. You might consider placing access-restricted files behind a password or moving them to another site with severe restrictions. Running both restricted and nonrestricted files on the same site can be the source of extra load.

> **TIP:**   If you run CGI scripts that require the use of a hostname to generate the proper response, use the `gethostbyname` call in each of those scripts. It's faster than relying on Apache to do it for you.

Content Negotiation

Turning off content negotiation is a dubious idea. Yes, it does speed up your performance a bit. However, you do lose the helpful capability to have Apache determine the file type requested and to send the appropriate document.

> **TIP:**   See Chapter 14, "MIME and Other Encoding," to learn more about content negotiation and why it's so useful.

The only time when you should even consider turning off content negotiation is when you're absolutely positive you only serve one kind of file in one language to people who know the precise URL they're seeking. If you turn off negotiation, your server won't be able to handle multiple versions of a file in different languages or to recognize when a browser requests the wrong file type.

You can speed up negotiation by removing wildcards from the DirectoryIndex entry in your configuration files, though. If you simply have a filename (without an extension) as the argument for DirectoryIndex, Apache still must work to determine what kind of files might be served under that name. Instead, supply the filename and all possible extensions you might use on your site as the argument, as in `filename.cgi` or `filename.html`. List them out on the DirectoryIndex line. This enables Apache to know the precise files that might be served in response to a browser request, saving some time.

Overrides

As with symbolic links, using the `.htaccess` file to set authorization for the files contained in a particular directory is a good idea that, unfortunately, adds additional time to a given request. `.htaccess` files can be kept in any directory and you can have one in every subdirectory on your Web site if you'd like. These files are used to allow overrides of the sitewide access policies (set with the mod_access module). By default, when a request comes in, Apache checks the `.htaccess` file to see whether this particular requester can view the data in that directory even if mod_access is configured otherwise.

TIP: See Chapter 5, "Apache Modules," to learn more about the mod_access module and its various options.

The problem lies not with the `.htaccess` file itself, but in how Apache performs these checks. Just as with symbolic links, Apache checks not only the requested subdirectory, but all directories in that file's path. So, if you get a browser request for access to the file **http://www.yoursite.com/mailing-list/archive/1998/may**, Apache calls up and checks the `.htaccess` file for all these directories

```
/www
/www/mailing-list
/www/mailing-list/archive
/www/mailing-list/archive/1998
/www/mailing-list/archive/1998/may
```

where each of those calls is an independent call to the operating system. Checking `.htaccess` files can be a drain, especially if you keep a lot of files in deeply nested directories.

To fix this problem, look in your configuration files for the AllowOverride variable. This is probably set to AllowOverride All, as that's the default. Change it to AllowOverride None to stop Apache from checking the `.htaccess` files and to use the sitewide access policies you set up elsewhere.

NOTE: You might have configured different override policies for different directories in your configuration file. Be sure to change the override setting wherever this is necessary, not only in the root directory's configuration.

UNNECESSARY MODULES

One of the easiest ways to streamline your server is to remove any modules that aren't important to you. Installing new modules and configuring as many as you can find can be exciting. Each of those modules takes up space and system resources, however, because all configured modules run all the time when Apache is up. If you have many extra modules just sitting there, they aren't doing anything for you except slowing the server and your machine down.

> **NOTE:** It's okay to keep modules you're practicing with or that have logs you find useful, even if they aren't called into play much. In this section, I'm talking primarily about modules you never use that don't have logging turned on, and that don't do anything that relates to the kind of traffic you get on your site. For example, if you don't serve any image maps on your site and you don't plan to, you might not need the image-mapping module.

In Chapter 5, "Apache Modules," you learned about the array of modules provided with your Apache download package. While many of these modules install by default, you don't need them all. If you're experiencing lag or server slowness, consider reviewing your installed modules. You may find you don't need particular services, based on the kind of site traffic you get, or you have several modules installed that do basically the same thing. This might be the case if you download new or experimental modules on a regular basis.

The whole reason behind Apache's construction as a modular server is that modular programs run better. The core program is much leaner because the ancillary functions are farmed out to individual modules, which need only be attached to the core server when that particular function becomes necessary. If you add a bunch of modules to your server, but you don't particularly need to use most of them, you're defeating the purpose of a modular program. Use the modules as they were intended, adding only the ones you want. Then, you can have system resources and speed to spare when something new and truly exciting surfaces in the module-building community.

> **CAUTION:** Some modules may appear unimportant, especially if you don't understand what they do. Before you delete any modules installed by default, be sure you know what the module does and why you don't need it on your system. It's better to start cleaning house with the optional modules or the ones you found on the Web, rather than the basic and core modules Apache installed for you.

LOAD BALANCING

If you serve a significant amount of traffic and data on your site, you might want to consider splitting your installation between two machines. In such a scenario, you would install identical copies of the site on each machine, with an identical Apache configuration. Both machines would be connected to the Internet through your regular connection.

> **NOTE:** No matter how spiffy the setup on your end, no configuration can make your Internet connection run faster. All performance tuning is limited by the bandwidth available. If you've done everything you can on the hardware and software ends of things and still see no real effect, then you're going to have to upgrade your connection before you get results.

Once you set up a multiple-machine site, you need to determine how to distribute incoming requests between the two machines. This is called *load balancing*.

Load balancing is a tricky technique. The ultimate aim is to have each machine handle exactly the same amount of traffic and use the same amount of system resources, to handle incoming requests as efficiently as possible. This is almost never the case, if only because different kinds of requests take varying amounts of time to answer. Some administrators do a form of load balancing by shunting particular kinds of files to one machine, such as CGI scripts or dense image files, to remove those overhead loads from the main server. True load balancing, though, is the use of multiple servers with the same data. The benefits are redundancy, the capability to handle many more requests at once, and less stress on an individual machine's hardware and operating system.

You can get balanced loads on your multiple-server site in several ways. You can build a machine that serves as a proxy, distributing requests to the other servers through the mod_rewrite module. You could simply set up the mod_redundancy module, which defines a backup server in case the main server fails. However, neither of these is a true balancing mechanism. The best way to get your loads balanced across multiple servers is to use the mod_backhand module.

TIP: Learn more about the mod_backhand module at its Web site, **http://www.backhand.org**. You can download the module from this site, as well as read documentation and learn how to write your own extensions to the module in Perl.

The mod_backhand module is designed to distribute incoming requests through a multiple-server cluster. It started as a class project at Johns Hopkins University and has evolved into the standard tool used for load balancing on Apache-served sites. The current version is 1.2, so it is out of beta testing and should be stable for whatever you need to do with it. You can run mod_backhand on several Unix variants, including Linux, Solaris, and the FreeBSD family.

NOTE: Administrators running Apache on MacOS X or MacOS X Server can also run mod_backhand because those operating systems are BSD based, but the module hasn't yet been ported to the Windows platform.

How does the module work? It contains a set of algorithms that constantly evaluate the available system resources across the server cluster. When a request comes in, the module considers the available resources and directs the request to the least-used machine in the cluster at that moment. Its work is unnoticeable to the requesting browser and it's extremely fast.

The trick is that mod_backhand works on individual requests, not on connections to the site. That is, if you connect to a site using mod_backhand, each request you make to the server may be routed to a different machine in the cluster. With other load-balancing techniques, like most commercial load-balancing tools available for specific operating systems, only your initial connection is routed. Each request you make stays on the same machine. If you happen to be making a lot of system-intensive requests, nonmod_backhand sites can't distribute those requests over the cluster to make loads more even, but mod_backhand can.

You need to do some work if you want to run mod_backhand on your site. It requires some configuration and can be complicated, depending on what kind of traffic you serve, the number of machines you have in your cluster, and the type of data you provide to visitors. Despite the time it requires to set up, however, mod_backhand is the way to go when you need to balance site load across multiple machines. It's quite sophisticated and worth serious consideration if you're running a multiple-server site. Also, mod_backhand is free, in both the Free Software and cost senses. Commercial load-balancing software can be quite pricey, so give mod_backhand a try first. Even if you don't like it, you'll have investigated the cheapest option first.

TRACKING SITE USE

Tracking use of your site is one of the most controversial topics in the Web community. User tracking is done with the use of *cookies,* small bits of data sent as HTTP headers between the browser and the server. Cookies, in and of themselves, are harmless bits of data. They can speed the interaction between browser and server, especially when used as identification cards. In that situation, having a cookie on the requesting machine means the user can bypass authentication forms and get directly to whatever material she wants to see.

Unfortunately, some people have figured out how to exploit cookies for their commercial benefit. At the same time, a loud protest has risen concerning cookies among users who think their travels through the Web should be anonymous and untracked. Meanwhile, administrators are being pushed to deliver accurate and detailed data about the people who visit the sites they run. All sides of this debate have valid points, though—as with any controversial issue—every side has its extreme reactions as well. If you're like a lot of administrators, you find cookies a useful tool when used on your own site, but you don't particularly like other sites to use them, especially when they're used for more than administrative purposes.

So, what is a cookie anyway? A cookie is an HTTP header, like the many other headers that accompany requests and responses. It has a particular format, which changes depending on whether it's a browser-supplied cookie or a server-supplied cookie. For cookies supplied by browsers, the format is

```
Content-type: text/html
Cookie: cookie-name
```

The browser simply sends the name of the cookie to the server. This is usually used to remind the server a particular cookie already exists on the browser's machine, so the server won't request reidentification.

For cookies sent by the server, the format is more complex:

```
Content-type: text/html
Set-Cookie: cookiename=value; path=/; expires Wed, 31-Dec-2001 23:59:50 GMT
```

The cookie contains both the name of the cookie and its value, which is what the cookie actually means on the server. In this example, the path is set as /, which means the cookie applies to the entire site. You can also set cookies to apply only to particular directories. Finally, the cookie carries an expiration date. Your cookies should expire with relative speed, so users are required to reidentify themselves on a somewhat routine basis. If you're merely tracking a user, like Amazon tracks its purchasers, you can let the cookie go longer; but if it's sent as part of password verification, you should expire the cookie quickly.

> **TIP:** Cookies are how Amazon and similar sites know it's you, provide recommendations for new things to buy, and offer tailored articles or information that meets your tastes.

You can use cookies on your site to get a lot of useful information. You can also use cookies to do other, financially beneficial, things. For example, one of the sites that gets mentioned a lot in cookie arguments is DoubleClick (**http://www.doubleclick.com**). *DoubleClick* is a marketing company with presences in the United States, Canada, and various European countries. It enters into an agreement with you to serve ads on your site and will also help you target your own ads on other people's sites. Thus, DoubleClick has a presence on many thousands of sites across the world because they serve the banners. Every time you go to a DoubleClick-enabled site, DoubleClick uses a cookie to identify you. These cookies are then used for specific demographic information, which is a valuable commodity these days. The problem lies in the fact that most people visiting a DoubleClick-enabled site aren't there for DoubleClick—they're there for online comics, discussion, news, or any of the other myriad forms of information you can find on the Web. However, they're tracked by DoubleClick and may be targeted for particular kinds of advertising at a later date. Depending on your feelings about online privacy and marketing, you may see this either as a gross invasion of your personal space or as a brilliant marketing technique.

> **NOTE:** If you don't like the idea of a third party tracking your movement through the Web, go to DoubleClick's site and opt out. They promise to honor the wishes of those who sign up for the opt-out policy. You can find the appropriate page at **http://www.doubleclick.com/** by clicking the Privacy Policy link. There are opt-outs for ads, catalogs, and e-mail. You should also read the policy itself to learn what exactly is tracked.

Don't be afraid to use cookies to track legitimate information on your own site. You can use them to speed responses for files that require authorization and to identify certain bits of data about your visitors, so you can customize the site they see. Cookies are a great way to streamline visits to your site. Remember, individual users can configure their browsers to reject your cookies, though, or to deny any cookies that don't come directly from you (like a DoubleClick cookie). The tradeoff is that they won't be able to take advantage of personalized content until they turn cookies back on.

> **CAUTION:** If you use cookies on your site, provide a privacy policy for your visitors. Tell them what information is tracked and what isn't, and how you use that data. If you have a contract with a third-party ad server like DoubleClick, provide a link to that company's privacy policy as well.

To program your own cookies, you need to learn the HTTP standard for cookies. Once you understand the specific form cookies take, you can begin to write them yourself. Cookies can be written in Perl, JavaScript, or one of several platform-specific languages like VBScript. (Of course, I recommend Perl, so you can share the cookie—if you want to—with the widest array of operating systems.) Visit CookieCentral at **http://www.cookiecentral.com** to learn more about programming cookies or to download existing cookies. The site also has excellent coverage of Web-related privacy issues and is well worth a regular visit.

NOTE: You can learn a great deal more about cookies from the excellent book, *cookies*, by Simon St. Laurent (McGraw-Hill). Unfortunately, this book is out of print and some of the information is slightly dated, given that the HTTP standard has changed since the book was released. Still, for a general overview and an in-depth explanation of how cookies work, it's worth trying to find this book in a used bookstore or online.

SUMMARY

If you run a popular Web server, you might need to make some adjustments to your Apache installation to get your server running as quickly and efficiently as possible. In general, performance tuning is recommended for administrators who get more than one hit per second, on average, or who feed an outgoing stream of more than 10 Mbps bandwidth. The first thing to do when you think you need to streamline your installation is to check your hardware and software. Do you have enough RAM, a fast-enough hard disk, and an optimized operating system with the latest TCP/IP patches? Is your Internet connection big enough to handle the volume of traffic you serve daily? If any one of these answers is no, fix your setup before you begin to work with Apache.

When you begin to tune your Apache installation, you'll make a number of adjustments to your configuration files. Apache provides one sample configuration in the same directory as your `httpd-std.conf` file, called `highperformance.conf`. You can run this file with only a few minor changes, but you'll probably want to edit your regular configuration file instead. Several options exist that, if configured correctly, can speed up your server response significantly because they reduce the number of times Apache must make a system call to answer any given request. You can also speed up your installation by removing any unnecessary modules that may have been installed, so Apache doesn't have to consult those modules each time a new request comes in. If you want to track your visitors and their habits on your site, you can issue cookies (small bits of data transferred through an HTTP header) to generate useful data. Be aware, though, that cookies are controversial because some cookie-serving sites use the data they acquire for commercial purposes, not administrative use.

CHAPTER 12

Dealing with Users

While some Apache administrators never have to deal with other people on their systems, most network administrators do. Whether you have coworkers in your department, people from other units in a larger company (who may or may not be at the same physical location), or simply friends with accounts, you probably have some other users on your system beside yourself. Although dealing with users is a broad topic that affects almost every aspect of working with a network, in this chapter, the focus is primarily on how to deal with users who want to use the Web resources you administer.

Depending on your situation, you might have a great deal of freedom in how you deal with your users or you might have very little at all. In large companies, the ultimate responsibility for working with users probably lies with a manager, not with the regular network administrators who may or may not have the initial contact with users and their issues. In smaller companies, there might be only one or two administrators, who probably shoulder more of the user issue themselves. If you're running a site over which you have complete control, you also have control over your user base.

NOTE: Some of the suggestions in this chapter may require more authority than you have. If you think something in this chapter is a good idea, but you aren't in a position to implement the concept at your workplace, bring it up with your supervisor. In quite a few companies, the people who enforce computer policies aren't actually technical employees themselves, so what seems like a logical and common-sense policy to the techies might not be so clear to management. It's your job to convey the importance of a good set of user policies to those who write and enforce them.

In this chapter, you find guidelines to help you define or refine user policies for the system you work with. Issues like network use and disk space are primary, but these aren't the only things to consider. You should also consider the kind of work being done by different sorts of users, and the types of files they want to put on your system. In the sidebar "When Your Users Are Losers," you learn about dealing with users who want to use your system as a haven for problematic activity.

THE HUMAN SIDE OF ADMINISTRATION

One of the biggest problems with network administration is people skills are rarely emphasized as much as technical wizardry. However, most network administrators have to work with other people, who often aren't technically inclined. This can lead to some significant problems. Administrators are often perceived as arrogant and rude, speaking another language, while they see users as unwilling to learn and deliberately slow. (If you want to know how one culture views another, look at its jokes. "Stupid user" jokes are legendary in the systems administration world.) While this attitude might be fun on Friday nights or with a group of peers, it isn't helpful when working with users.

Those who work with the Web have a unique set of user issues. If you run an official site for a corporation or other entity, you may not have individual user pages to deal with, but you do have designers, managers, and public relations people who each have ideas about how the pages should be served. Many times, these ideas are simply not pos-sible from a technical standpoint or they open security holes that can't be risked. If you work for an entity that provides personal Web service (whether through a workplace, like a university, or through an Internet service provider), you have users with a wide range of skills who may rely on you for help with everything from putting up pictures of their vacation at Disneyland to sophisticated little CGI scripts. No matter what kind of site you're running, unless you do everything yourself, you're going to have user issues.

The best thing to do is to create a good set of user policies, written clearly and under-standable to everyone. Make sure people read the policies. You may want to have indi-vidual users sign a copy of the policy before you enable their Web space, for example. Be available to answer questions and try to create an environment in which people can be comfortable asking about something before they do it. Be clear about the outcome if someone violates a point of policy, and be sure to do what you say you will do. Most im-portant, though, don't mistake authority for arrogance. A bit of attention to human behavior can go a long way toward defusing bad situations—and toward preventing them from happening in the first place.

SETTING QUOTAS

Those who work with a site that's 100 percent commercial probably don't have too much to worry about when it comes to disk space. After all, if you're working on a corporate home site, you probably don't have user pages and other personal material to deal with as well.

NOTE: The exceptions here are mostly Internet service providers. ISPs have their own corporate sites, as well as all the pages offered by their users. Sites that are big, like Earthlink or AOL, don't usu-ally have administrators working on both aspects of their Web presence, but smaller ISPs may very well have a "Web person" who handles it all.

Those who work on purely commercial sites are lucky. The Web server machine can be entirely devoted to the site, with little need to control the amount of data placed on the machine or served to browsers. The only curb is disk space, which is easily handled with a large disk.

TIP: Clean out files you aren't using anymore, though. If you work with a Web content team or Web designers, ask them to review their files periodically. Deleting old and unused content or images frees up disk space and helps Apache to run more efficiently. It also prevents viewers from seeing no longer current or accurate files or content.

Administrators with personal users, though, may need to set some limits. Data quotas are a common sight with ISP accounts. With many ISPs, the more you pay each month for the account, the more Web space you get. These days, most ISPs offer a 5MB quota for a regular dial-up account (roughly $20 U.S. a month), and go up to 10MB or more for "premium" or business accounts. In practice, few of an ISP's customers actually use up their allotted 5MB unless they're serving a lot of big image files or keeping a lot of data archived on the Web.

The kind of quota you set is determined by your available disk space and by the number of users. If you have a few users and a large disk, you might think it's overkill to establish disk quotas. Only you know the facts about your system, but I think it's a good idea to establish quotas anyway. You never know what might happen. You might get many more users or you might end up with a user who thinks "Hey, there's no quota, so I'll fill up this entire disk with disco MP3 files." If you don't have quotas in place, you can't enforce them later without causing a fuss and, possibly, hurt feelings or a real fight on your hands.

SETTING POLICIES

Having network or system policies in place is always a good idea. If you're setting up a new network, now is the best time to build these policies and introduce them to your users. If you work with an existing network, you may encounter some resistance from users, especially if the previous policies were essentially "anything goes." The sooner you set up policies the better, however, because people generally adapt to new regulations once some time passes.

TIP: If you have no real user policies in place and you want to introduce strict policies, you may need to go in stages. Know your user base. Some groups adapt better if the new policies are introduced gradually, while other groups do best if the new policies are introduced and required all at once. You might need to sacrifice some security for user compliance, at least until everyone is used to a half-way solution. If the situation is critical, however, don't dilute a required security precaution just because it annoys some users.

Web policies can be complicated or brief. At the least, they should explain the types of files permitted on your server, any existing disk quotas, traffic restrictions, or other requirements that might affect the kinds of files or requests handled on your site.

CAUTION: If you think you might go through user directories at some point, perhaps to see what files they're providing, put that in your Web policy. Even though it's generally the administrator's right to view every file on her machine, it's not a good idea to go through personal accounts unless you have a compelling reason to do so. Make your policies explicit, so your users know what to expect in terms of privacy.

More complicated policies might include a required format for pages on your site; a policy on commercial use; or a policy on *affiliate programs,* in which users promote a third party's business through a link on a noncommercial site.

Whatever your Web policy, you must make sure your users see and read it, so they can abide by your policy. If you're building a new system, you can make the policy part of the sign-up or account creation process. If you have an existing system, you might want

When Your Users Are Losers

Probably the biggest user problem you can have as an Apache administrator involves illegal files. If you permit users to upload files into their personal Web accounts—as many employers, schools, and service providers do—you might have a user who abuses that permission. Thousands of people on the Internet illegally share material over the Web, from software to music to video to text. Whether or not you personally feel that information should be freely shared, you're putting yourself (or your system's owner) at legal risk if you knowingly permit files to be shared illegally from your site.

The key here is copyright, but it's also money. In this context, "illegal file" usually means "file transferred without observing legal copyrights." Offering a bootleg copy of Office 2000 is a copyright violation, as is sharing an MP3 file of the latest Britney Spears single. (The Office 2000 bootleg also violates the license accepted by the original purchaser of the software.) Unfortunately, the Web—and the Internet in general—is suffused with such stuff, but none of it is legal. Even if you're not the person actually distributing the files, you may be considered responsible as the site's administrator.

Some types of copyright violation have gotten away from the Web as the main method of distribution. With the rise of Napster and Napster-like clones, finding Web archives of MP3 or other audio files is harder. Peer-to-peer software is simply better for transmitting these files and individual users are much less likely to be caught. The *warez* kids, who share software, do a lot of their trading over Internet Relay Chat (IRC) or on USENET, as do many of the porn folks, who simply scan images from girlie magazines and post them on binary newsgroups. The term "warez" (pronounced "where's") is slang, and basically means "software that isn't paid for." The community is primarily made up of males in their teens and early twenties. Still, there is an advantage to the Web: it's static. People don't have to search someone out on another part of the Internet to trade illegal files if they can find a hidden Web archive.

How can you tell if your users are sharing such files? As described in Chapter 9, "Logs," the Apache logs are your friend. You can see which pages get the most requests and whether any pages or files on your site draw an unusual amount of traffic. For example, if you find directories called /porn, /warez, or /mp3 in your user Web directories and you see a great deal of traffic to those directories, you can probably assume something illicit is happening. Likewise, if you see a lot of traffic to directories with nonsense or cryptic names, like /x829djw9, that's a clue to follow up on. You should have a good idea of the normal traffic flow on your site if you read your logs regularly, and you can catch significant problems early if you notice odd variations in your regular traffic pattern.

Make part of your user Web policies the requirement that any files or data shared through personal Web directories be legal. Monitor the flow of requests to the pages you administer. If you see unusual traffic flows to obscure pages, check them out. You have the ultimate responsibility over what gets distributed from your site. If your users are doing stupid stuff, your job is to make them stop or boot them from your system.

to e-mail the policy or place it on a page accessible only to internal users. Commercial sites might need employees or customers to sign the policy, while small or personal sites can probably omit that part. If you have other network policies—and you should, at least to cover important things like password policies and sharing accounts—you can fold the Web policy in with those.

UNIX USER MANAGEMENT

One good way to enforce user policies is to use native Unix functions that control user behavior. Under Unix, individual user accounts can be assigned to one or more groups. The groups can then be given access to particular programs or permissions. This is a good way to define who on your system can access certain files and who cannot. The most common use of groups is to keep some system functions available only to administrators—not to regular users—but groups can be used for much more than that. You can use groups to let your Web designers share files, to let all the Apache administrators have access to scripts, or to prevent your users from accessing critical system data.

TIP: Users can see what groups they belong to by issuing the command `groups` at the shell prompt. The names of all groups to which the user belongs will print to the screen.

Under most Unix variants, groups are defined in the file `/etc/group`. Every group already defined by an administrator has an entry in the file similar to this:

```
underwater:x:503:mobydick,willy,keiko,flipper
```

The first field, `underwater`, is the name of the group.

NOTE: In many versions of the Unix user management tool `useradd`, a group for each user is created at the time the account is made. If this is the case for your variant, don't delete these individual groups from `/etc/group`.

The second field doesn't do anything. This field is left over from earlier versions of the group concept. Don't delete this x, though, because it may cause problems with other programs that expect this field to be present to do their own work. The third field is the ID number for this particular group. The final field contains the user names of everyone else in this group.

To create a new group, open the file `/etc/group` in a text editor. (See Appendix B, "Working with a Unix Text Editor," if you need help with one of these programs.) In this example, you create a new group for your Web designers. Add a new line to the file and enter the following text on that line:

```
webdesign:x:814:jones,kao,garcia,suzuki
```

Save the file and exit. You now have a new group called `webdesign` with the four designers' user names included. The group has the unique identification number 814 (of course, check first to see that 814 isn't already an existing group number before you make this entry). You, or any of the members of the group, can now set file permissions, so only members of that group can access a given file.

TIP: To learn more about file permissions, see Chapter 6, "Configuring the Site."

Assume you gave the Web designers a particular directory on the server called `/usr/local/designers`, where they can store and share their files before publicizing them on the official site. If the Web designer Atsumi Suzuki creates an HTML document she wants to share with the other designers, she can place it in that directory. However, the document still has her individual permission settings on it. She can issue the command

```
ls -l /usr/local/designers/atsumi.html
```

to see what the permissions are. The output looks like this:

```
-rw----    1    suzuki    suzuki    1839028    May 15    10.31    atsumi.html
```

Note, the file only has read-and-write permissions, and only for Suzuki. Note, also, the file's group owner is `suzuki`, her personal group. She has to change both the file permissions and the group owner on this file before the other members of the `webdesign` group can see and work with the file.

To change the group ownership, Suzuki issues the command

```
chgrp webdesign /usr/local/designers/atsumi.html
```

This command moves the file from the `suzuki` group's ownership to the `webdesign` group's ownership. Now she can set the group permissions so other members of the `webdesign` group can get to the file, by issuing the command

```
chmod g+rw /usr/local/designers/atsumi.html
```

This command expands read-and-write access to the file for all members of the group that owns the file. However, Suzuki is still the file's owner and she's the only person who can change its permissions. The settings on the file now look like this:

```
-rw-rw--    1    suzuki    webdesign    1839028    May 15    10.31    atsumi.html
```

NOTE: Some Unix variants and non-Unix operating systems use a graphical administration tool to handle file permissions. For example, Solaris administrators can define groups and set file permissions with the `admintool` utility. Consult the documentation for your particular operating system to learn whether groups are permissible and how to set them up.

SUMMARY

Dealing with users requires a level of interpersonal skill that isn't always listed as part of an administrator's job requirements. You may have a large number of people who use your Web server, or you may have only a few who need it. Regardless of the size of your user base, working with users is easiest if you have consistent and clear user policies already defined. These policies should, at the least, contain statements about the file types, disk use, and traffic restrictions permitted on your system. More complex policies might define page format or include information about permissible content.

If you have a large group of users who receive Web space as part of their agreement with the network, either through work or as consumers, you may have to deal with users who put illegal materials on your site. These materials, usually copyright violations, can bring trouble both for the user and for the site administrator, especially if you know the files are there and don't remove them. Track your logs so you can tell when unusual traffic occurs and figure out which files are attracting the hits. Be sure your user policies state clearly that files in violation of copyright aren't permitted on your site and what the consequences are if such files are found.

Controlling access to certain files or functions and, thus, controlling user behavior, is easier with the Unix groups function. Unix operating systems allow user accounts to be placed into groups, which are then given particular permissions to read, write, or execute given files. You can limit access to Web files or other important data by setting file permissions, so only particular groups can get those files.

CHAPTER 13

Serving Compliant HTML

If you're going to go to all the trouble of running a Web server, why not use the server to provide pages and files that are technically correct? Hypertext Markup Language (HTML) is the coding language used to format documents and images so they can be seen on the Web. *Compliant HTML* is HTML that follows all the rules of the current HTML *standard*, the document that defines what is, and what isn't, acceptable use of HTML tags in a file. The standard changes as new techniques are developed, and, as the standard changes, pages should be rewritten to be compliant. Old tags are superseded and new methods introduced with each revision of the standard.

NOTE: Most browsers can handle outdated HTML tags. However, they won't do so forever; and, if your visitors are using a browser that requires compliant HTML—like the Opera browser—your pages won't load properly. Update your HTML as the standard changes in order to meet the needs of your visitors.

Why worry about compliant HTML? At the most basic level, using compliant HTML means pages and files coming from your server are more likely to be seen on a wider variety of browsers than noncompliant pages and files. Compliant HTML is more easily parsed by adaptive browsers, used by disabled Web viewers, and by text-only browsers, such as wireless-access-enabled cell phones or lynx, the Unix text-only browser. Writing compliant HTML isn't particularly difficult, though. If you use an HTML editor or a page design program, you might have to go back and confirm its output. Such editors often produce bad HTML, using outdated tags or appending their own unique (nonstandard) tags to your page.

In this chapter, you meet the World Wide Web Consortium, the body that produces standards for Web-related endeavors. Then, you see the table of contents of the HTML standard itself, with notes explaining what each section of the standard covers and how those guidelines are used in a regular Web page. The chapter ends with a brief discussion of server policies about HTML and why such policies are a good idea.

WHAT IS THE WORLD WIDE WEB CONSORTIUM?

At its most basic, the World Wide Web Consortium is an organization that manages and develops standards for various languages and protocols that constitute the World Wide Web, as it's generally thought of. The Consortium, usually called W3C, has both members and employees. The members aren't employed by the W3C, but are interested persons who sit on various committees, each of which is involved in some particular aspect of the Web. More than 500 W3C members exist around the world. The W3C also employs nearly 70 full-time workers in jobs ranging from programming to education and outreach. Its main offices are in Massachusetts (in Boston on the MIT campus), France, and Switzerland.

The W3C considers its mission "to lead the Web to its full potential," which it does by providing software and standards, as well as by leading discussions in the Web community about where HTML, HTTP, and the other core technologies should go next. W3C is also deeply involved in the Web accessibility issue, providing education to Web designers and software developers about the Web Accessibility Standard and how to make sites usable by the disabled. In the United States, this is especially important. Some in the computer news media have speculated that the Americans with Disabilities Act may be applicable to Web sites and software, as well as to physical facilities.

> **TIP:**   Learn more about accessibility and the Web Accessibility Standard in Chapter 22, "CSS—Cascading Style Sheets."

If you're running a Web site, you should be familiar with the work of the W3C. Its work defines how the software you use runs, how pages are transmitted across the Internet, and how browsers interface with your site. You don't have to join the W3C as an official member, but you might want to browse the various documents stored on the W3C site at **http://www.w3c.org**. Whether you're interested in programming languages, accessibility, newer ways to move multimedia content across networks, or new products that make the entire Web experience easier, check out the W3C.

HTML STANDARDS

If you have the opportunity to set policies about the kind of material served as Web pages from your Apache installation, consider requiring your Web page developers code that material to the HTML standard. Serving standard-compliant HTML means a wider variety of people can read your pages, regardless of the browser they're using, and your site is more likely to be accessible to people who use adaptive technologies to browse the Web. Writing compliant HTML isn't any more difficult than writing broken HTML.

Your Web page developers should be aware that some HTML editor software doesn't produce compliant HTML. For example, the Netscape Composer program (part of the Netscape browser) adds Netscape-specific tags to pages it creates. These tags aren't part of the HTML standard. The various Front Page extensions added when pages are built in the Microsoft Front Page HTML editor aren't compliant either. Also, any tags that tailor pages to one browser over another probably aren't compliant.

> **NOTE:**   Browsers are notoriously different from each other. Some pages display perfectly well on Internet Explorer, but barely load at all with Netscape. This may be a problem with the browser, with the HTML, or with the scripts running on the serving site (it's especially problematic with dynamically served pages). Always be sure to test your site on as many browsers as possible, because to require that all viewers use one particular browser isn't very friendly. This is especially the case if the browser you pick is Internet Explorer, as people using Unix-derived machines cannot run that browser unless they install a Windows partition.

The HTML Standard

If you like to read instruction manuals, the HTML standard is fascinating reading. Actually, it's interesting whether or not you're prone to technical books at your bedside. The current standard is HTML 4, and the current version is HTML 4.1.

TIP: You can always obtain the latest version of Web standards from the W3C Web site at **http://www.w3c.org**. The HTML 4.01 standard is available as plain text, a PostScript file, or a PDF file readable with Adobe's Acrobat Reader.

The main drawback to reading the HTML standard straight through is it's over 330 pages long! Therefore, this standard is better used as a reference when you have a question about a particular tag or way to structure pages on your site.

Rather than print the entire standard in this chapter, I opted to include only the Table of Contents for the document. The HTML standard is divided into multiple parts, each of which addresses a significant aspect of Web site operation and Web page development. If you see a section in the Table of Contents that looks like something you'd like to know more about, you can jump directly to that section in the standard itself.

```
1. About the HTML 4 Specification
        1. How the specification is organized
        2. Document conventions
                1. Elements and attributes
                2. Notes and examples
        3. Acknowledgments
                1. Acknowledgments for the current revision
        4. Copyright Notice
```

Most standards and specifications for Internet-related practices follow this pattern. The most important part to read is usually the Document Conventions section because it explains various typographical issues and other phrases that are used throughout the document. In the HTML standard, two critical phrases are DEPRECATED EXAMPLE and ILLEGAL EXAMPLE. A *deprecated* example is a code sample that shows a particular HTML use that's no longer encouraged. An *illegal* example is a code sample showing a particular HTML use that's no longer permitted under the standard.

```
2. Introduction to HTML 4
        1. What is the World Wide Web?
                1. Introduction to URIs
                2. Fragment identifiers
                3. Relative URIs
        2. What is HTML?
                1. A brief history of HTML
        3. HTML 4
```

```
      1. Internationalization
      2. Accessibility
      3. Tables
      4. Compound documents
      5. Style sheets
      6. Scripting
      7. Printing
   4. Authoring documents with HTML 4
      1. Separate structure and presentation
      2. Consider universal accessibility to the Web
      3. Help user agents with incremental rendering
```

If you're new to HTML in general or you haven't learned what makes HTML 4 different from HTML 2 or 3, read through this section. You'll find a great deal of information about HTML in general, as well as specific upgrades available in version 4. The accessibility information is particularly useful because the introduction of style sheets and other such functions have increased the probability that an adaptive browser can parse a standards-compliant HTML file with ease.

The section on authoring HTML 4–compliant documents is especially important for Web page developers to read. You'll find three major components, each of which is critical in this age of complicated and dense multimedia Web files:

▼ *Separate structure and presentation.* The W3C encourages developers to think of the page's (and site's) structure as a different thing than the way the page looks. This is a different approach than many page designers take. The W3C's position is this: HTML should be used to build a framework for the page, which is then filled with content and visual flash, but the two should be separate.

■ *Consider universal accessibility to the Web.* Not only should pages be easily parsed by alternative and adaptive browsers, they should be usable for people who don't have access to full-size monitors and Web browsers. Accessibility isn't just a question of getting access to the disabled, but also to those viewing your pages with text-only browsers or on palmtop computers, wireless–Web-enabled cellular phones, and other new and limited-bandwidth technology.

▲ *Help user agents with incremental rendering.* This point addresses the overhead Web browsing places on the viewer's machine, your server, and all network connections in between. If your pages are constructed modularly, the browser can download certain elements only once. This saves download time and the time it takes to draw the page in the browser. Elements like CSS are designed to emphasize this incremental rendering method.

```
   3. On SGML and HTML
      1. Introduction to SGML
      2. SGML constructs used in HTML
         1. Elements
```

```
          2. Attributes
          3. Character references
          4. Comments
      3. How to read the HTML DTD
          1. DTD Comments
          2. Parameter entity definitions
          3. Element declarations
                # Content model definitions
          4. Attribute declarations
                # DTD entities in attribute definitions
                # Boolean attributes

   4. Conformance: requirements and recommendations
       1. Definitions
       2. SGML
       3. The text/html content type
```

These sections explain how HTML uses various components of SGML. HTML is a language used to *mark up,* or format, plain text. SGML is the standard that defines how markup languages work in general.

```
5. HTML Document Representation - Character sets, character
       encodings, and entities
       1. The Document Character Set
       2. Character encodings
           1. Choosing an encoding
                # Notes on specific encodings
           2. Specifying the character encoding
       3. Character references
           1. Numeric character references
           2. Character entity references
       4. Undisplayable characters
```

This section describes acceptable methods of defining individual characters on the Web and how best to refer to those characters when building Web pages. The easiest way is to define a *character set,* or a batch of characters that share the same characteristics. The section also describes how characters are handled when they're unable to be displayed on the viewer's browser.

```
   6. Basic HTML data types - Character data, colors, lengths, URIs,
       content types, etc.
       1. Case information
       2. SGML basic types
       3. Text strings
       4. URIs
       5. Colors
```

     1. Notes on using colors
  6. Lengths
  7. Content types (MIME types)
  8. Language codes
  9. Character encodings
 10. Single characters
 11. Dates and times
 12. Link types
 13. Media descriptors
 14. Script data
 15. Style sheet data
 16. Frame target names

For those new to raw HTML, section 6 of the standard is important reading. It defines the various types of data HTML recognizes—from characters and text to colors and dynamic script data. If it's permissible in HTML, it's probably described in this section. Those developers used to working with graphical HTML editors may not have much experience working directly with HTML tags and should find this section and the following sections highly useful.

  7. The global structure of an HTML document - The HEAD and BODY of a
     document
       1. Introduction to the structure of an HTML document
       2. HTML version information
       3. The HTML element
       4. The document head
            1. The HEAD element
            2. The TITLE element
            3. The title attribute
            4. Meta data
                 # Specifying meta data
                 # The META element
                 # Meta data profiles
       5. The document body
            1. The BODY element
            2. Element identifiers: the id and class attributes
            3. Block-level and inline elements
            4. Grouping elements: the DIV and SPAN elements
            5. Headings: The H1, H2, H3, H4, H5, H6 elements
            6. The ADDRESS element

Earlier in the standard, HTML users were encouraged to divorce page structure from page content and appearance. Section 7 describes the various tags used to build the structure of a Web page. Much of a page's appearance can be handled with these structural tags rather than with image files or font experimentation. The more these structural tags are used instead of graphical substitutions, the more likely the page will display without complaint in the widest variety of browsers.

```
8. Language information and text direction - International
   considerations for text
      1. Specifying the language of content: the lang attribute
            1. Language codes
            2. Inheritance of language codes
            3. Interpretation of language codes
      2. Specifying the direction of text and tables: the dir
         attribute
            1. Introduction to the bidirectional algorithm
            2. Inheritance of text direction information
            3. Setting the direction of embedded text
            4. Overriding the bidirectional algorithm: the BDO element
            5. Character references for directionality and joining
               control
            6. The effect of style sheets on bidirectionality
```

As you learned when you configured Apache for your system, you can handle the language issue on the Web in many different ways. You may have specified a particular default language for files coming from your system, or you might have left that variable blank, so the files themselves could determine the language in which they're displayed. This section of the standard explains how to work with languages in the HTML files, rather than at the server level. You also learn how text can be oriented with the powerful dir attribute, which is used to change the orientation of text on the page: either left to right, as in English, or right to left, as in Hebrew or many Asian languages.

```
9. Text - Paragraphs, Lines, and Phrases
      1. White space
      2. Structured text
            1. Phrase elements: EM, STRONG, DFN, CODE, SAMP, KBD, VAR,
               CITE, ABBR, and ACRONYM
            2. Quotations: The BLOCKQUOTE and Q elements
                  # Rendering quotations
            3. Subscripts and superscripts: the SUB and SUP elements
      3. Lines and Paragraphs
            1. Paragraphs: the P element
            2. Controlling line breaks
                  # Forcing a line break: the BR element
```

```
        # Prohibiting a line break
  3. Hyphenation
  4. Preformatted text: The PRE element
  5. Visual rendering of paragraphs
4. Marking document changes: The INS and DEL elements
```

Text has always been the basic element of Web pages. In the earliest days, just when people were switching from text-only utilities like gopher and archie to Web pages, most files on the Web were pure text (and most still are). Although the role of text hasn't changed much since days of yore, however, the way in which it's handled in HTML has certainly changed. If you learned to write HTML by hand in the mid 1990s, you learned tags like <b> and <i>, which defined bold and italic typefaces, respectively. The bold and italic tags are no longer part of the HTML standard, having been replaced by <EM> and <STRONG>.

This section is critical because text is so important on the Web. If you or your developers routinely use an HTML checker program to test your tags, you'll probably find the majority of your HTML errors are text related. By combining the structural tags of the previous section with the text, line, and paragraph tags of this section, you can do a great deal of formatting in a standard-compliant way.

```
10. Lists - Unordered, Ordered, and Definition Lists
    1. Introduction to lists
    2. Unordered lists (UL), ordered lists (OL), and list items(LI)
    3. Definition lists: the DL, DT, and DD elements
        1. Visual rendering of lists
    4. The DIR and MENU elements
```

Lists aren't as common on the Web as they used to be, but the HTML standard has several options that create attractive and functional lists in your text documents. Six different list styles have their own tags, each described in this section. You may find the list features are an effective way to format some data, even if you don't want the traditional bulleted list on every page.

```
11. Tables
    1. Introduction to tables
    2. Elements for constructing tables
        1. The TABLE element
            # Table directionality
        2. Table Captions: The CAPTION element
        3. Row groups: the THEAD, TFOOT, and TBODY elements
        4. Column groups: the COLGROUP and COL elements
            # The COLGROUP element
            # The COL element
            # Calculating the number of columns in a table
```

```
                    # Calculating the width of columns
          5. Table rows: The TR element
          6. Table cells: The TH and TD elements
                    # Cells that span several rows or columns
       3. Table formatting by visual user agents
          1. Borders and rules
          2. Horizontal and vertical alignment
                    # Inheritance of alignment specifications
          3. Cell margins
       4. Table rendering by non-visual user agents
          1. Associating header information with data cells
          2. Categorizing cells
          3. Algorithm to find heading information
       5. Sample table
```

Tables have become a widespread phenomenon on the Web and are often used in ways the HTML standard doesn't permit. Many Web designers have turned to using tables as graphical design tools, rather than as organized presentations of data. The problem with this admittedly easy design method is it makes the page difficult to view in a nonstandard browser, and even some standard browsers have trouble displaying tables used for design instead of data. Learn the appropriate use of tables in this section, and find new ways to manage the shape and size of the tables you do use.

```
    12. Links - Hypertext and Media-Independent Links
       1. Introduction to links and anchors
          1. Visiting a linked resource
          2. Other link relationships
          3. Specifying anchors and links
          4. Link titles
          5. Internationalization and links
       2. The A element
          1. Syntax of anchor names
          2. Nested links are illegal
          3. Anchors with the id attribute
          4. Unavailable and unidentifiable resources
       3. Document relationships: the LINK element
          1. Forward and reverse links
          2. Links and external style sheets
          3. Links and search engines
       4. Path information: the BASE element
          1. Resolving relative URIs
```

It's not the Web without hypertext. Links are the one element that define a document as a Web page (apart from being written in HTML). For links to work, though, you must use the appropriate tags and syntax. All you ever need to know about links, whether absolute or relative, is contained in Section 12 of the standard.

```
13. Objects, Images, and Applets
     1. Introduction to objects, images, and applets
     2. Including an image: the IMG element
     3. Generic inclusion: the OBJECT element
          1. Rules for rendering objects
          2. Object initialization: the PARAM element
          3. Global naming schemes for objects
          4. Object declarations and instantiations
     4. Including an applet: the APPLET element
     5. Notes on embedded documents
     6. Image maps
          1. Client-side image maps: the MAP and AREA elements
               # Client-side image map examples
          2. Server-side image maps
     7. Visual presentation of images, objects, and applets
          1. Width and height
          2. White space around images and objects
          3. Borders
          4. Alignment
     8. How to specify alternate text
```

With the explosion of the Web, more and more pages that incorporate images into the core function of the page are being seen. Where images on the Web used to be single files placed in the middle of text, images are now used as navigational tools or animations. Rules about how images can be used in HTML documents and suggestions on the best way to add these visual features to your pages are in this section of the standard.

NOTE: The alternate text part of this section is critical. The *ALT text* is a short description of any image files you include on the page. Adaptive browsers, browsers with images turned off, and text-only browsers all rely on the ALT tag to provide information about the image that isn't being displayed. Any page containing images must have ALT tags for all images to be accessible to such browsers and those who use them.

```
14. Style Sheets - Adding style to HTML documents
     1. Introduction to style sheets
     2. Adding style to HTML
          1. Setting the default style sheet language
          2. Inline style information
          3. Header style information: the STYLE element
       4. Media types
```

3. External style sheets
   1. Preferred and alternate style sheets
   2. Specifying external style sheets
4. Cascading style sheets
   1. Media-dependent cascades
   2. Inheritance and cascading
5. Hiding style data from user agents
6. Linking to style sheets with HTTP headers

Style sheets are a new addition to the HTML 4 standard. With these sheets, you can define a set of visual parameters that affect every page on your site. The browser downloads this style sheet with the first page accessed on your site and uses the parameters to maintain visual similarity with each new page opened. Using style sheets speeds download times because individual browsers needn't download formatting information with each new page opened. They also make it easier for adaptive and text-based browsers because much of the formatting information is located elsewhere. Thus, the browser doesn't have to wade through code intended for visual browsers before getting to the actual data on the page.

15. Alignment, font styles, and horizontal rules
   1. Formatting
      1. Background color
      2. Alignment
      3. Floating objects
         # Float an object
         # Float text around an object
   2. Fonts
      1. Font style elements: the TT, I, B, BIG, SMALL, STRIKE, S, and U elements
      2. Font modifier elements: FONT and BASEFONT
   3. Rules: the HR element

Even basic text-only pages can have some visual splash if the coder incorporates some of the simple formatting possibilities included in this section of the standard. Some of these tags have been deprecated as other tags have been developed, though. Read this section and others pertaining to the same topic carefully if you want to use these tags.

16. Frames - Multi-view presentation of documents
   1. Introduction to frames
   2. Layout of frames
      1. The FRAMESET element
         # Rows and columns
         # Nested frame sets
         # Sharing data among frames
      2. The FRAME element

```
                    # Setting the initial contents of a frame
                    # Visual rendering of a frame
            3. Specifying target frame information
                    1. Setting the default target for links
                    2. Target semantics
            4. Alternate content
                    1. The NOFRAMES element
                    2. Long descriptions of frames
            5. Inline frames: the IFRAME element
```

Frames are one of the most popular ways to present Web data. Using a frame might help you keep a given visitor on your site longer, by showing external pages within a frame that's based on your own site. The unfortunate aspect of frames is they can be implemented wrongly and often simply annoy viewers. Learn the actual rules for frames in Section 16 of the HTML standard.

NOTE: Frames, like images, use the alternate text tag to describe, in words, what shows on the screen. Such tags are important for visitors who might not be using a graphical browser or who might have an adaptive browser that reads the page aloud.

```
17. Forms - User-input Forms: Text Fields, Buttons, Menus, and more
            1. Introduction to forms
            2. Controls
                    1. Control types
            3. The FORM element
            4. The INPUT element
                    1. Control types created with INPUT
                    2. Examples of forms containing INPUT controls
            5. The BUTTON element
            6. The SELECT, OPTGROUP, and OPTION elements
                    1. Pre-selected options
            7. The TEXTAREA element
            8. The ISINDEX element
            9. Labels
                    1. The LABEL element
           10. Adding structure to forms: the FIELDSET and LEGEND elements
           11. Giving focus to an element
                    1. Tabbing navigation
                    2. Access keys
           12. Disabled and read-only controls
                    1. Disabled controls
                    2. Read-only controls
           13. Form submission
                    1. Form submission method
```

```
      2. Successful controls
      3. Processing form data
            # Step one: Identify the successful controls
            # Step two: Build a form data set
            # Step three: Encode the form data set
            # Step four: Submit the encoded form data set
      4. Form content types
            # application/x-www-form-urlencoded
            # multipart/form-data
```

Forms are a useful way to get information and feedback from your readers, although admittedly in a fairly basic manner. If you don't want to load your site with scripts and fancy interactive functions, though, you can build simple forms using these tags and guidelines. You can use the basic form setup, which encodes selected data into a new URL, or you can use a more complex multipart mode that keeps the data out of the URL. If you don't have time or access to a scripting professional, these guidelines might be all you need.

```
   18. Scripts - Animated Documents and Smart Forms
         1. Introduction to scripts
         2. Designing documents for user agents that support scripting
               1. The SCRIPT element
               2. Specifying the scripting language
                     # The default scripting language
                     # Local declaration of a scripting language
                     # References to HTML elements from a script
               3. Intrinsic events
               4. Dynamic modification of documents
         3. Designing documents for user agents that don't support
            scripting
               1. The NOSCRIPT element
               2. Hiding script data from user agents
```

It seems like any job ad for a Web-related position these days specifies that applicants should know a scripting language. Scripting is certainly the basis for many of the complicated and densely coded pages available on the Web, and, used properly, it adds to the user experience. Learn about the standard's requirements for scripts in this section and learn how to shield your scripts from browsers that can't handle them.

TIP: If at all possible, keep a version of your site available that's text-only or with limited formatting. Many people have limited tolerance for sites jam-packed with technological wizardry or use browsers that simply can't display pages written that way. Give viewers an option: a plain hamburger or filet mignon stuffed with asparagus and drizzled with Bernaise sauce.

19. SGML reference information for HTML - Formal definition of HTML
    and validation
       1. Document Validation
       2. Sample SGML catalog

20. SGML Declaration of HTML 4
       1. SGML Declaration

21. Document Type Definition

22. Transitional Document Type Definition

23. Frameset Document Type Definition

These sections simply provide definitions for different kinds of files and document types. Such sections are common components of a standard. They probably won't affect the work you or your coders do, but they're useful references for programmers and others who need specific definitions of the various entities possible on a Web site.

24. Character entity references in HTML 4
       1. Introduction to character entity references
       2. Character entity references for ISO 8859-1 characters
            1. The list of characters
       3. Character entity references for symbols, mathematical
          symbols, and Greek letters
            1. The list of characters
       4. Character entity references for markup-significant and
          internationalization characters
            1. The list of characters

As you saw in Chapter 8, "Configuration Files," hundreds of different character sets exist, and it seems like a different set exists for every language and dialect in the world. (Some have more than one—Russian and Hebrew are two examples.) HTML has its own way of dealing with character codes, which is described in this section of the standard.

A. Changes

> **NOTE:**   This section, as printed here, was removed from the Table of Contents. This is a listing of all changes to the HTML standard since the release of the previous version.

B. Performance, Implementation, and Design Notes
       1. Notes on invalid documents
       2. Special characters in URI attribute values
            1. Non-ASCII characters in URI attribute values
            2. Ampersands in URI attribute values

```
3. SGML implementation notes
    1. Line breaks
    2. Specifying non-HTML data
            # Element content
            # Attribute values
    3. SGML features with limited support
    4. Boolean attributes
    5. Marked Sections
    6. Processing Instructions
    7. Shorthand markup
4. Notes on helping search engines index your Web site
    1. Search robots
            # The robots.txt file
            # Robots and the META element
5. Notes on tables
    1. Design rationale
            # Dynamic reformatting
            # Incremental display
            # Structure and presentation
            # Row and column groups
            # Accessibility
    2. Recommended Layout Algorithms
            # Fixed Layout Algorithm
            # Autolayout Algorithm
6. Notes on forms
    1. Incremental display
    2. Future projects
7. Notes on scripting
    1. Reserved syntax for future script macros
            # Current Practice for Script Macros
8. Notes on frames
9. Notes on accessibility
10. Notes on security
    1. Security issues for forms
```

Down here at the bottom of the standard is a most useful section. In this section, you can find notes on almost every aspect of a Web site. These notes are suggestions to coders and server administrators, and offer helpful information about good ways to run your site and build your pages. I encourage you to read the notes relating to any aspect of Web administration of particular concern to you, and to read all of them if you're interested in HTML in general.

SETTING APPROPRIATE SERVER POLICIES

Abiding by standards on the Internet is like following the rules when you're driving. Sure, a lot of people speed, make U-turns, and slide through stop signs, but it's risky. You could get in serious trouble if you break the rules routinely. So it is with the HTML standard. True, you probably won't get a ticket (unless courts decide to extend disability-access laws to Web sites) for distributing bad HTML, but it's not a good idea. Bad HTML means you might have angry customers or visitors who can't see your pages, or a site that regularly crashes one particular kind of browser.

You have a lot more leeway if you're the person who does all the coding, in addition to running the server. If you work for a larger company—especially if you're not the top dog in the Web administration—you might have a bit more trouble convincing people a good HTML policy is necessary. The policy should be that all pages served from your Apache installation must be HTML 4 compliant. Encourage your coders and designers to use page design tools that produce compliant code. Microsoft Front Page and Netscape Composer don't because both add unique tags that aren't part of the standard. Macromedia's Dreamweaver generates code that's reasonably clean and also has a tool that can check hand-coded pages (or pages generated by another program) against the HTML 4 standard. Adobe's GoLive also builds compliant code, but code-checking tools are available only in GoLive 5 and not in previous versions.

One of the best tests for HTML compliance is a program distributed by the W3C called the *HTML Validator*. You can either upload your pages to the validator or you can enter a single page's URL to check whether the HTML is compliant. Find the HTML Validator at **http://validator.w3.org**. If you run a random sample of your site's pages through the validator and find significant errors, this might be proof enough to institute a compliant HTML policy. Also, check your site's pages in a number of browsers to see whether cross-browser compatibility is on your site:

▼ Netscape and Internet Explorer—the two browsers most likely to be used to access your site.

■ Opera—a browser that only displays compliant HTML (**http://operasoftware.com**).

■ lynx—a Unix text-only browser.

■ WAP (Wireless Access Protocol)—any cellular or PCS phone that has wireless Web service enabled, or a palmtop computer with Web access.

▲ Any adaptive browser you can find—or, run your pages through the *Bobby validator*, which checks your page for HTML that blocks adaptive browsers (**http://www.cast.org/bobby**).

SUMMARY

Hypertext Markup Language (HTML) is the coding language used to produce Web pages. A standard exists for HTML that defines what is acceptable and what isn't when working with the language. The standard is developed and maintained by the World Wide Web Consortium (W3C), a nonprofit group that manages the many facets of the Web. The HTML standard is currently in version 4, which introduced many significant changes from earlier versions.

The goals of the HTML standard, as it currently stands, are the following: to separate a page's structure from its content through various page structure tags and conventions, to make pages more accessible to disabled viewers and those not using a standard image-based browser, and to reduce the number of requests for page configurations from the same site. All of these goals are addressed in the HTML standard and the methods suggested to attain each goal are described in detail. Although you probably won't want to read the entire document, the standard should be the first place you look for answers to an HTML question. The standard is a good basis for a policy requiring only compliant HTML on your Apache-served site. Compliant HTML makes your pages accessible to the widest pool of viewers and reduces the chance your pages won't display on a particular browser, whether it's adaptive or not.

PART IV

Beyond the Basics: Advanced Apache Topics

CHAPTER 14

MIME and Other Encoding

Different kinds of data are handled differently. Pretty obvious, yes? After all, files are generated by all sorts of programs, each with their own formatting quirks and data-encoding structures. You can't read a Microsoft Word document directly in a plain-text editor because of the formatting, and you can't run random Unix programs on a Windows or Macintosh computer without getting specially formatted packages. (MacOS X is different because it's essentially a Mac-flavored version of BSD Unix.)

However, the software industry has worked diligently over the last 20 years to blur the lines between data types. With an integrated office suite like Sun's StarOffice or Corel's WordPerfect Suite, for example, you can open database files inside word processors and view images inside e-mail clients. The trend is toward suites, or individual programs, that offer a number of functions traditionally associated with different data management techniques. That's the surface experience, though.

Inside all those integrated programs, deep in the code, are mechanisms that associate different kinds of data with special programs that make the data readable in the user environment. If you're working in a word processor and you want to insert images into your file, the image file is managed by a different mechanism than the text itself. The different kinds of data are called *types,* and the mechanisms are called *handlers.* Installing software that can deal with multiple data types without making the change between types obvious to the user is increasingly common.

What does all this have to do with the Internet? Well, the Internet is just a giant filing cabinet that holds millions of files in a wide range of data types. When you use an Internet tool like e-mail or a Web browser, chances are you're going to view multiple data types in that one client. E-mail and the Web are the two segments of the Internet that are most closely associated with data types because both are used to transfer files of various types. Unlike FTP or other file transfer modes, people using e-mail and Web clients want to view the files they're working with. How those different file types are translated to the screen is the job of the individual client's handlers and their understanding of the incoming files.

In this chapter, you learn about data types and their handlers, and what this has to do with Apache. The MIME standard manages data types and provides a framework for Web servers like Apache to use in determining the type of files being sent. You learn about the HTTP headers that control type designations, as well as how Apache works with HTTP and the requesting browser to display files correctly. Character sets are also covered because displaying pages in different languages requires unique MIME types to handle the appearance of written text.

WHAT IS MIME?

The Multimedia E-Mail Extensions (MIME) standard controls the way in which different data types are identified. These identifications, in turn, control the internal mechanisms that programs use to display the data to the user. MIME was originally developed to work with e-mail clients, as is evident from the name. Before the Web was developed, people used e-mail to transfer files back and forth. Early e-mail clients were plain text only, but users wanted to be able to attach different kinds of data to their text messages. Unfortunately, those clients couldn't understand the nontext data. Once the data types could be identified with the consistent MIME type tags, though, new clients could be developed that enabled users to see nontext files as well as text data in their messages.

NOTE: Most Windows and Macintosh e-mail clients are now fully featured programs that handle different MIME types with ease. Relatively few MIME-based e-mail clients exist for the Unix platform, however. The Pine e-mail client is the main exception. If configured properly, Pine can be used to view various kinds of data types in e-mail messages.

Generic MIME Types

Table 14-1 shows the generic MIME types that have been registered as formal MIME designations. You see some common file types and some unfamiliar ones, but all are valid data types and have handlers that can parse the data. Many vendor-specific registered MIME types also exist that haven't been included in this table, but you can see them in the complete list of registered MIME types at **http://www.iana.org/assignments/character-sets**.

NOTE: Despite the URL, that page contains the complete list of MIME types and not character sets.

NOTE: MIME types in Table 14-1, that begin with the characters "x-" aren't currently considered standards. They're going through a definition process that should ultimately result in a standard being issued for those types, but the current protocol used is likely to change in the future.

Type	Subtype
text	plain
	richtext
	enriched
	tab-separated-values
	html
	sgml
	x-server-parsed-html
	uri-list

Table 14-1.   General MIME Types

Type	Subtype
	rfc822-headers
	prs.lines.tag
	css
	xml
	rtf
	directory
	calendar
multipart	mixed
	alternative
	digest
	parallel
	appledouble
	header-set
	form-data
	related
	report
	voice-message
	signed
	encrypted
	byteranges
message	rfc822
	partial
	external-body
	news
	http
	delivery-status
	disposition-notification
	s-http
application	octet-stream

Table 14-1. General MIME Types *(continued)*

Type	Subtype
	postscript
	oda
	atomicmail
	andrew-inset
	slate
	wita
	dec-dx
	dca-rft
	activemessage
	rtf
	applefile
	mac-binhex40
	news-message-id
	news-transmission
	wordperfect5.1
	pdf
	zip
	macwriteii
	msword
	remote-printing
	mathematica
	cybercash
	commonground
	iges
	riscos
	eshop
	x400-bp
	sgml
	cals-1840

Table 14-1.   General MIME Types *(continued)*

Type	Subtype
	pgp-encrypted
	pgp-signature
	pgp-keys
	set-payment-initiation
	set-payment
	set-registration-initiation
	set-registration
	sgml-open-catalog
	prs.alvestrand.titrax-sheet
	prs.nprend
	hyperstudio
	vemmi
	prs.cww
	marc
	pkcs7-mime
	pkcs7-signature
	pkcs10
	EDIFACT
	EDI-X12
	EDI-Consent
	xml
	batch-SMTP
	pkixcmp
	ipp
	ocsp-request
	ocsp-response
	pkix-cert
	pkix-crl
	index

Table 14-1. General MIME Types *(continued)*

Type	Subtype
	index.cmd
	index.response
	index.obj
	index.vnd
	http
	sdp
	java
	x-csh
	x-sh
	x-tcl
	x-tex
	x-latex
	x-texinfo
	zip
	x-bcpio
	x-cpio
	x-shar
	x-tar
	x-dvi
	x-hdf
	x-x509-ca-cert
image	jpeg
	gif
	ief
	g3fax
	tiff
	cgm
	naplps
	png

Table 14-1.   General MIME Types *(continued)*

Type	Subtype
	prs.btif
	prs.pti
	x-xbitmap
	x-xpixmap
	x-xwindowdump
	x-xbitmap
	x-cmu-raster
	x-portable-anymap
	x-portable-bitmap
	x-portable-graymap
	x-rgb
audio	basic
	32kadpcm
	L16
	x-wav
video	mpeg
	quicktime
	/x-sgi-movie
	model
	iges
	vrml
	mesh

Table 14-1.   General MIME Types *(continued)*

How MIME Types Work

Content type negotiation is controlled by the Web server in response to requests from an external browser. When a browser makes a request, it also sends along information about itself. Such data might include the kinds of image files that a particular browser can show, the preferred types and language set by the browser's user as user preferences, or other configuration details that affect the files to be returned. In addition to this background data, the URL of the request itself will be used in negotiation. File extensions, such as the common .html or .jpg, identify particular MIME types.

Thus, when a request is received by the server, Apache considers the file extension to determine the MIME type of the requested file. It then considers the various configuration data sent by the browser along with the URL to see whether additional MIME types will be called into play. Using the mod_mime and mod_mime_magic modules, Apache identifies the appropriate files to return and sends them to the browser.

The vast majority of MIME types are identified by file extensions. In the next section of this chapter, "MIME Types and Apache Configuration," you see the mime.types configuration file. This file contains all types recognized by Apache, as well as any file extensions associated with those types. If you add a new MIME type to this file, be sure to add any extensions of which you're aware that go with this kind of file. It can make your server run more efficiently.

NOTE: Some file types don't use extensions or they advertise themselves in different ways. Read on to learn more about the mod_mime_magic module, which can identify file formats by actually reading the file's code and comparing it to known code strings.

MIME TYPES AND APACHE CONFIGURATION

Apache uses a configuration file to manage the MIME types it recognizes and sends. The file is called mime.types and is kept in the /docs subdirectory of your main Apache directory (for Apache 2.0 installations). The mime.types file uses a particular syntax for each entry, placing the general type before a slash and the specific type after. Thus, text/plain is the MIME type for plain text, while image/tiff is the type for TIFF image files. Some lines in mime.types also have a short character string after the type definition. These characters are common file extensions for that file type. Apache can figure out the appropriate MIME type based on file extension for any types with extensions listed in this file. The default mime.types file is printed in the following.

NOTE: The Apache mime.types file contains many vendor-specific MIME types, as well as many of the generic types described in the previous section of the chapter. You can recognize them by the vnd prefix.

```
# This file controls what Internet media types are sent to the client for
# given file extension(s). Sending the correct media type to the client
# is important so they know how to handle the content of the file.
# Extra types can either be added here or by using an AddType directive
# in your config files. For more information about Internet media types,
# please read RFC 2045, 2046, 2047, 2048, and 2077. The Internet media type
# registry is at
<ftp://ftp.iana.org/in-notes/iana/assignments/media-types/>.

# MIME type    Extension
application/EDI-Consent
```

```
application/EDI-X12
application/EDIFACT
application/activemessage
application/andrew-inset      ez
application/applefile
application/atomicmail
application/batch-SMTP
application/cals-1840
application/commonground
application/cybercash
application/dca-rft
application/dec-dx
application/eshop
application/htt
application/hyperstudio
application/iges
application/index
application/index.cmd
application/index.obj
application/index.response
application/index.vnd
application/iotp
application/ipp
application/mac-binhex40      hqx
application/mac-compactpro    cpt
application/macwriteii
application/marc
application/mathematica
application/mathematica-old
application/msword      doc
application/news-message-id
application/news-transmission
application/ocsp-reques
application/ocsp-response
application/octet-stream      bin dms lha lzh exe class so dll
application/oda      oda
application/pdf      pdf
application/pgp-encrypted
application/pgp-keys
application/pgp-signature
application/pkcs10
application/pkcs7-mime
application/pkcs7-signatur
application/pkix-cert
```

```
application/pkix-crl
application/pkixcmp
application/postscript      ai eps ps
application/prs.alvestrand.titrax-sheet
application/prs.cww
application/prs.nprend
application/remote-printing
application/riscos
application/sdp
application/set-payment
application/set-payment-initiation
application/set-registration
application/set-registration-initiation
application/sgml
application/sgml-open-catalog
application/slate
application/smil      smi smil
application/vemmi
application/vnd.3M.Post-it-Notes
application/vnd.FloGraphIt
application/vnd.accpac.simply.aso
application/vnd.accpac.simply.imp
application/vnd.acucobol
application/vnd.anser-web-certificate-issue-initiatio
application/vnd.anser-web-funds-transfer-initiation
application/vnd.audiograph
application/vnd.businessobject
application/vnd.bmi
application/vnd.canon-cpdl
application/vnd.canon-lip
application/vnd.claymore
application/vnd.commerce-battelle
application/vnd.commonspace
application/vnd.comsocaller
application/vnd.contact.cmsg
application/vnd.cosmocaller
application/vnd.cups-postscript
application/vnd.cups-raster
application/vnd.cups-raw
application/vnd.ctc-posml
application/vnd.cyban
application/vnd.dna
application/vnd.dpgraph
application/vnd.dxr
```

```
application/vnd.ecdis-update
application/vnd.ecowin.chart
application/vnd.ecowin.filerequest
application/vnd.ecowin.fileupdate
application/vnd.ecowin.series
application/vnd.ecowin.seriesrequest
application/vnd.ecowin.seriesupdate
application/vnd.enliven
application/vnd.epson.esf
application/vnd.epson.msf
application/vnd.epson.quickanime
application/vnd.epson.salt
application/vnd.epson.ssf
application/vnd.ericsson.quickcall
application/vnd.eudora.data
application/vnd.fd
application/vnd.ffsns
application/vnd.framemaker
application/vnd.fujitsu.oasys
application/vnd.fujitsu.oasys2
application/vnd.fujitsu.oasys3
application/vnd.fujitsu.oasysgp
application/vnd.fujitsu.oasysprs
application/vnd.fujixerox.ddd
application/vnd.fujixerox.docuworks
application/vnd.fujixerox.docuworks.binder
application/vnd.fut-misnet
application/vnd.grafeq
application/vnd.groove-account
application/vnd.groove-identity-message
application/vnd.groove-injector
application/vnd.groove-tool-message
application/vnd.groove-tool-template
application/vnd.groove-vcard
application/vnd.hp-HPGL
application/vnd.hp-PCL
application/vnd.hp-PCLXL
application/vnd.hp-hpid
application/vnd.hp-hps
application/vnd.httphone
application/vnd.hzn-3d-crossword
application/vnd.ibm.MiniPay
application/vnd.ibm.modcap
application/vnd.informix-visionary
```

```
application/vnd.intercon.formnet
application/vnd.intertrust.digibox
application/vnd.intertrust.nncp
application/vnd.intu.qbo
application/vnd.intu.qfx
application/vnd.is-xpr
application/vnd.japannet-directory-service
application/vnd.japannet-jpnstore-wakeup
application/vnd.japannet-payment-wakeup
application/vnd.japannet-registration
application/vnd.japannet-registration-wakeup
application/vnd.japannet-setstore-wakeu
application/vnd.japannet-verification
application/vnd.japannet-verification-wakeup
application/vnd.koan
application/vnd.lotus-1-2-3
application/vnd.lotus-approach
application/vnd.lotus-freelance
application/vnd.lotus-notes
application/vnd.lotus-organizer
application/vnd.lotus-screencam
application/vnd.lotus-wordpro
application/vnd.mcd
application/vnd.mediastation.cdkey
application/vnd.meridian-slingshot
application/vnd.mif        mif
application/vnd.minisoft-hp3000-save
application/vnd.mitsubishi.misty-guard.trustweb
application/vnd.mobius.daf
application/vnd.mobius.dis
application/vnd.mobius.msl
application/vnd.mobius.plc
application/vnd.mobius.txf
application/vnd.motorola.flexsuite
application/vnd.motorola.flexsuite.adsi
application/vnd.motorola.flexsuite.fis
application/vnd.motorola.flexsuite.gotap
application/vnd.motorola.flexsuite.kmr
application/vnd.motorola.flexsuite.ttc
application/vnd.motorola.flexsuite.wem
application/vnd.mozilla.xul+xml
application/vnd.ms-artgalry
application/vnd.ms-asf
application/vnd.ms-excel      xls
```

```
application/vnd.ms-lrm
application/vnd.ms-powerpoint ppt
application/vnd.ms-project
application/vnd.ms-tnef
application/vnd.ms-works
application/vnd.msign
application/vnd.music-niff
application/vnd.musician
application/vnd.netfpx
application/vnd.noblenet-director
application/vnd.noblenet-sealer
application/vnd.noblenet-web
application/vnd.novadigm.EDM
application/vnd.novadigm.EDX
application/vnd.novadigm.EXT
application/vnd.osa.netdeploy
application/vnd.pg.format
application/vnd.pg.osasli
application/vnd.powerbuilder6
application/vnd.powerbuilder6-s
application/vnd.powerbuilder7
application/vnd.powerbuilder7-s
application/vnd.powerbuilder75
application/vnd.powerbuilder75-s
application/vnd.previewsystems.box
application/vnd.publishare-delta-tree
application/vnd.rapid
application/vnd.s3sms
application/vnd.seemail
application/vnd.shana.informed.formdata
application/vnd.shana.informed.formtemplate
application/vnd.shana.informed.interchange
application/vnd.shana.informed.package
application/vnd.street-stream
application/vnd.svd
application/vnd.swiftview-ics
application/vnd.triscape.mxs
application/vnd.trueapp
application/vnd.truedoc
application/vnd.ufdl
application/vnd.uplanet.alert
application/vnd.uplanet.alert-wbxml
application/vnd.uplanet.bearer-choi-wbxml
application/vnd.uplanet.bearer-choice
```

```
application/vnd.uplanet.cacheop
application/vnd.uplanet.cacheop-wbxml
application/vnd.uplanet.channel
application/vnd.uplanet.channel-wbxml
application/vnd.uplanet.list
application/vnd.uplanet.list-wbxml
application/vnd.uplanet.listcmd
application/vnd.uplanet.listcmd-wbxml
application/vnd.uplanet.signal
application/vnd.vcx
application/vnd.vectorworks
application/vnd.visio
application/vnd.wap.sic
application/vnd.wap.slc
application/vnd.wap.wbxml        wbxml
application/vnd.wap.wmlc         wmlc
application/vnd.wap.wmlscriptc        wmlsc
application/vnd.webturbo
application/vnd.wrq-hp3000-labelled
application/vnd.wt.stf
application/vnd.xara
application/vnd.xfdl
application/vnd.yellowriver-custom-menu
application/whoispp-query
application/whoispp-response
application/wita
application/wordperfect5.1
application/x-bcpio        bcpio
application/x-cdlink       vcd
application/x-chess-pgn        pgn
application/x-compress
application/x-cpio        cpio
application/x-csh        csh
application/x-director        dcr dir dxr
application/x-dvi        dvi
application/x-futuresplash        spl
application/x-gtar        gtar
application/x-gzip
application/x-hdf        hdf
application/x-javascript        js
application/x-koan        skp skd skt skm
application/x-latex        latex
application/x-netcdf        nc cdf
application/x-sh        sh
```

```
application/x-shar          shar
application/x-shockwave-flash       swf
application/x-stuffit       sit
application/x-sv4cpio        sv4cpio
application/x-sv4crc         sv4crc
application/x-tar       tar
application/x-tcl       tcl
application/x-tex       tex
application/x-texinfo        texinfo texi
application/x-troff         t tr roff
application/x-troff-man      man
application/x-troff-me       me
application/x-troff-ms       ms
application/x-ustar         ustar
application/x-wais-source       src
application/x400-bp
application/xml
application/zip       zip
audio/32kadpcm
audio/basic       au snd
audio/l16
audio/midi        mid midi kar
audio/mpeg        mpga mp2 mp3
audio/prs.sid
audio/telephone-event
audio/tone
audio/vnd.cns.anp1
audio/vnd.cns.inf1
audio/vnd.digital-winds
audio/vnd.everad.plj
audio/vnd.lucent.voice
audio/vnd.nortel.vbk
audio/vnd.nuera.ecelp4800
audio/vnd.nuera.ecelp7470
audio/vnd.octel.sbc
audio/vnd.qcelp
audio/vnd.rhetorex.32kadpcm
audio/vnd.vmx.cvsd
audio/x-aiff       aif aiff aifc
audio/x-pn-realaudio       ram rm
audio/x-pn-realaudio-plugin       rpm
audio/x-realaudio       ra
audio/x-wav       wav
chemical/x-pdb       pdb
chemical/x-xyz       xyz
```

```
image/bmp        bmp
image/cgm
image/g3fax
image/gif        gif
image/ief        ief
image/jpeg       jpeg jpg jpe
image/naplps
image/png        png
image/prs.btif
image/prs.pti
image/tiff       tiff tif
image/vnd.cns.inf2
image/vnd.dwg
image/vnd.dxf
image/vnd.fastbidsheet
image/vnd.fpx
image/vnd.fst
image/vnd.fujixerox.edmics-mmr
image/vnd.fujixerox.edmics-rlc
image/vnd.mix
image/vnd.net-fpx
image/vnd.svf
image/vnd.wap.wbmp       wbmp
image/vnd.xiff
image/x-cmu-raster       ras
image/x-portable-anymap       pnm
image/x-portable-bitmap       pbm
image/x-portable-graymap       pgm
image/x-portable-pixmap       ppm
image/x-rgb        rgb
image/x-xbitmap       xbm
image/x-xpixmap       xpm
image/x-xwindowdump       xwd
message/delivery-status
message/disposition-notification
message/external-body
message/http
message/news
message/partial
message/rfc822
message/s-http
model/iges        igs iges
model/mesh        msh mesh silo
model/vnd.dwf
model/vnd.flatland.3dml
```

```
model/vnd.gdl
model/vnd.gs-gdl
model/vnd.gtw
model/vnd.mts
model/vnd.vtu
model/vrml          wrl vrml
multipart/alternative
multipart/appledouble
multipart/byteranges
multipart/digest
multipart/encrypted
multipart/form-data
multipart/header-set
multipart/mixed
multipart/parallel
multipart/related
multipart/report
multipart/signed
multipart/voice-message
text/calendar
text/css          css
text/directory
text/enriched
text/html          html htm
text/plain          asc txt
text/prs.lines.tag
text/rfc822-headers
text/richtext          rtx
text/rtf          rtf
text/sgml          sgml sgm
text/tab-separated-values          tsv
text/t140
text/uri-list
text/vnd.DMClientScript
text/vnd.IPTC.NITF
text/vnd.IPTC.NewsML
text/vnd.abc
text/vnd.curl
text/vnd.flatland.3dml
text/vnd.fly
text/vnd.fmi.flexstor
text/vnd.in3d.3dml
text/vnd.in3d.spot
```

```
text/vnd.latex-z
text/vnd.motorola.reflex
text/vnd.ms-mediapackage
text/vnd.wap.si
text/vnd.wap.sl
text/vnd.wap.wml        wml
text/vnd.wap.wmlscript      wmls
text/x-setext      etx
text/xml      xml
video/mpeg      mpeg mpg mpe
video/pointer
video/quicktime      qt mov
video/vnd.fvt
video/vnd.motorola.video
video/vnd.motorola.videop
video/vnd.vivo
video/x-msvideo      avi
video/x-sgi-movie      movie
x-conference/x-cooltalk      ice
```

Although `mime.types` contains almost all known registered MIME types (and many others as well), you might occasionally need to edit this file. Perhaps your company has defined a particular file type for one of your products and you want to serve those files on your site, or maybe you've read about a new MIME type in a technical journal and want to add that capability to your server.

To edit `mime.types`, open the file in a text editor (see Appendix B, "Using a Unix Text Editor," for more information). You can add a new entry in the alphabetically appropriate place or you can simply stick it at the end. The mod_mime module probably runs a bit more cleanly if you put the entry in with others of its general type, however. Entries in `mime.types` take the syntax

```
mime-type extension extension
```

For example, the entry for MPEG movie files looks like this:

```
video/mpeg      mpeg mpg mpe
```

video/mpeg is the MIME type definition, and mpeg, mpg, and mpe are all permissible file extensions, which cause Apache to recognize the file as an MPEG movie.

NOTE: If you don't know the relevant file extensions or if no particular extensions are associated with the type, you can place the type definition in the file. In this case, it's unlikely that Apache can determine the file type unless the requesting browser sends the appropriate type request and the correct filename is specified in the URL.

mod_mime_magic

As explained in Chapter 5, "Apache Modules," Apache uses the mod_mime module to determine the MIME type of a given file named in a browser request. Apache also uses the mod_mime_magic module to help with MIME type distinction, but mod_mime_magic works differently than mod_mime. Where mod_mime checks the file extension to see whether it maps on to a known extension contained in mime.types, the mod_mime_magic module actually checks the first few data bits in the requested file. The module then attempts to match those bits with a known format described in the MimeMagicFile configuration file, stored in the /docs subdirectory along with mime.types and other configuration files.

The default MimeMagicFile is printed next. This is an astoundingly technical document because each entry defines the actual data that appears at the start of a file formatted in a particular manner. This document is extremely useful, however: when mod_mime can't figure out a type, the magic module often can. Entries for a number of file types are here, though more are being developed all the time (it takes time to figure this stuff out!). If you want to work with this file, don't change any of the syntax, which is specific and must remain in the same format for the module to work properly.

```
# Magic data for mod_mime_magic Apache module (originally for file(1)
# command)
# The module is described in htdocs/manual/mod/mod_mime_magic.html
#
# The format is 4-5 columns:
#    Column #1: byte number to begin checking from, ">" indicates
#       continuation
#    Column #2: type of data to match
#    Column #3: contents of data to match
#    Column #4: MIME type of result
#    Column #5: MIME encoding of result (optional)


#------------------------------------------------------------------------
# Localstuff: file(1) magic for locally observed files
# Add any locally observed files here.
#------------------------------------------------------------------------
# end local stuff
#------------------------------------------------------------------------
# Java

0          short       0xcafe
>2         short       0xbabe      application/java


#------------------------------------------------------------------------
# audio:  file(1) magic for sound formats
#
# from Jan Nicolai Langfeldt <janl@ifi.uio.no>,

# Sun/NeXT audio data
```

```
0       string          .snd
>12     belong     1    audio/basic
>12     belong     2    audio/basic
>12     belong     3    audio/basic
>12     belong     4    audio/basic
>12     belong     5    audio/basic
>12     belong     6    audio/basic
>12     belong     7    audio/basic

>12     belong     23   audio/x-adpcm

# DEC systems (e.g. DECstation 5000) use a variant of the Sun/NeXT format
# that uses little-endian encoding and has a different magic number
# (0x0064732E in little-endian encoding).
0       lelong     0x0064732E
>12     lelong     1    audio/x-dec-basic
>12     lelong     2    audio/x-dec-basic
>12     lelong     3    audio/x-dec-basic
>12     lelong     4    audio/x-dec-basic
>12     lelong     5    audio/x-dec-basic
>12     lelong     6    audio/x-dec-basic
>12     lelong     7    audio/x-dec-basic
#                                       compressed (G.721 ADPCM)
>12     lelong     23   audio/x-dec-adpcm

# Bytes 0-3 of AIFF, AIFF-C, & 8SVX audio files are "FORM"
#                                       AIFF audio data
8       string     AIFF   audio/x-aiff
#                                       AIFF-C audio data
8       string     AIFC   audio/x-aiff
#                                       IFF/8SVX audio data
8       string     8SVX   audio/x-aiff
# Creative Labs AUDIO stuff
#                                       Standard MIDI data
0       string     MThd   audio/unknown
#>9     byte   >0    (format %d)
#>11    byte   >1    using %d channels
#                                       Creative Music (CMF) data
0       string     CTMF   audio/unknown
#                                       SoundBlaster instrument data
0       string     SBI    audio/unknown
#                                       Creative Labs voice data
0       string     Creative\ Voice\ File    audio/unknown
## is this next line right?  it came this way...
#>19    byte   0x1A
#>23    byte   >0       - version %d
#>22    byte   >0          \b.%d

# [GRR 950115:  is this also Creative Labs?  Guessing that first line
```

```
#   should be string instead of unknown-endian long...]
#0      long     0x4e54524b     MultiTrack sound data
#0      string   NTRK           MultiTrack sound data
#>4     long     x              - version %ld

# Microsoft WAVE format (*.wav)
# [GRR 950115:  probably all of the shorts and longs should be
# eshort/lelong]
#                               Microsoft RIFF
0       string   RIFF     audio/unknown
#                                - WAVE format
>8      string   WAVE     audio/x-wav

#----------------------------------------------------------------------
# c-lang:  file(1) magic for C programs or various scripts
#

# XPM icons (Greg Roelofs, newt@uchicago.edu)
# ideally should go into "images", but entries below would tag XPM as C
# source
0       string       /*\ XPM      image/x-xbm      7bit

# this first will upset you if you're a PL/1 shop... (are there any left?)
# in which case rm it; ascmagic will catch real C programs
#                               C or REXX program text
0       string       /*      text/plain
#                               C++ program text
0       string       //      text/plain

#----------------------------------------------------------------------
# compress:  file(1) magic for pure-compression formats (no archives)
#
# compress, gzip, pack, compact, huf, squeeze, crunch, freeze, yabba, whap,
# etc.
#
# Formats for various forms of compressed data
# Formats for "compress" proper have been moved into "compress.c",
# because it tries to uncompress it to figure out what's inside.

# standard unix compress
0       string   \037\235     application/octet-stream     x-compress

# gzip (GNU zip, not to be confused with [Info-ZIP/PKWARE] zip archiver)
0       string   \037\213     application/octet-stream     x-gzip

# According to gzip.h, this is the correct byte order for packed data.
0       string   \037\036     application/octet-stream
#
# This magic number is byte-order-independent.
```

```
#
0      short     017437        application/octet-stream

# XXX - why *two* entries for "compacted data", one of which is
# byte-order independent, and one of which is byte-order dependent?
#
# compacted data
0      short     0x1fff        application/octet-stream
0      string    \377\037      application/octet-stream
# huf output
0      short     0145405       application/octet-stream
# Squeeze and Crunch...
# These numbers were gleaned from the Unix versions of the programs to
# handle these formats.  Note that I can only uncrunch, not crunch, and
# I didn't have a crunched file handy, so the crunch number is untested.
#               Keith Waclena <keith@cerberus.uchicago.edu>
#0     leshort   0x76FF        squeezed data (CP/M, DOS)
#0     leshort   0x76FE        crunched data (CP/M, DOS)

# Freeze
#0     string    \037\237      Frozen file 2.1
#0     string    \037\236      Frozen file 1.0 (or gzip 0.5)

# lzh?
#0     string    \037\240      LZH compressed data

#----------------------------------------------------------------------
# frame:  file(1) magic for FrameMaker files
#
# This stuff came on a FrameMaker demo tape, most of which is
# copyright, but this file is "published" as witness the following:
#
0      string    \<MakerFile         application/x-frame
0      string    \<MIFFile           application/x-frame
0      string    \<MakerDictionary   application/x-frame
0      string    \<MakerScreenFon    application/x-frame
0      string    \<MML               application/x-frame
0      string    \<Book              application/x-frame
0      string    \<Maker             application/x-frame

#----------------------------------------------------------------------
# html:  file(1) magic for HTML (HyperText Markup Language) docs
#
# from Daniel Quinlan <quinlan@yggdrasil.com>
# and Anna Shergold <anna@inext.co.uk>
#
0      string    \<!DOCTYPE\ HTML     text/html
0      string    \<!doctype\ html     text/html
0      string    \<HEAD              text/html
```

```
0       string          \<head                  text/html
0       string          \<TITLE                 text/html
0       string          \<title                 text/html
0       string          \<html                  text/html
0       string          \<HTML                  text/html
0       string          \<!--                   text/html
0       string          \<h1                    text/html
0       string          \<H1                    text/html


#--------------------------------------------------------------------
# images:  file(1) magic for image formats (see also "c-lang" for XPM
# bitmaps)
#
# originally from jef@helios.ee.lbl.gov (Jef Poskanzer),
# additions by janl@ifi.uio.no as well as others. Jan also suggested
# merging several one- and two-line files into here.
#
# XXX - byte order for GIF and TIFF fields?
# [GRR:  TIFF allows both byte orders; GIF is probably little-endian]
#

# [GRR:  what the hell is this doing in here?]
#0      string          xbtoa       btoa'd file

# PBMPLUS
#                                       PBM file
0       string          P1          image/x-portable-bitmap     7bit
#                                       PGM file
0       string          P2          image/x-portable-greymap    7bit
#                                       PPM file
0       string          P3          image/x-portable-pixmap     7bit
#                                       PBM "rawbits" file
0       string          P4          image/x-portable-bitmap
#                                       PGM "rawbits" file
0       string          P5          image/x-portable-greymap
#                                       PPM "rawbits" file
0       string          P6          image/x-portable-pixmap

# NIFF (Navy Interchange File Format, a modification of TIFF)
# [GRR:  this *must* go before TIFF]
0       string          IIN1        image/x-niff

# TIFF and friends
#                                       TIFF file, big-endian
0       string          MM          image/tiff
#                                       TIFF file, little-endian
0       string          II          image/tiff

# possible GIF replacements; none yet released!
```

```
# (Greg Roelofs, newt@uchicago.edu)
#
# GRR 950115:  this was mine ("Zip GIF"):
#                                   ZIF image (GIF+deflate alpha)
0     string        GIF94z     image/unknown
#
# GRR 950115:  this is Jeremy Wohl's Free Graphics Format (better):
#                                   FGF image (GIF+deflate beta)
0     string        FGF95a     image/unknown
#
# GRR 950115:  this is Thomas Boutell's Portable Bitmap Format proposal
# (best; not yet implemented):
#                                   PBF image (deflate compression)
0     string        PBF        image/unknown


# GIF
0     string        GIF        image/gif


# JPEG images
0     beshort       0xffd8     image/jpeg


# PC bitmaps (OS/2, Windoze BMP files)   (Greg Roelofs, newt@uchicago.edu)
0     string        BM         image/bmp
#>14  byte          12         (OS/2 1.x format)
#>14  byte          64         (OS/2 2.x format)
#>14  byte          40         (Windows 3.x format)
#0    string        IC         icon
#0    string        PI         pointer
#0    string        CI         color icon
#0    string        CP         color pointer
#0    string        BA         bitmap array


#-----------------------------------------------------------------------
# lisp:  file(1) magic for lisp programs
#
# various lisp types, from Daniel Quinlan (quinlan@yggdrasil.com)
0     string        ;;            text/plain     8bit
# Emacs 18 - this is always correct, but not very magical.
0     string        \012(         application/x-elc
# Emacs 19
0     string        ;ELC\023\000\000\000      application/x-elc


#-----------------------------------------------------------------------
# mail.news:  file(1) magic for mail and news
#
# There are tests to ascmagic.c to cope with mail and news.
0     string        Relay-Version:      message/rfc822     7bit
0     string        #!\ rnews           message/rfc822     7bit
0     string        N#!\ rnews          message/rfc822     7bit
```

```
0       string      Forward\ to        message/rfc822     7bit
0       string      Pipe\ to           message/rfc822     7bit
0       string      Return-Path:       message/rfc822     7bit
0       string      Path:              message/news       8bit
0       string      Xref:              message/news       8bit
0       string      From:              message/rfc822     7bit
0       string      Article            message/news       8bit
#-------------------------------------------------------------------
# msword: file(1) magic for MS Word files
#
# Contributor claims:
# Reversed-engineered MS Word magic numbers

0       string      \376\067\0\043     application/msword
0       string      \333\245-\0\0\0    application/msword

# disable this one because it applies also to other
# Office/OLE documents for which msword is not correct. See PR#2608.
#0    string          \320\317\021\340\241\261      application/msword
#-------------------------------------------------------------------
# printer:  file(1) magic for printer-formatted files

# PostScript
0       string      %!      application/postscript
0       string      \004%!  application/postscript

# Acrobat
# (due to clamen@cs.cmu.edu)
0       string      %PDF-      application/pdf


#-------------------------------------------------------------------
# sc:  file(1) magic for "sc" spreadsheet
#
38      string      Spreadsheet      application/x-sc


#-------------------------------------------------------------------
# tex:  file(1) magic for TeX files
#
# XXX - needs byte-endian stuff (big-endian and little-endian DVI?)
#
# From <conklin@talisman.kaleida.com>

# Although we may know the offset of certain text fields in TeX DVI
# and font files, we can't use them reliably because they are not
# zero terminated. [but we do anyway, christos]
0       string      \367\002                application/x-dvi
#0      string      \367\203                TeX generic font data
#0      string      \367\131                TeX packed font data
```

```
#0      string      \367\312                TeX virtual font data
#0      string      This\ is\ TeX,          TeX transcript text
#0      string      This\ is\ METAFONT,     METAFONT transcript text

# There is no way to detect TeX Font Metric (*.tfm) files without
# breaking them apart and reading the data.  The following patterns
# match most *.tfm files generated by METAFONT or afm2tfm.
#2      string      \000\021        TeX font metric data
#2      string      \000\022        TeX font metric data
#>34    string      >\0             (%s)

# Texinfo and GNU Info, from Daniel Quinlan (quinlan@yggdrasil.com)
#0      string      \\input\ texinfo        Texinfo source text
#0      string      This\ is\ Info\ file    GNU Info text

# correct TeX magic for Linux (and maybe more)
# from Peter Tobias (tobias@server.et-inf.fho-emden.de)
#
0       leshort     0x02f7          application/x-dvi

# RTF - Rich Text Format
0       string      {\\rtf          application/rtf


#----------------------------------------------------------------------
# animation: file(1) magic for animation/movie formats
#
# animation formats, originally from vax@ccwf.cc.utexas.edu (VaX#n8)
#                                             MPEG file
0       string      \000\000\001\263    video/mpeg
#
# The contributor claims:
#   I couldn't find a real magic number for these, however, this
#   -appears- to work. Note that it might catch other files, too,
#   so BE CAREFUL!
#
# Note that title and author appear in the two 20-byte chunks
# at decimal offsets 2 and 22, respectively, but they are XOR'ed with
# 255 (hex FF)! DL format SUCKS BIG ROCKS.
#
#             DL file version 1 , medium format 160x100, 4 images/screen)
0       byte    1       video/unknown
0       byte    2       video/unknown
```

It's unlikely you'll ever need to edit this file. If new entries are released, you can always grab a new copy of the file from the Apache download site. If you simply want to add a new entry that's been posted to an Apache news site or you've found in some other way, open the file in a text editor and add the entry at the appropriate place. Note, some entries need to precede other entries. You'll be warned if this is the case.

CHARACTER SETS

File data isn't the only thing controlled by MIME type. The character sets used for different languages are also defined by MIME type and can be called by a browser that has its preferences set to designate a particular language as its preference.

NOTE: If the server doesn't offer documents in the specified language, the browser receives the page as it exists. Pages cannot be translated on-the-fly. A page must be available in that language for one to be served.

As Internet access and availability has spread throughout the world, additional languages have been added to the MIME database. In Table 14-2, you can see a list of the languages currently identified with two-letter codes, used by HTTP to identify the preferred language of the requesting browser. Some languages also have three-letter codes, but the two-letter codes are most important for Web administrators.

Language	Two-Letter Code	Character Set (charset)
Afrikaans	af	iso-8859-1
Albanian	sq	iso-8859-1
Arabic	ar	iso-8859-6
Basque	eu	iso-8859-1
Bulgarian	bg	iso-8859-5
Byelorussian	be	iso-8859-5
Catalan	ca	iso-8859-1
Croatian	hr	iso-8859-2
Czech	cs	iso-8859-2
Danish	da	iso-8859-1
Dutch	nl	iso-8859-1
English	en	iso-8859-1
Esperanto	eo	iso-8859-3
Estonian	et	iso-8859-15
Faroese	fo	iso-8859-1
Finnish	fi	iso-8859-1

Table 14-2. Character Set and Abbreviations for Major Web Languages

Language	Two-Letter Code	Character Set (charset)
French	fr	iso-8859-1
Galician	gl	iso-8859-1
German	de	iso-8859-1
Greek	el	iso-8859-7
Hebrew	iw	iso-8859-8
Hungarian	hu	iso-8859-2
Icelandic	is	iso-8859-1
Inuit/Eskimo languages	(no code)	iso-8859-10
Irish	ga	iso-8859-1
Italian	it	iso-8859-1
Japanese	ja	iso-2022-jp
Lapp	(no code)	iso-8859-10
Latvian	lv	iso-8859-13
Lithuanian	lt	iso-8859-13
Macedonian	mk	iso-8859-5
Maltese	mt	iso-8859-3
Norwegian	no	iso-8859-1
Polish	pl	iso-8859-2
Portuguese	pt	iso-8859-1
Romanian	ro	iso-8859-2
Russian	ru	iso-8859-5
Scottish	gd	iso-8859-1
Serbian	sr	iso-8859-5
Slovak	sk	iso-8859-2
Slovenian	sl	iso-8859-2
Spanish	es	iso-8859-1
Swedish	sv	iso-8859-1
Turkish	tr	iso-8859-9
Ukrainian	uk	iso-8859-5

Table 14-2.   Character Set and Abbreviations for Major Web Languages *(continued)*

Language on the Web is usually controlled by users and browsers. Web browser preferences include the option to set a particular language as the preferred language. Whenever that browser accesses a site, it sends additional data saying "the preferred language of this browser is Turkish" (or whatever it's set as). If the server has a Turkish version of its pages, that version is then served in place of the regular page. The browser uses the preference setting to reconstruct the URL sent as a request. If the page requested is index.html, for example, the URL requested would be **http://www.your.site/index.html.tr**. Apache reads URLs from right to left, so the .tr extension would be the trigger that generates the correct file.

CAUTION: Make sure to name nondefault language files with the language extension as the final component because this is how browsers request them. If you rename them to make your directory listings look nicer, Apache could get confused and serve the wrong language or return a "404—Page Not Found" error.

Apache is configured to serve the default language of English, as you saw in Chapter 6, "Configuring and Testing Apache." If you want to use another language as your server default, simply change the DefaultLanguage setting in apache.conf or httpd-conf, depending on your Apache version. Use the appropriate two-letter code to identify the language.

NOTE: Unlike other programs, Apache uses a single "English" code to define the various English variants. Some software differentiates between American English, Australian English, British English, and Canadian English. No difference exists in the actual character set used for all four, though, so the simple "English" is sufficient.

While you're in apache.conf or httpd-conf, check the entries that define the various languages your server provides. The AddLanguage entries contain all the language-related file extensions your Apache server recognizes. If you want to add a new language to your site, simply add a new entry. AddLanguage entries take the syntax

```
AddLanguage two-letter-code file-extension
```

Thus, a new entry for French would read

```
AddLanguage fr .fr
```

Apache Server 2.0: A Beginner's Guide
Blueprints

Table of Contents

This book is intended for readers who might not have extensive experience with Internet server software, or with networks that routinely transmit data through the Internet. These blueprints contain diagrams of some of the more common configurations described in this book, from the basic function of the Apache server to more complex security-related network designs.

How Apache Works

Web pages are handled with a traditional client/server interaction. The visitor's Web browser is the client, which requests specified files from your Apache Web server.

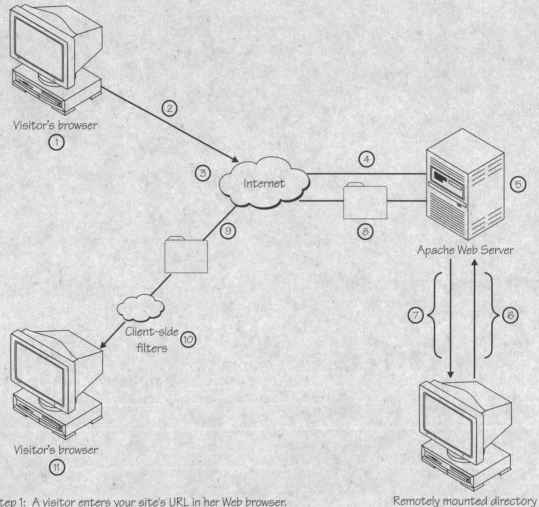

Step 1: A visitor enters your site's URL in her Web browser.

Step 2: The browser sends a request for that URL.

Step 3: The request is routed through the Internet, using the shortest path between her site and yours.

Step 4: The request arrives at your Web server.

Step 5: Apache parses the request's HTTP headers and identifies the correct file(s) to be sent.

(Optional) Step 6: Apache contacts another machine on the internal network to obtain the files.

(Optional) Step 7: The files are sent to Apache for any final review or filtering.

Step 8: Apache sends the files, with appropriate HTTP headers.

Step 9: The file is routed through the Internet, using the shortest path between the server and the requesting browser.

Step 10: The requesting browser performs any client-side filtering or actions, as determined by the HTTP headers or file type.

Step 11: The requested file displays in the visitor's browser window.

Virtual Domain Hosting

One of Apache's many features is the capability to host more than one Web site from a single server. The number of sites you can host is limited only by your bandwidth and by the traffic your combined Web sites generate. From the visitor's end, the transaction looks the same as the one shown in Blueprint 1, but it may be a more complex process on the Apache end.

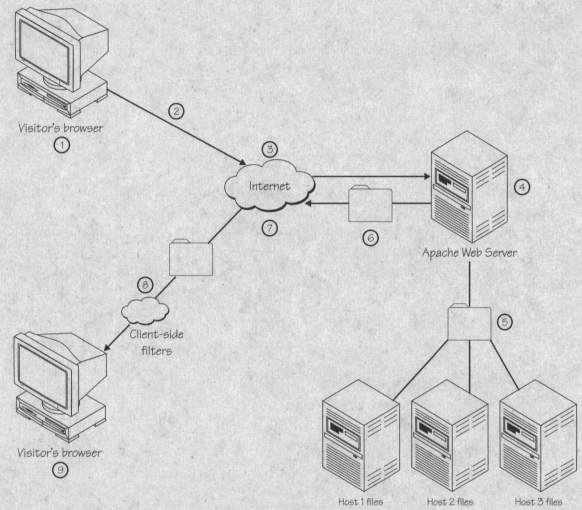

Step 1: A visitor directs his browser to one of the sites you host virtually.

Step 2: The request is routed through the Internet, using the shortest path between his site and yours.

Step 3: The request arrives at your Web server.

Step 4: Apache parses the request to determine where that site's files are located.

Step 5: Apache obtains the requested files.

Step 6: Apache sends the files, with appropriate HTTP headers.

Step 7: The files are routed through the Internet, using the shortest path between the server and the requesting browser.

Step 8: The requesting browser performs any client-side filtering or actions, as determined by the HTTP headers or file type.

Step 9: The requested file displays in the visitor's browser window.

Performance Tuning Possibilities

Asking Apache to resolve hostnames for every incoming request can be a drag on your system's performance. In this diagram, you see the extra steps required to resolve hostnames each time a request is received. Turning off this function eliminates those extra steps from the procedure and speeds up your response time.

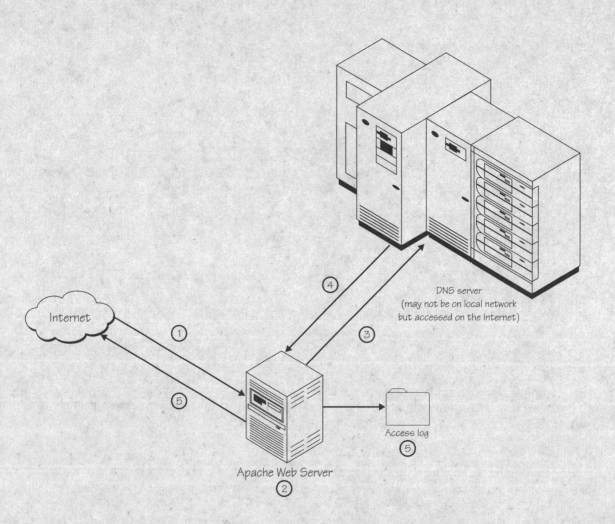

DNS server
(may not be on local network
but accessed on the Internet)

Internet

Access log
⑤

Apache Web Server
②

Step 1: An external request for one of your Web pages arrives from the Internet.

Step 2: Apache sees the IP number of the requesting browser.

Step 3: Apache contacts an external DNS server to request the text hostname associated with that IP.

Step 4: The DNS server responds with the hostname.

Step 5: Apache processes the request, while writing the hostname to the access log.

Performance Tuning Possibilities

If you serve a very popular site, or set of sites, you might need to distribute the load across several Apache servers. The mod_backhand module makes it easy to manage the load over the whole server farm and enables incoming requests to be answered as quickly as possible.

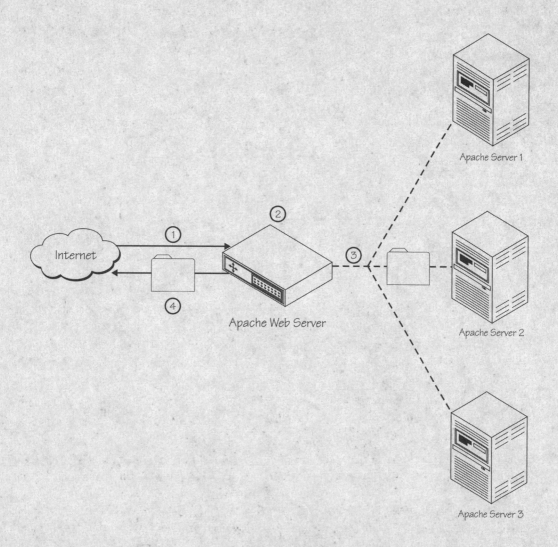

Step 1: An external request for one of your Web pages arrives from the Internet.

Step 2: The mod_backhand module on your Apache server evaluates the load conditions of the entire Apache server farm.

Step 3: mod_backhand directs the request to the server with the lightest load.

Step 4: That server provides the requested data, which is sent back to the requesting browser.

Firewalls vs. Proxies

Firewalls are an excellent way to protect your internal network from harmful data or intrusion. You can also configure a firewall to filter incoming and outgoing packets so that only certain kinds of data will be allowed into your network. Firewalls combined with proxies or with other machines, like routers, can form a sophisticated security bulwark around your network.

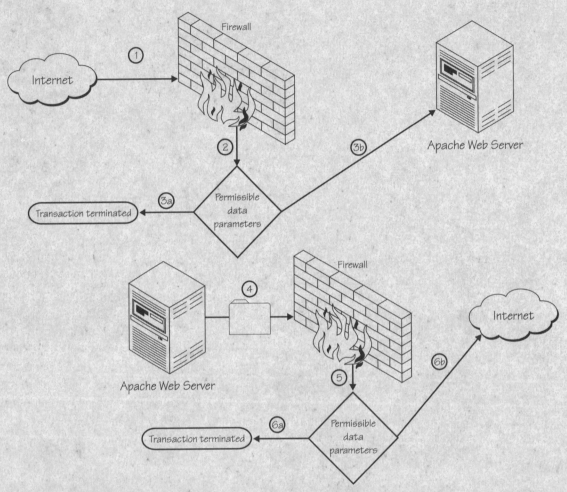

Step 1: An external request comes from the Internet, destined for a machine on your internal network.

Step 2: The request arrives at the firewall machine, which determines whether the request meets your defined parameters.

Step 3a: If the request is not permitted under the firewall's configuration, it is rejected.

Step 3b: If the request is allowed, the firewall passes the request into the internal network to the appropriate machine (in this case, the Apache server).

Step 4: Apache fulfills the request and sends the requested files back.

Step 5: The requested data arrives at the firewall machine, which determines whether the request meets defined parameters.

Step 6a: If the data is of a type not permitted to leave the network, the transaction aborts.

Step 6b: If the data is allowed, the firewall passes it back to the Internet, to be delivered to the appropriate requesting browser.

Firewalls vs. Proxies

Proxies are also a good way to protect your internal network. With a proxy, no contact is allowed between the internal network and any external networks. Rather, the proxy passes requests between the networks and poses as the intended recipient (or sender) for each transaction.

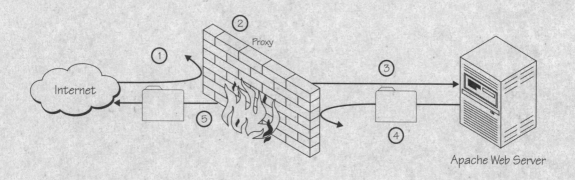

Step 1: An external request comes from the Internet, destined for a machine on your internal network.

Step 2: The request arrives at the proxy server, which determines what kind of request is being made.

Step 3: The proxy server makes a separate request for the same data to a server on the internal network, as if it were the requesting client.

Step 4: The internal server provides the requested data to the proxy server.

Step 5: The proxy server provides the requested data to the external client, as if it were the internal server itself.

SSL Transactions

Transactions using the Secure Socket Layer (SSL) protocol are simple, yet extremely secure. SSL-enabled clients and servers encrypt and decrypt the data stream as it enters and leaves, keeping the data secure as it travels through the Internet.

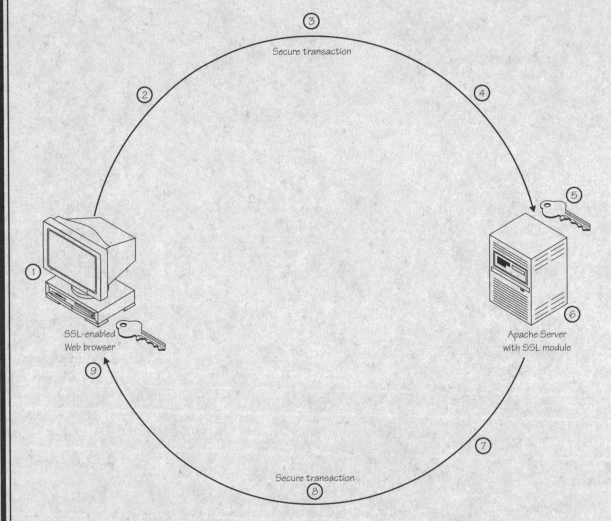

Step 1: A visitor enters a URL in her browser, using the https:// URL prefix that alerts the browser to use SSL when transmitting data.

Step 2: The browser encrypts the request as it leaves the client.

Step 3: The request travels through the Internet, secure from eavesdropping.

Step 4: The encrypted request arrives at the Apache server.

Step 5. The server's SSL module decrypts the request.

Step 6: Apache finds the requested file and serves the request.

Step 7: The SSL module encrypts the response as it leaves Apache.

Step 8: The encrypted data travels through the Internet.

Step 9: The requesting browser decrypts the response and displays the file.

SUMMARY

The different kinds of data transferred across networks, like the Internet, are defined as particular types so browsers and servers can transfer and show the data correctly. The Multimedia E-Mail Extensions (MIME) are used to define these types. Hundreds of MIME types exist, most of which are registered as official types, but some of which are vendor specific and aren't necessarily registered. Each type has its own handler—usually installed on the viewer's computer—which transforms that file into something that can be seen in the browser or as a new window on the viewer's machine. Most of the common MIME types have a unique file extension that Apache uses to locate the correct file and serve it back to the browser.

You can configure Apache to recognize new MIME types by editing its configuration files. The mod_mime module is the primary method by which Apache associates file extensions with MIME types, though the mod_mime_magic file can be used to discover a file's type by scanning the first few bits of the file to see if it matches a known pattern. You can also use Apache configuration files to define the various languages your site serves in response to browser preference data.

CHAPTER 15

CGI: The Common Gateway Interface

Way back in the misty days of old, when the Web was primarily a textual interface and there wasn't a whole lot of interactivity, Web pages were static. They didn't change and little opportunity existed for you to work with the data on a given site to find an answer or run a program. These days, the Web is a lot different. Almost every site has interactive features, ranging from guestbooks to shopping carts or stock quotes. In fact, one of the reasons for the Web explosion of the late 1990s was the rapid growth of interactive Web applications. Once people realized they could actively participate in the Web, rather than passively surf and look, the Web's popularity boomed.

While many different mechanisms bring these interactive programs to life, the majority of Web applications use the Common Gateway Interface (CGI). CGI scripts are small programs that respond to input and send their output to the requesting browser as a Web page. CGI scripts power a variety of Web features ranging from the simple—like a radio button form that sends its output to the Web administrator—to the complex—like a fully featured shopping cart linked to an online catalog. Regardless of the operating system or the browser that Web users employ, CGI scripts run cleanly. They may not be as sexy as programs written in the latest and hottest new programming technique, but CGI programs are reliable and take relatively few system resources. CGI is a technique all Web administrators should understand and use, if possible, to make their sites as powerful as they can.

TIP: Even if you don't want to program your own CGI scripts, you can download many CGI programs from Web archives. Many of these scripts are reliable workhorses and can be used on your site with little alteration.

In this chapter, you learn more about the CGI and how it works with Apache to serve browser requests with individualized information. You also discover some popular uses for CGI and the scripts behind these features, such as message boards, personalized error pages, and other handy functions. In addition, you learn about the security risks inherent in using CGI and how to minimize the chance that CGI will provide unauthorized entry to your Web site. The last section of the chapter, an introduction to writing your own CGI scripts, tells you how to debug and share your scripts with other Apache administrators.

THE COMMON GATEWAY INTERFACE

The CGI is less of a particular code specification than it is an agreement between programmers. At its most basic, CGI is—as its name implies—an interface between external programs, like browsers, and internal programs, like servers. In practice, the only servers supported by the CGI are Web servers like `httpd`, Apache, or Microsoft's Internet Information Server (IIS).

TIP: The true benefit of the CGI is that one program can be run on multiple kinds of Web servers and the output can be viewed on multiple kinds of browsers. The interface enables Web users and designers to view and provide files without needing to care about which server is running or what browser is being used, as the CGI scripts should work regardless of platform or program.

What does CGI do? It translates certain kinds of browser requests for the server and translates certain files on the server for the requesting browser. These files may be Perl or C programs, files from a database like Microsoft Access or SQL, responses to an HTML form, or several other kinds of data. What these files have in common is this: the browser and the server cannot both interpret the data in the same way. The data must be translated in some way to make it usable for both the server and the recipient.

The CGI works most closely with HTML headers included in files destined for the Web, but that the requesting browser doesn't show. Some CGI programs actually convert files into HTML, adding the appropriate headers as the file is translated. Others respond to URLs that are formatted in a particular way. That format may trigger a particular module to parse the requested file as a script instead of as a text file.

CGI AND APACHE

You needn't do much to run CGI scripts from your Apache Web server. The CGI standard has been part of Web servers since the days of the NCSA `httpd` server and it's also part of Apache. If you read the list of modules contained in the default Apache download, as described in Chapter 5, "Apache Modules," you may remember seeing a number of CGI-related modules that are part of the base installation. Table 15-1 contains a list of the base modules that are CGI-centric and their functions. Be sure these modules are installed and configured properly if you plan to serve CGI scripts on your server.

To serve CGI scripts from your Apache installation, you must add a few other pieces of software to the server machine. First, you need a program to interpret the scripts before they process input data. Depending on the type of programming language used to write the scripts, you may need a compiler or an interpreter. (See the "Programming Languages" sidebar later in this chapter for more information on languages used to write

Module	Function
mod_actions	Identifies file types that should be run as CGI scripts
mod_cgi	Enables CGI and maintains an error log of CGI-related incidents. Uses the standard core modules of Apache 1.3.*. (Don't run mod_cgi and mod_cgid at the same time.)
mod_cgid	Enables CGI and maintains an error log of CGI-related incidents. Uses the threaded core modules of Apache 2.0. (Don't run mod_cgi and mod_cgid at the same time.)
mod_env	Sets environment variables, such as software libraries, required by the CGI compiler.

Table 15-1.   CGI-Related Apache Modules

CGI programs.) If you have CGI programs written in different languages, you need an interpretation program for each language represented. In addition to a compiler or an interpreter, you need the appropriate software libraries required by each language. These *libraries* contain frequently used shortcuts and functions individual programs can call on, rather than including those functions directly in the program.

TIP: When a Unix program fails, this is often because the required libraries are missing or are somehow corrupted. Reinstalling libraries or adding them if they aren't there should be your first line of troubleshooting.

Choosing a Compiler

If you choose to use CGI scripts written by others, you'll have relatively little choice about what kind of compiler or interpreter to place on your Apache machine. You needn't go out and get compilers for every single programming language in existence, however. Only a few languages are used for the vast majority of CGI scripts. In fact, the Perl scripting language is used for most scripts so, if you choose wisely, you need install only the Perl interpreter.

TIP: Even though most CGI scripts are written in Perl, consider installing a C compiler if you have the space on the machine. CGI scripts written in C are less common, but they certainly do exist. If you find a script that does exactly what you need on your site, it's probably easier to install the appropriate compiler than to rewrite the script in another language (unless programming is your hobby anyway).

What about compilers for less-frequently used programming languages in the CGI environment? You can certainly install as many compilers as you want, but they do take up a lot of disk space. A better idea is to limit the languages used by your scripts, instead of installing seven or eight different compilers—that's space you could use for Web files or other important administrative data. If you need them, though, there's no reason not to install the compilers appropriate for your site. You might consider some of these compilers in addition to a Perl interpreter and a C compiler:

▼ **Any UNIX Shell** Some people enjoy writing CGI programs as Unix shell
  scripts. If you have the file /bin/sh on your system, then you already have
  the *Bourne Shell,* one of the more common shell environments. (The *shell
  environment* is the program that provides an interface between you and the
  operating system. Command prompts and visual displays are part of the shell,
  as are programming functions and other administrative features.) You're
  unlikely to find a lot of shell scripts in CGI archives, though. They tend to be
  written for particular situations by longtime Unix administrators who try
  to do as much as possible with shell scripting.

- **Visual Basic**   If you work with a lot of Windows programmers, they may want to write scripts for you in Visual Basic. Don't let them. The language isn't appropriate for CGI's needs. While they could use VBScript, this is useful only with Microsoft's Active Server Pages (ASP) dynamic content program run on Internet Information Server (IIS). Visual Basic and VBScript aren't particularly useful for the Unix platform or the Apache administrator.

▲   **Java**—Java isn't a good idea for CGI. You can't use Java to write CGI programs because Java has its own unique way of executing programs. If you want to get fancy and complicated, you could write a script that used CGI to invoke the Java Virtual Machine, run the Java program, and then translate the output for the requesting browser. Imagine the server overhead! Much simpler to learn Perl.

 NOTE: One of the newest scripting languages is Python. *Python* is getting a lot of press now because it's quite elegant and amazingly powerful. It's sort of a combination of the best elements of a scripted programming language and a compiled programming language. You can certainly use Python to write CGI scripts and installing a Python interpreter isn't a bad idea. If you don't know any scripted languages, however, Perl is slightly easier to learn than Python, and most CGI scripts are written in Perl anyway. Learn Perl first, and then concentrate on Python later.

Installing Perl

You may already have Perl installed on your machine. Perl is part of most recent Unix distributions. If you're running Linux or a BSD variant, you almost certainly have Perl installed. To see if you already have the correct files on your system, issue the command

```
which perl
```

at a command prompt. If Perl is already on your machine, you should see output consisting of a single directory path like /usr/bin/perl.

 TIP: If you do get a directory path, jot it down. You'll need it later.

Next, issue the command

```
perl -v
```

at the system prompt. The output tells you what version of Perl you have installed. The current version is 5.6.1 at press time, though 5.005.* versions of Perl are also quite common. You needn't upgrade as long as you have Perl 5 or higher. Earlier versions don't have all the nifty features you might need.

If Perl isn't on your machine, you get a much longer output that looks more like this:

```
/usr/bin/which: no perl in
(/bin:/usr/bin:/usr/bin/X11:/usr/local/bin:/usr/bin:/usr/X11R6/bin:
/home/kate/bin:/sbin:/usr/sbin:/home/kate/bin:/sbin:/usr/sbin:/usr/X11R6/bin:
/home/kate/bin:/sbin:/usr/sbin)
```

This indicates the various binary directories searched (some several times) for the Perl executables, which weren't found.

NOTE: If you're running Windows, chances are much slimmer that you already have Perl installed. Skip to the "Installing Perl on Windows and MacOS" sidebar, later in this section, for information about your operating system and Perl. Those who run Mac OS X already have Perl installed by default.

To install Perl, you must get the software packages. The best place to get the latest versions of the language is at **http://www.perl.com**, unsurprisingly enough. No matter what kind of Unix you're running, you should be able to find appropriate Perl packages at this site. Click the Downloads link to select the best package. As with Apache downloads, you can choose between source code and precompiled binary packages for most Unix variants. Unlike Apache, though, installing Perl binary packages is recommended. Perl is complicated and needs to be installed exactly right—the binary packages do all the work for you, unlike source code. If binaries are available for your operating system, grab them.

Install the binary packages or the source code using the directions contained in the README or INSTALL files included with the downloaded software. In general, the binary packages have a self-installer program, which may require some response from you, but runs quietly the rest of the time. The source code must be installed using the three-step `Configure` / `make` / `install` process described for Apache 2.0 source code installation in Chapter 3, "Installing Apache." You can usually accept all the default configurations in the first step because little reason exists to configure a basic Perl installation beyond the default.

CAUTION: Before you install Perl, be sure you have every other piece of software required for the installation. In particular, you should have a working C compiler and all appropriate standard C software libraries. Almost all Unix variants have these programs and libraries already installed for you.

When the installation is finished, check to make sure the program installed cleanly. Just as you did when you were checking to see whether Perl was on your system already, issue the command

```
which perl
```

at the system prompt. You should get back output that contains the directory path of the main Perl executable, such as `/usr/bin/perl`. If you don't get such output, you may need to reinstall.

Installing Perl on Windows and MacOS

If you're running Windows or MacOS and want to install Perl, you have a slightly different path to follow. Windows users can download Perl packages from **perl.com**, but you'll have better luck with the ActiveState Perl distribution. This distribution is much easier to install and work with than the Windows version of regular Perl. Get ActiveState Perl downloads at **http://www.activestate.com**. The distribution comes in precompiled binaries, so you need to install it as you would install any other Windows program. This is easy and involves little hassle. The same is true for MacPerl, a Perl distribution designed for the MacOS. Get MacPerl downloads at **http://www.macperl.com** and install the package, just as you would install any other Macintosh program.

CAUTION: If you, for some odd reason, must install Perl on a Windows machine using source code downloads, you have a more difficult task. First, be sure you have a working C compiler already installed on the machine. Borland's compiler is one of the most popular for the Windows platform. Download the source code package from **http://www.perl.com** and unZip it. Locate and read the file README.win32. You must follow all the steps in this document explicitly to get source code Perl installed correctly.

Windows users need to have certain software on your machine before you can proceed with the ActivePerl installation. Windows 2000 and Windows Me users needn't add any software, as everything you need (except a compiler) is already part of the operating system. Windows NT 4 users need these three programs:

- ▼ Service Pack 5+
- ■ Microsoft Windows Installer 1.1+ (**http://download.microsoft.com/download/platformsdk/wininst/1.1/NT4/EN-US/InstMsi.exe**)
- ▲ Internet Explorer 5+ (**http://windowsupdate.microsoft.com**)

Windows 98 users need these three programs:

- ▼ Microsoft Windows Installer 1.1+ (see previous paragraphs for download information)
- ■ Internet Explorer 5+ (see previous paragraphs for update information)
- ▲ DCOM for Windows 98 (**http://www.microsoft.com/com/resources/downloads.asp**)

Windows 95 users need these four programs:

- ▼ Microsoft Windows Installer 1.1+ (see previous paragraphs for download information
- ■ Internet Explorer 5+ (see previous paragraphs for upgrade information)
- ■ DCOM for Windows 95 (**http://www.microsoft.com/com/resources/downloads.asp**)
- ▲ MSVCRT (**ftp://ftp.microsoft.com/softlib/mslfiles/msvcrt.exe**)

Testing Perl Scripts

Once Perl is installed and you've checked to make certain it runs properly, you can use it in several ways even if you don't want to learn how to program in the language. Most CGI scripts you download are probably written in Perl, so you can use the built-in interpreter to translate the programs on-the-fly as they're sent from your Web server.

TIP: You can also download many other Perl programs from various software archives. Many of these programs are simply short administrative shell scripts that automate some routine task. These scripts can be quite helpful and save you a lot of time, especially if you don't have a good handle on shell scripting or if you simply don't have space in your day to program. Be careful to make any configurations needed for your particular network or machine before you run the script. Never run scripts you haven't looked through first.

Before you put Perl CGI programs on your Apache machine and let them go out to an unsuspecting public, though, you should test the scripts to be sure they work. CGI programs are all executable files anyway, so you can run them just as you would run any other Unix program or script. To test a CGI script before using it on your site, simply type the program's name by itself at a command prompt. For example, if the program is called `messageboard`, issue the command

```
messageboard
```

at the prompt. The program should execute cleanly. Most downloaded scripts don't work perfectly right out of the bag, however, and you'll have to do some basic configuration first. See the following section, "Obtaining CGI Scripts," for more information on script configuration and troubleshooting.

NOTE: If you download a Perl script and you already have Perl installed, the script should run with only its name used as a command. If you download a script written in C or in another compiled language, though, you'll have to compile the script before you can run it. Follow the directions included with your C compiler.

OBTAINING CGI SCRIPTS

If you don't want to write your own CGI scripts, you must get them from somewhere. Luckily, CGI script archives are almost as common as regular Unix software archives, so you have several choices. Note, some scripts may appear in multiple script archives, either because the developer submitted her work to several places or because the script is so popular it gets uploaded by its users to different archives, so it's as widely distributed as possible.

The kinds of scripts contained in most CGI archives are wildly varied. You can find a ton of scripts for the everyday features that many Web administrators like to have: guestbooks, message boards, databases and database interpreters, and Web forms of various sorts. You can also find extremely specialized scripts that may only be useful for the site of the guy who wrote it, or scripts so general they don't seem to have much function at all. Both of these latter types are also useful, though more as examples for your own programming than as something you might want to run on your own server.

TIP: If you're teaching yourself to program CGI, looking at existing scripts is one good way to study. You can see how other people set up a given function and how well—or not—the resulting script works. Looking at multiple scripts that do the same thing is a great way to learn that Unix programming isn't always a case of "the right way" to do something, but a case of personal style and, in the best cases, elegance and flair.

So how do you find these helpful repositories? Plug "CGI script" into your favorite search engine and you'll get a slew of sites that offer a few CGI scripts or a ton of them. When you're just starting out with CGI, concentrating on the really big archives is best. These archives have a lot of turnover and some enable users to rate the scripts they've downloaded. Plus, the big archives tend to get the newest scripts and keep copies of old-but-good programs around as well.

NOTE: Read the documentation that accompanies any script you download. Some scripts require you to place a note on your site giving credit to the script author, while others let you use the scripts quietly and without attribution. Some scripts are shareware (pay a small fee) or have other payment requirements. Check out the rules before you install. If you can't live with the requirements, don't use the software.

Here are some of the more popular CGI script archive sites:

▼   **http://www.worldwidemart.com/scripts**   Matt's Script Archive is part of a larger site that offers a wide range of Web programs and features. Most of the scripts here are written by the site's host, Matt Wright. Matt's software runs on thousands of Web sites. This may not be the most sophisticated software, but it's a good place to start and the stuff usually works right away.

■   **http://www.cgi-resources.com**   If you're eager to learn more about CGI programming in general or to download scripts from the simple to the complicated, the CGI Resources site is a good place to start. You can run most of the scripts without attribution and a good assortment of functions is here.

■   **http://www.scriptsearch.com**   The folks at ScriptSearch claim they have the world's largest archive of scripts: CGI, shell, and other types. Whether this is true or not, they certainly have a whole bunch of them, sorted by type and function. You can use this site as one-stop shopping for Web scripts, administrative scripts, and any other kind of script for your network.

▲   **ftp://ftp.ncsa.uiuc.edu/Web/httpd/Unix/ncsa_httpd/cgi/**   This is the script archive maintained by NCSA, the National Center for Supercomputing Applications. NCSA invented the first Web server, `httpd`, and manages online resources for a number of Web topics. This isn't the biggest archive, but you can find tried-and-true scripts here, as well as others submitted by authors who like the idea of having their scripts living at NCSA. (Whether the archive is currently being maintained is unclear, however.)

Once you find a script you like, download it. Be sure to get the appropriate format for your operating system. Some scripts offer different variations for different Unices, while others have a single Unix code version. Place the download in the `cgi-bin` directory under your main Apache directory and unpack it using `tar` and `gzip` on a Unix platform or the appropriate unpacking software for your operating system.

Open the script in a text editor (see Appendix B, "Using a Unix Text Editor," for help). Make sure the first line of the script—if it's a Perl script—points to the appropriate directory on your system. This is where you need the directory path that appeared when you tested your system for Perl earlier. If this isn't right, change the directory path to the correct location. You may need to make other alterations to the script, placing URLs for your domain in the proper place and specifying log files and other administrative details. The script should have a README file and possibly an INSTALL file, which tells you the minimum configurations that must be made before you can run the script.

When you make all the appropriate configurations, save the file and exit the text editor. Be sure all the script's files are in the proper locations: CGI in the `cgi-bin` directory and HTML in the appropriate directories of your Web server. Once everything's configured and situated properly, you can test the file. Simply call up the script in a Web browser and see whether it works. The README and INSTALL files should offer additional troubleshooting tips specific to the script you installed.

USES FOR CGI ON YOUR SITE

While you can use CGI for a number of functions on your site, the most popular reason to use CGI is usually for interaction among the people who visit your pages. These people may want to interact with each other, through message boards related to your site's topic, or may want to leave messages for you (or your company) in a guestbook. You can also use CGI to serve pages and data from a database to your visitors, depending on the pages they request, rather than keeping each page in static form on your site. Finally, you can use CGI to interact with the visitors by creating individualized error pages that appear when something goes wrong, whether it's a server error or a user error, such as typing the wrong URL or misspelling filenames.

When you search CGI script archives for new programs, you find a large number of files in the archive are devoted to these programs that encourage interaction and involvement among visitors to a given site. In this section of the chapter, you learn a bit more about some of these Web tools. If you read about something that interests you, download a few different versions from an archive. Different scripts offer a different "look and feel" in a browser, as well as varying in administrative or configuration difficulty.

NOTE: CGI and related technologies have been a big part of the "Web explosion" in the past few years. In the early days, the Web wasn't interactive—visitors to the same page had no real way to have a conversation. Now, Web boards are more numerous than USENET news groups and, by some reckonings, are more popular as well. A number of professionally developed programs offer a sophisticated interface for these user-oriented functions. In this chapter, we discuss the low-tech and freely available versions, but know the elaborate (and often expensive) versions use much of the same technology.

Forms

Working with Web forms is the best way to learn how CGI actually works. Different components of forms use CGI—HTML pages that provide the framework and page formatting around the CGI script—and they use CGI to pass input to the server and output back to the requesting browser. In this section of the chapter, you learn the mechanics of each component and the basic concepts behind CGI—the GET and POST HTTP headers.

HTML Pages

To create the HTML page that will show your form to site visitors, you need to make sure the <FORM> tag is placed at the top of the file. This tag indicates to HTTP that the data returned from this page should be parsed with CGI. Throughout the page, every time you want to receive data from the person filling out the form, you apply an ACTION attribute to those segments. Other attributes you should include in the form are METHOD, ENCTYPE, and TARGET, as well as the <INPUT> tag, which actually creates the various form fields. These tags and attributes all influence how the data is encoded and how it will be displayed on the page itself.

You can pick from a variety of page elements to help build the form. Many forms use radio buttons and check boxes to give users the option of choosing from several selections. Radio buttons require one answer, while check boxes permit multiple answers. Text entry fields enable users to enter character strings, such as names or e-mail addresses. Depending on the size of the text entry field, they may even be able to write several pages of input (just be sure you're aware of your maximum buffer size, as described in "CGI and Security," later in the chapter). Regardless of how you design the form, it needn't be boxy and unattractive. You can include form elements on an HTML page, and still keep it elegant and usable.

TIP: Any good HTML design book contains information on designing forms. One such book is *HTML: A Beginner's Guide*, by Wendy Willard (Osborne/McGraw-Hill, 2000).

CGI and Forms

Once you build an HTML form, how does it work? To understand this, first you must understand how a Web server handles incoming and outgoing data. An HTTP server understands three request types: GET, POST, and HEAD. A browser request is a GET request, as are many other kinds of data transfer on a Web server. Most CGI forms use GET as their primary input method. Some CGI forms use a POST request because it creates more elegant URLs than those generated with GET. (HEAD requests identify data that will be sent as an HTTP header.) When you begin to build the CGI that works with your form, you must choose between the GET and POST methods.

When a person fills in a form that uses GET requests, the information provided in the form is returned to the server in the URL. That is, everything the person entered is passed into a new URL in a new browser request. The server, through the mod_cgi module and others, parses that URL to strip the input data and process it in whatever manner is prescribed. Some administrators feel using GET requests opens a security hole because the URL contains everything the respondent has entered. Others think GET URLs are ugly and inelegant. The fact remains, though, writing CGI that uses GET is easy, and most CGI on the Web uses that request method. Forms that use the POST method encode all the respondent's data into a new browser request, but the data may not be included in the URL. (Usually, the URL contains the data whether or not GET is used, but some sophisticated CGI constructs new URLs that don't contain any response information.)

Which method should you choose? It doesn't really matter. If you run Perl CGI scripts, they'll be interpreted with the CGI.pm library, which doesn't care which request method was used. For scripts called by clicking a hyperlink, GET must be used. If the form requires or allows lengthy input—like a message board—POST gets around character limitations on URLs imposed by some browsers. Any CGI reference gives you a long list of limitations on both methods, but many of those limits don't apply to garden-variety CGI forms or scripts.

CAUTION: If you don't want data-rich URLs to be captured in your Apache Web logs, use the POST method. This is especially important if you use a Web form for logins and passwords. Never allow passwords to be logged in plain text.

If you're downloading CGI scripts to use with your own forms and you edit them to contain references to your particular form, you probably needn't worry about the request method used. However, many people learn CGI programming because they can't get a downloaded script to work with their home-grown forms. CGI form scripting is the easiest way to get started with the language. If you have some knowledge of a programming language already, you're well on your way to writing sophisticated and unique forms for your site.

Databases

The most exciting use of CGI, however, is to integrate data stored in a database with your Web site. You can use a flat database, which merely stores information in a single file, or you can use a relational database, which stores data in tables with cell addresses. Both types of database can contain relatively few entries or thousands upon thousands of entries. If you have a CGI script that knows how to work with your database and how to locate data within it, you have a way to serve that information to people visiting your Web site. Add a CGI form that formats the data in HTML as it passes through a filter and you expand the amount of information available on your site from a small array of artistically designed static HTML files to as much data as you have stored in the database.

NOTE: The interface between CGI and databases is a complex one. If you're interested in learning more about this field, consider taking a course in SQL, the Standardized Query Language.

Flat Databases

Flat databases store individual records in plain-text files, with each component of the record separated by a delimiter character. The *delimiter character* is usually a standard punctuation mark, selected because it probably won't appear as part of one of the records. For example, the colon and question marks are often used as delimiters in flat databases. While flat databases are easy to construct, retrieving data from them is less easy. The retrieving program must know how to read the individual records to obtain the desired data and return it to the requester.

CGI scripts can be used to retrieve data from flat databases and provide that data to a requesting browser. The script contains a series of actions that search the database file, identify appropriate information, and return that information. CGI scripts that work with flat databases must also have the capability to *lock* the database file. Because the entire file may take some time to process, especially if it's large, the script must have sole access to the file. If another script attempts to sort the file while the first search is going on, both scripts are likely to crash.

While some situations occur where a flat database is the best way of retrieving information for visitors to your Web site, if you have a lot of data, better options exist. Relational databases, described in the next section, are much faster and take far less system overhead while scripts search for specified data. Flat databases are still extremely useful, however, for small database files and for particular types of data. The message board programs described later in the chapter use flat databases to store the posts made by individual visitors. Because of the way in which message board scripts handle these posts, a flat database meets the data storage needs without unnecessary disk use.

Relational Databases

If you have a vast amount of information you want to share with your users, you probably already have it stored in a relational database. The databases sold today are all relational, whether they're marketed by Microsoft, Oracle, Sybase, or other major software companies. Relational databases store individual data units in tables, with identifying marks on each unit so it can be retrieved quickly and precisely at a later time. Although relational databases are far more complex than the simple plain-text flat database, searches are much faster, and it's possible to do a lot more with the data stored in a relational database.

CGI scripts that work with relational databases do so through the Structured Query Language (SQL), which is a standardized language capable of making queries to any relational database formatted to understand SQL. The major databases work with SQL queries seamlessly. You may find some CGI scripts that work reasonably well, regardless of the brand name on the database they're searching. SQL is an immensely complicated language, though, and no software company has yet released a database that is 100 percent standards-compliant. This means you must know enough about SQL—or find someone who does—to tinker with downloaded CGI scripts until they work appropriately with whatever database is used on your site.

NOTE: If you're hoping to use an internal database as the source for Web data, but the database is either quite old or was written explicitly for your company, you may run into some trouble. Relational databases that don't conform—at least in the major part—to the SQL standard can cause a lot of trouble when other programs try to interact with the database. If at all possible, your company should upgrade to a current-generation SQL database. The benefits will be felt by many in the company, not only by you and your CGI scripts.

Message Boards

Message boards are an amazingly popular feature on many Web pages. Message board scripts are quite complex and certainly not for the beginner CGI programmer, but many possibilities exist in the CGI script archives. A *message board* is simply a sophisticated version of a bulletin board. Users come and make posts, and other users reply to those posts or start new topic threads of their own. Message boards are a more visually pleasing version of text-based newsgroups. Some message-board software even permits posters to use animations and sound files in their posts, though doing so can create some server load.

Most message-board software is actually a combination of several scripts that interact each time a post is made to the board. The number of scripts depends on how many features the message board offers. All boards require at least two scripts: one to manage and display a list of message topics, and another to handle new messages. If the board *threads* message topics, keeping messages with the same topic together, a third script will likely be necessary. All scripts rely on a graphical form, with particular tags associated with the various fields on the form. For example, the $topic tag might be associated with the character string entered into the Web form field labeled TOPIC, and then that string is parsed according to the rules defined for topics in the CGI script.

Adding a CGI-based message board to your site is one way to encourage repeat visits and increase the stickiness of your Web site. (The *stickier* your site, the longer an individual visitor remains before leaving for another site. Sticky is good.) Real user communities can develop around Web message boards, but the community can be fickle. If your software acts up frequently or it simply doesn't offer the range of features users are accustomed to finding at other sites, you might realize the message board isn't improving site retention and hit count as much as you thought it would. In that case, consider keeping the message board function, but changing the software.

A number of CGI message board programs are available that are far more sophisticated than what the average amateur CGI programmer can generate. Many of them are available in CGI archives, but some of them are commercial programs that offer technical assistance and reliability for a price. One of the most popular commercial boards is the Ultimate Bulletin Board (UBB). UBB boards can run on almost any platform and with almost any Web server. Many UBB boards run happily with Apache and Unix, Apache and Windows, and Apache and MacOS X. You do have to pay for the UBB software, but it's highly customizable and offers a huge amount of flexibility for the Web administrator. UBB also has the reputation of being responsive to its customers and answers a lot of questions on its own Web boards.

TIP: Find out more about UBB, and look at a UBB board in action, at the Ultimate Bulletin Board Web site: **http://www.infopop.com/business/business_ubb.html**.

Customized Error Pages

When you installed and configured Apache, you enabled a certain set of pages that show up whenever someone makes an error in requesting a page from your site. These pages also come into play when your server makes a mistake. While the default error pages are serviceable, they're kind of boring, being simply text on a white background with a big black error code. The default error pages also don't contain links back to your main site, so a frustrated visitor might simply go elsewhere rather than return to the site and try again to find the correct page. Many administrators choose to supply more customized pages when an error occurs, so visitors can be kept on the site longer and get more information about errors. Table 15-2 shows some of the common error codes your visitors might encounter.

These custom error pages can be either HTML files or CGI scripts. While HTML files are easy to build, they have one drawback: no matter what the visitor has done to generate that particular error code, such as a "404—Page Not Found" error, the same error page will display. With CGI error pages, however, you can serve documents that reflect the kind of mistake the visitor made, which then enables him to make a better choice and go elsewhere on your site. At the very least, you can use CGI error pages to generate a

Code	Meaning
400	Bad Request—either the page requested doesn't exist or the person requesting the file hasn't been authorized to view it.
401	Unauthorized—the requesting browser hasn't provided required encrypted authorization data, so access is denied.
403	Forbidden—the user hasn't entered a password, so access is denied.
404	Not Found—the Web server can't find or identify the requested file.
500	Internal Error—Apache has experienced a software error and can't complete the request.
501	Not Implemented—this installation of Apache doesn't provide the feature being requested (often with new technologies or dynamic content requests).
502	Service Overloaded—too many browsers are requesting information from the server, so access is denied.
503	Gateway Time-Out—the connection between the requesting browser and the server has expired because too much time has elapsed.

Table 15-2.   Common HTTP Error Codes

page that contains a link back to the most recent page visited on your site by that browser. You can get far more complicated with error pages, as well. For example, you could write a script that took the mistaken URL, parsed it, and returned several possible pages on your site that might fit the viewer's needs.

TIP: How does Apache know what kind of error has been made, to serve the proper page? When a missing page is requested, Apache generates several environment variables that define the incorrect URL, the form of the browser request, and the status that would have resulted if the request had been successful. Apache takes the data from these variables and generates the appropriate error code and linked page.

You can find some custom error page scripts in the CGI archives previously mentioned. Once you download and configure the scripts for your particular site, you must enable them in your Apache configuration. Open the `.htaccess` file, found in your main Apache directory, in a Unix text editor. Find the line beginning with `ErrorDocument`. This line uses the syntax

```
ErrorDocument error-code document-location
```

You have four choices for the document location: print a message provided by Apache (default), print a specified message that you write, redirect to a local document, or redirect offsite. If you are using CGI-generated error pages, you'll redirect to a local document. Thus, for a "404—Page Not Found" error, you might edit the `ErrorDocument` entry to read

```
ErrorDocument 404 /cgi-bin/404_errorpage.cgi
```

Now, when a 404 error occurs, Apache redirects the browser request to the CGI script `404_errorpage.cgi`, which lives in the `cgi-bin` subdirectory of your main Apache directory. Save the file and exit the text editor.

NOTE: Be sure you have overridden the `FileInfo` variable in your Apache configuration files. Apache won't call `.htaccess` unless it knows you want to override that variable.

CGI AND SECURITY

Although many, many reasons exist to use CGI scripts on your Web site, there's one extremely good reason to be wary. CGI is notorious for being the gateway to Web site abuse. This is because people don't generally test CGI scripts as rigorously as they test other software on the server. After all, a CGI script can be only a few lines long, right? How much damage can be done in a few lines? An awful lot, unfortunately. Exploiting CGI is one of the first lines of attack any Web cracker tries. If you rely on scripts you downloaded from Web archives, you have no guarantee they are either secure or well programmed. Be especially careful if you don't write your own CGI scripts.

CAUTION: Here's a worst-case scenario that, unfortunately, does occur. Imagine you are of a malicious mind and you're a pretty good programmer. You can write a useful CGI script that happens to contain a security hole, which you know how to exploit. You upload your script to all the big archives and watch as it becomes popular (because you took care to write a good script in the first place). Now, all you need to do is figure out what sites are using your script—a good search engine can help here—and your free time is occupied for days on end with a long list of sites you can break into. Scary? Yes! Learn enough about how scripts are written to see gaping security holes before you install anything.

Of course, the first thing you need to do is to ensure your own site and server are as secure as possible. The various approaches outlined in Part V, "Security and Apache," are the best place to start. Make sure your own house is tight and well guarded before you introduce any exploitable items like scripts. Remember, a CGI script is a program that runs on *your* machine. You give external visitors the right to run programs on your server when you offer scripts. In itself, this isn't the most secure situation. The tradeoff is reasonable, though, because CGI scripts tend to be small and don't take much system resource overhead, and scripts make using your site easier. Just be aware of the security issue and enforce your existing security policies before you introduce scripts into the mix.

One way to manage CGI scripts in a secure manner is to make sure all CGI scripts running on your site are housed in the same directory. Traditionally, this is the `cgi-bin` subdirectory kept in your standard Apache directory, or `apache/cgi-bin`. The `cgi-bin` directory is the first place Apache looks when it's alerted a CGI script is needed. Apache knows everything in that directory should be executed as a program, instead of sent as raw text to the requesting browser. Maintain a server policy that all CGI must be kept in the appropriate directory and enforce it.

CAUTION: No matter how intuitive it seems to keep CGI scripts in different folders near the HTML pages they work with, don't do it. Keep them in the `cgi-bin` directory where you can control file and directory permissions, and where Apache won't be forced to guess whether a particular file is an executable.

Another way in which CGI scripts can be compromised is when a user's input causes a buffer overflow. The *buffer* is the allocated amount of memory for user input. For example, when you write a script for a guestbook, you might allocate 2,048 bytes of memory for each guestbook entry. If someone writes an entry longer than 2,048 bytes, the buffer overflows because no more room exists for the additional data. Buffer overflows aren't security risks in and of themselves, but they do usually cause the program to fail completely. Depending on how the program is written, a crashed script can leave some holes open, which a savvy cracker can easily exploit. If you're writing your own scripts, don't allocate hard buffers if possible. Instead, allocate memory dynamically, so the number of bytes needed fluctuates with the size of the entry.

NOTE: Buffer overflows are far more common in CGI scripts written in C, C++, or some other compiled language. They aren't as frequently found in Perl or Python scripts. You needn't avoid compiled scripts, but you should be aware of the buffer overflow issue.

The last thing to be aware of is something that can't be helped. When CGI scripts run, they use the HTTP functions GET and POST. These functions determine how data is sent to the server for input into the script. Because of the way GET works, the data being sent is encoded into the URL of the resulting CGI output. If you ever looked at the URL window in your browser as you use a CGI script (perhaps a user form or a message board), you probably saw a long string of characters containing your responses to the questions or the title of the post you're reading. This is how GET handles data. (POST is more opaque, but it's simple to capture the script and determine how to exploit it.) You can't change how CGI transfers data, but be aware that a determined user with basic knowledge of your site and how GET works can construct a new URL that might give her access to things she shouldn't be able to see. It's a good argument for keeping your Web files on a separate machine apart from the main network administrative data.

Don't let security fears keep you from running CGI scripts. They are immensely useful and add a great deal to the user experience on your site. You do need to be aware that CGI is often an overlooked part of site design, however, and can be exploited if it's not properly constructed or maintained. Keep an eye on what's running on your site and how it operates. Learn enough programming to scan the scripts and see if anything looks out of place. And, be wary of scripts you downloaded from public archives until you review them for security measures.

WRITING YOUR OWN CGI SCRIPTS

Like many Web administrators, you may grow frustrated with the scripts available in Web script archives. You might think the scripts need too much configuration to do what you want them to do or you might be irritated with the security risks each script you download seems to contain. If you find yourself spending a lot of time working with each script and wishing you could simply write your own, you're ripe to learn a new skill.

Script writing is programming, but scripts are generally short, have a limited number of functions, and require less skill than long programs that run to many megabytes of code. Scripting is a good way to get your feet wet in programming and it's a useful skill that can help you in system administration, as well as in Web administration. (Plus, knowing how to script looks good on your resume when it's time to change jobs.)

When you decide to learn scripting, you need to pick a language to learn. The sidebar "Programming Languages" offers some options and describes the possible choices. If you're going to focus your programming efforts on CGI scripts, it's best to learn Perl first because you'll have the widest range of examples to download and review from the various archives. Programming in Perl—and the niceties of writing CGI scripts—are beyond the scope of this book, but there are a number of good resources available in your local bookstore's computer section. Find a good introductory book for each topic and work through them. You don't need a vast array of skills to start writing usable scripts and each succeeding script hones your skills until you feel fully competent as a scripter.

Programming Languages

When you decide to write your own CGI scripts, you must first decide what programming language you'll use to write them. A number of choices are out there and, depending on your previous experience with programming, the decision can seem rather overwhelming. Only a few languages used in the vast majority of CGI scripts are found on the Web, however, so the choice needn't be as difficult as it may seem. And, if you choose the right language, neither does the programming itself.

Before you pick the language you're going to use, you need to decide whether you want to use a compiled language or a scripted language. *Compiled languages*, like the traditional programming languages C and C++, must be compiled before you can run programs written with them. The compiling process is identical to the process used in installing Apache from source code. The written program is run through a compiler and turned into machine-executable binary code. *Scripted languages*, however, don't require a compiler. Instead, you use a known syntax and set of commands to write your programs, which are then run directly on the machine using particular software libraries to execute the scripted action. Advantages exist to both, but CGI scripts tend to be small, so scripts written in compiled languages may be a bit unwieldy and time-consuming.

TIP: If you don't already have a strong background in compiled language programming, pick a scripted language to learn first. The learning curve is shorter and you'll be programming faster and adding new features to your site.

If you're picking a language out of a hat so you can learn it and learn to program CGI scripts, pick Perl. Earlier in this chapter, I recommended you install the Perl compiler and libraries on your Apache server machine, so you can serve CGI scripts from script archives. Because the vast majority of CGI scripts are written in Perl anyway, why not choose it as the language you'll learn for CGI projects? Perl is easy to learn. You can teach yourself with one of a number of excellent Perl resource books. Look for reviews and online information at **www.perl.com**. The CGI scripts in this chapter are all written in Perl.

If you don't want to learn a scripting language, try the C programming language. C is one of the grand old programming languages and is widely used in Unix programming. CGI scripts written in C run quickly because they've already been compiled and are sitting on your server as executable binaries. Scripting languages, however, must be interpreted (compiled) each time they're run. Thus, C CGI programs require less server overhead and can make your server respond more quickly. You can use C to write all sorts of programs and it's definitely a useful skill, but C takes a lot longer to learn than Perl. Take your time and programming skills into consideration when you begin to think about learning a new language.

TIP: Perl's a hot topic these days, so lots of beginning Perl books are on the market. The granddaddy Perl books are those written by Larry Wall and Tom Christensen for O'Reilly & Associates: *Learning Perl* and *Programming Perl*. If you get involved in the Perl community, you'll be expected to own and know these books. (*Learning Perl* is known as "the llama book" and *Programming Perl* as "the camel book" because of O'Reilly's distinctive cover designs. The animal names are used more frequently than the actual book titles.)

SUMMARY

One of the most popular functions on many Web pages are features and programs that run using the Common Gateway Interface (CGI). CGI scripts use a standardized method of dealing with data that enables site visitors to interact with the site itself or with other visitors. CGI translates browser requests encoded in particular ways, often taking the information in the URL as the data to feed a program that parses the information and returns a customized page to the requesting browser.

Many kinds of CGI programs exist and you can download thousands of CGI scripts from online script archives. Scripts range from popular site features like guestbooks and message boards to information-gathering tools like forms. You can also use CGI to customize some of the default settings in your Apache installation. Perhaps the most powerful use of CGI, however, is in providing information stored in a database to site visitors, according to their interests. CGI can work either with plain-text flat databases or with the most sophisticated relational databases on the market. Adding a database and CGI scripts to your site expands the amount of information available through your pages, without requiring countless hours of HTML design and configuration.

CGI scripts are written in traditional programming languages. You can use either compiled languages like C and C++, or scripted languages like Perl and Python. The vast majority of existing CGI scripts are written in Perl or C, though, and, of those, most are written in Perl. So, if you're interested in writing your own CGI—or even if you're only going to run scripts downloaded from Web archives—you need to have a Perl interpreter and a C compiler installed on your system and available to the CGI modules.

CHAPTER 16

Image Maps

As the Web developed and visual presentation became more important, textual navigation inevitably came to be seen as boring and old-fashioned. After all, simple text links had been part of Web pages since the first days of HTML, and you can only do so much with text appearance and color. Web designers began to use images as clickable links, giving the entire image a reference tag that turned it into an active part of the page.

Individual images have many of the same limitations as text links, though. You're still limited to one link per image, and the images must be quite small if more than one of them appears on a page. As the HTML standard developed and as Web servers became more sophisticated, a new form of image-based navigation was born: the image map.

An *image map* is a graphical file that contains at least one link, though most image maps contain multiple links and serve as the main navigation tool for a given page or site. The beauty of image maps is that individual links may not be delineated in the file. Just by looking at it, you can't tell what's a working link and what's simply attractive to look at. In many image maps, certain elements of the graphic function as links; while in others, the links are hidden and must be searched out.

TIP: If you're confronted with an image map where you can't find the links, roll your mouse cursor across the image. Do this methodically, from side to side. The cursor should change shape when it passes over a link. If the map was designed well, the image changes with a rollover to identify the link. If the map doesn't change, look in the corner of your Web browser to see the actual URL the link's connected to.

While image maps are a leap forward in Web design, they do bring problems along with their flexibility and attractiveness. For those who use adaptive browsers or text-only browsers, an image map can be a stumbling block preventing further exploration of the site. For those who have bad fine motor control, using a densely packed image map can be an exercise in frustration. Finally, for those who dislike fussing around with a site's graphic design and prefer to get straight to the content, an image map could seem a waste of time. While all of these are valid points, ways exist to incorporate both sound navigation and image maps into a well-designed and navigable site.

This chapter introduces image maps from three perspectives. First, you learn about the construction of image maps and how they're built. Even if you never plan to design a single component of the pages you serve, you should know how image maps work, so you can administer them properly on your site. Next, you learn about the mod_imap module, which Apache uses to serve image maps correctly when they're requested by a visitor. mod_imap is reasonably straightforward, though particular configurations exist that you can make to the module to serve your maps most efficiently. Finally, you learn about accessibility and navigability, and whether a site can be both accessible and visually appealing.

NOTE: You might feel image maps have little place in a book about Web server administration, and it's true they aren't precisely an Apache topic. Image maps are a fact of Web design, though, and it's certainly an administrative duty to make sure all files are served properly on your site, as well as to make sure nobody is excluded from visiting the sites on the server.

WEB NAVIGATION

The Web is built on navigation. Without a method of moving from page to page and site to site, the Web wouldn't be what it is. For visitors to move easily through a site and to find the information they're seeking, the site needs navigation tools that are easy to understand and simple to use. A site with complicated navigation may drive visitors away, because finding a completely different Web site on the same topic is often easier than fighting a badly designed site navigation setup.

Much Web navigation hasn't changed since the early days of HTML. Simple text links were initially the only navigation tools Web designers and users had, and links were clearly designated: usually, links were a different color (bright blue, back in the early days) and underlined. While browsers can now be configured to change the colors for links, both clicked and unclicked, and can even remove the underline, textual navigation is still a large part of many Web sites' design strategy.

Textual navigation has its place no matter how sophisticated and visually appealing a site's design may be. As you'll read in the "Maintaining Accessibility" section of this chapter, textual navigation provides needed hooks for various browsers and new technologies that provide a low-image interface to Web pages. In some ways, the newest advances in Web technology have pushed site design back to the early days. You can have a site that incorporates the latest in both design and technology, however, and still appeals to the eye as well as to the brain.

TIP: Although image maps are a completely different technique of Web page construction than cascading style sheets, using style sheets on your site can make your site as accessible as possible to the widest range of visitors. See Chapter 17, "Using Apache to Save Time—SSI and CSS," for more information on this additional Web design tool.

In addition to the plain-text links found on almost every Web site in the world, several types of nontextual Web navigation exist and you might find all of them incorporated into the pages you serve. Simple graphic images, such as arrows or representative images like pens (for MailTo links), are common, where the entire image is an active link. Most sites use some form of this nontext navigation, whether it's in a Next button or an image of the corporate logo that serves as a link back to the `index.html` page.

Some sites take the graphic image navigation technique to the extreme, presenting only a page of icons—each an active link—but no text. Sites like this need to provide ALT text for each of those icons, so the links are clear in a nongraphical browser. If ALT text isn't provided, a browser like lynx might display the following:

```
[flower.jpg]
[smiley.jpg]
[doggy.gif]
[purpleflower.gif]
[cube.jpg]
```

The filenames give no clue to what the link might actually be. With ALT text, though, lynx might display something more like this:

```
Photos of my garden
Photos of my family
Photos of my dogs
Daily journal
Guestbook
```

Both displays show the five images as clickable links, but only the second display actually explains what those links represent.

Image maps are simply a more sophisticated version of the simple graphical navigation images, encompassing many links into one image. As with any visual component, image maps can be parsed by text-only or adaptive browsers as long as they're configured properly. Building image maps is relatively easy and they're an effective method of nontext navigation. Image maps are popular for a reason: they look good, and, if designed well, they're simple to use. A judicious blend of textual and nontext navigation can make your sites memorable and functional, which increases the likelihood of return visitors and added stickiness.

CONSTRUCTING IMAGE MAPS

Building an image map can be complicated or it can be amazingly easy. This all boils down to the software you're using to design your Web pages. In most modern page design programs, such as Macromedia's Dreamweaver or Adobe's GoLive, image-map construction is a feature that comes with its own tools and helpful guidance. In Dreamweaver, for example, you can create a sophisticated image map with the correct HTML placed in the page code in less than ten minutes. As with most page design software, you need never read the code produced by your mouse and keystroke activity.

Because image-map construction techniques vary dramatically from program to program, however, this section of the chapter describes only the "hard way" of building image maps: plain old HTML coding. It's good to know how image maps are built with HTML, in the off chance that you have to edit one of your site pages in a text editor rather than in a page design program.

TIP: If you plan to design a lot of image maps, invest in a good page design program. They exist for almost every operating system and offer a wide range of features that should suit almost any design whim you have. Yes, you can code image maps by hand and it's good to know how to do it. This takes time, though, and you might forget a crucial tag that can render your image map useless. As with much software, knowing how to code HTML by hand is useful, but the right software makes it a lot faster.

Create the Image

To begin building an image map, you need an image. This can be any kind of image file, as long as it's in a recognizable image file format. The best choices are GIF or JPEG, simply because they're most likely to work with the widest number of browsers. Even though PNG files are attractive and smaller than GIFs, the PNG format isn't supported in older browsers. TIFF files are beautiful, but the files themselves are huge. Stick with GIF or JPEG unless you know your visitors can handle other formats and you don't care about downloading giant image files.

The image needn't be a particular size. It need only be large enough to hold all the *hotspots* (areas that act as links) for the links you want to embed in the image. If you plan to have six or eight links in one image, make sure the image is large enough to allow you enough room for each link. Visitors can get frustrated if it's hard to hit the link because the hotspot is so small, so give each link enough room for even the most casual of clickers.

NOTE: For those using a page design program, you might find your software enables you to build irregularly shaped hotspots as links. You might be able to trace the outline of a particular element in the image, for example, rather than draw a geometrical shape. If you want to have your links follow the shape of various image elements, use a page design program. This is simply too complicated to do by hand because you'd have to enter a vast array of pixel coordinates to define each link.

Build the Imagemap File

Once you select the appropriate image to serve as the image map, you must create a new file to hold all the settings for that particular map. This file, known as the *imagemap file*, can be a plain-text file or can use HTML tags to format the structure of the document. You needn't use HTML unless you really want to because the file works equally well without HTML coding.

NOTE: If you plan to change the value of the ImapMenu directive, explained in the "mod_imap Directives" section of the chapter, be aware the unformatted value requires HTML tags to serve a formatted menu in case of an error with the map file.

The imagemap file, as with other Apache configuration files, processes directives in the order they appear in the file. That is, the directives must be presented sequentially, so the map can be built properly in the requesting browser. Six directives can be used in the imagemap file. These directives aren't HTML tags, but are structural definitions that set the shape and size of a field in the image, which then becomes a link to the associated URL.

Base

The *Base directive* is used to define the base URL for links in the map. Any links given as relative links use the base URL as part of their absolute location. That is, if the base URL is set as **http://www.yoursite.ext** and a link is defined as **/text/helpfiles/apache**, the link is defined in the HTTP header as **http://www.yoursite.net/text/helpfiles/apache**. If you defined a base URL elsewhere with the ImapBase directive (explained later in this chapter), any setting you make in the imagemap file override an ImapBase setting.

> **NOTE:** Don't include a trailing slash in the Base value unless you need one. mod_imap doesn't let mod_dir reparse URLs with or without trailing slashes before resolving the absolute URL, so use trailing slashes only when they're needed.

Default

The *Default directive* defines what happens if the imagemap file contains coordinates that don't fit any of the geometric directives used to define a link. If no value is given, the default value is nocontent, generating a 204-No Content HTTP header. The visitor won't see an error page, but the link won't work. The Default directive can take any of the values shown in Table 16-1. These values are also defined in the "mod_imap Directives" section later in this chapter.

Poly

The *Poly directive* defines an irregularly shaped area of the image as a link. You can provide a range of coordinates (with at least three separate points, but as many as 100) used to define the border of the link area. If the visitor clicks anywhere within this area, the link

Value	Meaning
URL	Takes viewer to the defined URL
map	Takes viewer to the actual imagemap file, not the image file used for the map. A menu is generated according to the value of ImapMenu.
menu	Generates a menu of links in the map, taken from the imagemap file, formatted according to the value of ImapMenu.
referer	Returns viewer to the page that referred to the image map.
nocontent	Generates a 204—No Content header. The page won't change in the viewer's browser.
error	Generates a 500—Server Error HTTP header, which might call up an error page if Apache is configured to do so.

Table 16-1.   Values for mod_imap Default Directive

is followed. Use the Poly directive if you're trying to define particular segments of the image as a link, such as figures in the image itself.

NOTE: The Poly directive is the most difficult way to define a link area in the image file. This is one place where page design software makes the task much simpler because it automatically defines the pixel coordinates you select.

Circle

The *Circle directive* defines a round area of the image as a link. To build a circular link, you must provide two coordinates: the center of the circle and a coordinate somewhere on the perimeter of the circle. From those coordinates, mod_imap determines the correct circle size. If the visitor clicks anywhere within the circle, the link is followed.

Rect

The *Rectangle directive* defines a rectangular or square area of the image as a link. Which corners are provided doesn't matter. mod_imap extends lines from those points until they intersect to provide the remaining two corners. If the visitor clicks anywhere inside the rectangle or square so defined, the link is followed.

Point

The *Point directive* defines a single point of the image as a link. If the visitor clicks somewhere close to the point, but not directly on the point, the closest link defined by a Point directive is followed. Be aware, though, that the Point directive overrides any settings for the Default directive; so if a visitor clicks in error, she might not see any result.

CAUTION: Clicking a precise pixel coordinate on an image map is difficult for users. Avoid defining single points if at all possible because the link will be hard to click.

Imagemap File Coordinates

Coordinates are required to define the various shapes that constitute links in an image map. Without accurate coordinates, mod_imap has no way to place the link in the correct location. As with any mathematical coordinate, imagemap coordinates are expressed as two numbers on an *X-Y* axis. That is, the coordinate value

```
15,230
```

defines the point 15 pixels up the *X* axis and 230 pixels out the *Y* axis. Imagemap coordinates are always expressed as *X,Y* and use the comma to separate the two values. For directives that require a series of coordinates, each individual coordinate pair is separated by spacebar characters, as in

```
15,230 20,185
```

> **NOTE:**   The coordinate 0,0 is a special case. If a user clicks the 0,0 coordinate on the image map, mod_imap responds as if no selection had been made. This enables the lynx text-only browser to move past the image map and not get stuck because the map cannot be processed.

Text In Imagemap Files

While text isn't usually part of image maps, you might want to provide some anyway. The text you enter in the imagemap file is used when an image map cannot be built and a menu must be provided instead. (See the ImapMenu entry in the "mod_imap Directives" section later in this chapter.) You needn't provide text for menus, but it's one more layer of redundancy if your map doesn't function properly.

To add text to an entry in the imagemap file, first define the link and provide the required coordinates. On the same line, you can then add the menu text you want to show when a menu is generated, enclosed in double quotes. Thus, the entry

```
circ http://www.cnn.news 8,55 15,75 "CNN News"
```

would generate the entry

```
CNN News
```

in a menu listing. If you don't provide text between the double quotes, the value of the link is printed in the menu instead. So, if the links you provide are descriptive, you needn't add additional text. This is useful mainly in situations in which the URL might not indicate the actual function of the link, or when you want to be sure of the text in an error menu.

Creating an Imagemap File

Entries in the imagemap file take one of several forms, but each entry has consistent components. An imagemap file entry must contain at least three elements:

▼   The directive being defined for this link

■   The value of the link, which is the URL of the destination page

▲   The coordinates needed for this directive

For example, the entry

```
rect http://www.apache.org 2,45 20,80
```

defines a rectangular link with opposite corners located at the coordinates 2,45 and 20,80. When a visitor clicks this area of the image, the requesting browser is sent to the main Apache Web site.

The directive and its URL value must always be the first two elements in any given entry, but you can add other elements in any order after the value. If you want to provide extra text, as in the menu text previously described, you could place the text after the value or after the coordinates. As long as the directive and value are in place, the coordinates and any other information in that entry needn't be in a particular order.

TIP: As with any other Unix script or program, you can add comments to your imagemap files. Just use hashmarks to precede any comments, so they won't be parsed by mod_imap when the map is called. Comments are a great way to remember what you're doing. For example, you might use a comment with the Poly directive to remind yourself what section of the image is being used in this particular link. Comments might be printed when an error menu is generated—depending on the value of the ImapMenu directive, so keep them topical and useful (or set ImapMenu to unformatted).

Here's a sample imagemap file,

```
#A sample imagemap file that defines three areas on a graphic
#ImapMenu is set to "semiformatted" so menu text is included
base http://www.mysite.ext
circle http://www.apache.org 25,20 35,40 "Apache Web Server"
poly /text/otherlinks.html "Some other Apache links" 2,2 15,80 18,50 21,8
```

and so on, with additional entries for each link to be added as part of the image map.

ENABLING IMAGE MAPS

Once the imagemap file is created and associated with the image, you needn't do much more work with the map itself. Apart from configuring Apache to serve image maps properly, all that's left is to make sure the new image map is called correctly in every page on the site that will use the map. This is done with a regular HTML <A HREF> tag, the same tag you would use to build any other sort of link in your coded pages.

NOTE: If you've gone to the trouble of building a complex image map, plan to use it on multiple pages throughout the site. A well-designed image map can create visual continuity across your site, giving each page an identity that proclaims it as part of the site. One of the aims of good Web design is to create a sense of flow throughout the entire site, regardless of the content on each individual page. Image maps are a big part of that continuous flow.

As I mentioned in Chapter 7, "Managing the Apache Server," the best way to organize your Web files is like with like. That is, CGI scripts all go in the cgi-bin directory, images go in the image directory, and so on. If you're using image maps, the individual map files should be kept in a map directory, so they're all together. Once you define the appropriate directory for your map files and for image files, you can begin to use the HTML code that sets up the map.

On every page where you want the map displayed, insert a link to the map and map file that looks like this (substituting the appropriate directory path and filenames, of course):

```
<A HREF="/map/image-map-main.map">
<IMG ISMAP SRC="/images/image-map-main.jpg">
</A>
```

Note, the tag takes the same form as a regular link, but the SRC tag is formatted a little differently than a regular SRC link. The HREF tag defines the imagemap file, which contains the actual links and the pixel parameters for each link, while the SRC tag links the appropriate image (and defines it as an image map) to the map file.

SERVING IMAGE MAPS: MOD_IMAP

To serve the image maps you or your page designers create, you need to enable the *mod_imap module,* which is designed to support server-side image map processing. Luckily, mod_imap is considered a base module by the Apache developers, so it should compile by default when you install Apache for the first time. To make mod_imap work most efficiently, though, you need to configure the module and provide the information it needs to serve your maps.

TIP: To learn more about working with Apache modules, see Chapter 5, "Apache Modules." In this chapter, you can find more information about how modules work with Apache, as well as how to install and configure new modules.

The mod_imap module is used when Apache detects the file extension *.map on an outgoing file. This extension, as explained previously in this chapter, denotes an imagemap file. Because of the way Apache handles file and data types, the *.map extension is associated with the imagemap file format (see Chapter 14, "MIME and Other Encoding," for more information on data types and encoding). Because mod_imap is a base module, you might already have the *.map extension associated with the proper file type in your mime.types file. Check, just to be sure, by opening the mime.types file in your favorite text editor. Look for the line

```
application /x-httpd-imap map
```

If the file isn't there, you can add it using the directions found in Chapter 14.

You should also enable a handler for imagemap files. Open the configuration file httpd.conf in the text editor and search for an AddHandler directive that refers to *.map files. If no such directive is in your configuration file, add the line

```
AddHandler imap-file map
```

to `httpd.conf`. Save the file and exit the text editor. You need to restart the Apache server to take advantage of the changes you made. Issue the command

```
apachectl graceful
```

to restart the server without cutting off any active connections.

The mod_imap Directives

Although you can probably run mod_imap fine with its existing configuration, understanding how mod_imap is configured can help, in case you need to change something at a later time or in the rare instance that mod_imap doesn't properly serve your image maps. As with other Apache modules, mod_imap is configured through various directives, which can take certain values. These directives are placed in the appropriate configuration file and tell the module how to handle particular types of input.

TIP: You can use these directives either in a module configuration file or in the individual .htaccess file found in each directory on your site. If you use the .htaccess file method, the values you provide for these directives only apply to the directory with which that particular .htaccess file is associated.

mod_imap has three directives: ImapMenu, ImapDefault, and ImapBase. Each of these directives has a unique syntax and function. If, for some reason, you need to change or add a directive to mod_imap's configuration, be sure to use the appropriate syntax for that directive. Misconfigured directives won't work, and, in the worst-case scenario, might crash Apache altogether.

ImapMenu

The *ImapMenu directive* controls how the information in an imagemap file is provided, if the coordinates in the file are incorrect. Four possible settings exist—each of which places an increasing load on Apache as the module must perform all required formatting before delivering the information to the requesting browser.

none   If the value of ImapMenu is set to the *none* option, nothing happens when an incorrectly formed image map is requested. The image file is served as normal, but the links won't appear in the correct places. This is the lowest setting for this directive.

unformatted   If you built your imagemap files as HTML documents, the *unformatted* option is for you. Anything that's coded with HTML tags appears as intended in the resulting menu, but mod_imap won't apply its own formatting to the file. That is, if no paragraph breaks or designated header styles are in the imagemap file, the links and comments appear exactly as they were written in the file. Don't select this option unless you already coded the imagemap file with HTML tags.

semiformatted   The *semiformatted* option for this directive produces a menu with little formatting, that has no header or other graphical distinction. The links in the file are listed, with any blank lines in the file turned into paragraph breaks. Any comments contained in the file are shown in this option.

formatted   The *formatted* option for ImapMenu produces a basic menu with some standard formatting, generated from the information in the imagemap file. The menu has an <H1> header and a plain ruled line, and then a list of links. This is the nicest output from ImapMenu and, if you want to change the setting of this directive, formatted is an excellent choice. Unlike the semiformatted option, any comments in the imagemap file won't be printed in the formatted menu, which is simply a list of the links that are part of the image map.

ImapDefault

The *ImapDefault directive* defines the default HTTP response sent by the server to a client for the imagemap file associated with the requested image map. As with the ImapBase directive, this setting is automatically overridden by any default settings in the imagemap file, so there is little reason to change the value of the directive in a configuration file. There are five possible values for this directive.

error   The *error* setting returns a 500—Server Error HTTP header to the requesting browser. This produces either the standard 500 pages configured in Apache or any custom page you might have provided in place of the default. The image map won't remain displayed if an error occurs.

nocontent   The *nocontent* setting returns a 204—No Content HTTP header to the requesting browser. Because 200-level errors don't generate special error pages for the visiting browser, Apache continues to display the image map, but won't move to the specified link.

map   The *map* setting for the ImapDefault directive returns the URL of the imagemap file, not the image associated with the map. Depending on the setting of ImapMenu, a directory listing might be generated. If ImapMenu is set to none, no list is generated because the map setting of ImapDefault doesn't send coordinates for the links.

referer   The *referer* setting causes the browser to return to the referring page, rather than continue to view the image map's image. The Referer: header is a regular HTTP header but, if the server cannot find the header or parse the information contained in it, the default setting is **http://www.server.ext**, as your site is defined in `httpd.conf`.

URL   If ImapDefault is set to *URL*, you can provide a different URL to be used if an error occurs. This URL can be relative, as in **/maps/image-map-fallback.map**, or absolute, as in **http://www.yoursite.com/errormap.html**. You can also substitute other HTML link formats, like **Mailto:** if you want to enable an e-mail response when an error occurs.

ImapBase

The ImapBase directive defines the root URL used in the imagemap file called by the requesting browser. Three setting are possible, though this directive shouldn't be changed unless you have a good reason to override the imagemap file designed for each individual map served on your site. If no value is given for this directive, the root URL always defaults to **http://www.servername.ext** as defined in `httpd.conf`.

map   The *map* value for this directive sets the base URL to one defined in the specified imagemap file. Because the default value of the ImapBase directive can be overridden by the base URL value specified in the associated imagemap file, little need exists to use this value.

referer   Setting the ImapBase directive to *referer* means the URL of the referring page is used as the base URL for the image map. This works only if the image map is always obtained from a particular page.

URL   You can set an absolute URL to be used as the base URL for the image map by defining the ImapBase directive with this value and the appropriate URL.

> **CAUTION:**   As noted earlier in this section, don't change this directive's value without knowing exactly how this is going to affect the maps on your site.

MAINTAINING ACCESSIBILITY

While image maps can add a level of sophistication and visual appeal to your site, which is hard to match with text-based navigation, beware of overreliance on image maps. Maps don't always parse properly in various browsers, whether they're text-based browsers like lynx or adaptive browsers used to assist Web users with various disabilities. They can also be frustrating to older visitors or those with less-fine motor control, because clicking within a fairly small defined area—especially if the area isn't bordered so the boundary of the link is visible—might be a difficult task for people unfamiliar or uncomfortable with a mouse.

To meet the needs of as many users as possible, consider using image maps as one part of your site navigation, but not as the sole navigation mechanism. For example, you might run a small text navigation bar underneath the image used as an image map, or you could add a constant navigation menu to the side of every page on your site. You might also consider providing a complete text-only version of your pages, which visitors can select on the front page of the site. Providing alternative navigation methods makes your site friendly and usable for everyone, including people who prefer text links. When designing your pages or working with those who do design your site, be aware of the browsers used to see your site and the capabilities those browsers have.

TIP: If you're interested in learning whether your site is currently adaptive-browser friendly, consider running your pages through the Bobby. The *Bobby* is a *validator*, a program that reviews Web pages to see whether they comply with some standard. A number of validators are available on the Web, and the Bobby checks pages to see whether they're friendly to adaptive Web technology. Find the Bobby at **http://www.cast.org/bobby**. If you like the program, you can download a copy of it to use on your own machine. The Bobby is written in Java, so it should work on a variety of platforms. Get it at **http://www.cast.org/bobby/index.cfm?i=316**.

SUMMARY

Image maps are an advanced form of Web navigation. Rather than using text links to other pages or Web sites, an image map has various defined areas that act as links. These areas can be of any shape and are defined in a separate imagemap file, which is linked with the image file in an HTML coded file. Image maps can be used in conjunction with textual navigation or used alone. To configure an image map, you need an image file and an imagemap file. The imagemap file is used to define the separate areas and to link them with the appropriate URL, using pixel coordinates on the image file. Image maps are served by Apache through the mod_imap module. mod_imap is a base Apache module, but you can make additional configurations that define how map errors are to be handled, among other directives.

Although image maps are an excellent way to improve the appearance of your site, be aware they might not be the best way for some visitors to navigate. Consider adding text navigation bars along the side or bottom of each page on your site, especially the pages that have image maps. With text links, as well as the visual links, your site can be friendlier to those using adaptive or text-only browsers, and to those whose motor skills or eyesight prevent them from locating the appropriate link in an image map.

CHAPTER 17

Using Apache to Save Time: SSI and CSS

Everyone who designs and administers pages for a Web site would like to save time. Coding pages in HTML takes time, and writing new CGI scripts requires another chunk of the clock that you can't spend running your site. Even the people who access your site would love to spend less time downloading complex pages with a lot of formatting. Unfortunately, we're all stuck with the HTML and CGI tools we have, right?

Not so. As the HTML and HTTP standards have evolved over the last few years, new ideas have been developed that can save us all some precious time. Whether it's an intermediate stop between plain HTML and full-blown CGI, or a way to economize on the HTML headers that are sent with every requested file, the Web development community has come up with methods that fill the needs of every participant in a Web transaction: the person who designed the pages, the programmer who coded the server, and the user who is looking at your site with her browser.

In this chapter, you learn about two of the newer ideas in Web design: SSI and CSS. SSI, or server-side include, occupies the space between vanilla HTML and tutti-frutti CGI. You can use SSI in your regular HTML pages and, when the page is requested, the server automatically includes specific data as part of the page. This is seamless on the visitor's end, and it saves a lot of time both for you and for the people designing the pages on your site. An additional benefit of SSI is that it's easier to learn than a new programming language, which you'd need to start writing your own CGI scripts.

CSS, or cascading style sheets, also save time. These sheets are primarily a designer's trick, but they help you out in your role as an administrator. With CSS, a designer can set the visual appearance of a particular set of pages, but he only has to do it once by coding a style sheet. The sheet goes along with the first page requested by a visitor and alerts the visitor's browser that particular visual rules must be followed with these pages. The browser gets much less of a chance to override your carefully selected design. Your server can provide pages more quickly and your visitors needn't download identical style information for each subsequent page they see on your site. In addition, CSS helps adaptive browsers and other technologies used by the disabled on the Web.

SERVER SIDE INCLUDES

Server-side includes are small functions embedded into regular HTML pages. When a page including an SSI is requested by an external browser, Apache grabs the file before it's sent. Apache parses the file, finding the server-side include, determining what it requires, and providing the necessary information before sending the file to the requesting browser. This is a relatively quick transaction and doesn't put a great deal of stress on your Web server machine.

Apache knows a file contains an SSI only if you place the correct extension on that file. The most common file extension associated with SSI is *.shtml. When Apache detects a file with the *.shtml extension, it knows the file contains an SSI function and additional data must be supplied before the file can be sent out of the site. While you can use other extensions—even the standard *.html and *.htm extensions associated with ordinary static pages—this isn't a good idea. Using these common extensions for both SSI and non-SSI pages means Apache will waste system cycles processing every single file served by your site, whether or not it actually requires the server to include additional data. Keep your SSI files easily identifiable, and use a consistent file extension to mark them.

You can use SSIs for all sorts of data. They can save you quite a bit of time, especially if you use SSI to provide data that's constantly changing or being updated. You need only change the data that's included, not the HTML file itself. This can be quite a break, especially if it's data that appears on every page in an extensive site. What if, for example, you run a site that prints the local directory path of each file on the bottom of the file when it's served as a Web page? You could type that path in each document as the document was coded, which seems reasonable. However, what if the path changes? What if you reorganize your site? You must go back and retype that path on every single page of your site.

Instead, you could embed an SSI command at the bottom of each page. This command would cause Apache to pull the document's path, as it currently exists when the page is requested, and add the path to the correct position at the bottom of the page. While you might not need to use complete directory paths on each page of your site, consider the possibilities. You might want to add date, time, a copyright notice, the local weather, contact information, or any of hundreds of possible data bits. When the data changes, you only need to change one thing (and, for some of these options, you don't have to change anything at all) instead of editing hundreds or thousands of individual HTML documents. Table 17-1 shows the

Variable	Function
DATE_LOCAL	The time and date of the request as defined by your operating system. (The clock on your system must be accurate for this to be a true value. If your clock is wrong, this variable will also be wrong.)
DATE_GMT	The time and date of the request, as expressed in Greenwich Mean Time.
DOCUMENT_URI	The local directory path of the requested document (includes filename).
DOCUMENT_NAME	The full name, including the extension, of the requested document.
DOCUMENT_PATH_INFO	The requested document's full path, including CGI variables.
LAST_MODIFIED	The timestamp of the document.
QUERY_STRING_UNESCAPED	Same as DOCUMENT_PATH_INFO, but without HTML's special character codings.
USER_NAME	The user name (login name) of the requested file's owner.

Table 17-1.   Native SSI Variables (Not Including CGI Variables)

variables SSI already knows how to parse and that can be dropped directly into SSI commands embedded in HTML files without additional coding.

NOTE: SSI can also handle almost every CGI variable as well, so consider those functions before you code your own. Although a complete list of CGI variables isn't included in this book, you can find one in any good CGI reference.

CONFIGURING SSI

To use SSIs on your Web site, you must have the mod_include module installed and properly configured. mod_include is installed by default with your regular Apache installation. If you removed that module for any reason, you must recompile Apache, including mod_include, before you can work with SSI.

NOTE: Learn more about Apache modules, including mod_include, in Chapter 5, "Apache Modules."

Once you determine you have mod_include available and it's properly installed, you must configure it to recognize SSIs as they're passed through the server. To do this, you need to complete a series of tasks to enable the SSI component of mod_include. These tasks use the AddHandler function of Apache. This directive forces Apache to recognize new file extensions and coding, like SSI.

Adding a New Handler

To alert Apache to a new activity it must perform, such as processing SSIs, you need to tell Apache what files need this activity and what files don't need it. Generally, you can tell Apache what files must be examined and it then ignores all files without the appropriate extension.

NOTE: As noted in the previous section of this chapter, using the file extension *.shtml as the identifier for files with SSIs is best. If you use the standard *.html or *.htm extensions for files that include SSI, Apache then must parse both files that include SSI and files that don't. SSI places enough of a drain on the system, so avoid adding additional stress where possible.

Give Apache this information by amending your configuration files.

For Apache 2.0, open httpd.conf in your favorite text editor and search for the section containing AddHandler directives:

```
# AddHandler allows you to map certain file extensions to "handlers",
# actions unrelated to filetype. These can be either built into the server
# or added with the Action command (see below)
```

```
#
# If you want to use server side includes, or CGI outside
# ScriptAliased directories, uncomment the following lines.
#
# To use CGI scripts:
#
#AddHandler cgi-script .cgi

#
# To use server-parsed HTML files
#
#<FilesMatch "\.shtml(\..+)?$">
#    SetOutputFilter INCLUDES
#</FilesMatch>
```

Uncomment the final three lines by removing the hashmark at the start of each line, as directed in the file's comments.

TIP: If you plan to use CGI scripts on your site as well, uncomment the AddHandler line concerning CGI. Doing all these edits at one time—while you have the file open—is easiest. Learn more about CGI in Chapter 15, "CGI—The Common Gateway Interface."

Leave the file open because you'll need to edit another section in the next step.

Adding a Handler Under Apache 1.3.*

For Apache 1.3.* installations, you need to edit `httpd.conf` in a slightly different manner. As previously described, open the configuration file in a text editor and search for the section that contains AddHandler directives. Your file should contain a commented-out line for SSI documents. If it doesn't, add the line

```
AddHandler server-parsed .shtml
```

at the appropriate location.

Adding a New File Extension

Once you add the appropriate AddHandler directive, you must add a new file type. As described in Chapter 14, "MIME and Other Encoding," Apache uses MIME types to identify different kinds of data, each of which is handled differently as it passes through the server. SSI-enabled documents are no exception. They must have a MIME type enabled in Apache configuration to be parsed correctly.

NOTE: You can also edit the `mime.types` file directly if you choose, but it's far easier to use the AddType directive. `mime.types` has a unique syntax and organization, and making an error in that file may cause trouble with Apache when it restarts.

In the configuration file that you already have open, locate the section dealing with MIME types:

```
# AddType allows you to tweak mime.types without actually editing it, or to
# make certain files to be certain types.
#
# For example, the PHP3 module (not part of the Apache distribution - see
# http://www.php.net) will typically use:
#
#AddType application/x-httpd-php3 .php3
#AddType application/x-httpd-php3-source .phps

AddType application/x-tar .tgz
```

In the default `httpd.conf` file, this section is directly above the AddHandler section. Editing the configuration file with the AddType directive is simpler than closing this file and working directly with the `mime.types` file, and it lessens the chance you'll make an error, which will cause trouble when the server restarts.

Add a line at the end of this section that reads

```
AddType    text/html        .shtml
```

Save the file if you like, but don't exit the editor. You still have one final configuration to make before SSI is enabled on your site.

NOTE: Apache 1.3.* installations use this procedure as described.

Enabling Specific Directories for SSI

To enable SSI fully for your Apache installation, you must tell Apache the directories that are going to include SSI-enabled documents. You can enable SSI globally or you can restrict its use to particular subdirectories on the site. If you want to enable it globally, you need make only one entry in `httpd.conf`. If you decide to limit SSI to individual subdirectories, you need to make an entry in the configuration sections for each of the desired directories.

Locate the appropriate directory sections in the configuration file. These are usually at the top of the document. In `httpd.conf`, for example, the global directory settings are found directly after the ServerRoot variable.

```
# Each directory to which Apache has access, can be configured with respect
# to which services and features are allowed and/or disabled in that
# directory (and its subdirectories).
#
# First, we configure the "default" to be a very restrictive set of
# permissions.
#
```

```
<Directory />
    Options FollowSymLinks
    AllowOverride None
</Directory>


#
# Note that from this point forward you must specifically allow
# particular features to be enabled - so if something's not working as
# you might expect, make sure that you have specifically enabled it
# below.
#


#
# This should be changed to whatever you set DocumentRoot to.
#
<Directory "@@ServerRoot@@/htdocs">

#
# This may also be "None", "All", or any combination of "Indexes",
# "Includes", "FollowSymLinks", "ExecCGI", or "MultiViews".
#
# Note that "MultiViews" must be named *explicitly* --- "Options All"
# doesn't give it to you.
#
    Options Indexes FollowSymLinks MultiViews

#
# This controls which options the .htaccess files in directories can
# override. Can also be "All", or any combination of "Options", "FileInfo",
# "AuthConfig", and "Limit"
#
    AllowOverride None

#
# Controls who can get stuff from this server.
#
    Order allow,deny
    Allow from all
</Directory>
```

Add a new line, within the appropriate directory container, that reads

```
Options +Includes
```

Now you can save the file and exit the text editor. Note, you need to place the Options entry into each subdirectory's individual configuration section if you don't want to enable SSI across the site. You must also enable AllowOverride for each of those directories, however, or Apache won't be able to parse the files for includes. Note, AllowOverride doesn't identify the directories that contain SSI commands. Instead, AllowOverride enables the .htaccess file to define the individual directories with SSI commands in their files, overriding any global settings. When you check your AllowOverride settings, you should also check .htaccess to make sure the correct directories are identified there.

> **NOTE:**   You can use this same configuration to enable SSI on sites you administer as virtual hosts. Simply place the configuration into the appropriate virtual host section of the configuration file. To learn more about virtual hosts, see Chapter 18, "Virtual Domain Hosting."

You must restart the Apache server to take advantage of the new settings. To restart gracefully, forcing Apache to reread the configuration files, issue the command

```
apachectl graceful
```

> **TIP:**   To learn more about the `apachectl` command, consult Chapter 7, "Managing the Apache Server."

Adding a MIME Type Under Apache 1.3.*

Apache 1.3.* administrators need to place this directive in the `access.conf` file if they want SSI enabled globally on their site or in the individual directory configuration sections of `.htaccess` if they want to limit SSI to certain directories. As with Apache 2.0, be sure to enable AllowOverride for each individual directory in which you enable SSI, or Apache won't be able to parse the individual files and include the requested data. Remember, only the directories identified in the .htaccess file will be checked for SSI, so enabling AllowOverride ensures .htaccess can define that directory as one containing SSI commands.

WORKING WITH SSI VARIABLES

Working with variables in SSI is much like working with variables in scripting languages or even in the shell environment itself. You can use preexisting variables, like those previously shown in Table 17-1, or you can create your own by using those preexisting variables and additional data of your own. To create your own variables, you need to provide both a name for the variable and a starting value. For example, if you want to create the SSI variable "TimeStamp," you would add the following variable definition to the SSI command embedded in the HTML for a particular page:

```
<!--#set
    var="TimeStamp"
    value="This file was last modified at $LAST_MODIFIED."
-->
<!--#echo var="TimeStamp" -->
```

This block of code sets the name for the new variable, and then sets the value of the variable. As you can see, I used one of the basic SSI variables and added some text of my own. Now, whenever I add SSI to one of my Web pages, I can include the variable TimeStamp to pull in this line of text and Apache will automatically add the LAST_MODIFIED data as the page passes out to a requesting browser.

NOTE: Variables always start with the dollar sign, $, when used as part of a script. The $ sign denotes that the following character string is a placeholder for a particular defined value, rather than being part of the text as it's written. If you need to use a dollar sign as part of the actual text of your variable's value, place a backslash in the space just before the dollar sign.

SSI COMMANDS

SSI is fairly easy to write. If you have a grasp of programming fundamentals, you can pick up SSI in a short time. If you're completely new to programming, you'll need to consult a more extensive introduction to SSI programming than can be included here. Do be aware that, if you're experienced in scripting languages like Perl or Python, you may find SSI somewhat frustrating because you cannot use normal scripting functions in SSI commands. Some people get quite irritated by this and simply leave off SSI in favor of CGI or some other scripting-friendly mechanism. However, if you remember that SSI commands aren't full-fledged scripts, you can probably get past the annoyance and save yourself a lot of time instead of writing CGI scripts.

You can incorporate seven major SSI commands into the commands embedded in an HTML page. Table 17-2 shows six of them. The seventh—the config command—has a

Command	Function
echo	Prints the value of a specified variable `<!--#echo var="WEB_ADMIN" «-->`
exec	Runs a specified script or shell command, including the output in the HTML page (this is usually disabled for security reasons so intruders don't assume the server's privileges and begin issuing commands to the machine) `<!--#exec cgi="/cgi-bin/doohickey.cgi" «-->`
fsize	Prints the size of the requested file, taking the data from an operating system call `<!--#fsize file="/documentation/HOWTO-Install.html" «-->`
flastmod	Prints the timestamp on the requested file `<!--#flastmod file="/docs/HOWTO-Install.html" «-->`
include	Adds the contents of a specified file to the requested file `<!--#include file="/data/copyright.html" «-->`
set	Creates and defines a given variable `<!--#set var="WEB_ADMIN" value="web@yoursite.com" «-->`

Table 17-2.   Selected SSI Programming Commands

number of options and is treated separately after the table. Note, each of these commands must be inserted into the SSI command in a particular format. You cannot simply type the command and let it go. Most of these commands also require some additional information, like a definition, to operate correctly.

The SSI Config Command

Unlike the commands previously shown in Table 17-2, the config command has a wide array of variables built into the command itself, rather than relying on externally defined variables or filenames. The config command is used to define the value of a config variable, of which there are three:

▼ `errmsg` The text of the error message that will be sent if any problems are encountered while Apache parses the SSI and appends the appropriate information

■ `sizefmt` Determines whether file sizes will be reported in bytes, kilobytes, or megabytes

▲ `timefmt` Specifies the format for various time and date variables

Each of these variables has its own syntax and set of already identified character strings that can be used to compose a complete variable with config.

errmsg

The `errmsg` variable is easy to configure. You can make this variable as complex or as simple as you want, but you should create one. Apache automatically generates error messages for regular HTML files, but not for SSI-enabled files. So, if you want your visitors to see an error message when things go wrong, you must create your own. The `errmsg` variable takes the syntax

```
<!--#config errmsg="Place the text of your error message here." -->
```

You can also include previously defined or default SSI variables, as in

```
<!--#config errmsg="An error has occurred while processing this document. Please
send mail to $WEB_ADMIN if you have questions." -->
```

sizefmt

The `sizefmt` variable defines how file sizes will be displayed on your site when called with an SSI command. You can choose between regular bytes or kilobytes and megabytes. The byte option simply prints a number, but the kilobyte and megabyte option is followed by a *K* or an *M*, respectively, depending on the file size. The `sizefmt` variable takes the syntax

```
<!--#config sizefmt="bytes" -->
```

To set the kilobyte and megabyte option, issue this command instead:

```
<!--#config sizefmt="abbrev" -->
```

timefmt

The `timefmt` variable determines how time and date information will be displayed in any output from an SSI command. This variable has a number of possible elements, each of which is called by a particular character string. The syntax of `timefmt` is quite basic:

```
<!--#config timefmt="string-of-elements" -->
```

as in

```
<!--#config timefmt="%A%B%d%Y" -->
```

resulting in the output

```
Tuesday June 23 2001
```

Table 17-3 contains the complete list of character strings the `timefmt` variable accepts.

Character String	Meaning
%A	Name of the current weekday, as in Monday
%a	Abbreviated name of the current weekday, as in Mon
%B	Name of the current month
%b	Abbreviated name of the current month
%c	Date and time stamp as taken from the current machine settings
%d	Number of the current day of the month, as in 17
%H	Current hour on a 24-hour clock, as in 8 or 23
%I	Current hour on a 12-hour clock, as in 3 or 11
%j	Day of the year on a Julian calendar, as in 285
%M	Current minute, as in 34
%m	Current month expressed numerically, as in 7
%p	AM/PM identifier, used with a 12-hour clock
%S	Current second, as in 12

Table 17-3.   Character Strings for the timefmt config Variable

Character String	Meaning
%U	Current week expressed numerically, as in 44, with Sunday denoting the first day of the week
%W	Current week expressed numerically, as in 44, with Monday being the first day of the week (the year begins with Week 0)
%w	Current day of the week expressed numerically, as in 3, with Sunday being Day 0
%X	A complete time stamp expressed in the time zone of the machine's location, as in 11:15:32 EDT
%x	A complete date stamp expressed in the time zone of the machine's location, as in Monday, 25-12-00
%y	Current year, printing only the final two digits, as in 00
%Y	Current year, printing all four digits, as in 2001
%Z	Current time zone

Table 17-3.   Character Strings for the timefmt config Variable *(continued)*

CASCADING STYLE SHEETS

While SSIs are an effective way to add current information to your static Web pages as they pass through Apache on their way to the requesting browser, they aren't the only tool to speed up your request times. Cascading style sheets (CSS) are a new Web specification that provide a greater deal of flexibility in page design than was formerly available through plain HTML. CSS don't require a great deal of attention on your part as an administrator but, if you design your own pages, you should learn about these useful new methods of page design.

TIP: Using CSS is a great way to increase the accessibility of your site for those visitors using adaptive browsers or low-graphic browsers, like the text browser lynx or the Wireless Web–enabled devices, like cellphones and palmtop computers.

CSS are a way to centralize the codes that define the appearance of pages on your site. The style sheet is transmitted with the page when a browser makes a request, but this is separate from the actual HTML document. Each style sheet contains a set of rules that tell the receiving browser how the page should be displayed. Instead of loading your pages with strings of HTML codes, you can accomplish the same thing by creating one rule in a style sheet. For example, let's say you have a page with a number of main title headings. You want each heading to be bold, italic, underlined, and green. In HTML, you'd have to use the <H1> tag, and then add four additional tags to add your extra elements. You'd also have to close all those tags after the title text and repeat these steps for every title in the page! With CSS, however, you can define one rule that applies to all H1-coded lines on the page:

```
H1 (color: green; font: italic bold Arial, sanserif; text-decoration: underline;
background: white; border: 3px solid blue;)
```

In this example, I've even added a background color and a border to anything coded with an H1 tag on this page. Because I didn't have to type all these tags in with every H1 tag, I can add more elements while still saving time. Of course, you can add additional rules for every other structural element you plan to use in that page—and you needn't code any of it individually!

Why CSS Matters

To understand why CSS are so important, you must know what the Web was like in the early days. For the first few versions of the HTML standard, HTML was a lean and simple coding mechanism that emphasized page structure, not appearance. You couldn't do much with it, except change the format of the page by altering font, alignment, and text appearance. Pages with images were considered "fancy." How times have changed! As the Web became more popular and pages began to be designed by people with actual artistic background (instead of computer geeks who didn't care what things looked like), designers started to stretch the HTML code and use various elements in ways never intended. The common tricks of using a table to set up a page's appearance, or the one-pixel transparent image used to block graphic elements into the correct position, aren't technically correct uses of HTML, but they are found on almost every site with some sense of graphic design.

With CSS, Web design has, in a sense, gone backward. HTML can once again be a structural mechanism rather than a graphic design method (something HTML is badly designed to do). Instead of cluttering your coded pages with hundreds of individual tags defining the appearance of each structural element and repeating those tags every time that element appears again, you can write one single rule for each element and be sure you'll get the same appearance each time the element appears. In contrast, coding HTML for visual appearance runs the risk that you'll forget a tag or forget to close a tag, causing the remainder of the page to look wrong. CSS saves time—a lot of time.

You can use CSS on a single page or across an entire site. Imagine you have a site with several hundred pages. Not unthinkable in this era of full-information Web sites. Of course, you want the pages to maintain a unique visual identity, so visitors are aware each page is part of your site. In the "old days," you'd have to make sure each page was coded identically. But—horrors—what happens when the marketing team decides to change the visual identity of your site? Many hours of recoding and pages that invariably get forgotten. This is never the case with a CSS site: simply change the rule and the entire site changes.

NOTE: Unfortunately, browser development hasn't kept pace with new Web standards like CSS. A lot of still-popular browsers don't handle CSS-enabled sites well, because of miscoding or plain misunderstanding of the standard. Opera, a browser that only shows compliant HTML, does CSS quite well. Microsoft's Internet Explorer, in versions 4.* and 5.*, can handle most CSS and is far better at doing so than the 3.* version. Netscape, alas, has had trouble with CSS since version 4.*. While the newer versions of Netscape handle CSS somewhat better, the 4.7 version is still widely used across the Internet. Be sure to preview all CSS-enabled pages in a variety of browsers before you deploy the site, and consider providing a bare-bones HTML-only alternative for people whose browsers simply can't deal with style sheets.

So, you might be saying, I understand the style sheet concept, but what's "cascading" got to do with it? The cascading part is the truly ingenious part. You can set a rule that applies to the entire site: let's call it Rule H1. With this rule, all the H1 elements on every page of the site share the same appearance. On a particular subset of pages, however, you don't want to use those colors or settings. All you must do is to provide another style sheet and attach it to those specific pages. On the new style sheet, you can set Rule H1-A. The original style will still apply to every other page on the site, but the pages with the new rule display H1 elements with the new settings.

NOTE: The term *cascading* means you can set a global array of styles for the elements on your site, but you can also provide new style sheets as a visitor drills down through your files. The new sheets may only affect one or two page elements, so the original style sheet is still used for all other page elements. Think of it as a waterfall, or a cascade, of formatting instructions.

CSS for Site Administrators

For those readers who aren't page designers, the entire concept of CSS might seem an academic discussion. After all, you're not sitting around marking up HTML documents—you're a systems administrator and you're too busy to care about what things look like, as long as the server is running. True, but take a minute to think about this. If you look at your Web directories and all the pages you serve, how much disk space do the Web files occupy? And what is the average size of a single document on your site? If you run a site with a certain amount of visual appeal, those files might be quite large.

What makes those files so big is the amount of HTML coding required to get them looking the right way. All those individual tags you read about a few pages ago take up space and add to the file's size. Multiply that by a few hundred—or however many pages you have on the site—and the disk commitment to HTML-designed files becomes quite significant. Compare that to the size those files would have if the HTML tags were gone, except for the few tags needed to designate structural elements, and all visual appearance was managed by CSS. You could see a startling increase in free disk space if the files you serve were gradually converted to CSS, rather than HTML design. Smaller pages serve faster, taking less overhead both in Apache and in your system load.

TIP: Don't forget to look at the sizes of the sites you host virtually. While I'd never recommend decreasing the size of your hard disk, you might be able to put off purchasing a new disk for a while if you can free some space on the existing machine by converting all your sites to CSS documents.

MAKING WEB PAGES ACCESSIBLE

While CSS certainly helps with both page design and Apache operation, another aspect of style sheets often goes unnoticed. You can use CSS to make your Web pages far friendlier to those using adaptive browsers or other minimally visual Web technologies. These browsers rely on the basic HTML structural codes to determine how a given page should be presented to the user. Where people using Netscape or Internet Explorer won't notice or care that an HTML tag has been used improperly to create a particular visual effect, those using adaptive browsers might find misused tags cause crashes or simply prevent the page from being visited.

In addition to removing a lot of bad HTML from Web pages, CSS also enables individual users to create their own style sheets, which can override the style sheet contained with the browser. That is, if a visitor prefers certain page elements to be extremely large and a bright color, she can create a *reader style sheet,* which applies that style to CSS-enabled pages, even if the designer didn't intend the element to look like that. Reader style sheets can go a long way toward making the Web more accessible, even if visitors aren't using adaptive browsers. Many visual impairments simply need an adjustment to be accommodated, such as color-blindness or uncorrected vision.

Another useful accessibility trick in CSS is the capability to provide an aural style sheet. Some adaptive browsers speak the page aloud as it's parsed (another reason to provide the correct elemental structure). With an *aural style sheet,* you can design the sound that comes from the speakers, changing elements such as volume, pauses, and added cues. By configuring an aural style sheet correctly, you can make your site sound as unique as it looks.

TIP: If you want to design aural style sheets, consult someone who uses an audio browser, or someone familiar with recorded print material designed for visually impaired or dyslexic people. Some conventions exist, such as audio cues, that might be helpful in creating the soundscape of your site.

Regardless of the specific options you select, using CSS can add a new level of flexibility and accessibility to your site. If you enable accessibility properties as well as visual design properties, you'll increase the number of people who can visit your site successfully, and also improve your skills. Web design for accessibility is a growing trend, and administrators familiar with accessibility techniques can find a welcome market for those skills.

NOTE: For more information about Web accessibility, visit the World Wide Web Consortium's Web Accessibility Initiative site at **http://www.w3c.org/WAI/**.

SUMMARY

Whether you code your own pages or simply administer the Web server for your site, you probably want to save time. Several techniques can speed response time to browser requests on your system. Two of the best methods are to implement server-side includes, or SSIs, and cascading style sheets, or CSS. Server-side includes are a method that requires Apache to parse outgoing files and add bits of designated data as the pages pass out. Although it does require input from Apache, SSI commands are faster than CGI scripts and save time in the design and updating of the files on your site.

Cascading style sheets save time because your server doesn't need to send lengthy sets of HTML tags, which define the appearance of the page in the requester's browser, along with each document. Rather, HTML is used only to set the structure of the document (as the coding language was originally intended to do). Style sheets, which are sent along with the requesting file, define the appearance of each structural element. In addition to speeding transmission and rendering of Web files, CSS makes it easier for adaptive browsers to render your Web pages in whatever format the end user needs.

CHAPTER 18

Virtual Domain Hosting

A day may come in your life as a Web administrator when you think, "Hey, running one Web site is a lot of fun. I want to run lots of Web sites!" Or, you might get a call from your boss, who will say: "We've decided to set up another Web site for our summer promotion. Go ahead and put that together, will you?" A third person might have a friend who owns a domain, but has no place to put it, who will ask, "Can you run my Web site for me?" No matter how the subject comes up, multiple Web sites are a reality for many Web professionals.

Luckily, answering all those questions affirmatively isn't complicated. While you could build a complex network in which each of the sites you want to host has its own server machine and its own connection to the Internet, you needn't spend the money and time pulling such a giant complication together. Instead, you can turn to your trusty Web server and use the virtual domain hosting feature of Apache.

With virtual domains, you can administer a number of sites from one machine. Those sites can even share an IP number! Apache, with the appropriate configuration, can recognize requests for each of the sites as they come into the server, direct the requests appropriately, and serve the resulting pages back to the requesting browser. The person on the other end of the connection will probably never know the site she's looking at doesn't have its own network—or even its own machine! In fact, you probably have no idea whether your favorite sites are administered directly on a server machine of their own or they're virtually hosted on someone else's network.

NOTE: While this chapter is primarily concerned with the virtual hosting of Web sites, a number of other Internet services can be administered virtually. The final section of this chapter addresses some of these services, which you may want to offer in conjunction with virtual Web site hosting.

In this chapter, you learn the ins and outs of virtual domain hosting. First, we introduce the concept and explain exactly how virtual domains work and why you can't tell a virtually hosted Web site from an actual one. Next, we ask some of the hard questions about virtual hosting: is it for you? What are the drawbacks, as well as the benefits, of providing virtual host services to other people—or of purchasing virtual hosting services yourself? Once you decide virtual hosting is for you, you need to know how to configure the new sites. This is a two-part process, involving configurations both with the Domain Name Service servers you have access to and with Apache itself. The chapter ends with a discussion of virtual e-mail hosting, a service you might want to provide to people whose sites you administer or host. This is a feature many virtual host customers want because they prefer to have administrative addresses that mirror their virtual site's domain name.

VIRTUAL DOMAINS

A *virtual domain*, at its most basic, is a Web site without its own physical presence. On the Web, the site doesn't look different from any other site. Its links work the same way, files are transferred in the same manner with the same HTTP headers, and all the regular commands are still functional. The only difference between a virtually hosted site and a nonvirtual site is the nonvirtual site is situated on an actual network with the same domain name, while the virtual site exists only in an Apache configuration file.

For example, the site **www.yahoo.com** is an actual Web site. An entire server farm in the San Francisco Bay Area is devoted to serving the pages of Yahoo!'s Web site. However, Yahoo! also offers Web-based e-mail groups. The site **groups.yahoo.com**, which is the home of those groups, may or may not be virtual. We don't know from looking at the site. In all likelihood, this is a virtual site that doesn't have its own IP number, but relies on Apache to distribute its requests appropriately. If the groups site is, indeed, virtual, Yahoo! saves time and energy. Yahoo! doesn't have to devote an extra machine just to group requests. Instead, Yahoo! can distribute requests for groups-related pages across its server farm and use an existing IP number for what appears to be a completely different site.

> *NOTE:*   In fact, running **groups.yahoo.com** through WHOIS, the database of registered domain names and their IP numbers, produces no result. This increases the probability that the site is virtually hosted by Yahoo!'s Apache server and not a stand-alone server with its own `httpd` process.

Virtual hosting can be a lot of fun. You can serve a number of wildly different sites or closely related ones, from a single Apache installation and using a single IP number. Apache makes configuring virtual hosts easy. The only limitation is your bandwidth and the amount of RAM you have installed in the server machine. While you need to answer some questions before you decide whether virtual hosting is for you, this is a technique worth trying, even if you decide not to continue offering the service.

SHOULD YOU HOST VIRTUAL DOMAINS?

Whether or not you should host virtual domains is a question that calls into play a number of variables. You should ask yourself the following questions and see whether you're comfortable doing the extra work that hosting virtual sites requires. In addition, you might be limited by your terms of employment or by the contract you signed with your Internet connection. Some places won't let you run any servers at all, while others only want you hosting your own sites (often a safeguard against you making money on someone else's commercial bandwidth). For starters, here are the basic questions you should ask—and answer—before you commit to hosting virtual sites.

▼   What sort of hardware and software are you running on your network now?

You should have as much RAM and as fast a chip as you can afford. You'll probably need a larger hard drive to store the files for virtual sites, especially if they're graphics intensive or offer file archives. Make sure your operating system is updated and has the latest patches, and the same for Apache and any other Internet services you plan to offer.

▼ How fast is your Internet connection and how much bandwidth is at your disposal?

Virtual sites will multiply the traffic you already get on your main site. Are you prepared to double your Web traffic for one additional site, or triple or quadruple it if you take on more virtual sites? How will you manage the traffic that comes to your main site if the connection is slow or if your bandwidth becomes saturated with hits for the new site? Do you have the money to pay for an increase in bandwidth or a new method of connecting to the Internet?

▼ Are the sites you will host sites that are somehow related to the site you're already administering, or would you be hosting completely unrelated sites for people with whom you don't work or who aren't your friends?

If the sites you want to host are closely related to the site you already run, such as additional sites for your company or sites similar to your personal Web presence, you'll be more able to predict visitor traffic and the system resources needed for each site. If you're hosting sites as a favor to friends, will you charge them for the privilege? If you plan to offer hosting as a service to people you don't know, are you setting up a legitimate business, or will you be doing this as a backyard hobby? You may pique the curiosity of the Internal Revenue Service if you run a backyard business, especially if you're charging for services on the same bandwidth as part of your legitimate daytime business, but not counting your virtual host income as part of your business income.

TIP: If you're planning to charge, consider filing with your local authorities and doing the paperwork to become a real company. Not only may you be able to deduct some of the hardware, software, and connection costs of doing business, but you'll have a stronger legal position if you must pursue your customers for nonpayment or for violating your Terms of Service. See your attorney and accountant for more information on starting your own business and on the tax implications of charging for virtual host services.

▼ Are you charging to host the sites? Will that income be a significant part of your income stream and something you need to stay afloat?

If you decide to charge others for the virtual domain host services you offer, how much will you charge? Does that cost cover your overhead or are you charging a token payment to keep your friends from abusing your generosity? If you need to rely on virtual host charges to keep your network alive, consider what you'd do if your customers all vanished or went to other hosting providers.

▼ How do you feel about having people access your machines to upload files or about doing the work yourself if you don't want to give others access?

Security is an issue when you give other people access to machines for which you're responsible. How will the people who own the virtual sites get their Web data online? You might set up an FTP server for them, using password authentication, so they can upload their own data and manage their own Web files. If you're genuinely concerned about security, you could require that they send you all the files from another network, and then you can upload the data to the site yourself. Note, however, this is unwieldy and can take a great deal of your time, especially if you have a client who likes to redecorate his Web page every week or month.

▼   What will you do if one of the sites you host distributes illegal material or disseminates material that violates someone else's copyright?

As the ultimate owner of the server machine, you may be liable for damages or criminal prosecution if you knowingly allow someone to distribute illegal files on your site. Illegal files range from many MP3 music files to archives of scanned magazine images to copies of articles or excerpts from books, all protected by United States copyright laws. (If you're in another country, depending on the conventions signed by your home nation, you may still be subject to United States copyright protections. See your attorney.)

Those are some of the disadvantages of virtual hosting. Note, most of them stem from the particular problems posed by selling virtual host services or agreeing to host your friends' sites on your own network. If you're doing virtual hosting as part of your regular job routine, you shouldn't have much to worry about except the hardware and software issues, and possibly the site policies you need to set up.

Regardless of the social or legal implications of virtual hosting, some technical advantages exist to using Apache's virtual host mechanism if you're responsible for multiple Web sites. First, obviously, you needn't set up and administer single machines for each site you host. You can put all the sites on one machine and let Apache do the work while all the sites share the same Internet connection and bandwidth. You rarely have to edit more than one configuration file for the whole lot of sites (unless you choose to give each site its own httpd daemon, as described later in the chapter). You also save time when you upgrade software or hardware. You only have to install one new stick of RAM, for example, to benefit every site you host. If you had those sites on individual machines, you'd have to buy and install RAM for each one. Not only does that get expensive, it takes time.

As you can see, the answer to "should I host virtual Web sites on my machine?" isn't always easy to find. If you have the resources and the time, though, this can be a great learning experience. Hosting virtual Web sites saves money and streamlines administrative tasks, and it's a great way to multiply your presence on the Web without a lot of expenditure. It can even be a way to bring in extra revenue if you decide to sell space on your machines. Whatever reason you choose as your motivator, virtual domain hosting is a great feature of Apache and it's fun to do.

WORKING WITH THE DOMAIN NAME SERVER

Before you can begin configuring a virtual domain on your site, you must spend some time with the Domain Name Service. As you might already know, the Domain Name Service

(DNS), is the mechanism through which IP addresses get resolved into domain names, and vice versa. Every time you pull up a Web site with a domain name, such as **http://www.cnn.com**, your browser must contact a DNS server to determine the actual IP address of CNN's Web site. Every domain represented on the Internet—whether on the Web or not—has a DNS record. If you want to add a virtual host to your site, you must ensure that the new host also has a DNS record; it doesn't matter whether the site is virtual or not.

To use a domain name on the Internet, it must have a related IP number. You'll usually get the IP number from the upstream site that provides your Internet service. If you work for a company that's purchased a significant data pipe, you might be able to select from an array of IP numbers that belong to your company. For others with more limited resources, you might be restricted to one IP that comes as part of your connectivity package, or you might be able to purchase individual IP numbers for an additional price. You need to provide the IP number when you purchase the domain name.

Under the current method for obtaining domain names in the United States, you must contact a third-party company and purchase the name. For names in the major top-level domains (TLDs) (.com, .org, and .net), you usually buy rights to the name for two years. You need to renew at that time if you want to keep the name. If you don't pay on time, you could lose the name to someone who's quicker with the cash. Other domains have different rules. Because many small countries now sell names within their own domains as a way to bring cash across their borders, you could get a good deal if you're willing to settle for a TLD that isn't as recognizable as .com.

CAUTION: Some domain-name registries now purchase your requested domain name themselves, and then lease it to you for the two-year period. Network Solutions now does business this way. Although I'm in no way affiliated with them, I find the domain service provided by Register.com speedy and reliable—and, with Register, you actually own your domain name. You can find a complete list of accredited registrars at **http://www.internic.net/regist.html**.

Get your IP number, go to a domain name registry, and purchase the domain name you want. (Most of the good ones are gone, though.) If your upstream provider will handle DNS registration for you, all you need to do at this point is tell the upstream folks you have a new domain name and what IP it will use. Most providers do handle DNS registration because they run their own nameservers. If you can't get your upstream provider to add the new domain name to its database, ask what you need to do. Writing DNS database entries is an art unto itself and isn't something to be done without careful attention to DNS documentation.

NOTE: If your upstream provider won't handle your DNS, you're far better off purchasing DNS service from another company than you are trying to do it yourself. DNS companies handle this data all the time and they refresh their nameservers regularly. It's okay to outsource DNS.

CONFIGURING VIRTUAL DOMAINS

Once you have the correct DNS settings configured for the virtual host, you can turn to Apache. Apache also needs to be configured for virtual hosts, both to deliver browser requests properly and to serve the appropriate pages. If you want virtual host data logged, that also needs to be configured at this point.

NOTE: You needn't configure virtual host logs separately from those for the main server. Errors, in particular, affect the main server whether or not the error-causing request is for the actual site or a virtual site. You'll probably want to track accesses separately for each site you host, however, so be sure to configure separate `access_log` files. You can also set up custom logs that only track browser requests directed at the virtual host. Learn more about Apache logs and how to set them up in Chapter 9, "Logs."

You can configure virtual domains on your server in two ways. You can either force separate `httpd` processes—one for each site (virtual or not)—or you can handle all sites you host under a single daemon process. While advantages exist to the former configuration, most people find the single daemon is sufficient for their needs. In general, if you would need different `httpd.conf` settings for each site, such as the `ServerRoot` variable or other basic information, you need to run separate processes. Apache can't handle multiple values for a given variable in the configuration file. If the basic information is the same for the virtual site as well as the actual site, though, you can run both sites off a single process. Most sites can use the single-process option.

Configuring a Virtual Host with a Single Daemon

Using a single Apache process is a somewhat complex configuration, but it is much simpler to administer than the multiple-daemon setup described in the next section of this chapter. This also produces much less stress on the machine because only one process is the parent and has control over the incoming requests. Each site, virtual or not, gets its own spawned child processes. You can use Apache to listen for requests on an unlimited number of IP numbers or domain names, but be aware of the total amount of traffic you're pumping through your Internet connection. No matter how carefully you configure the server, you're still limited by the bandwidth you have available, and you can't make your bandwidth bigger or faster without throwing money at the problem.

To configure your existing Apache installation so it recognizes virtual hosts, you simply need to work with the configuration file you've already seen many times throughout this book: `httpd.conf`.

NOTE: If you don't have Apache installed yet, go do that right now. Complete directions for installation are in Chapter 3, "Installing Apache," and basic configuration is covered in Chapter 6, "Configuring and Testing Apache." Test your server to make sure it's running properly before you begin to work with virtual hosts.

Open the appropriate configuration file for your version of Apache in your favorite text editor, using the help in Appendix B, "Using a Unix Text Editor," if necessary. Scroll past the basic configurations for your core site and the general server settings until you find the virtual host section of the file:

```
### Section 3: Virtual Hosts
```

You need to complete each of the following steps for each site you want to host virtually. In making these configurations, you're building individual "containers" for the sites. Each container will hold specific configurations and other information about that site. Using this technique means you can have different parameters or settings for each of the sites you host. They needn't be identical, and your visitors won't be able to tell the site isn't actually hosted on its own personal machine with its own httpd daemon.

```
#
# VirtualHost: If you want to maintain multiple domains/hostnames on your
# machine you can setup VirtualHost containers for them. Most configurations
# use only name-based virtual hosts so the server doesn't need to worry about
# IP addresses. This is indicated by the asterisks in the directives below.
#
# Please see the documentation at <URL:http://www.apache.org/docs/vhosts/>
# for further details before you try to setup virtual hosts.
```

Please consult this site before you begin working with virtual hosts. Although the information in this book is as current and accurate as we could make it, things do change, especially around the time of a new version of the software. While virtual hosting should not change significantly between press time and the time Apache 2.0 is released as stable, checking is always wise, especially if you're charging for the privilege of having a site hosted virtually on your server.

```
#
# You may use the command line option '-S' to verify your virtual host
# configuration.
```

This tip should be toward the end of the configuration, because it's something you'll want to do after you finish configuring all your virtual sites. (If you're paranoid about getting things right, as I am, you probably want to save and exit the configuration file after you build each container, test the settings, and then return to build another site's container.) Simply issue the command

```
httpd -S
```

at the prompt in your Apache directory to test the configuration of virtual sites. The output that prints to the screen tells you whether a problem exists. If you follow the directions in this chapter and in the configuration file itself, you should be fine.

```
#
# Use name-based virtual hosting.
#
#NameVirtualHost *
```

Name-based virtual hosting is a good example of advances on the server side that aren't always mirrored well on the client side. With *name-based virtual hosting,* the sites you host virtually can share a single IP number. That is, if you host the site **www.foo.bar** and the site **www.2foo.bar**, you can let them both share the same IP number. A particular HTTP header, Host:, should be sent by the requesting browser to indicate which site is being asked for—even if the request uses the IP number. This is a great way to economize on IP numbers, which are becoming increasingly scarce as more of the world's population moves online.

Not all browsers send the Host: header correctly, though. If the header is missing or malformed, Apache automatically serves the site listed first in the configuration file as listening to that IP number. So, if **www.foo.bar**'s container is placed ahead of the container for **www.2foo.bar** (and their Listen or BindAddress directives are identical), **www.foo.bar** is always served to a request with a missing or malformed Host: header.

TIP: To be nice to your visitors, place a link to the other sites that share the same IP number on the index.html page of that first site using the shared IP. Forcing your visitors to use HTTP 1.1–compliant browsers isn't always possible, so you might as well offer some help if they become lost because of a software problem.

Uncomment the name-based virtual hosting line if you plan to host sites that will share the same IP number. If you don't plan to do this, you can leave the line as is. Whether or not you choose to use name-based virtual hosting, you must still create a complete virtual host container for each site you plan to host virtually, including its domain name.

```
#
# VirtualHost example:
# Almost any Apache directive may go into a VirtualHost container.
# The first VirtualHost section is used for requests without a known
# server name.
#
#<VirtualHost *>
#    ServerAdmin webmaster@dummy-host.example.com
#    DocumentRoot /www/docs/dummy-host.example.com
#    ServerName dummy-host.example.com
#    ErrorLog logs/dummy-host.example.com-error_log
#    CustomLog logs/dummy-host.example.com-access_log common
#</VirtualHost>
```

This set of lines is the core of a virtual host configuration. The line that reads <VirtualHost *> is the beginning of the host container and the line reading </VirtualHost> is the end of the container. For any given host, you must place all the configurations specific for the host between those two lines. The sample configuration is quite clear: simply replace the placeholder data, such as dummy-host, with the actual data for the host you're setting up. For example, assume you're setting up a virtual host for a site called **www.paperclipmania.org**, as well as another site for pencils with a different IP number. The container might look like this:

```
<VirtualHost 198.16.0.1>
    ServerAdmin webmaster@www.paperclipmania.org
    DocumentRoot /www/docs/www.paperclipmania.org
    ServerName www.paperclipmania.org
    ErrorLog  logs/www.paperclipmania.org-error_log
    CustomLog logs/www.paperclipmania.org-access_log common
</VirtualHost>

<VirtualHost 198.16.0.3>
    ServerAdmin webmaster@www.pencilfunforeveryone.org
    DocumentRoot /www/docs/www.pencilfunforeveryone.org
    ServerName www.pencilfunforeveryone.org
    ErrorLog  logs/www.pencilfunforeveryone.org-error_log
    CustomLog logs/www.pencilfunforeveryone.org-access_log common
</VirtualHost>
```

Note, the full domain name is included in every setting. This is because the site doesn't actually have any machines. You're creating the only name by which the site will ever be known. The first line of the container contains the IP number on which Apache listens for requests concerning this site. Be sure this is identified with a Listen directive in the general configuration settings.

CAUTION: Don't put a domain name in the first line of the container instead of an IP number. Apache must contact the DNS server to resolve the IP number from the domain name every time this site has requests, which can eat up server resources and slow response time. Always use a valid IP number in the header of a virtual host container. You can use the domain name in every other line. You definitely have to put the full domain name as the value of the ServerName variable, so Apache knows which requests are directed to this virtual host and which are sent elsewhere.

This container has specified logs to be kept only for this server, which is an excellent idea. You don't need a separate error log, but it doesn't hurt. Remember to review the error log regularly because errors on this virtual host will no longer appear in the general Apache error_log file.

Continue in this vein, making new containers for each virtual site you plan to host. When you finish with the configuration file, save it and exit the text editor. You need to restart the server before the new configurations take effect. Do this by moving into your main Apache directory and issuing the command

```
apachectl graceful
```

to force a restart without disconnecting anyone currently connected to your main server process. If you don't have anyone connected, issue the command as

```
apachectl restart
```

When the server restarts, test each newly configured virtual site with a regular browser (you might need to throw up a basic index.html file, so the site can be accessed). If at all possible, have someone outside your network test the sites as well. You should be able to see everything on the site, whether you're using the IP number assigned to the virtual host or the complete domain name.

Configuring a Virtual Host with Multiple Daemons

Configuring a virtual host that will have its own Apache process is simpler than the process in the previous section. However, it takes up more space on your hard disk because you must create a completely new server for each site you host. To set this up properly, make sure you have a clean download of the latest version of Apache (either beta or stable, depending on your needs and risk tolerance).

CAUTION: Running multiple Apache daemons is going to eat your system resources like a hungry person faced with delicious snack foods. Just the daemons alone can suck up a good chunk of overhead. And, if any of these sites get a lot of traffic, it'll be even worse. If you're setting up virtual hosts with their own daemons because you expect to get a lot of traffic on one or more of your sites, consider whether you should give each site its own server machine. Although putting each site on its own machine is usually overkill, in the case of high traffic and multiple daemons, this might make the most sense.

Install as many copies of Apache as you need to serve each of the sites you host. Obviously, you need to put them in different locations on the hard drive, so each new installation doesn't simply overwrite the previous copy. Open the configuration file for each installation and make all the changes you need to make, such as defining the site and setting appropriate values for all the variables. You must use the `Listen` directive in `httpd-std.conf` to set the IP address or domain name to be used by the particular iteration of `httpd` that uses that configuration file.

NOTE: If you want a particular installation to listen for connections on only one IP number, you can use the `BindAddress` directive instead. With `Listen`, however, you can set multiple ports, IP numbers, or domain names for that daemon to answer.

Edit each installation's configuration file and make sure no duplications exist in the `Listen` or `BindAddress` directives. If two separate daemons are listening on the same port, you might have problems as the two processes both try to answer the single request. Save the files and exit your text editor, making sure to keep the appropriate configuration file in the appropriate directory.

TIP: Even though multiple daemons are going to slow your machine, you can cut some of the system overhead by using only IP numbers in the configuration files. If you use resolved domain names, Apache must resolve those names back to IP numbers before it can continue with the request.

Be careful when you're managing the multiple-server processes. Before you issue any commands that involve only one of the processes, check the `httpd.pid` file to be sure you know which process identification number refers to that daemon. To be absolutely positive you're issuing commands for the correct server, use the full path when you type the command, instead of relying on any settings in your PATH environment variable.

VIRTUAL DOMAIN SERVICES: E-MAIL

If you provide virtual domain hosting to people who aren't normally part of your user base, you'll probably need to provide e-mail services to them as well. People who are part of your regular user community, such as other employees of your company, don't need access to specially configured e-mail accounts for the virtually hosted sites. Providing e-mail services as well as Web hosting is a good idea. Site visitors generally expect administrative e-mail accounts for a given site will share the same domain name. This looks more professional, and it makes the distinction between virtually hosted sites and physical sites less obvious.

Configuring your e-mail server is beyond the scope of this book. Please consider your choices of e-mail server programs carefully.

NOTE: If you're a Web administrator at a company large enough to pay you just to do Apache, there's probably an e-mail administrator or two around the corner. Find that person and ask how to configure e-mail accounts for your virtual host clients. Far better to annoy someone else than to poach on their territory without permission or an advanced knowledge of the software being used!

`sendmail`, the grand-daddy of all e-mail servers, is highly functional and can do nearly anything you want to do with e-mail. `sendmail` is also an absolute bear to configure and it's opaque to administer. Many administrators have switched to the smaller and faster `qmail` program. Under `qmail`, if you have accounts that are mail-only, you can store them in a database, which is much faster for the server to process when mail comes in. `sendmail`, however, offers some elegant and advanced settings that let you configure different ways to deal with mail coming in to different addresses for each of your virtual sites. Many more mail servers are also available beyond just `sendmail` and `qmail`. The best thing to do is to obtain a large and comprehensive Unix reference that includes a section on Internet services, including e-mail. Pick the one easiest for you to configure and manage.

> *TIP:* Learn more about `sendmail` at **http://www.sendmail.org** and about `qmail` at **http://www.qmail.org**. The `sendmail` site has a page devoted to virtual domains and e-mail at **http://www.sendmail.org/virtual-hosting.html**. If you want to learn about mail servers in general, try the Linux Administrator's Security Guide e-mail server section at **http://howto.tucows.com/LDP/ LDP/lasg/lasg-www/servers/email/**. Despite its name, this document is useful as an overview for administrators of all Unix variants and it isn't completely restricted to security topics.

No matter what mail server you end up using, you should enable as many addresses as necessary for the sites you're hosting. At the minimum, you should create a `webmaster@virtual.site` address, as well as an `abuse@virtual.site` address. Even though `abuse@` isn't a required address, many people have become accustomed to the address and it's rapidly becoming a convention. Your individual virtual host clients may have other addresses they also want configured. Try to avoid creating a slew of personal addresses for people who don't otherwise have accounts on your site (and, thus, aren't necessarily bound by your regular user policies). Keep the virtual e-mail accounts administrative in nature, unless you're prepared to offer a complete e-mail hosting service as well. Most Web administrators aren't interested in also running mail servers, so save yourself the work and simply build administrative accounts for any virtual hosts you create.

> *TIP:* If you're creating administrative e-mail accounts for virtual sites under your control, set those accounts to forward to your regular in-box. This way, you needn't remember to go to a different in-box to read Webmaster mail, but visitors can use the virtual domain name to send administrative or abuse queries.

SUMMARY

You can host more sites on your Apache server than only the one main site. Each of these additional sites can operate without having a dedicated server machine or even any other physical presence besides the domain name used to request files from the site. Such sites are called virtual domains. You can host an unlimited number of virtual domains with any given Apache installation, as long as the domain name is properly registered and you abide by any regulations from your upstream Internet connection.

To configure a virtual domain, you simply need to add a container with the domain's identifying information into your regular configuration file. When you restart the server, the new domain will be accessible from a Web browser. The sites can share the same httpd daemon process and the same IP number, or you can configure Apache to start individual processes for each site and assign individual IP numbers. The latter option takes an inordinate amount of system resources and scarce IP numbers, however. Depending on the electronic mail server program you're running, you can also configure virtual e-mail, so the various administrative addresses for each virtual domain reflect the domain's name.

CHAPTER 19

E-Commerce

No book about Apache or the Web would be complete without at least one chapter on e-commerce, and this book complies with that de facto requirement. E-commerce is what everyone's talking about. It was the Next Big Thing for much of the mid-90s, and now—in the aftermath of the tech stock crash—people are wondering whether e-commerce was only another flashy hype-filled movement that's going to fade as quickly as the idea that people want to surf the Web inside their sunglasses as they drive down the highway. (Okay, that does sound like fun, but you get the idea.)

The fact is, e-commerce is here to stay. Although the high-profile implosions of some heavily advertised Web sites has dulled some of the initial infatuation, many companies have seen their Web division increase in importance and add to the bottom line. For every **Pets.com** or **Kozmo.com** that fails spectacularly, there's a company like Patternworks (**http://www.patternworks.com**), a yarn store in New York that has transferred much of its successful catalog business to a Web model. The real successes in e-commerce are small companies who might do most (or all!) of their business on a Web site or larger companies that see a Web presence as yet another sales location, but not as the savior of the business.

Should you care about e-commerce? Probably. Even if the sites you run are 100 percent static and one directional, taking no feedback from visitors and providing only information, you're probably an e-commerce consumer on some level. If you work for a company and administer the corporate Web site, you're involved in e-commerce at some level. You might not be running shopping carts and credit card software, but e-commerce is more than just shopping. The fact is, if you spend any time on the Web, you're affected by e-commerce. Your favorite sites are funded through various models, including advertising contracts. You might check your bank balance online or browse **Amazon.com** for gift ideas. You may just curse banner ads and pop-up windows that interfere with your regular browsing habits, but you're still involved in the e-commerce equation. In the world of Web advertising, you're still another set of eyeballs staring at the banners, even if you never click one.

TIP: To learn more about the world of e-commerce from both business and technical perspectives, see *eBusiness: A Beginner's Guide,* by Robert C. Elsenpeter and Toby J. Velte (Osborne/McGraw-Hill, 2001). It's in the same series as this book, the Network Professional's Library.

In this chapter, we introduce the world of e-commerce from a Web administrator's perspective.

NOTE: In all likelihood, if you work for a company that has a significant e-commerce presence, the person running the Apache server is probably not the same person in charge of administering the e-commerce services. This is a good thing, because each has a unique set of skills and attitudes that complement each other, but are hard to implement simultaneously. (No matter how involved or uninvolved in your company's e-commerce arm you might be, you should still understand what's at stake, both financially and technologically.)

We begin with a set of possible definitions of "e-commerce" and move directly to security: one of the main reasons people won't shop online, whether justified or not. Next, you learn how to add e-commerce elements to your site whether or not you process entire transactions locally. Finally, you learn about third-party e-commerce providers and whether you should hire one to handle certain aspects—or all—of your e-commerce Web presence.

WHAT IS E-COMMERCE, ANYWAY?

Ask 20 people to define e-commerce and the first reaction most of them have will probably be "Buying stuff online." That's certainly the model we're all most familiar with because it's the core of many newspaper and television stories about e-commerce. It's also the aspect that gets the most attention when a sales site shuts down: **eToys.com**, anyone? Business troubles often bring out the naysayers who ask, "Just how many people are going to buy kitty litter online, anyway?" (Not many, as **Pets.com** would tell you.) As I write this chapter, the big story on business pages is the rapid series of home grocery delivery sites that are shutting down. In New England, the year started with four or five grocery delivery options: in July, only one remained—and Peapod is backed by a large regional grocery chain, which, in turn, is bankrolled by an international food-services conglomerate.

The glamour of shopping online has faded. The market is shaking out, and it's becoming more apparent that certain sectors do well online and other sectors don't. Sure, you can order a pizza online in some markets, but the CGI form simply delivers your order to a person at a telephone, who then calls your local franchise and places the order for you. Pizza's not the way to use the Web, but what about airline tickets? Price comparison sites and travel auctions are booming, and travel agents are feeling the squeeze. Airlines make more money when they sell tickets directly, rather than relying on agents to broker the deal. Travel is a great e-commerce sector.

Up to this point, we've been discussing consumer-oriented e-commerce. When you log onto Amazon or the Borders online site to buy some books, you're Jane Doe with a credit card. You aren't going to buy more than one or two hundred dollars' worth of merchandise at a time, and the site needs to turn over thousands of transactions like yours a day to break even. Selling to consumers is a risky world because individual consumers are fickle and like to browse, compare prices, and buy on sale. The profit margin for online sales to consumers can be thin, and it's no surprise that the hyped failures of the past year or two have all been sites targeted at consumers.

NOTE: This doesn't mean consumer-oriented e-commerce sites can't succeed. The ones that do make it, however, are sites that have figured out their market and targeted the site accordingly. WalMart has an online presence, but it does the vast majority of its business in the physical stores. Amazon is floundering because it has lost focus on what made it famous—books—and expanded into kitchen equipment, lawn and garden accessories, and other items that don't fit the general perception of **Amazon.com**.

A whole other world of e-commerce lies beyond the online versions of your favorite mall shops. The business-to-business model, commonly called B2B, is far more successful than the consumer-oriented model. B2B e-commerce is based on the theory that businesses have to buy goods and services to do their own business. For example, a manufacturer must buy raw materials, new machinery, and packaging to make and market its items. In earlier times, these materials were marketed by salesmen and catalogs. In the B2B era, a company can put its materials on the Web and sell to other businesses with lower overhead (no traveling salesmen or expensive four-color catalogs!). B2B sites have different needs than consumer-driven sites—for example, they might not have a credit card–processing mechanism, because customers might require invoices instead. They also rely much less heavily on third-party advertising or flashy visual layout designed to draw an individual consumer into the site. Businesses must buy to sell, so half the sales battle has already been won by the time a purchasing manager arrives at a B2B site.

TIP: If you want to see how B2B sites differ from consumer-oriented sites, pick up any true trade magazine. The ads are mostly for B2B sites. Advertisements in airports are also B2B oriented because the majority of air travelers are there on business.

Beyond consumer-oriented sites and B2B sites, other aspects of e-commerce still might affect your site and how you market your data or the products you sell. Some of the other facets of e-commerce might not even seem like "online business" to you at first, but they all count if you're defining e-commerce as business transactions involving the Internet:

▼ Online bill paying services

■ Online billing for utilities, insurance, and credit cards

■ Web access to bank accounts

■ Web applications for mortgages, home equity loans, and other credit

■ Online credit reports

■ Banner advertisements

■ Tracking software that generates contact lists

■ Demographic analysis of site visitors

■ Web-only account management for Internet service providers

■ Virtual domain and e-mail hosting

■ Payroll and accounting services

▲ Price comparison services for large corporate or governmental purchases

Many more ways exist in which people do business using the Web. The stereotypical e-commerce site, a consumer-oriented site with no physical presence, is a relatively small fraction of the complete e-commerce picture. Even if your company doesn't sell products directly online, it might still participate in an e-commerce activity.

SECURITY AND E-COMMERCE

If you're offering the capability to purchase items or information over the Internet, you *must* be absolutely obsessive about security. No excuses are accepted. When someone buys something from you, that person entrusts you with critical personal information: name, address, even credit card numbers or governmental identification like a Social Security number. If this information is stolen or otherwise compromised, your customers' credit ratings and identities may be ruined—and you'll be spending time in court explaining where your security policies failed.

Data theft is a depressing fact of life, as well as a guaranteed ratings hook for local news media who seem to run identity theft stories regularly every three months. Unique data that identifies each of us as individuals is worth quite a bit on the black market. If someone can get hold of your Social Security number, your name, and your address, they can become you. The credit-rating databases have no idea what you look like. They make their decisions and scores based on that set of data. It doesn't matter if someone else is posing as you. If they have your information, they can get credit cards and spend thousands of dollars you can end up owing. Erasing the scars of an identity theft from your permanent credit records takes a lot of time and effort, and catching the perpetrators is extremely difficult.

Scary? You bet. But that's the risk we all take by shopping online. Your job as an e-commerce Web administrator is to make that scenario as impossible as you can, by locking down sensitive information on your site and making each connection to the site as secure as possible. Running a secure e-commerce site that meets shoppers' needs while protecting their identification is certainly possible. This simply takes time and attention, and a little help from software.

NOTE: If you contract any of your e-commerce services out to another company, you need to know what security precautions they take. Someone who visits your site and has her security compromised may not care if it wasn't your machines that failed. She was visiting *your* site, not your contractor's. While you may be technically in the right, your job is to police your vendors, as well as your own site.

Luckily, you can call several security mechanisms into play on your site to provide as much security as possible, while still letting your site function as it should.

NOTE: As you see in the next part of the book, "Security and Apache," the only truly secure machine is one that's not connected to any other computers, including the networks of the Internet, which is locked in a room where only you have the key—and that's secure only because I'm assuming you won't do anything nefarious!

The remainder of this section of the chapter introduces security considerations primarily related to e-commerce implementations. If you take each of these methods into account, along with the various methods described in Part V of the book, you'll have a reasonably secure system. Pay special attention to the e-commerce software and files on your machine, and you should be able to run commercial transactions with little trouble, as long as you stay vigilant for any sign of illegal entry or compromised data.

Public Key Infrastructure

The Public Key Infrastructure (PKI) is a suite of elements that constitute the security framework of the Internet. *PKI* is a general term that applies to encryption, digital signatures, certificates of authority, and registration. The more of these elements you incorporate into your site and publicize to your users, the better level of trust you'll have with those users. Trust, as you've read throughout this chapter, is the key to successful and sustained consumer relationships.

Encryption is the most well-known segment of this suite of security elements. As you probably know, *encrypted data* is simply data that has been changed, according to a predetermined code. If you know the code, you can unlock the data. If you don't know the code, you can only get the data through brute force, applying all sorts of known codes or algorithms to the data until the code is broken.

NOTE: Some encryption codes are ridiculously simple. You probably used simple encryptions in primary school, substituting letters for letters. For example, you might have substituted *C* for *A*, *D* for *B*, *E* for *C*, and so on, simply jumping ahead two letters. This is fun and complicated for a seven-year-old, but the software used to break encrypted data is far more sophisticated now. Encryption algorithms used for security purposes generate random codes each time the software is installed and configured.

A lot of data on the Internet, and especially in e-commerce situations, is encrypted. Any e-commerce software you buy should encrypt authentication data, and especially credit card numbers. With an appropriate encryption and decryption algorithm, you won't ever need to see the actual numbers or store them unencrypted on your site.

Certification programs and digital signatures both take advantage of a particular kind of encryption technology: the public key. With *public key encryption,* installing the encryption software generates a public code, or key. The key is small enough that it can be placed in the .signature file of an e-mail program. Anyone can get your key, insert it into their own encryption software, and generate an encrypted piece of data that only you can unlock. The public key is tied to a private key, which only you have, buried in your own encryption installation. Public key encryption is both easy to use and highly secure.

TIP: The best-known public key encryption program is PGP, or Pretty Good Privacy. Learn more about PGP at **http://www.pgp.com**.

When you apply for a certificate of authority or identity, you receive a software key that says "this company is who it says it is." Certificates are sent as headers in a regular Apache transaction, and individual users can configure their browsers to require certificates or ignore them. In practical terms, certificates are less useful than they seem, although they're quite heavily used in certain B2B sectors. Digital signatures, on the other hand, are growing in popularity as the United States legal system struggles with the best way to accept electronic transmissions as valid documents. Digital signatures also provide a public encryption key and travel as HTTP headers.

NOTE: The Secure Socket Layer (SSL) uses encryption to protect the data stream as it flows from your server to the requesting browser and back again. Chapter 22, "SSL—Secure Socket Layer," explains the basics of SSL and why you might want to use it on your site. SSL is a type of encryption that's more transparent than deliberately encrypted files and it's quite easy to use once you configure it properly.

Consumer Security Confidence

You can put all the time and money in the world into your e-commerce site, making it as secure as possible, but there's one element of security over which you have little direct influence. The public opinion and perception of your site is something you can work toward affecting, but this isn't something you can shape directly. Unfortunately, public opinion is not always based on fact, but can be altered by rumor, misinformation, or plain meanness.

NOTE: If you think that public rumors are not going to have much effect on your business, think about Proctor & Gamble, the Ivory Soap people. For the past 20 or 30 years, Proctor & Gamble has been the victim of a persistent rumor that the company is run by Satanists. The rumor stems from the P&G logo, which is an image of a crescent moon and stars. Of course, Proctor & Gamble is a staid blue-chip company interested in selling you shampoo and bodywash, not a hotbed of esoteric religious practice. Still, the rumor persists. Both columnists for Ann Landers and Dear Abby have debunked it numerous times, and I've received e-mail warning me about P&G's Satanic activity at least twice during 2001 already. If P&G can't shake the public relations nightmare, what will you—a much smaller company or individual—do if a rumor gets started about what you do with consumer information? Look at DoubleClick's PR problems, described in Chapter 11, "Performance Tuning."

More specifically, you need to worry about how your potential and existing customers see your site. Do they think you're secure? Do they worry about the way in which their information is used after they visit the site? Are you losing customers to other sites with different security protocols? You don't know unless you ask, and, sometimes, even then you won't get an accurate answer.

You can do a lot to give your visitors an accurate understanding of site security. Place a link to your site security policies on the front page and keep a link available on every page of your site: put it down at the bottom with your copyright policy and help link. Explain how you handle sensitive data like credit card numbers. Do you encrypt? Delete after a certain time? Never store numbers after the order has been processed? If you use cookie logs or order forms to build a database of information about your visitors, explain that, too. Give customers the ability to opt out—or better yet, to opt in—for your e-mail and direct mail solicitations. The more control you give customers over how you interact with them and use their data, the more likely they are to return because you've built an extra level of trust.

The key concept for e-commerce is trust. You trust your customers to provide accurate information when they purchase a product on your site. They trust you to build a secure environment in which they can share sensitive information with you to make that purchase. Everything you do that increases this level of trust—from asking before you mail a catalog to destroying encrypted credit card data after a certain period of time—can keep your customers happy and glad to do repeat business with you. They'll even recommend their friends or place links to your site on their own Web pages if you make the experience good enough. Isn't that better than the alternative of losing customers and public confidence if you don't have effective security policies and practices in place on your site?

ADDING E-COMMERCE ELEMENTS TO YOUR SITE

Even if you don't run a complete e-commerce setup on your site, you can use some e-commerce elements to add extra functions and assistance your visitors can appreciate. For example, you might set up a shopping cart to handle requests for printed information. Visitors can fill their electronic carts with the brochures they want to receive through the mail and conclude the session by giving you a mailing address. This is far faster and easier to deal with than a simple HTML form that generates output in an extended URL. Although both the form and the shopping cart can use the CGI format, the shopping cart makes it easier on your end to process the transaction.

If you decide to outsource your e-commerce transactions, you could save money by handling some of the elements locally. For example, you might design your own online catalogs and shopping cart in-house. Then, you can outsource only the credit card processing task, which is best left to a specialist anyway. By blending internal design and responsibility with external resources to handle difficult tasks, you can get the benefits of professional assistance combined with the cost savings and product familiarity in using your own staff.

CAUTION: Be sure the company to which you outsource permits you to use homegrown e-commerce elements on your site. Some providers sell only "whole package" contracts, where they're responsible for all elements of your commercial presence. If you want to retain the most control, make sure you can host everything on your site and outsource only the parts that don't make sense for you to do, like credit card processing and shipping.

E-commerce sites offer good lessons for any Web administrator or designer, even if you don't sell things off your site. E-commerce sites know how to handle heavy traffic and adopt the technologies that keep high hit counts while not impacting the individual user experience. Look around a busy e-commerce site—using the code-view features of your browser—and see what kind of software the site is using. It's probably dynamic page serving software, like PHP, combined with some savvy page design and well-placed links to other parts of the site.

NOTE: PHP is actually an embedded scripting language. It's used with regular HTML files to serve requested pages dynamically. Instead of setting up your entire site with static links, you can customize both the content and structure of your pages depending on certain variables or input from visitors. Learn more at **http://www.php.com**.

What can you take back to your own site? Perhaps you can change the way in which files are served, or you can provide additional functions for your visitors that enhance their experience at your site (and, thus, increase the likelihood of return visits or longer stays).

Catalogs

Catalogs are the core of many consumer-oriented sites and of B2B sites as well. As you know, at its most basic, a catalog is simply a list of products for sale and their prices. The catalogs you get in the mail, part of the multimillion dollar direct-mail industry, are glossy visual feasts carefully designed to get you in the mood to buy. Online catalogs are no different. If you visit the Web sites of companies that also have a thriving print catalog business, you see sophisticated sites that integrate the best elements of the Web and of traditional catalog marketing.

TIP: On your Web catalog tour, visit Lands' End (**http://www.landsend.com**), LL Bean (**http://www.llbean.com**), Crate & Barrel (**http://www.crateandbarrel.com**), and Peapod (**http://www.peapod.com**). The first three sites also have successful print catalogs. If you've seen these catalogs in the past, note how carefully the online presence meshes with the print presence. The fourth site is an online grocery service. See how sparse the design is? Groceries aren't as "sexy" as clothes or home furnishings. The sites fit the material they're selling.

In designing your catalogs, you probably want to use a dynamic page delivery mechanism. With such software, you needn't redesign static catalog pages every time the inventory changes. Rather, the catalog pages themselves have placeholders and spaces for whatever items need to be rotated forward. The actual information is pulled from a database when the page is requested.

NOTE: For Apache administrators, the dynamic page delivery system of choice is PHP. While ASP (Active Server Pages, Microsoft's scripting language used for dynamic page delivery) has a strong presence on the Web, it's designed to work with Microsoft's Internet Information Server. Open Source and Free Software users should focus on PHP, which is reasonably easy to learn if you have a handle on how databases are constructed and an understanding of the HTTP standard.

As an administrator, your main concern is on delivering the catalog content rather than designing the catalog itself, unless you work in a small shop where you handle a range of Web tasks. Catalogs can consume quite a bit of your system resources, especially because they're graphics intensive, and might require CGI or PHP processing from Apache as well as the regular server tasks. E-commerce sites, in general, need as much hardware power as you can provide because they perform a number of additional routines along with Web operations.

Shopping Carts

Almost all e-commerce sites, except for the most minimal ones, use some form of shopping cart software to handle orders on their site. A shopping cart program works much like the cart at your grocery: the visitor clicks around your site, adding items into the cart as she finds things she likes. At any time, she can visit her cart and delete items, change the number of items she's buying, or conclude the transaction. A shopping cart is a great boon to Web shoppers because it encourages browsing—you're not forced to buy an item as soon as you select it, which means you might buy more.

Shopping cart programs are usually CGI scripts. They rely on a complicated relational database containing all necessary information about the items sold on the site and they usually pull various bits of tracking information from each transaction for later marketing use. Most shopping cart programs mesh with an order program, which actually manages the purchase, but some shopping carts include order functions along with the cart itself. A wide number of shopping cart scripts is available on the Web or for purchase from commercial software companies, and they vary greatly in terms of ease of use or functions you can enable.

TIP: If possible, get a shopping cart that lets customers leave the site and return later to find the same items there. **Amazon.com** uses such a cart with a several-month expiration. It's not unusual for me to return to Amazon a month after filling my cart, but not concluding the transaction, and realize I still want those same books. Letting data stay in an individual shopper's record (using cookies to track authentication and access) could increase your sales in the long run.

Buying or downloading a shopping cart is much easier than programming one yourself. Writing a shopping cart program requires a good understanding of your chosen scripting or compiled programming language, how relational databases work, and how to mesh three or four individual scripts together to offer all the functions the cart needs. Most shopping cart programs have various subroutines to handle number of items, valid values (like color or whether the item is in stock), and price. To display the current cart contents on the screen, the program uses yet another subroutine to call all the current values and print them to the screen in the correct format. Get one from a trusted vendor and save the headaches you'd have in fixing your own coding errors. You can force a vendor to fix problems, rather than working around the clock to do it yourself.

TIP: For those administrators with limited time who still want to offer shopping cart convenience to their visitors, go ahead and get a commercial or downloaded cart. You should be able to customize enough of the program to make it work for you. The most important use of your time, though, is keeping the relational database updated with the appropriate items, descriptions, prices, and stock availability. Nothing irritates an online shopper more than completing a lengthy transaction, and then getting an apologetic e-mail the next day informing him that eight of the eleven items he bought are out of stock, and the ninth is only available in mustard yellow. Your time is almost always best spent keeping the database on target, rather than programming your own unique scripts.

Contact Lists and Marketing Information

The marketing staff at your company has a different view of success in e-commerce transactions than does the technical staff or even the sales staff. To marketing professionals, getting information about visitors and customers is as important as selling things. After all, if you can contact your visitors and previous customers on a regular basis, you can entice them back to the site with sales and special offers, so they'll become repeat customers and build loyalty to your site.

You can gather that information about your site visitors in several ways. Of course, you can use the custom logs and cookie information described in Chapter 9, "Logs," and Chapter 11, "Performance Tuning." These Apache techniques give you information about your visitor's IP address and browser settings, but not a great deal of marketable information about the visitor's personal likes and dislikes. You can get much better information about a consumer by tracking what he buys each time he visits. For example, look at the **Amazon.com** recommendations strategy. Based on what you bought in the past and ratings you provide for books you've read, Amazon can build a set of recommendations that appear when you visit the site. The more you visit and rate, the more accurate the recommendations become. The Amazon model is so successful, it's been adopted by other sites as well. Netflix, which rents DVDs through the postal service, uses an almost-identical rating and recommendation system to point out movies you might enjoy. The ratings are popular because it's fun to pass judgment on movies and books, and people like to see the recommendations get better focused as more data is entered.

Of course, your marketing strategy will include shopping cart contents. Part of the shopping cart data is the purchaser's name and address. While many sites (as well as print catalogs and physical stores) simply take the name and address, and then add it to a mailing list, some online privacy groups disapprove of subscribing people automatically to any sort of list. When it comes to advertising, a conservative approach almost always plays better with your customers than the aggressive marketing campaign your company may want to mount. When you ask people for name and address, include a check box or two where the purchaser can select whether to receive material through the mail or through e-mail. Requiring your customers to opt into receiving such communications is a better trust mechanism than assuming they'd love to get your messages.

CAUTION: Despite all the publicity and media hype that surrounds online privacy issues, many people still believe they're invisible on the Internet unless they choose not to be. This simply is not the case. However, it's a pervasive belief and something you must deal with if you get into the user-tracking and e-commerce end of Web administration. You can go a long way toward ensuring a happy interaction with your visitors if you allow them to initiate contact or request to be added to a list. Unsolicited commercial e-mail (even if "unsolicited" means "the user didn't deselect the E-mail Me check box") gives consumers a bad taste and might cause them to stop visiting your site. It's all about perception.

CHOOSING AN E-COMMERCE PROVIDER

About ready to scream? Realizing there's no way you can administer an e-commerce site with the attention it deserves, along with all your other administrative duties? Join the club. Many administrators and companies have decided that handling their own e-commerce transactions is simply too complicated, and requires too much work and specialized knowledge. Instead of tearing their hair out, they whip out their checkbooks and hire a third-party company to handle an e-commerce presence on the Web. You, too, can take this route; it's certainly easy. You have to ask some questions and gather some information before you decide to outsource any of your e-commerce activities, but, for many companies, outsourcing is the most efficient way to sell product or information over the Web.

In this section of the chapter, you learn more about Application service providers (ASPs). Like Internet service providers (ISPs), ASPs range between the bare-bones and the full-service. You need to be a savvy consumer and know exactly what you need—as well as what you don't want—before you sign a contract. The advantage of using an ASP is that the headache of running a secure e-commerce site is off your shoulders: either completely, if you outsourced the whole thing, or partially, if you retained control over certain aspects of the site.

What's Included?

If you did any comparison shopping when you picked an ISP, you might remember that different providers offer different packages. From one provider, you might get eight e-mail addresses, 10MB for a personal Web site, and unlimited access time. From another provider, for the same price, you might get one e-mail address and no Web space, but a blazingly fast connection. Picking the right ISP involved making tradeoffs until you found the intersection between price and services that worked best for you.

Shopping for an ASP is like that. The services offered by different companies can vary wildly. Some companies only sell a *turnkey* system, where you buy the software and set it up on your own machines with your own Internet connection, configuring and administering it yourself. Other companies sell a one-size-fits-all system, in which you upload your entire site to their server machines: they administer everything, and your only responsibility is keeping the files updated and fulfilling the orders. Still other companies sell only part of the e-commerce package, such as credit card processing or order fulfillment. The ASP you ultimately select will be the company that offers services you need at a price you can afford.

> **NOTE:**   You might find you can't afford the services you need. In this case, you might want to pull back and retain control over some of the major chunks of your e-commerce presence: managing your own catalog pages, writing your own shopping cart program, or downloading Free or Open Source software that costs less than the proprietary programs. At the minimum, you should pay someone to handle credit card orders for you. If you're an extremely small company, though, you might be able to get away with a merchant account on a system like PayPal (**http://www.paypal.com**), the payment system beloved by eBay sellers. You could also accept only mailed orders, but you'll lose a lot of the impulse purchases that keep Web sites solvent.

Even if you never comparison shop for anything, do so when you're purchasing ASP services. If a company gives off a weird vibe, go elsewhere. Just as with a bank, you want your ASP to be filled with conservative, safety-conscious people who understand the magnitude of the data they're handling for you. When you sign an ASP contract, you're essentially bringing the ASP in as a partner in your business. The ASP has that much influence over your bottom line.

It's relatively easy to do homework on an ASP. Check the Better Business Bureau (BBB) in the state or city where the ASP is headquartered. While many people don't make BBB complaints about Internet businesses, it's a special flag if complaints are on file because someone had to go to the trouble of tracking down the correct BBB. You can also check the various trade papers and sites for ASP professionals, including these three:

▼ **http://www.aspindustry.org**   The main trade association for ASP professionals

■ **http://www.aspnews.com**   A news site with insightful columns about ASP issues

▲ **http://www.aspisland.com**   Another news site that offers many press releases and other information from companies involved in the industry

Making the Decision

Once you find a company you're comfortable with, it's time to make your decision. Should you outsource? What should you outsource and what should you keep on site? The answers depend on the kind of business you run and the resources available to you. Obviously, if you're the only technical person at your company, you'll probably want to outsource much of the work. But, you should ask yourself a number of questions before you're ready to make the final commitment to an external e-commerce service provider:

▼ How much money do I have available?

   If you don't have the money to purchase fast servers and pay employees or consultants to configure an e-commerce site for you, an ASP may be the right solution. Just be sure you're not paying for things you don't use or you're not paying more than the going market rate for e-commerce features. Again, do your homework to know what the rates are before you sign a contract.

▼ How soon do I need to have this site up and running?

You can probably get an ASP-served site up faster than you can build one from scratch, especially if you don't already have a relational database in place filled with the information about your products. ASPs are experienced in taking raw data from their clients and putting it into a workable sales format. If you aren't under particular time pressure, though, and you enjoy designing your own sites (or you have a team of Web designers who need something to do), consider outsourcing the connectivity and the operations, but not the design.

▼ Do I work well with vendors?

Some people hate handing off their intellectual property to others, especially if the only control over the other company is a contract. Other people don't do well with vendor relationships. They end up micromanaging the vendor; bossing their technical staff around; or taking up endless hours on the phone with tiny complaints, questions, or needs for reassurance. Still others don't feel comfortable speaking up when something is wrong, especially if their own knowledge of the e-commerce world is slight. Before you sign a contract as important as one with an ASP, you need to reach an understanding about how you and the ASP will interact with each other on a regular basis and when there's a crisis (and who defines a "crisis," as well).

▼ Do we have special needs?

As described earlier in this section, not every e-commerce package is the right solution for your company. How much extra configuration will you have to pay for, and who decides when the configuration and customization is finished? If it's you, you might have to pay more for extra work. If it's the ASP, you might not get the site you want.

NOTE: If the ASP does the programming, ask what its policy is on accessibility. Given the choice between an ASP that pays attention to Web accessibility and one that doesn't, pick the one that does. You'll feel better about your site and you'll open the doors to a consumer segment who might be unable to visit your competition's sites.

▼ Who retains control?

This is the big one. You need to retain control over your data. Be absolutely positive and confident that your ASP has appropriate back-up mechanisms in place and that it has enough redundancy built into the system so your site won't suffer if there's a power outage or hardware failure. *Always keep a copy of your complete site on your own network or in your office.* Also, make sure you know what the grievance procedures are in case you have a problem that can't be solved. While this isn't nice to think about, it's *your* livelihood at stake.

When Not to Outsource

Don't outsource anything you're not willing to lose control of. It's fine to outsource credit card processing, for example, but you might not want to cede control over your marketing strategy to someone else. You can't influence the practices of another company the way you can influence the policies and employees of your own business.

Be wary of any company that refuses to let you buy only the elements you need from an e-commerce package. Even if you do need all the services they offer, that kind of pressure may indicate a problem you'll face down the road when you want to change your account structure or bring some elements of the site back under your direct control. Remember, you're giving the ASP access not only to your customers' data, but to your own. The amount of money you make via the Web, the precise sales numbers from your site, and the kinds of things that sell well for you are all valuable pieces of information. The vast majority of ASPs are honorable companies who behave ethically, but there's always the risk of landing a contract with the one ASP that's Jimmy's E-Commerce and Fender Repair Solutions. Do your homework before you sign anything.

You might also want to reconsider outsourcing if you can't find an ASP or an e-commerce package that suits your needs. This is usually more of a problem for extremely big companies that have unique requirements or large catalogs. If you're going to have to pay the ASP to reconfigure and reprogram its basic software to handle your business, why not pay that money to your own programmers—or to contractors—and customize your site in-house? A company big enough to afford this is a company that can afford to purchase all the right hardware, software, and security precautions necessary to run a hard-core e-commerce presence.

SUMMARY

Running a site that provides commercial transactions is a different world than running noncommercial Web sites. E-commerce has become an integral part of the American business world, and—despite the highly publicized crashes of some e-commerce businesses in the past few years—it's rapidly becoming yet another way to do business. Whether you're an e-commerce administrator or merely an interested consumer, the special rules for e-commerce sites are both interesting and critical.

The primary concern of every e-commerce Web administrator must be security. There's simply no excuse for treating your customers' personal identification in a cavalier manner. You must install the highest level of security possible and patrol your site constantly to keep your data safe. If you don't think you have the skills or interest to pay such close attention, you can always contract with another company to handle your e-commerce needs. Application service providers (ASPs) offer a range of services as wide as that in any business. Do your homework before signing a contract. Even if you don't run your own e-commerce site, though, you can still benefit from some business software to add extra functions to your own noncommercial Web presence.

PART V

Security and Apache

CHAPTER 20

Basic Security Concerns

No matter who you are, you should be concerned about system security. Whether you're a single user on a single machine or one of many network administrators on a large system, you have many of the same concerns. Anyone connected to the Internet or another network, in fact, has security concerns—even if they don't know they do.

What's all the fuss about? Well, you've probably seen or heard plenty of news stories about prominent Web sites that have been hacked and vandalized, or you've read about people who are serving lengthy jail sentences for illegally accessing someone else's computer. Some people in the world are interested in exploiting other people's access or hardware for nefarious purposes and some people out there like to break into systems for fun. Whether you're dealing with a professional cracker or a 13-year-old script kiddie, the end result is the same: someone wants to use your system without your permission.

NOTE: This chapter might frighten you or make you think there's no use in running a Web server (or any other server) because it makes you too vulnerable. You don't have to feel that way. A few basic precautions, and a good dose of thinking about your network and how secure you want it to be, can go a long way toward making your system less vulnerable. Yes, the risk is there, but take it as a challenge instead of a menace.

In this chapter, you read about the basic areas of security concern: access to the system, availability of tempting items, resources and how they can be exploited, and some programs and practices that can increase the security of your network. You also find some detailed examples that show how a small system can become secure and information on ways to protect your larger network. Let's begin with a self-evaluation: how secure do you want or need to be? The answer may surprise you.

NOTE: If you feel your network is too large, or your data too precious, to protect with the simple ideas in this chapter, consider consulting a security specialist. You'll pay handsomely because these folks are in high demand, but you can probably get a system closer to bullet-proof than not. Be aware that some security specialists are merely salespeople for particular software and be wary of anyone who proclaims one particular program is the solution for any given problem.

SECURITY SELF-EVALUATION

Yes, such a thing exists as being too secure. The most secure computer in the world is one that isn't connected to any network and is locked in a room with only one key, which you hold. Unfortunately, such a secure computer isn't useful at all. The goals of security and of access are diametrically opposed. Your job, as a security-minded administrator, is to figure out how much security you can trade for ease of use and how many barriers to free use you're willing to stand to keep the network safe.

In writing this book, I've made some assumptions about you, the reader. These assumptions affect this part of the book more than any other. People who run Web servers are likely to have systems that are far more attractive to intruders than people who don't. You probably have a static IP address, a fast connection to the Internet, and multiple computers—all of which have various user accounts and the capability to get to the Internet from each machine. If you had evil plans in mind, wouldn't that sound like a great site to try and exploit?

Because you have these resources, you need to decide how strongly you want to protect them. Security procedures are often annoying, which is a fact of life. Security methods are designed to place baffles between the user and her intended goal, whether it's demanding she verify her identity with a password or deciding whether to grant her access based on the location of the machine where she's logged in. If you have a large user base, you'll get complaints every time you implement a new security policy. I hope you also have supportive superiors who will back you up.

Defining Risk Tolerance

So, how do you decide what your security risk tolerance actually is? Given that you have some attractive resources at hand, your tolerance is lower than that of many other administrators. With a static IP address, you're a sitting duck. People who must rely on dynamic IP assignments—such as those with cable modems, dial-up modems, or some DSL—have the luxury of being hard to target because their location changes frequently.

You could take the hard-line approach that security is your main concern. In this case, you'd introduce rigid password policies and install software to enforce the new rules. You'd place strict quotas on the disk space each user can have and require that no executable files be placed in any public Web directories. You might add machines to your network, placing a single server on each machine and locking down access to each server machine, so only a handful of trusted people could actually get to the server. You'd certainly install a firewall and a proxy server.

Your counterpart at the company next door, though, might take a different approach. His attitude might be that security is well and good, but his users' needs are the main concern. Security approaches must be built around ease of use for the user base. In his office, users have access to the Web server, so they can add and edit Web files without having to bother anyone else. He encourages strong passwords and frequent change, but doesn't enforce the suggestion. If the Web site itself isn't too large, the server may share machine space with other servers, which may or may not be partitioned off on the disk. Firewalls and proxies can be annoying when doing a lot of work on the Internet, so he doesn't use them.

Neither of these sample policies is exaggerated. Plenty of sites work like one or the other of these scenarios and plenty of others are worse (depending on which description made you more uneasy). There are gonzo sites and lackadaisical sites, and reasons exist for both. The fact is, it's somewhat of a gamble, but the sites with less security may win and not be cracked. If they are cracked, though, the damage is likely to be greater. You have to look at your own situation to decide what your risk tolerance is.

NOTE: If you're in doubt, opt for the more-secure choice in whatever situation you're facing. Users dislike getting used to new policies that are more strict than the previous rules; but if you define strict policies from the beginning, a problem rarely occurs. See Chapter 12, "Dealing with Users," for more about introducing new policies to a user base.

ACCESS

Access is often overlooked, but it's a critical part of designing a good security program for your network. Access is both physical and electronic, both internal and external. Whenever you think about how your system is designed and how its security is managed, you need to think about access along with everything else.

Much of the access issue is common sense. Pay attention to your machines and your user base, and you'll knock out 95 percent of the problem. Walk around and inspect the machines every day, just to make sure things are okay. You might even catch a hardware problem before it becomes critical, like a banging fan or a CPU that's running too loudly. As with most security regimens, regular attention is the best way to head off problems.

Physical Access

Physical access is probably the most forgotten part of the security equation. No matter how strong your software and policies, they're pretty much useless if someone can simply pick up a machine and take it home, or pop the case open and tear out the hard drive. Your servers should be in a secure location. In larger companies, servers are often kept in a *server room,* an isolated room with a locked door and a good cooling system to deal with all the CPU heat. Server rooms are good ideas if you have the space. Distribute keys only to those who have actual job tasks in the server room. (Your server room shouldn't be a stopping point on the company tour path.)

If you don't have room or a real need for a separate server room, at least place the server machines in as secure a location as possible. You might investigate one of the many tethering or locking systems now available, which let you connect the computer to a large immovable object. Some of these systems have loud piercing alarms, letting you know if someone is trying to take the computer, though that may be overkill if the servers are in a room with lots of foot traffic and the alarm is sensitive to vibration. You may not want to have a keyboard attached to the server machines all the time, to discourage people from thinking it's a workstation.

Internal Access

Those who administer smaller systems have the luxury of knowing the people who log into the network. Administrators of big networks don't have that opportunity and a drawback exists. Just as your external access security is only as good as your user passwords, internal security is only as good as your users. If you have a user who is determined to make mischief, it's a tricky situation. After all, the person is a legitimate user of your system, so he won't trip intrusion detection software when he logs in.

Most internal access issues are due only to sloppy behavior, whether it's yours or your users'. If you permit bad passwords and don't pay a lot of attention to file permissions, then you're responsible for any problems that ensue. If you have good policies, but only enforce them sporadically, you're at fault. If your users ignore your policies to do something easier, however, it's your job to educate them and to eliminate the sloppiness.

If you have bad users, though, then you have a different problem. The vast majority of your users will follow system policies, however grudgingly. A user intent on making trouble follows the policies, at least enough to fly under your radar, but then does things you might never have thought of including. The only solution, barring catching the person in the act, is to pay constant attention to your network. Familiarize yourself with your users and what they habitually do when logged in. When something unusual pops up on the screen, you can take care of it right away.

AVAILABILITY

Is your network easy to get into? Do you leave ports unmonitored or run servers that don't get checked often? Do your users have sloppy password habits? All of these are security holes that make your system attractive because it's available. As with access, fixing availability problems is easy and mostly requires regular attention, rather than complicated scripts or new hardware.

Of course, you can spend money if you want to. Installing a firewall or a proxy server, as described in Chapter 23, "Firewalls and Proxies," will probably involve new hardware. You can also purchase a commercial software package to check your ports or you can use one of the many free programs available in software archives. (Unix administrators can find free programs more easily than non-Unix administrators.) No matter how much you spend, though, you can get the best results if you put aside some time every few days to review your system.

NOTE: In the upcoming "Software and Practices for Secure Operation" section, I introduce port scanning software and intrusion detection software. Both of these program types can automate a big part of your availability routine by running constant sentries. If someone tries to get into your system through an unsecured port, you're alerted by the program. These are good and low-cost ways to add an extra level of security to your network.

Passwords

Passwords are the first thing to consider. Of course, you should have a good policy about passwords for your users. Be careful that your policy isn't too strong, though! If you devised an extremely secure policy involving passwords of at least eight characters, which include both uppercase and lowercase letters as well as numbers, and you require those passwords to be changed every 14 days, you've written yourself a problem, as well as a strong password policy.

The problem is human nature, not the password. People hate to change passwords and every administrator knows this. Not only does this policy require the password be changed every other week, but it requires a complicated construction. The outcome here is likely to be a number of users who write down their passwords and keep them in a convenient location, like stuck to the monitor or in the pencil tray of their desk's top drawer. Not a particularly secure outcome, is it?

You need to come up with an intermediate solution that can satisfy both security and user behavior. Certainly, a 14-day changeover is too much for most situations unless the passwords are for a machine containing highly secret or important data. The uppercase/lowercase requirement may be overkill if you also require numbers. The important thing is to build a password that isn't in the dictionary, to slow down crackers working with crack programs that use unabridged dictionaries as their database.

RESOURCES

What do most crackers and intruders want? They want what they don't have and what you do have. Most of the time, they want your connection to the Internet. Some crackers want to use your CPU cycles, however, and a few want the data you have. Others just want to toy with you, perhaps vandalizing your Web files or moving things around without damaging the data. Just as with any other criminal activity, the reasons behind computer intrusion are myriad.

Connection Theft

Do you have high-speed Internet access that's always on? If you have a cable modem or DSL, or anything better than that (like a T1 or T3 line), you're a target. Crackers want to get into your system and use your machine as a relay point. Some intruders want to disguise large batches of unsolicited commercial e-mail, or *spam,* making it appear as if you're the one soliciting business for the stupid porn site of the week or the business opportunity that will have dollar bills flowing into your mailbox. Others want to use your system to send massive floods of data at particular sites, flooding their machines with ping requests for tiny answering packets. Still others want to use you as a shield while they go into other machines, building a twisty trail to cover their tracks as they approach their ultimate goal machine.

The faster and more constant your Internet access, the more careful you need to be about security. It's unlikely that someone connecting to the Internet with a 2,400-baud modem over dial-up is going to be an attractive target, but anyone reading this book is probably working with a constant and speedy connection (there's no other way to manage Apache and a constant Web presence). Pay careful attention to the firewall and proxy chapters.

Data Theft

Data theft is the thing everyone is frightened of. Several kinds of important data exist: some run on every computer and some do not. The kind people worry about is the latter. If you are an e-commerce site, for example, and you store huge files containing customer credit card numbers, then you have attractive data. Not every site has that kind of data, so crackers looking for credit information target their intrusions at sites that do—and often at smaller sites with more lax security habits than the big sites. (Of course, every once in a while, you see a story about some familiar e-commerce site that had a glaring security hole, leading to credit theft. No matter who you are, you're vulnerable!)

Even if you don't have obviously important data on your computer, like credit card numbers, you do have valuable data. Most important, you have passwords. If an intruder can figure out your user passwords, then he can get into your system and do whatever he wants—all the while, looking like one of your normal users. Intrusion detection software, as described in the "Software and Practices for Secure Operation" section of this chapter, can't tell the difference between `fred`, your regular user, and someone pretending to be Fred.

Encourage your users to change their passwords frequently and to use different passwords for each machine or site where they're required. Passwords shouldn't be dictionary words and the best ones contain a mix of letters and numbers. Password policies are discussed in more detail in Chapter 12, "Dealing with Users." Crackers often look for the `/etc/passwd` file on a Unix system, which contains all user passwords in an encrypted format, and run the encrypted data against a dictionary program that can identify dictionary-word passwords. Passwords are golden keys to your system and they're only as secure as the strength of the password itself. Protect your system from password data theft by requiring strong passwords from your users.

Vandalism

Anyone who's been around the Web business for a while knows the stories that seem to pop up regularly, especially around election time. Web site vandals are a unique type of intruder. They don't actually take anything away and their target is your public presence, not your system. Despite the relatively benign reaction vandals get in the media ("Hey, at least they didn't steal credit card numbers!"), Web vandalism is still an illegal entry into an unsecured system that results in damage to your data.

NOTE: If your site is vandalized, treat it like you would any other illegal system entry. Shut down vulnerable holes and vow to beef up security.

Web vandalism attacks range from the clumsy to the sophisticated. The most unskilled vandals merely add scrawled slogans to the index.html file or pop in new images. More skillful vandals may add a redirect, sending visitors to pages opposed to your company or viewpoint, or they may change out your pages altogether. The complexity of a site vandalism often depends on the time the vandals have available.

TIP: If you find a site you read often has completely changed, check the calendar before you leap to the phone and notify the site's administrator. The Internet has always delighted in April Fools' Day jokes, and a common Web-based joke is to spoof a vandalism. If the calendar says April 1, hold off on panic until the 2nd or 3rd.

If your site is vandalized, follow the procedures described in Chapter 21, "What to Do When You've Been Cracked." Be sure to keep copies of the altered pages and of any files added to the site, as well as copies of relevant log files and reports from intrusion detection software. If you or your company want to press charges or ask law enforcement to help you find the vandals, you need that data for the case.

NOTE: Obviously, you should always keep a backup copy of your entire site, updating the backup each time the site changes. The most secure way to do this is to copy the site to some sort of removable media, whether it's a Zip disk or a writable CD-ROM. The next best solution is to keep a copy on a machine that's not actually connected to the network. If you keep the backup on the same network that hosts the site, someone who breaks in has access to your backup as well.

SOFTWARE AND PRACTICES FOR SECURE OPERATION

Once you figure out the level of security you want to employ on your system and determine which resources need the most protection, you can begin to design an array of software and good practices to bolster the fences around your data and machines. Several types of software are useful to the security-minded administrator. Even easier than installing new software is the simple adoption of good habits and strong user policies.

CAUTION: You can adopt the most stringent security policies on the planet and follow them diligently yourself, but if you have users who ignore your rules, your work may be for nothing. You are only as secure as your least-secure practice. Chapter 12, "Dealing with Users," offers some hints and strategies for working with your users to develop both effective and workable policies. Users balk at requirements that seem irrational or needlessly complicated. Just as you wouldn't write the root password on a Post-it note and stick it to your monitor, don't make your security stratagem so complicated that your users ignore it.

Because security is such a big deal these days, a lot of programs are available to network administrators that claim to automate much of your security routine. Some of these programs make claims that seem a bit unrealistic, but excellent programs are out there that do what they say they do. Security software can be divided into a few general categories: intrusion detection software, port scanners, and firewalls and proxies.

NOTE: Firewalls and proxies are covered in Chapter 23, "Firewalls and Proxies." This chapter introduces intrusion detection and port scanning software only.

Intrusion Detection

Obviously, it's good to know whether someone is breaking into your system. The simplest way to detect intruders, though it requires a hefty bit of good luck, is to check your logged-in users frequently. Issue the command w at the system prompt to see a printout of current users. The printout looks something like this:

```
2:16pm up 24 days, 5:11, 3 users, load average 0.05,0.10,0.07
USER     TTY     FROM   LOGIN@    IDLE    JCPU     PCPU     WHAT
fred     tty1    :0     11:04am   3:01    0.14s    0.05s    trn
wilma    pts/0   :3     2:02pm    1.43s   0.25s    0.10s    perl
betty    tty2    :2     12:15pm   40.1s   0.12s    0.07s    pine
```

The w report shows you who's logged in to that particular machine, where they're coming from, and what they're doing. You can also see how long they've been connected and how long they've been idle. This is an easy way to keep an eye on machine use, but you're limited to the users who are currently logged in. If user barney, for example, had logged out moments before you issued the w command, you'd have no idea barney had been there at all from this report. So, w is useful, but it's not particularly efficient.

The w report is especially inefficient if you have a halfway-intelligent intruder. Most intruders are capable of hiding themselves from something like w, which is a command intended to display legitimate users. You can still use w as a checkpoint, though, if you know what your routine system load is.

TIP: *System load* is the measurement of how busy a particular machine is at a given point in time. The numbers, shown at the right end of the first line in the w report, indicate how many idle CPU cycles exist and how many cycles are occupied. A load of 1.0 means all cycles are occupied, but no commands are waiting to be executed. Loads higher than 1.0 mean commands are queued up, while loads lower than 1.0 mean all commands are being executed efficiently and the CPU isn't being used to capacity. If you routinely see loads near or over 1.0, consider adding a second CPU or upgrading the one you have.

Once you've been checking the load for a while, you'll know when something is out of whack. A machine with routine loads below 0.20, for example, carries loads above 0.6 infrequently. High load may be legitimate. Perhaps you have a user who's testing programs, or some automatic administrative task has started to run and needs a lot of cycles to do its work. In other cases, though, load spikes might mean you have someone on your machine using up your processor cycles for nefarious purposes.

If the load looks odd to you, issue the `top` command at the system prompt. The `top` program is what you use to see the processes that are currently occupying the CPU. The name is an acronym for table of processes. From the `top` report, you can see what processes are running, who ordered them, and how much they're consuming, and so on.

```
2:18pm up 24 days, 5:13, 3 users, load average 0.05,0.10,0.07
58 processes: 57 sleeping, 1 running, 0 zombie, 0 stopped
CPU states: 0.7% user, 3.5% system, 0.0% nice, 95.8% idle
Mem: 257902K av, 217385K used, 40517K free, 597382K shrd, 902837K buff
Swap: 498275K av, 517K used, 497758K free, 98079K cached
```

PID	USER	PRI	NI	SIZE	RSS	SHARE	STAT	LIB	%CPU	%MEM	TIME	COMMAND
8372	fred	11	0	3829	3829	2829	S	0	3.4	1.2	1:18	trn
7712	root	6	0	14599	14M	2651	S	0	4.1	1.1	2:14	X
1	root	0	0	352	348	272	SW	0	0.0	0.1	0.21	init
2	root	0	0	0	0	0	SW	0	0.0	0.0	0.0	kflushd
3	root	0	0	0	0	0	SW	0	0.0	0.0	0.0	kupdate
4	root	0	0	0	0	0	SW	0	0.0	0.0	0.0	kpiod
245	wilma	4	0	864	864	668	R	0	1.1	0.3	0:00	top

The `top` report continuously refreshes itself as processes change. To sort the output by CPU use, type **P** while `top` is running. It then resorts into a list ordered by the %CPU field. In this way, you can see what processes are consuming the most cycles.

Be aware that most savvy intruders can disguise themselves and hide from w and `top`. They might even go so far as to replace your login program with one that makes them invisible; and most crackers run *log scrubber* programs, which erase any mention of them or their activities from your system logs. Still, w and `top` are useful tools to learn more about your system, and they can help you catch the unwary, neophyte, or simply stupid cracker.

Intrusion Detection Programs

Okay, so w, `top`, and system logs might not be of much use in detecting security breaches. But what is a bewildered administrator to do? Get some new software. Several packages are on the market that scan your system and report unauthorized access. One of the better intrusion detection programs is called AIDE, or Advanced Intrusion Detection Environment. I like AIDE because it's Free Software and is also available free of charge.

AIDE, like several of these software packages, works by building a database. The database contains critical information about the files on your system and can be used to determine whether the files that exist on your system at some later date are actually the same files that existed when the database was created. This is useful because no intruder can replace a file or program with identical characteristics, so you can tell whether files have been compromised.

Whether you choose AIDE or another intrusion detection program, you should install one. If at all possible, you should install it on a new system before it's ever connected to other machines, either directly or over a network. This gives the database the best chance to create a pristine image of your files. Intrusion detection is difficult to do manually. Running software designed for the task is a great way to step up your security surveillance without much more work on your part.

> **TIP:**   You can get AIDE and other intrusion detection software at most major Unix software archives on the Web.

Port Scanning

Before an intruder breaks into your system, he probably spent some time scanning ports before choosing your machine. *Port scanning* is the use of a specialized program sent out across a network to a particular IP address. The program goes down the list of ports—thousands of them on any given machine—and tries to connect to each one. If a connection is successful, then your machine becomes an attractive target for illicit entry.

Port scanning happens all the time. That is, if you're connected to the Internet right now with an individual IP (that is, a cable modem, a DSL or aDSL, an ISDN, or a direct pipe), you've probably been scanned in the last 24 hours. It's a fact of life on the Internet: crackers are hungry for connections, and you have one. As discussed in the previous "Resources" section, a connection is a valuable item. And, if it's a high-speed connection, so much the better.

> **NOTE:**   The only crack that's ever happened on our home office network came from a port scan. People using the @Home cable modem service are notoriously susceptible to port scanning, in part because services that are so easy to set up don't take the time to teach users how to protect their machines. We thought we had ample security precautions, but our system was pretty rudimentary. Now we're firewalled and have switched to DSL.

Port Scanning Software

Two types of software deal with port scans. One type alerts you if you're being scanned and the other actually scans the ports. Using both is best because they have different aims. An alert program tells you what's going on, but a port scanner helps you close off vulnerable ports. Be aware that port scanners, especially, are revised and upgraded all the time. Crackers can usually stay one step ahead of those chasing them, so make sure you have the most updated versions of your port scanning software.

To check your own ports for vulnerability, you need to get a *port scanner*. This is the same software the intruders use to run scans. Dozens of port scanners are available on the Web. They all have different features, and many of them are constantly being revised. Look on any Unix software archive to find some of these programs; the search term "portscan" often pulls up quite a few. **http://www.freshmeat.net** usually has a pretty good selection for Linux machines.

Once you download a port scanner, install it, preferably on a computer that isn't connected to your network. You get the most accurate results if you work like a cracker and attack your system from outside. Sometimes finding a machine outside your network to scan from is difficult. If you know an administrator on another network, offer to trade port scans. You can both benefit from such an agreement. Any ports that turn up as available should be shut down immediately. You may need to turn off some services or limit the kinds of connections that can be made to that port. Be especially vigilant about ports higher than 1024 because many administrators pay no attention to these thousands of ports and they're frequent targets.

After you scan and seal your ports, you should install a *port-scan alert* program. Such programs keep a constant eye on all your ports. If someone attempts to scan you from outside the machine, the software alerts you immediately, so you can trace the scan (if possible) and shut down vulnerable ports. As with port scanners, many port-scan alert programs are available. One we installed on our home office network is called PortSentry. It's free of charge, though it isn't completely Free Software. The developers of PortSentry also have other good security programs available on their Web site.

TIP: Find PortSentry at **http://www.psionic.com/abacus/portsentry**.

SUMMARY

Anyone who administers a machine or network must be concerned about security issues. The assessment of risk is an individual choice and involves variables like Internet connection speed, number of users, and data kept on the machine. If a choice exists between a secure option and a less-secure option, administrators should generally select the secure path. One of the easiest ways to enhance a network's security is simply to pay attention to what happens on the network routinely. Then, if an unusual activity or load occurs, you're more likely to notice it.

Security can also be enhanced by effective user policies, which aren't too complicated and yet require users to make conscious efforts in vulnerable activities, like password selection. Policies should be appropriate for the type of network you're running. You can also help your security regimen by installing security software, such as port scanners or intrusion detection software. With these programs, you're alerted when someone tries to break in to the network or when the network is scanned for vulnerability. An effective security regimen uses all these mechanisms and more to guard against illegal access and misuse of data or other system resources.

CHAPTER 21

What to Do If You Get Cracked

For many administrators, security is a theoretical concept. Sure, putting up some protection and defining some system policies about secure behavior is a good idea, but it's not like anything is ever going to happen, is it? Well, it might. As Chapter 20, "Basic Security Concerns," explains, many attractive things exist on even the smallest networks. Good security habits are like automobile insurance: the chance of you having an accident in any given year is quite small; but if you do get into an accident, it's wonderful to have the reassurance of a paid-up policy. Even if you never get into an accident, the money you spent on insurance isn't wasted money. Insurance, like network security, is both a bet and a safeguard. The bet, expressed in your policy rate, expresses how likely the insurance company thinks you are to have an accident. The safeguard is, even if you pay low rates, you're covered in the event of an expensive mistake.

NOTE: Why the use of "crack" instead of "hack" throughout this book? Hackers are the core of both Unix and Internet cultures. A *hacker* is simply a person who likes to work with code—writing it, fixing it, or taking it apart to see how it works. *Crackers*, on the other hand, are people who try to "crack into" other systems. Blame the movie *Hackers* for creating much of the confusion, and for robbing an old and honorable term of most of its meaning.

Just like automobile accidents, security breaches can happen to anyone, no matter how well insured your network is. If you minimized the vulnerabilities on your network, you might feel even worse if you get cracked than if you've never done anything about security at all. In contrast, if you ignored security issues, a crack may be a devastating reminder of your lapse. If you inherited an insecure system from a predecessor, you might become irate with an unfair situation for which you aren't responsible.

NOTE: No matter how much attention you paid to security—or not— nothing is quite like the feeling when you realize your system has been cracked. As with any intrusion, whether virtual or real, you may feel a wide range of emotions from anger to fear, violation to revenge. All these feelings are normal and you might cycle through all of them in a relatively brief period of time. Your users and supervisors might also face these same reactions.

Regardless of how you deal with the crack personally, you need to take some immediate steps. In this chapter, you learn how to notice you've been cracked, how to find the vulnerable spot, and how to close any open holes you might have inadvertently left open. The aftermath of a crack runs fast and furious, with a lot of activity in a short time. If you have external users relying on your site for information or product, you're under even more pressure to solve the problem and get the site running again.

NOTICING THE CRACK

For many Web administrators, the first glimmer that something has been cracked is an unusual entry in the logs. For others, it's a routine look at the site that reveals the wrong file, whether it's a defaced version of your own index.html or a completely new document. For a few unfortunate souls, someone else—the press, the president of the company, an early-bird user—might discover the problem and spread the news before you have a chance to do early triage on the situation.

Regardless of the media's love for stories about defaced Web sites, that sort of malicious vandalism isn't the primary kind of crack on the Internet. Unless your company is involved in controversial activities, or you work for a political figure or party, you probably don't have enough angry and tech-savvy people who are interested in making you look bad. Any site is vulnerable, though. People are on the Internet who are just happy to break into any site they can figure out how to crack, and they'll deface your site for fun. Even if you offer the most benign information in the world, you might still be the victim of a random crack.

NOTE: If you *do* work for a company that does something unpopular—cigarette manufacturing, animal testing, making chemicals in poverty-stricken areas—or you administer a political site, add another task to your regular site maintenance. Try to view every page on your site on a frequent and regular basis. Sometimes, site vandalism happens on secondary pages, not on the highly visible index page. Combine checking the logs with checking your pages to catch the widest range of vandalism possibilities.

You can have the best handle on your system if you review it regularly. Check your logs daily, both Apache's and other system-generated logs. Get an idea of what business-as-usual looks like on your system so, if something goes awry, you can check it.

TIP: Chapter 9, "Logs," explains what normal Apache logs look like. Chapter 9 also explains how to set up custom logs, which might help you customize your security routines further to make your site as tight as possible.

If your site has been exploited as a shield for an attack on a third network, you might get a phone call from the administrator at that network. Most savvy administrators realize that, just because a ping flood or other Denial of Service attack is coming from Network A, it's not necessarily the people at Network A who're bombing Network B. A quick e-mail or call to Network A's offices is a professional courtesy, as well as a plea for help. If you get such a call, respond quickly. In addition, if you notice you're being attacked by a machine on another network, place a similar call to their administrators. Chances are, they've been cracked themselves.

No matter how you find out about the crack, take immediate action. If the crack is currently going on, such as a Denial of Service (DoS) attack on another network, shut off the machine's connection to the Internet. If you're lucky enough to have backup servers, put those into service for the time it'll take you to fix the main server machines. The larger your network, the more likely you can fix big chunks of the problem without taking down the entire network's access to the Internet.

TIP: Many network attacks take place at night, which is a blessing in disguise. Crackers know vulnerable networks can have few or no administrators around 24 hours a day. If you get paged in the middle of the night to respond to a security breach, at least you needn't take down the network in the middle of the workday.

FINDING AND FIXING VULNERABILITIES

Read your logs. (You knew I was going to say that.) Not only the Apache logs, but all the administrative logs that record what s happening and what has happened on your system. Check access logs, intrusion detection software logs, and server logs. If you're lucky enough to be cracked by a relatively slow and old-fashioned intruder, you might be able to see him with the w command or with `top`. Look at the most obvious possibilities first: open ports, software with known exploits, servers you don't use often, or malicious users.

CAUTION: Remember, cracks aren't always external. Inside jobs can be just as devastating, perhaps more, because we're inclined to believe in the better sides of our users. Be careful if you make allegations against a user, and be sure to save log files and other evidence.

If you have open ports, shut them down. This is especially important if you have high-speed constant access to the Internet. Open ports are the easiest way for someone to get into your network and cause mischief. If you don't keep an eye on your upper ports, a lot of activity could pass unnoticed until something serious happens. It's easy to firewall off the ports you don't use and to lock down anything that's open. If you then see log activity coming from a port you know isn't in use, you can start to fix the problem.

Shut off any services you don't use. Most administrators don't intentionally run unused servers, but they can happen anyway. For example, if you work with a network that has a different server machine for each service, the Web server machine shouldn't be running a mail server, and the mail server machine shouldn't be running an FTP server. Sometimes these servers get installed by default, however, when a new operating system is installed on the machine. Double-check after every installation to be sure you aren't inadvertently running a server nobody pays attention to.

If you're running multiple servers on one machine, even if they're on different partitions, give strong consideration to a multiple-server network instead. Placing servers on individual machines, isolated from other servers and network traffic, makes dealing with security breaches much easier. If someone cracks your Apache machine, for example, you can lock down the Web server and take it offline while you fix the problem on that machine. If Apache runs on the same machine—or even the same partition—as `sendmail` or your NFS server, you might have to bring down the whole network to deal with a single problem.

CAUTION: Multiple servers on the same machine also make a cracker's job easier. If he gets access to one server, he can move across the disk into other critical system areas or other services. Keeping the servers separate from each other and from administrative tools and files minimizes the damage that can be done.

When People Crack

Psychologists are interested in human behavior under stress, and there's little more stressful at the workplace than dealing with an invasion. After all, it's your network and you're expected to keep it running—when vandals drop by, you might have to deal both with your own feelings and with an attitude that you should have prevented the invasion. In many cases, your network was probably as secure as you knew how to make it. Those who like to enter systems illegally enjoy a good challenge and often have top-of-the-line skills and abilities.

One of the side effects of a public or devastating crack, though, are the Monday morning quarterbacks. Whether it's a supervisor or someone who isn't employed in a technical position, people who second-guess your work and suggest the crack was your fault aren't helpful. If you work with people whom you think might blame you for a security breach, a good idea is to document your entire security regime long before it becomes an issue. In fact, this is a good idea even if you never get cracked. Even if the document is only used by the person who takes your job someday when you move on, it will be worthwhile.

If you're the one who's cracking, take a deep breath and a step back. Yes, it can be a horrible feeling to learn you've been cracked, but this isn't the end of the world and, most likely, this isn't the end of your job (unless you took absolutely no security precautions at all, despite being instructed to do so). Do what you need to rebuild the walls around your system. Explain to your supervisors and user base what happened, and then move on. Dwelling on a crack isn't healthy—no matter how spectacular it was—unless you happen to run systems that control nuclear missiles or the IRS database or something equally grave.

One of the best ways to deal with the emotional aspects of a security breach is education. Perhaps your employer would pay your entrance fees for a security conference or two, or bring in a security consultant to work with you in building better defenses. This is also an opportunity for you and the technical staff to educate the larger user base, from front-line employees to senior management, on the facts of computer security and how your network is protected, as well as any new changes that have taken place since the security breach to make the system even stronger.

PREVENTIVE MEASURES

If you don't have any security-related software on your system, get some. If the software you do have is old, get updated versions. Many kinds of security software are available to the network administrator, some of which are described in Chapter 20, "Basic Security Concerns." Depending on the kind of security breach you experienced, you might want to concentrate more on one kind of software than another. However, just because you had a password crack on this occasion doesn't mean the next attempt will also be a password crack. Throwing all your administrative eggs into the password basket could make you vulnerable to a port invasion instead. Be balanced in your choices and try to cover the main areas of concern equally.

You might have discounted some of the most useful preventive measures earlier. Before a network is violated or attacked, setting up a firewall machine or implementing proxies might seem like too much trouble. An attempt on your network, however, might be enough to change your mind about whether these methods are appropriate for your system.

> **TIP:**   You can learn more about these security measures in Chapter 23, "Firewalls and Proxies."

Another good idea is to run a port scan immediately after an attack, even if you do this on a regular basis every few months. Someone might have opened a port inadvertently, or you might be running formerly secure software that has just been exploited and the bypass posted on the Internet. As suggested in Chapter 20, find an administrator at another network who is willing to trade port scans with you, so you can get the most complete look at your system from outside.

SECURITY BREACH CHECKLISTS

Because the time surrounding an attempt on your network is so stressful, having a checklist of necessary steps can be extremely helpful. Such lists help to remind you of every step and precaution that should be taken to secure your system. In this section of the chapter, I provide a basic security breach checklist, which should work for most systems. Be sure to add any steps you know are important on your own network, whatever your network might look like. For example, you might want to lock down an internal firewall if you have one, so the compromised machine is walled off from the rest of the network.

Get Offline

First things first: get the affected machine off the network and off the Internet. If you have the capability to firewall that machine from the rest of your network, do so. If your gateway machine contains firewall and/or proxy software, you might have to bring down the entire network's connection to the Internet. You can leave the rest of the network running, if necessary, but you need to get the affected machine off the connection.

> **CAUTION:**   Unfortunately, this can disrupt your network's normal work, especially if the Internet is a big part of your work or that of your coworkers. However, security is the primary consideration. Don't be tempted to rush a poorly configured backup firewall into service. If you disrupt an intruder's work, he might try to get back into your system right away—putting an untested or identical firewall up in place of the affected machine could be foolhardy. After all, the intruder has already cracked you once. Why give her a second chance?

Online Checklists

If you're looking for checklists to print out and keep near your main terminals, several useful lists are on the Web. One such checklist is provided by CERT, the Computer Emergency Response Team, which is one of the most respected security teams on the Internet. CERT has a set of checklists at these URLs:

▼   http://www.cert.org/tech_tips/intruder_detection_checklist.html

■   http://www.cert.org/tech_tips/root_compromise.html

▲   http://www.cert.org/tech_tips/security_tools.html

With these three lists, you should be able to deal with any critical site intrusion. Although they aren't Web specific, there's no reason to treat Web intrusions any differently than other system break-ins.

Other checklists and online intrusion-detection resources you might find useful can be found at the following URLs:

▼   http://www.sans.org/newlook/resources/IDFAQ/ID_FAQ.htm

■   http://www.cerias.purdue.edu/coast/ids/

■   http://www.incident.org

■   http://www.linuxsecurity.com/resources/intrusion_detection-1.html

■   http://www.networkintrusion.co.uk/

▲   http://secinf.net/iidse.html

Don't turn the machine off, though, or reboot the system. You need to leave it up long enough to make a backup. No matter how tempting, don't leave the machine connected as you try to track the intruder. You might be watched and the intruder can learn more about how you handle crisis situations than you should want her to know. Just get the machine offline and secured away from the rest of the network.

TIP: If you're determined to get some information while you think the intruder is still in your machine, run the `ps x`, `w`, and `top` commands, and then pipe the output to text files. Then, get the machine offline. Those three commands generate enough information about current connections to satisfy your immediate needs, and then you can get on with securing the system. Don't play detective when your primary role needs to be technical administrator.

Make a Backup

Before you make any changes to your system, but after the compromised machine is safely disconnected from the Internet, make a backup of the entire machine. Doing a full backup is a great way to document exactly what happened on the machine, or at least to preserve a snapshot of the machine as it was before you took any additional steps to trace the intruder or seal off back doors. If you need to involve local or national law enforcement, such a snapshot could be of great assistance to the investigation.

Especially important is to make a backup before you reboot the machine. Some processes that can indicate the presence of intruders or their tools can disappear at a reboot, even though the tools might remain hidden for future attempts on your network. As long as you're not connected to the rest of the network, you should be safe enough in making a full backup. Include the entire machine in your backup. You never know where an intruder will hide tools or evidence. The less likely the spot, the more vulnerable it is to exploit.

NOTE: If possible, use a permanent medium, like a writable CD-ROM disk, rather than a magnetic tape backup. There's no telling how many times the backup will be accessed or installed and, the more permanent the medium, the better. Be sure to label the disk, so nobody mistakes it for an actual backup and uses it to restore the system to "pristine" condition!

Inform Appropriate People

No matter what kind of break-in you're dealing with, you need to inform someone of the event and how you're handling it. If you administer a corporate site, you probably need to contact your managers and possibly senior administration (depending on how severe the break-in was). If you're closing down services, you might have to notify users that certain functions won't be available for some time. You might also need to contact your upstream Internet provider if you feel the break has been significant enough so they should be on guard.

Depending on your local and state laws, you might need to contact local law enforcement to file a report and be put in contact with the appropriate officials. If the break-in has certain characteristics, such as terrorist threats or the impersonation of senior public officials (the United States President, the Canadian Prime Minister, and so forth), you might need to contact federal or national authorities. For example, if you have an intruder who's pretending to be the United States President, the Secret Service will want to know. If threats are being made, the Federal Bureau of Investigation (FBI) may need to be called. The FBI also handles certain computer crimes that occur across state lines. Those readers who work for a company should consult their legal division for advice.

NOTE: Obviously, not every break-in or intrusion will be of interest to the FBI or other government agencies, but certain intrusions do warrant their involvement. Check the FBI's National Intrusion Protection Center at **http://www.nipc.gov** and the Secret Service at **http://www.treasury.gov/usss**. The Secret Service investigates financial fraud, including fraud over the Internet.

Read Your Logs

Now that you've pulled the machine off the Internet and your local network and you've alerted the appropriate people, it's time to take a deep breath and get to work. From the immediate backup you made, pull all administrative log files. You might also need to pull log files for each Internet service you offer, such as Apache or FTP. If you piped system information to text files, as suggested in the first step, it's time to look at those files as well.

Review your logs. Look for anything out of the ordinary: users logged in who should not be, suspicious processes under `top` that are taking up chunks of CPU time, processes running under unusual user IDs, entries in your logs that don't make sense, or significant chunks missing from log files. All these are standard cracker tools. Even if you can't identify the origin of the crack, you can often find some suspicious connections or programs in your log files. Truly thorough crackers use log scrubbers to erase their presence from your logs; but if you surprise someone before the log scrubber can finish, you might catch a lucky break.

NOTE: As I noted elsewhere in this book, reading your logs in a security breach is only helpful if you know what "normal" looks like on your system. You can't define "out of the ordinary" processes or cycles if you don't know what ordinary looks like.

Look for Back Doors

Once you've gone through all your log files, including those from Internet services and firewalls or proxies that might be running, it's time to study the rest of the system. Crackers might modify your regular administrative tools, install new programs, or leave back doors on your machine that they can use later. These back doors, or Trojan horses, are much more of a security risk than any damage that may have already happened. You're on high alert now, but if the cracker can hold tight and wait out your enthusiasm, there'll be plenty of time to exploit your system later.

CAUTION: Check `/etc/passwd` or your operating system's password storage file, immediately. Assume password security has been compromised and you must change all passwords used to access this machine. Because `/etc/passwd` is often encrypted, you probably won't be able to tell whether a particular entry has been changed, but you should be able to detect any changes in the number of entries. You might want to change to a shadow password scheme, if one is available for your operating system.

Sniffers

One of the most common—and dangerous—programs a cracker can install is a sniffer program. *Sniffers* track the data that moves across your network, whether by logging it or by performing basic packet filtering. Sniffers are usually hidden files and often encrypt their output, so they can be hard to find. You can often find sniffers by watching for their log files, however. Sniffer logs grow quickly and dramatically because they track so much data.

Sniffers are particularly dangerous when they're used to capture user names and passwords, which might be sent in cleartext when transferred internally. A sniffer log that contains password information is as valuable as a hacked login program, because it gives the cracker the luxury of logging in as a regular user, whose presence on the system would not seem out of the ordinary to you.

TIP: Check for logs and programs kept in strangely named directories, such as those using dots, white space, or unusual characters. Many Trojan horse programs live in the /dev directory on a Unix system, so you might find log files or unknown programs hiding there as well. Check *all* your directories when you clean up after an intrusion, not only /usr or /.

Altered Binaries

If you can name an administrative Unix program, chances are it's been modified illegally on some system. Crackers use all kinds of programs to get access to your machine or to find important data, and those programs can also be altered to permit later access and abuse. You might be unable to tell whether a binary program has been changed or reinstalled insecurely, so the best reaction is to reinstall all the basic programs (this can be done by reinstalling the operating system, as suggested later in this checklist).

CERT notes a number of regular and popular programs that have been found in compromised versions on cracked systems, including

- ▼ login
- ■ su
- ■ Telnet
- ■ rlogin
- ■ ifconfig
- ■ ls
- ■ find
- ■ netstat
- ■ inetd
- ■ syslogd
- ■ ftp
- ■ du
- ■ libc
- ■ sync
- ▲ df

and others. In fact, most of the commands listed in Appendix D have been compromised at some time or another. Get a clean version from a trusted source (not from a backup you've made in the past), and reinstall any utility you suspect.

TIP: If you use a program like AIDE, described in Chapter 20, "Basic Security Concerns," you should be able to use the AIDE database to determine whether a utility has changed since it was initially installed and the AIDE database created. This is an easier solution than reinstalling all your utilities.

ID Programs

Savvy crackers often try to alter your group ID or user ID files, known as `setuid` and `setgid`. Look for any stray files—especially root-owned files—that aren't where you expect them to be, or files that don't contain the data you want them to contain. Look for extra entries, extra users placed into groups, and other alterations to your user base and group setup. You can also run the `ncheck` utility to find `setuid` or `setgid` files across your network or on the local machine, which might be easier than scanning each directory by hand, especially if the files are hidden or renamed.

> *TIP:*   Issue the command as `ncheck -s`. The `-s` flag identifies only files and processes that have `setuid` mode. If you want to check individual file systems one at a time, issue the command as `ncheck -s filesystem`. This could make it easier to read the output or to make notes of the files you find.

Check Your Services and Configuration Files

Are any services running that you didn't explicitly enable? Some crackers may start idle servers to provide an easy entry back to the system. Administrators who don't pay attention to the servers or daemons running on their systems are particularly susceptible to this trick. Check all running processes and open ports to see whether anything is running that you didn't intend to have open.

After you check for running processes, look through your configuration files. Pay particular attention to any files used to configure the services that start when the system reboots, such as the `rc.d` files used to configure various Linux run levels, or `/etc/inet.d`, which determines the programs started by the `inet` daemon. A cracker might give up immediate access for a Trojan horse entry into your system hidden deep in your bootup configuration scripts. You won't find the cracker at the time you find the intrusion and, if she is patient, the cracker might let your system lie for a long time before exploiting the tool left in `rc.d` or `inet` configuration files.

> *TIP:*   Learn more about Unix bootup configuration scripts in Chapter 7, "Managing the Apache Server." Consult a reference for your particular Unix variant to learn the specifics of such scripts on your system.

Study the Network

When you're satisfied you have everything you can get from the compromised machine, turn your attention to the rest of your network. Depending on the size of the network, this might take some time or it could be a relatively quick process. As with the compromised machine, check the logs on each of your networked machines and look to see whether critical system binaries have been altered, as well as whether unauthorized daemons are running or ports are left unsecured. This is especially important for any network running NFS or NIS, both of which are protocols with known security risks.

If you have an extensive network, allocate your time appropriately and work outward from the compromised machine. For example, if you keep all your Internet server machines on one part of the network—outside an internal firewall—examine all those machines before you examine the internal firewall machine and, finally, the machines beyond the internal firewall. Work logically, checking the machines most closely linked to the Internet connection before you begin to work out to less likely machines.

CAUTION: If you allow dial-ins to individual workstations or you have a modem pool for your users, you must treat all those machines as if they were the initially compromised machine. Allowing people to dial in behind the firewall isn't good security, no matter how trusted those people are. And, it's human nature to forget the firewall isn't necessarily protecting every entry into your network.

Take the time to examine every file on your Web site, as well as any database files or other important data files that live on the compromised machine. If user files are there, ask your users to check carefully whether a change occurred in their personal data. A malicious cracker might want nothing more than to be a nuisance, and changing data is a good way to annoy administrators and users.

Reinstall the Operating System

Some may argue that it's overkill to reinstall the operating system when you have a security breach, but I think it's reasonable. If hidden system files are altered or Trojan horses have been implanted, the easiest way to fix all that is to reinstall the operating system. Install from the same disks you originally used to install the OS or obtain a new and clean version from your OS vendor. Don't simply reinstall an old backup, although you can reuse old configuration files from a preintrusion backup if you know they're clean and trustworthy.

One advantage to obtaining a new copy from your operating system vendor is that you can get any recently released security patches. Even if you reinstall from disks you already had, get the latest patches, so you can run the tightest operating system possible—especially if the patches fix known security risks, which might have been how your machine was exploited in the first place.

TIP: Be sure to change all your network passwords. You can force individual users to change their passwords as well, but be doubly sure to change your own administrative passwords, including the root password.

Contact Vendors

As with your operating system, contact each vendor whose software you run on your machine. If you're running mostly Free or Open Source software, check the Web site or mailing list archives for the program to see whether new security patches exist or an update version is available. With commercial software, see whether patches are available and report the intrusion, especially if you know how the program was exploited.

Take the opportunity to update all your software as you rebuild the machine. The newer the software and the more current the security patches, the less likely you'll be cracked through a known exploit. Be aware, though, brand new versions (those that are *.0 or *.1 releases) often have their own security issues, which are often tied to new features. Installing patches for a reliable version is better than upgrading to something not yet fully tested. It's always good to keep your machine running with a lean suite of programs you actually use, rather than loading up with unused software that leaves an inviting doorway for illicit entry.

TIP: While you're contacting your vendors, consider subscribing to e-mail alerts or adding a bookmark to your Web browser for up-to-the-minute security information. Often, a security breach can occur before an administrator makes time in his schedule for security news, but, when you're aware of new problems, it's easier to guard against them than to clean up afterward.

Renew Your Commitment

After you scour your machine, check the network, reinstall your operating system and any necessary software, and clean your configuration files, you can reconnect to the network and the Internet. Also, be sure to check and clean any firewall machines that might have been affected. If you don't already have a firewall in place, consider building one before you reconnect the compromised machine to the network.

Don't forget to update your system policies. If you suffered because of a user error or a sloppy habit, include those errors and habits in your system security policy. Some policies describe exploits that already happened on the network. I'm not sure this is the best idea, though, because it could give ideas to the crack-inclined. Use the intrusion as an opportunity to renew your emphasis on secure procedures and to ensure your users know why security is so important.

TIP: CERT suggests that you tally the cost of recovering from the intrusion, especially if you have managers who won't approve money for additional security mechanisms or training. When you add up all the hours of your time spent on examining and reconfiguring the machine and the network, plus the cost of any new software or repairing damaged data, you might have a persuasive accounting that can buy you some help.

SUMMARY

Learning that your network's security has been violated is a stressful time. Not only must you deal with the practical realities of an intrusion, but you must also deal with the emotional fallout whether it be yours, your supervisor's, or members of your user community. Remember, no such thing exists as a 100 percent secure network. Even single machines aren't completely secure unless they're never connected to any network, including the Internet, and are kept in a locked closet. As long as you take reasonable precautions about your network, you're probably less to blame for the intrusion than you are, sadly, a victim of chance.

When you learn you've been cracked, you must do several things right away. First, isolate the machine that's been violated. If necessary, shut down the network. If you have servers on individual machines, however, you can probably shut down only the machine that has been cracked and leave the rest of the network running. Next, locate the problem. Perhaps you have open ports or servers that aren't used regularly, or you have vulnerable passwords. Finally, take preventive measures to ensure that future cracks are harder to make. Whether you choose to install intrusion detection software, build a multiple-machine network, or hire a security consultant, taking positive steps to bolster your network security can help you move past the psychological stress of a security breach and build a better network for your users.

CHAPTER 22

SSL: The Secure Socket Layer

If you're worried about security on your Web site, you're not alone. Every good Web administrator spends time thinking about security and planning new ways to keep her site safe. While many site administrators don't need the heaviest of security and can get away with the reasonable steps outlined in Chapter 20, "Basic Security Concerns," many sites must take the most conservative possible approach to security.

One technique that can help those in need of the tightest security is the Secure Sockets Layer (SSL). *SSL* is an on-the-fly encryption tool that can transform data into an encoded format as it leaves your server, to be decrypted by an SSL-enabled client program on the other end.

TIP: Most current browsers are SSL-capable. If people are unable to contact your SSL-enabled site, they might need to upgrade their browsers to take full advantage of your security precautions.

SSL deals with all types of HTTP data, including headers, CGI data, and cookies. SSL doesn't encode the TCP/IP headers used to direct the data back to the requesting browser, but it does take care of almost everything else.

In this chapter, you learn how the SSL works and why it's one of the best things you can do to secure your site. You read about the many benefits of SSL, and learn the basics of how the technology actually works. We cover security issues that relate to SSL, including some things you must do to ensure your SSL-enabled site remains secure. The chapter concludes with a look at emerging security technologies and a discussion of encryption in general.

NOTE: While SSL is the Cadillac of Web security technologies, you must be prepared to experience a significant increase in system response time. SSL takes a big chunk of system resources as it works. While this is a good trade-off in terms of the peace of mind you'll get from running an SSL-enabled system, it might also be time to upgrade your hardware and operating system to counteract some of the drain inherent in running SSL.

WHAT IS SSL?

At its most basic, SSL is a protocol like the other protocols described in this book. The SSL protocol describes a mechanism that creates a truly secure connection between two computers connected on a network. The connection, or channel, shields the data passing between the two machines by encrypting the data stream as it moves over the network. Although the data leaves Machine A unencrypted and arrives at Machine B unencrypted, SSL scrambles the data as soon as it enters the channel, and then descrambles it on the other end. This is known as a *transparent* channel because neither Machine A nor Machine B sees the data as encrypted.

The beauty of the SSL concept is that it doesn't require any special encryption plug-in capabilities in the user clients at each end of the connection. The transmission mechanism itself—the SSL channel—does all the work with the help of some code buried in the most popular TCP client programs. This means you, as an administrator, needn't install special versions of your favorite software, as long as you and the machine you're connecting to both have an up-to-date SSL installation.

> **NOTE:**   As you see later in this chapter, Apache has two SSL modules—mod_ssl and ApacheSSL. Using a module encrypts the file data as it leaves the server. This speeds the transmission and makes sure everything is encrypted before it heads to the requesting browser. If Apache had to call an additional SSL program to send data through the channel, it would increase response time significantly and probably have deleterious effects on your system resources while the data was encrypting.

Note, at no point in this description has SSL been defined as a "Web encryption" protocol. In fact, SSL can work with any service that transfers data over TCP because of the transparency of the connection. If you begin working with SSL as a Web security tool, but you also run other TCP services, you might find you want to start using SSL with those services. This is a great way to enhance the security level of data running through your machines.

Although SSL does work with any TCP service, it was originally designed to work with the Web. (This still doesn't mean it's a Web protocol, but it does work most closely with HTTP because that was its initial function.) In recent years, the SSL protocol has been adapted into the Transport Layer Security (TLS) model. *TLS* is an attempt to synthesize the disparate approaches to connection security proposed by Netscape and Microsoft. TLS is controversial because it uses an encryption scheme that can't be exported outside the United States. Currently, Internet Explorer supports the TLS protocol, but Netscape doesn't.

> **NOTE:**   I mention TLS only because you might hear the term if you delve further into Internet transmission security realms. Because of the nature of Open Source programming and development, Apache-oriented security work has been done with SSL and not with TLS. This chapter focuses on the work of the OpenSSL group and on the Apache::SSL initiative. All major browsers support SSL technology.

SSL's development started in the mid-1990s at Netscape. Netscape had started providing a full suite of programs bundled with their popular Web browser, Navigator. Instead of only using Netscape to browse the Web, you could now use Netscape products to handle your e-mail and read USENET news, too. This was also the era when e-commerce had started to grow in popularity. The result was that Netscape needed a security solution for protecting its clients' data in all the bundled programs, especially for protecting data sent as part of an e-commerce purchase. So, Netscape's developers came up with the SSL concept and did all the work on the project, up to the point where SSL was submitted as an open protocol to the Internet Engineering Task Force (IETF).

TIP: You can read the current SSL protocol draft, if you want to see the nitty-gritty details, at **http://www.freesoft.org/CIE/Topics/121.htm**.

SSL has gone through several versions since its initial development at Netscape. The average SSL administrator doesn't need to know the story behind each version or the squabbles that follow each change in a protocol (not unique to SSL, but a common feature of every protocol revision), because most of us don't work directly with SSL code. In the case of Apache, understanding how SSL works is far more important than understanding why it works that way instead of in a different manner.

NOTE: If you're interested in the history of SSL development or in more advanced information about the protocol, I recommend the excellent book *SSL and TLS: Designing and Building Secure Systems* by Eric Rescorla (Addison-Wesley, 2000). This book has a good introduction to the SSL protocol and its history, as well as some highly technical information about coding and cryptography.

SSL Features

SSL is an attractive method of securing data transmissions for a number of reasons. The protocol offers a variety of features, each of which is either an excellent security activity or makes administration of SSL-encrypted transmissions much easier. If you choose not to use SSL for some reason, consider whether you can duplicate these features with the security method you select instead. For many people, the system load of running SSL is still a good trade-off compared to myriad programs or hours of programming time required to duplicate what SSL can do.

Transparency

As described earlier in the chapter, a transparent connection is one in which the data sent is the same data that's received. That is, the data being sent as a Web file is the same data the requesting browser receives at the end of the transaction. Neither the client nor the server knows whether anything has happened to the data while it was moving between the two machines. In the case of an SSL connection, that data was encrypted so it could be sent across the network without passing the file contents in cleartext. The data was decrypted, however, before displaying in the browser window.

Because the data isn't encrypted at either end of the transaction, you can use the SSL channel to transmit all sorts of data over TCP connections. The data needn't be restricted to the Web. For example, Netscape's USENET news client uses SSL to transfer articles from the server to the individual user's newsreader. While nothing on USENET is particularly confidential or even deserving of encryption (USENET is, after all, a public medium), this is certainly a valid use of SSL channels. Most Internet aspects use TCP connections to transfer data, so SSL can also be used to secure whatever form of Internet traffic you want to provide or receive.

Confidentiality

The point of encryption is confidentiality. An encrypted piece of data is confidential because it isn't open for public view. To decrypt an encrypted piece of data, you need to have the appropriate key and know how to use it. SSL was designed as a confidentiality tool, primarily to secure online business transactions. Without SSL and technologies like it, Internet e-commerce would never have become as popular as it is now. This is because there would be no way to ensure that the only viewer of your credit card or identification data is the person or company you are sending it to.

While a connection is open between two machines and the data is flowing across it, the data is unprotected. Crackers can use tools like packet sniffers to look at the bits of data and, possibly, steal or copy useful information as it transmits. While this is far more difficult than breaking into a machine and simply taking files of valuable data, data transmission is an inherently insecure mechanism because the administrator of either machine can do little.

Well, at least little could be done until SSL! Because SSL encrypts the data as it flows through the SSL channel, the stream is safe. A cracker who intercepts the data stream gets encrypted bits, not cleartext, and is unable to decode the pieces he's pulled. The average consumer expects her information is confidential, and, with an SSL connection, it is.

CAUTION: Confidentiality is the main reason why you should *never* make an online purchase that isn't secured by SSL. Your browser should have an indicator, like the lock icon in the lower-left corner of Netscape Navigator, that shows when you're connected over an SSL channel and when you're not. Never send personal financial or private information over an unsecured connection because you can't know who's listening.

Authentication

Authentication is a major concern of Web transactions, even apart from the special needs of e-commerce. If you look at the various modules available in the Apache Module Registry, as shown in Table 8-1 of Chapter 8, "Dealing with Apache Innovation (mod_perl: A Case Study)," you can see the vast majority of modules are somehow related to authentication using different methods of achieving that goal. Knowing whom you're sending data to and identifying yourself appropriately are a big part of ensuring accurate transactions over the Web.

Certainly, SSL takes this into account. SSL has its own authentication tools that check to see where information is going and whether the specified end is appropriate for the data being sent. The primary method of identification for a Web server is the certificate. *Certificates,* somewhat like cookies, are pieces of data that confirm identity. Servers issue certificates that prove their identity, and then those certificates are accessed and verified during an SSL transaction. SSL can also authenticate clients, either through a password mechanism or through one of the several methods permissible under the SSL protocol.

Regardless of how SSL is configured to authenticate the machines on both ends of the channel, the authentication is prelude to the actual channel being built and the data being sent to the recipient. Combined with an appropriate authentication mechanism on your Apache installation for nonencrypted transmissions, you should have a good suite of methods to ensure that client requests can be identified and authorized appropriately, and that you send your machine's identity and certificates in a way client programs can understand. Sending confidential data to the correct location is as important as making the data confidential in the first place.

Spontaneity

Spontaneity is related to authentication. In a traditional authentication scenario, the client must have contacted the server before, in a session concluded before the session involving an authenticated transaction takes place. Assume, for example, you want to buy a brass-plated widget from **http://www.groovybrasswidgets.com** for Father's Day. Because you've been to Groovy Brass Widgets before to browse the catalog, you have a certificate for its server. When you connect a second time to order the particular widget you want for your father, the server and your browser recognize each other and the transaction proceeds normally and securely.

What if you're having one of those last-minute shopping frenzies, though? Perhaps you got your dad just the right thing for Father's Day, but you're having a hard time finding something for your Mom before her birthday hits. There's not a single brass widget that would make her happy, so you're browsing frantically across the Web, hoping to find the right thing. Finally, you run across **http://www.shinyshinythings.com** and there it is—the perfect shiny thing for your mom. But, wait a minute! You've never been to this site before. How will the transaction be authenticated so you can pay for the shiny thing?

This question is at the heart of spontaneity. To make e-commerce truly useful and financially rewarding (by making impulse purchases possible), browsers and servers must conduct secure transactions without having ever been in contact before. SSL handles these situations seamlessly, so you can buy your gift without having to leave the site and return to complete the authentication process. Your last-minute purchase is finished and the transaction was completely secure. Now, if you ever visit that site again, you can go through regular authentication because the correct certificate was exchanged.

Cryptographic Algorithms

Because an *algorithm* is a mathematical expression, it wouldn't be particularly secure if all encryption, worldwide, was done with one or two algorithms—no matter how many random keys could be generated by those expressions. The more choices for an encryption model, the more secure the ultimate encryption is, because it'll be less easy to determine which algorithm was used to generate the code. To provide this enhanced security, later versions of SSL support a number of different encryption algorithms.

A number of encryption methods are available today and more being developed all the time. Encryption is a topic of great interest, not only to the Internet and software development communities, but also to corporations, governments, and those who resist governments. *Encryption* is the way to keep your private data truly private. Even if the data stream is intercepted, a sufficiently strong algorithm keeps the code from being broken for a long time. Whether you're transmitting personal or financial information, defense strategies, a plan for revolution, or confidential and copyrighted information, encryption suits the needs of everyone who wants to keep things private while they move across a public network.

> **NOTE:**   Not surprisingly, encryption is a hot-button political topic as well. Until recently, the United States government prevented the distribution of encryption software of a certain strength outside the American borders. Although the laws were relaxed greatly in early 2000, most existing cryptographic software is weaker than it could be because of the previous requirements. In addition, there are frequently renewed calls to force encrypters to hand over their keys to the government so that, if encrypted data is suspected in a terrorist or other criminal act, the government can decrypt the data and see what it says. The Internet cryptography community, a hotbed of radical libertarian philosophy indeed (amid the generally libertarian Internet community as a whole), is understandably outraged. What's the point of encrypting if you give away the key? Stay tuned: this debate is likely to rage for years.

Even though you'll probably never need to know the dirty details of encryption, knowing what the different methods are that generate encryption codes and keys is useful. Some of these methods are far more popular than others. Some became popular because they could be exported, while others are used because they're strong and difficult to break. The remainder of this section of the chapter introduces the most popular forms of encryption.

RC2

The *RC2 algorithm* is a *block cipher,* meaning blocks of data are encrypted by randomly assigned encryption from another block in a table. (A table doesn't actually exist, but what would be the various cells in the table are generated by the cipher.) The RC2 algorithm was written by the same person who wrote the RC4 cipher described in the next entry. RC2 is unique because it can be configured in two ways. Not only can you set the length of the key, you can also set the effective key length. This means, while you might have a 256-bit key, the effective length might only be 64 bits. While this might not be interesting to most people, it does mean the RC2 algorithm could be exported under the draconian encryption export laws previously in effect in the United States. SSL support for RC2 always uses a 128-bit key and effective key length, making it relatively undistinguishable from other encryption methods.

RC4

The RC4 algorithm is a *stream cipher,* meaning each byte of data in the data stream is encrypted separately. *RC4* is a trademark of the RSA Data Security company, but it has also been reverse-engineered, and you can find the cipher on the Internet under other names.

RC4 doesn't have a set key length, so you can use a key of varying sizes: at least 8 bits, but less than 2,048. RC4 is a fast algorithm that codes and decodes quickly, regardless of key size. When SSL uses RC4, the key length is always 128 bits.

RSA

RSA encryption uses yet another methodology, public key encryption. As you might have read in Chapter 19, "E-Commerce," *public key encryption* relies on two keys: one public, easily shared along with the encrypted document, and one private, generated by the encrypting software and not shared with anyone. Although the method was patented for many years, the patent has now expired and this form of encryption is now the basis for a number of other encryption programs. Public key encryption is a bit complicated for normal Web traffic, though Apache and SSL can handle it if you need it. You need to ensure that a public key travels with the encoded data, so the recipient can decrypt the file on the other end.

TIP: If you're interested in encryption for things other than Web traffic, consider Pretty Good Privacy (PGP), a public key encryption program, which is also Open Source. PGP is popular in various Internet communities and the software is free. Learn more at **http://www.pgp.com** or at **http://www.pgpi.org** if you're outside the United States.

DES

Like the RC2 algorithm described previously, the Data Encryption Standard (DES) is a block cipher. DES is the most widely used cipher in the world and was invented by IBM nearly 30 years ago. DES keys are always 56 bits, while the data blocks are always 64 bits. You can probably find DES support in any program that offers encryption support, though you should consider using another algorithm if the program can handle more than just DES.

CAUTION: DES isn't the best choice when you're trying to secure critical data. Although it's been around forever, that has also given time to both curious and malevolent people. DES keys can now be cracked in under a day with the right hardware. This is no longer a good solution, except for situations where encryption is used as more of a discouragement than a solid defense.

3DES

If you like the idea of a block cipher, but aren't thrilled about the low security offered by DES, consider 3DES. As its name implies, *3DES* is a scheme that runs the DES algorithm three times on the data to be encrypted. All three repetitions can be encryptions, but most people who use 3DES use it as encryption-decryption-encryption, each with a separate key. This leads to a thoroughly jumbled piece of data, far more secure than a plain DES encryption. The drawback to 3DES is that it's slow (perhaps obviously, because it's repeating the same action three times in a row). You'll find 3DES support in a number of programs because it's been adopted as a more secure encryption by people who are used to DES and don't want to change their habits.

DSS

Digital Signature Standard (DSS) is theoretically similar to RSA but, in practice, works somewhat differently. Developed by the National Security Administration, DSS is intended as an encryption strategy that doesn't irritate the government because it's a fairly restricted algorithm. The government knows how to break DDS because they invented it in the first place. DDS is also freely exportable under the old laws. The point of DSS is to create a digital signature, a key that identifies the sender and the document, and allows the data to be decrypted. Unlike RSA, you can't use DSS to generate a public key. You see DSS support in some programs, though it's not widely accepted because the more paranoid members of the cryptography community don't see the point in encrypting something with government technology.

TCP Protocol Compliance

The final feature of SSL that makes it such a great protocol is that it's completely compliant with the TCP protocol. TCP is the main way in which information is transferred over the Internet. As with most protocols or programs that require other people to program in a certain way, a TCP API (Application Programming Interface) exists. We discussed the Apache API in other chapters of the book. SSL is written to the API for TCP. (Aren't acronyms fun?) What this means is that SSL can work seamlessly with TCP-transferred data, without confusing or breaking the servers and clients at each end of the transaction.

NOTE: While SSL is primarily intended for TCP transport, other versions of the protocol have been developed. If, for some reason, you aren't using TCP to transfer certain forms of data, SSL variants are also available for you. For example, the UDP protocol sends bits of data as datagrams rather than as the packets used by TCP. Wireless applications use datagrams, and a form of SSL has been developed to provide secure transmissions over wireless devices.

HOW SSL WORKS WITH APACHE

Although SSL was designed to work with the HTTP standard to secure data transmissions across the Internet, SSL isn't a seamless occurrence. Instead, a series of steps exist that both the server and the client must execute before the channel can be opened and encrypted data sent through the link. Not all Web servers can provide an SSL channel and not all browsers can execute all variations of the SSL standard.

NOTE: The older the browser, the less likely SSL can work fluidly. Just as you can't force your visitors to use a browser that handles style sheets (see Chapter 17, "Using Apache to Save Time—SSI and CSS"), you can't force them to use one with SSL capabilities that match those of your server. As with anything else, configure to meet the needs of the majority. You can't foresee every possible browser problem your site might prompt.

Any browser-Apache transaction, not only SSL transactions, begins with a new TCP connection. The browser contacts the server through that TCP link and makes a request for a particular file. Whether the person behind the browser has supplied the appropriate URL or has clicked a link on your site, the document that needs to be sent over SSL must be requested in a particular format. The https:// URL prefix must be used in place of the http:// prefix, or else the server won't know to open an SSL channel.

Once the server knows an SSL connection is being requested, the SSL handshake process can begin. The *handshake* is the series of communications between browser and server that include identification and authentication, culminating in the creation of the secure channel. The handshake has four components:

1. The encryption algorithm to be used in this particular session is defined. This is the most sophisticated transaction of the handshake because the browser and server must decide which of the many supported ciphers are to be used, how the key should be generated, and whether a digital signature is to be generated as part of the transaction.

2. The key is generated and shared with both the server and the browser. This step is where you notice the most lag on your system because generating a random key can take some time. The random key is usually created in a directory built for that purpose, often /dev/random. If you find that key generation is dragging your system to nearly unworkable levels, consider changing the configuration of your SSL module or program to require smaller keys.

3. (Optional) The server is authenticated to the client. This is usually done with a certificate, as previously described. Certificates vary in reliability. You can issue a self-signed certificate or get one from a low-cost or free certifying authority, but be prepared to lose some connections because the certificate you provide isn't sufficient. The only way to get a high-quality certificate is to buy one from a reliable company, such as Verisign (**http://www.verisign.com**). Verisign is currently charging $349 for a regular certificate ($249 renewal each year) and $995 for an e-commerce certificate ($895 renewal).

4. (Optional) The client is authenticated to the server. As with the previous step, this is done with a certificate. The server sends a CertificateVerify HTTP header to the client, requesting it return identification based on a private key corresponding to the certificate (usually granted in an earlier session). Because this requirement limits SSL channels to people who have visited your site before and have obtained the appropriate certificate, it's often disabled and server authentication might be the sole authentication (unless you choose not to enable that step either).

Once the authentication process is finished, the channel can be opened and the encrypted data sent to the browser. The key generated in step 2 is used to encrypt the data, and then the browser uses the same key to decrypt the data before displaying it.

TIP: While the channel is open, the browser usually displays a particular icon designating a secure connection. On Netscape, this icon is a small padlock in the lower-left corner. For insecure connections, this icon is outlined in blue and open; and, for secure connections, it's bright yellow and locked. With Internet Explorer, a small yellow padlock appears in the lower-right corner when an SSL connection is open. If visitors complain that the padlocks don't appear when they're expected, check through your SSL configurations, but don't worry too much. This problem is usually found with Netscape, where the various components of the SSL connection don't communicate as quickly as they could. The connection is still secure.

The channel remains open until the data finishes transmitting, which could be some time if the browser continues to request secure documents. Generally, you should provide an Exit or Logout button on any pages that use SSL channels, so visitors deliberately close the SSL channel when they finish. If a particular visitor wants to revisit a secure page after she leaves, the entire handshake process repeats (though possibly more quickly if certificates are needed).

USING SSL AS A MODULE

The best way to add SSL support to your Apache installation is to use a module. Two different Apache SSL modules exist, both of which have adherents and are used on many Web sites around the world. The ApacheSSL module (**http://apache-ssl.org**) was the first SSL module to be distributed to the Apache community. The mod_ssl module (**http://www.modssl.org**) was developed from Apache SSL and is now administered and run as a completely separate project.

Although no reasons exist to avoid using ApacheSSL, I recommend you use mod_ssl as your first ApacheSSL module. This is a reasonably arbitrary recommendation, but I find the user documentation for mod_ssl is a bit easier to understand. If you have a problem with the module, you can usually find the answer without too much trouble—either in the extensive FAQ or in other documents on the mod_ssl Web site. (Of course, there's nothing wrong with installing both—on separate Apache installations, please, lest Apache grow confused and crash—to see which you like better.)

TIP: Learn more about Apache modules in general in Chapter 5, "Apache Modules." This chapter introduces the concept of modularity and provides information about compiling and configuring modules for your installation.

Obtain the mod_ssl module from **http://www.modssl.org**. Make sure you download the correct version for your Apache installation. The module version must be the same as the Apache version, or you won't be able to get it to work. Install the module as you would install any other Apache module and restart the server by issuing the command

```
apachectl graceful
```

or

```
apachectl restart
```

if you have no current connections to the server.

Once you have mod_ssl working cleanly with Apache, you can begin to configure the module. Because every site has different configurations and different needs for encryption, working through the user documentation yourself as you set up and test mod_ssl is best. Luckily, the project has compiled an impressive User Guide, which contains both a FAQ and a truly exhaustive HowTo section. I recommend you read through the User Guide before you install the module. The User Guide should answer any questions you might have, as well as providing information you didn't know you needed.

SSL Without Modules

Interested in SSL, but don't want to enable it as an Apache module? You might not want to run SSL all the time, or maybe you're not too sure whether your machine and Internet connection can handle the load. Plenty of reasons exist not to use modules for various Apache-related functions, and SSL is no exception.

Instead of using a module, consider downloading OpenSSL (**http://www.openssl.org**). *OpenSSL* is the "big kahuna" of nonpatented encryption and SSL projects, and the software is thoroughly tested and undergoes ongoing development. The OpenSSL software includes support for several versions of SSL, as well as for TLS, if you want to implement that technology for use with Internet Explorer–using visitors. You can use any kind of encryption method you like with OpenSSL, including RSA. This became the case when RSA's patent expired in 2000.

The downside to using OpenSSL is that you need to do a lot more work than you would by using ApacheSSL or mod_ssl. OpenSSL is technically a *toolkit*, a program configured with functions of interest to programmers and developers. It could be too much for your needs—or it could help you tinker with your own coding projects that incorporate SSL technology.

Depending on your operating system, you could already have OpenSSL. Many BSD and Linux distributions include OpenSSL on the CD-ROM or in the download, so double-check that you have the latest version and install the software. OpenSSL is currently in beta release, though the beta appears almost ready to migrate to stable status. If you have no experience with SSL, I recommend you start with an Apache module, and change to OpenSSL if you find the technology fascinating and you plan to code SSL programs.

TIP: The most common problem with SSL modules seems to be that browsers sometimes hang when requesting pages. The fix is simple: SSL-enabled pages must be called with the prefix **https://** instead of **http://**.

SUMMARY

The Secure Socket Layer (SSL) provides an on-the-fly encryption mechanism that can protect data flowing into and out of your site. SSL is most commonly used in e-commerce installations, but is valuable to administrators of all Web site types. If you handle sensitive, personally identifying, or financial data, you probably need to use SSL to protect the information as it passes through your server on the way to a requesting browser. SSL supports many encryption methodologies: stream ciphers, block ciphers, and public key strategies.

SSL connections, or channels, are constructed through a five-step conversation between the requesting browser and the server. First, the browser requests a secure page with the URL prefix https://. The browser and server then negotiate an appropriate encryption algorithm and generate a key to be used for these particular connections. If you choose to add an additional layer of security, SSL can require the server to provide authentication to the browser, and vice versa. SSL authentication is usually handled through certificates, which can be purchased from a reputable third-party company or self-signed, though the self-signed certificates don't carry the same legitimacy as a commercially obtained certificate. You can install SSL as a module in your existing Apache server or you can download a separate program and run SSL as a stand-alone. No matter how you add this feature to your Web site, it's a necessity for any administrator who manages sensitive data.

CHAPTER 23

Firewalls and Proxies

In the other chapters contained in this part of the book, you learned about various security precautions you can take to protect your data and your site. Some of those solutions are integrated into your server installation, like SSL, while others involve user behavior and setting appropriate policies for your network. In Chapter 20, "Basic Security Concerns," you learned about some basic physical precautions, such as using a locked server room.

In this chapter, you're introduced to security options that combine both software and hardware. While firewalls and proxies might seem complicated to set up, they offer a level of security that's hard to match with other methods. Combined with an encryption technology like SSL, a good set of user policies, and some intrusion detection software, firewalls and proxies contribute to a site that's about as secure as you can get without spending all your time or money on an even more secure strategy.

A firewall, at its most basic, is simply a roadblock. It intercepts traffic going into your network and traffic coming out, passing the data or rejecting it based on a set of criteria you identified when you set up the firewall. Firewalls can be simple, checking only that packets on the bandwidth stream conform to expected parameters (such as requests for Web sites coming in on the appropriate ports). On the flip side, firewalls can be immensely complex networks of filters, checking IP numbers, authentication, encrypted data, and almost anything else that can be ascertained from a data stream.

Proxy servers, like firewalls, are roadblocks of a sort. Rather than verifying the data that flows through the roadblock like a firewall does, however, proxy servers do the work themselves. When a request comes in to a proxy server, the server holds that request instead of letting it pass through to the other side of the proxy. Then, the proxy itself gets the requested information, brings it back to the waiting request, and provides the appropriate data. Proxy servers help to balance the load on your network and can actually speed Apache response times because the proxy can cache frequently requested data directly on its own machine, rather than requesting the data from Apache each time it's needed. While proxies aren't as intended for security purposes as firewalls, you can use proxies to shield your actual server machines from browser requests or to control the sites your internal users can visit outside the network.

WHAT IS A FIREWALL?

At its most basic, a *firewall* is simply a defense mechanism. It sits at the entry to your network, at the juncture between the external world (your Internet connection) and the internal net of machines and servers. A firewall is a gatekeeper that can be as benevolent or as stringent as your circumstances require.

TIP: The term "firewall" comes from modern construction. A firewall is a specially fabricated wall that's fire resistant. If a fire breaks out in one part of the building, the firewall is intended to prevent the flames from getting into other parts of the structure. While physical firewalls are, indeed, protective, the gatekeeper analogy is more accurate in describing how Internet firewalls work.

Firewalls can be configured to provide a number of services, which, in turn, can be set to operate at different levels of security. A firewall might control the way in which people can access the internal network, by restricting logins to the firewall machine alone. Likewise, a firewall can be used to ensure that you know when people leave the network, if users must log out of the firewall, as well as their internal account. A firewall can provide a barrier so intruders must fight through the firewall before gaining access to your data and network. The extra layer might take enough time that your network becomes too risky to crack. Finally, a firewall can be used to analyze the data that flows through it, in both directions, and permit or deny that traffic based on the characteristics you defined.

Although the popular conception is of a firewall as a single computer, into which the Internet connection is plugged on the front end and the network is plugged on the back end, this isn't necessarily the case. You can build a firewall from a spare machine, of course. Depending on the configuration of your network, however, your firewall may comprise several pieces of hardware or be built primarily of software. In the section "Firewall Structures" later in this chapter, a number of firewall configurations are described.

NOTE: If you purchase a firewall from a security company, you'll probably purchase hardware from them as well. Be sure you buy from a company that will work with you to configure the firewall for your system, not leave you with a one-size-fits-all installation that doesn't do what you need (and might do a lot of things you don't need). As with any third-party purchases, do your homework and pay only for what you need and will use.

What Firewalls Can Do

Firewalls can do a lot. You can use them to enforce system policies, as well as to track what your users do. Depending on how you configure the firewall, you can make it an integral part of your administrative work, or you can use it merely as an imposing presence at the gate of your network. No matter how much time and effort you put into configuring the firewall, it is likely to save you many times that amount in preventing unwanted activity.

The most important thing a firewall can do is enforce your site security policies. Because the firewall locks down access to your network, so that entry and exit must traverse the firewall, you can use the firewall to ensure your site policies are followed.

▼   Interested in enforcing password authentication? Require a separate password for the firewall and one for the user account.

■   Want to log internal use of the Internet during work hours? Track the firewall logs to see who's surfing the Web or using other Internet features. You can associate activity with users by cross-referencing the IP numbers in the logs with the IP numbers of individual machines on your network. (You can't prove that User X was sitting at Machine Y, but you can say Machine Y was used at a particular time to access Web site Z.)

■ Need to limit access to certain parts of your network? Define the firewall so certain users have permission to log in to certain network machines, but not to others.

▲ Worried about confidential information or files leaving your network? Configure the firewall to scan outgoing data for particular markers embedded in the files. (Obviously, this won't stop someone from saving confidential files to a floppy disk and walking out the door, but it should prevent someone from e-mailing such files to an outsider.)

Of course, the reason most people think about implementing a firewall is plain old security. If you're running a firewall, you limit the amount of exposure your network has to the outside world, where evils lurk and security threats are common. By using the firewall, you present only the firewall to the Internet connection, not the individual faces of the four or forty (or four hundred) machines on your network. By limiting your exposure, you limit the damage that can be done.

What Firewalls Can't Do

Although firewalls are a key component of any security scheme, understanding what they cannot do as well as what they can do is important. The most critical thing to remember is that a firewall cannot protect your network against malicious users. If someone with a legitimate account on your system decides to cause trouble for you, the firewall can't do anything unless that user tries to transfer data through the firewall and your data parameters are triggered. If you have users who are intent on misbehavior, this is an issue for your internal policies and your administrative attention. The firewall is unlikely to be of much help in a situation like this.

TIP: See Chapter 12, "Dealing with Users," for more information on site policies and how to handle your user base. Chapter 10, "Disk Management," offers some software-based solutions for working with your users.

Be aware that firewalls aren't universal solutions, either. While a well-configured firewall is a marvelous way to bolster your network security, it does have drawbacks. The more you require from a firewall, the more time it takes to pass data through. That is, connections to the external world are likely to be slower if you have the firewall examining your data stream for a variety of triggers. You may hear some grousing from your internal users about the slowdown, or you may find your Apache response time has grown through no fault of Apache's.

It's certainly possible to break through a firewall. If a cracker is determined enough, and has enough time to work unnoticed, your firewall can be breached. The best defense against such a situation is the same admonition you've read countless times in this book: pay attention. If you watch your system logs, keep an eye on the firewall and its traffic, and know what regular traffic and activity on your network looks like, you're far more likely to catch an intruder before things go terribly wrong. Combine careful attention with appropriately chosen and configured software, like the intrusion detection software described in Chapter 20, "Basic Security Concerns," and your firewall will be stronger because you've surrounded it with effective administration. Software alone can't save your network from harm, but software combined with good practices can go a long way toward keeping the network safe.

CHOOSING A FIREWALL

To build an effective firewall, you must first determine what kind of firewall you need. How secure do you need to be? What is the optimum balance between access and protection for your network and the kind of data you have, as well as the amount of traffic that goes between your internal network and the Internet on a regular basis? Those who offer large amounts of data over the Web will have different firewall needs than those whose network needs little contact with the Internet.

TIP: You can build internal firewalls as well as external ones. If you want to lock down everything but your Web server, for which you want reasonably free access to the external world, build an internal firewall that offers easy access to the Web server, but not to anything else.

One way to narrow the decision about firewalls is to consider the various forms of firewall architecture. Certain setups are best for some kinds of networks, while other forms excel in other areas. Several choices of architecture exist, and you can change between them, if necessary. Don't panic over picking the "right firewall" because, like everything else on your network, you can edit and configure the firewall until it works for you. Having any firewall, regardless of its structure, is better than having none.

For many networks, usually corporate ones, purchasing a firewall from an external vendor is the optimal solution. If you and your fellow administrators don't have the time to learn about firewall technology or you don't have the knowledge required to program extremely secure software, buying a firewall may be the best way to enhance your site security. Firewall technology is specialized and people interested in security code often make it their career field. For those who plan to work on their own firewalls or to build them in-house, a good idea is to have a security specialist on call if you can't hire one to work full-time.

You can build firewalls many ways. The single machine sitting at the Internet gate is one method, but it's not the only way to construct your defenses. While a role certainly exists for the single box firewall, it might be less secure than your data requires. To select the appropriate architecture for your network, you need to know what your network does and how much of that must be secured. Before you begin to think about building a firewall, ask some questions and take all the answers into account as you decide

▼   Is this network single purpose or used by everyone at this site?

■   What services (besides Apache, obviously) do we provide to the Internet?

■   What kind of Internet traffic comes to our network?

- How many users do we have and how do they use the network?

- How many machines are on this network?

- How much extra hardware do we have lying around?

- How much money do we have allocated for site security?

- Do our administrators have the appropriate skills for working on the firewall?

- Is contact with the Internet critical to our work? (The answer is yes if you're running Apache.)

- How popular are the Web sites we host?

- What other security measures are in place?

▲ How well do our users comply with existing security policies?

Different kinds of networks require different firewall structures. Those who provide popular Internet services, like hosting high-traffic Web sites, need a much stronger level of security than those who run a basic internal network that doesn't generate much stress on the Internet connection. You must be particularly aware of how much money is allocated for security purposes. Firewalls, proxies, and other security mechanisms tend to expand to the limits of their budgets, because it's always possible to be a bit more secure if you spend a bit more.

NOTE: Answer these questions and similar ones that come up while you're reviewing your site before you make any decisions. Also a good idea is to review the questions and your answers on a regular basis to see if anything has changed, and whether you need to update your security measures in response.

FIREWALL STRUCTURES

You can construct a firewall in a number of ways, but most firewall methods can be divided into two categories: single box architectures and screened architectures. The single box method is the one most popularly called a "firewall," but for many networks it isn't an appropriate selection. The firewall types under the screened architectures category can be complex and may be overkill for smaller sites. Regardless of the site you have, you need to strike a balance between the security needs of your network and your data, and your own capabilities to manage and maintain the firewall itself.

Single Box Firewalls

As its name implies, the *single box firewall* is just that: a single box sitting between the internal network and the external world. Single boxes can take on several forms. The box might be a regular computer with a normal operating system, running security software, or it could be a specialized piece of equipment. It could even be a multipurpose computer that has a security partition. Single boxes aren't the most secure choice in firewall architecture, but they are the firewall of choice for many networks around the world.

TIP: If you're running a small network, such as a home network or one that supports a noncommercial Web site, the single box firewall might be appropriate for you. As long as you don't have a large amount of traffic going between your network and the Internet, a well-configured single box could serve your needs. Those who get high traffic to their Web site, whether or not it's commercial, might need to consider another architecture to protect their data.

Multipurpose Computers

The least secure single box firewall is one built from a computer that also serves other functions on the network. Some people try to save money and time by using a regular network machine as the local firewall, creating a new disk partition and loading it with firewall software. The problem is that this "solution" is about as secure as having no firewall at all. If someone enters the firewall partition on that machine, it's quite easy to get into other areas of the disk and into the other machines on the local network. If you notice an intrusion on the firewall partition, there's no way to isolate that intruder without shutting down the entire machine, which removes any chance that you can trace him or make any other real-time attempts at defending your system. This isn't an appropriate firewalling technique.

A slightly more secure method of firewalling with a multipurpose box is to have the machine handle both firewall actions, like packet filtering and proxy actions. (See the proxy sections of this chapter for more information.) While this can be a good way to consolidate security precautions on a small network, it's not amazingly secure if you're providing outgoing Internet services like a Web server. The main drawback is that doing both firewall and proxy activity on the same machine might lead to a false sense of security if leaks or missed communications exist between the two mechanisms. You'd notice the problems if there were separate machines, but when there's only one, this isn't so easy.

Routers

If you're connected to the Internet with an always-on connection, you're probably using a router. A *router* is simply a piece of specialized hardware that considers incoming traffic and directs it to the appropriate machine, and that does the same for outgoing traffic. Routers can be complex systems, requiring extremely specialized knowledge. To understand the importance of specialized router lore, you need only look at the popularity of the Cisco router certification. The Cisco certification is hard to get and a useful thing to have on your resume, because routing jobs are hard to get and lucrative.

Using a router as a firewall is tempting, and some routers are capable of doing the extra work. However, you need to know the specifics of your particular router before you can decide whether to use it as a firewall. Does your router have packet-filtering capabilities? Can you program it yourself, or do you need to get a specialist? If you're comfortable with the security functions provided with your router, this is certainly a reasonable option for the right kind of network.

NOTE: Web administrators might find the router a good firewall option in certain cases. If you can build a private internal firewall that locks off the rest of your system, you could use a router as the only defense between your Web site and the Internet. Because you need to offer reasonably open communication if you're going to serve Web pages, a router might be the correct level of security. Don't let the router provide all the security for your entire network, but consider it if you can separate the Web site from the other machines on the network. In addition, if your Web site has its own Internet connection, a router should be sufficient as long as you maintain general security practices.

Dual Homed Host Systems

The final single box architecture you might consider is the dual homed host. As with the other methods in this section of the chapter, a *dual homed host* relies on a single machine at the gate between the Internet and the local network. Unlike the router, the host machine is a regular computer. Unlike the multipurpose machine, this host machine only has one job. Under this architecture, the host machine is plugged into the Internet on one end and into the local network on the other end, but no communication occurs between the Internet and the network. That is, the dual host machine doesn't function as a router, but as a block to direct data transmission.

While this might seem like a great idea at first, blocking all packets between the Internet and the internal network can lead to some problems. First, you experience lag. For the dual host machine to process all of those packets and direct them to the correct location takes a lot of work. Second, if you're providing direct access to certain servers (like your Apache server), you defeat the purpose of having the dual host in the first place. Finally, if you have users with individual accounts on the network, they're going to have to log into the dual host machine, and then into their personal machines, every time they log in from outside the network. Even the most saintly of users will grow tired of this, especially if the user machines are all non-Unix boxes, and the firewall is a Unix machine with unfamiliar software and arcane commands that don't resemble anything installed on the user machines.

So, how can you get the effectiveness of a dual-homed host machine without running into all the problems inherent in the architecture? Combining the firewall capabilities of the dual-homed host architecture with a set of proxy services can make the most of this particular single box architecture. With a layer of proxy functions, your users won't see the dual host machine in operation, but they'll feel as if they're executing Internet connections without the additional security controls. For more information, see the proxy sections of this chapter.

CAUTION: No matter how tempting, don't run Apache on the dual-homed host machine. Apache is insecure by nature and a dual-homed host machine is a single point of failure. If someone cracks Apache, they can then access your network. This is especially important if you use CGI, SSI, or any form of dynamic content. Moving Apache to its own small network, perhaps with a router as a single-box firewall, is a far better solution than installing it on your dual-homed host firewall box.

Screened Architectures

For those networks where a single box isn't appropriate or secure enough, a *screened architecture* might make more sense. Under this kind of setup, at least two machines are between the internal network and the Internet. For example, the Internet connection might be plugged into a router, which directs packets to an internal firewall host, called the *bastion host*. The bastion host then filters the incoming packets and directs them to the appropriate places on the network. Individual machines on the network might need to go through the bastion host to access the Internet or, for some defined functions, might go directly to the router to place requests. The incoming data supplied as a response to that request, though, must go through both the router and the bastion host before it can be transferred to the individual user's machine.

As you can see, a screened architecture is much more secure than some of the methods described as single box architectures. The drawback to screened architectures is primarily financial. Running a router and a designated bastion host, as well as administering the rest of your network, can be quite expensive. Consider, though, whether spending money to protect your data is a better value than replacing that data in the event of a break-in. In addition, certain types of screened architectures are more secure than others. The simple router-bastion host example previously described is more secure than a single router or multipurpose machine scenario, but if someone manages to crack the bastion host machine, the entire network is compromised.

Screened Subnets

You can get an extra layer of security on a screened architecture firewall by implementing a screened subnet instead. With a *screened subnet architecture,* you build an extra network on the perimeter of your regular network, enclosing your internal network in a complete shell. This perimeter network has its own routers and bastion host, and can manage all incoming and outgoing traffic to keep the internal network as secure as possible. While setting up a screened subnet is time-consuming and might add extra time to incoming and outgoing requests, it is extremely secure.

Building a minimal screened subnet isn't too complicated. You need two routers (or two computers configured as routers) and a separate bastion host machine with proxy capabilities. Set up one router as the connection between the Internet and the bastion host machine, and the second router as the connection between the bastion host and the internal network. Any packets intended to go from the internal network to the Internet, or vice versa, need to travel through three separate machines before they reach their destinations. This is an opportunity for three different packet filters to check the data before it can get into the internal network and cause problems.

Why is the screened subnet such a good idea? It works because no single point of failure exists. In the single box firewalls, if the firewall machine is compromised, there's no more defense for the network. In a plain screened architecture, if the external router is bypassed and the bastion host is cracked, no more defense exists for the network. This is quite possible if you're running services on the bastion host machine. With a screened subnet, though, a third machine is added to the mix. It can take some time for a cracker to force his way through a router, the bastion host, and a second router. If you have your in-trusion detection software calibrated correctly and you're paying attention to the network, it's unlikely a cracker can make it all the way through.

TIP: To configure a screened subnet architecture even more precisely for your Web needs, you can install specialized proxy code on the bastion host that transfers HTTP requests and the resulting files with a minimum of fuss.

Split-Screened Subnets

If the single screened subnet isn't secure enough for you, consider a *split-screened subnet*. You get all the benefits of the screened subnet with an additional perimeter network (or more than one) for extra security. The various perimeter networks are managed with dual-homed host machines located between the two screened subnet routers, rather than by a single bastion host. Or, you could have multiple bastion hosts between the routers, each handling a different kind of traffic.

The split-screened subnet might be an appropriate solution for administrators of Web sites that get a lot of traffic and are located on networks that also see a great deal of traffic passing through to the Internet and back (non-Web related). If you want to wall off your Web site, give it its own bastion host or dual-homed host between the routers. Then configure the packet filters, so data with HTTP headers is the only kind of packet data allowed to pass to the Apache server and back out again.

TIP: This also keeps a wall between Apache and the rest of the network if a security breach occurs, but allows the Web site to share an Internet connection with the rest of the network through the external router.

Independent Screened Subnets

The last type of screened architecture described in this chapter is the independent screened subnet. Like the split-screened subnet, the *independent screened subnet* is more complicated than a simple screened architecture firewall. However, the independent screened subnet has the advantage of extreme redundancy. If you have more than one connection to the Internet, such as two fractional T-1 lines, you can give each connection its own external router and handle the traffic separately.

NOTE: Having more than one external connection only makes sense when the two connections go to different places. For example, you might have one fractional T-1 that connects your local network directly to a larger network for all your company offices around the world, and another pipe that handles general Internet traffic. Both these connections need to be secured, but they don't carry duplicate traffic. By giving each one a separate set of routers and perimeter networks, you can keep one external connection going if the other one happens to fail or if a security breach occurs on one of the perimeter networks.

Internal Firewalls

Although the most common use of a firewall is to protect internal networks from direct communication with the Internet, at times, an internal firewall is a more appropriate security precaution. Perhaps you want to keep most of your internal network secure and protected, but you offer services—like Apache—to the external world, and you want your visitors to have a relatively open interface with your server machines. You might also want to lock down machines containing secure or confidential data, like credit card numbers or other e-commerce–related material. Regardless of the reason you're configuring one, an internal firewall might be an equally good solution for some of your network security priorities.

You can set up an internal firewall using any of the methods already described in this chapter. For example, you might add an additional bastion host or dual-homed host to handle Web traffic onto an existing perimeter network, and configure the external router to filter data with HTTP headers to that new host. Or, you might add a second connection to the Internet altogether (registering any domain or IP changes with the appropriate registry, of course), with a new router that feeds onto the same perimeter network—or onto a completely different one. You could even set up the Apache server machine as a second single box firewall with packet-filtering software that keeps HTTP data on the Apache machine and sends other data through to another router—but this would not only be highly insecure, it would also introduce another single point-of-failure into the network.

NOTE: As with the external firewall, determine why you're creating an internal firewall, and then draw the appropriate architecture from that. Don't decide on an architecture, and then determine how to fit your data and your network into it.

ADMINISTERING A FIREWALL

Once you have your firewall in place, as with any other software running on the network, you must keep working with the firewall for it to give you the service you need. Firewalls, in particular, require careful attention and regular maintenance, so they can protect your data and keep your network secure. Anyone who sells you a firewall and promises it's low-maintenance (or no-maintenance!) is either a fool or is lying to you.

When you build the firewall, pay careful attention to the functions that can make firewall maintenance easier. Know where the firewall sends its logs and where it will e-mail any urgent messages you need to handle immediately.

CAUTION: As with Apache, be sure to read the firewall logs and know what regular log entries look like. If you ignore the logs, you're relying on the firewall to protect your network for you, instead of working with the firewall to keep the network secure. The firewall is only software and hardware. Human eyes and intuition are as necessary as the code in creating a secure network.

Remember to keep your logs on a separate machine. If the firewall logs to itself, then any intruder who can get into the firewall machine can read your logs. If you configure reports to go to a particular e-mail address, be sure it's an account that's read routinely. It might even be a good idea to configure alarm reports to be sent to an e-mail address linked to your cell phone or pager. If someone is cracking your firewall, that's important enough to get beeped.

In addition to logging and getting regular updates and reports, backing up the firewall on a regular basis is important. I assume you're backing up your Web site and other critical data routinely, probably with an automated backup utility. Add your routers, single box firewalls, and bastion or dual-homed host machines to the utility. Reconfiguring a router if it gets hosed for some reason is a real bear. This is one of the reasons a router certification is so useful. If you have a copy of the files, this won't be so bad. Automated backup utilities are worth every penny you pay for them, even if you buy a high-powered commercial program. Compare the cost to the number of hours it would take to duplicate the data on your system at the regular salaries of everyone involved. Backup utilities are cheaper—get one.

Shutting Down Unused Services

If you want to help your firewall work more efficiently—and who doesn't, especially if you laid out a lot of money to buy a good one—you can do one thing to make your site even more secure: shut down any ports or services you don't use. One of the easiest ways for a cracker to slip into your system is through services or open ports you don't monitor regularly, or you don't even know are running. If you followed the directions in Chapter 20, "Basic Security Concerns," you might have run a port scan on your network from an external location. Any ports that popped up on the port scanner as available, which you aren't using for explicit reasons, should be shut down. Any services running that you don't use should be disabled.

You needn't make your firewall and proxy software work doubly hard to prevent intrusions on unused services. If you don't use an e-mail server, don't run one. If you don't provide USENET news to your users, don't run a news server. Install and run servers only for services you actually provide and that your users need. Keeping ports open for traffic types you don't get is an invitation to enter the system through a side door or a cracked window. If you've gone to the trouble of installing a firewall, don't expect the firewall to make up for sloppy administration. Do your part to run a tight ship, and your firewall will work much harder for you.

WHAT IS A PROXY?

Where a firewall is a physical bar between the external world and the internal network, a proxy is a different beast. A proxy is, in some ways, sleight of hand. When a request from the Internet comes into a proxy on your network, the external client thinks it's actually accessing the service it wants to use. However, the proxy merely appears to be that service. The *proxy* takes the request and sends it to the correct internal machine or server, and then relays the asked-for data back to the external client. Proxies aren't filters, in that they don't reject certain data streams based on their characteristics. Rather, proxies act as butlers or receptionists, responding to both internal and external requests without allowing the two realms to meet.

When you interact with services on the Internet, chances are good you're actually dealing with proxies, not with those services directly. Proxies are a common security precaution and have administrative uses beyond the security help they provide. With a proxy, you can protect your internal network from external intrusion in much the same way as the firewall does, but without the explicit actions of going through the firewall. Proxies run quietly and visitors might never know they've been proxied through a gateway machine or firewall, rather than contacting an internal machine directly. If you have users who complain about logging into a firewall machine and then, from that machine, logging into their personal machines, consider a proxy mechanism on your firewall. The login will seem much easier, and your users probably won't even notice it. On the flip side of that scenario, you can also force the use of regular user account names and passwords, rather than creating special accounts on the firewall machine itself. Proxies don't require explicit logins, so they're harder to detect and hack.

TIP: One of the better reasons to use a proxy, apart from the security aspect, is that you can spread one IP number across your entire network. Assign the IP number given to you by your upstream Internet provider to the proxy, and use private-class IP numbers (like the 192.168.0.* range) on the other machines in the network. This is much easier and cheaper than paying for additional IP addresses, especially because the proxy is the only thing that will ever contact the Internet directly.

How Proxies Work

As with the other systems described in this book, proxies use a client-server architecture. For the proxy to work as intended, a proxy server and a proxy client must exist. For security scenarios, the proxy server usually runs on the firewall machine or on some other gateway machine, so it can intercept incoming data and relay it to the internal network, or vice versa for requests leaving the network and going to external services.

Proxy servers can be configured to do many of the same things firewalls can do. Proxy servers can handle user authentication, if you prefer the proxy do it instead of the firewall or a third program. Because the proxy has to handle the connection anyway, authenticating it is merely a bit more work to do with the same item the proxy is already working on. Proxy servers can filter data streams even more efficiently than some firewall software, especially for HTTP data. Web administrators may be especially attracted to proxy servers because they handle HTTP headers and various data types quite well.

TIP: For more information on data and content types, and why you might want to filter certain types from others, see Chapter 14, "MIME and Other Encoding."

Another aspect of proxy servers of interest to Web administrators is the capability to cache. If certain files are requested frequently, the proxy server can cache those files locally. Then, when a request comes in for one of the files, the proxy server sends it out right away. No need exists for an additional request to the internal server or for the output to get back to the proxy before being delivered. Instead, the proxy server handles the entire transaction, saving time and preventing an additional contact to the internal network (thus, removing one possible interaction that might be a security risk). Not only is caching a slight aid to security, it speeds things up. The request is answered more quickly and there's no stress on the Web server, so system load isn't affected.

Of course, nothing in the administrative world is without fault. Proxies do have some disadvantages. Primary among these is there simply isn't enough support on the client end for proxying. The older the service or client you're using, the less likely that proxy support is built into it. Luckily for us, Web clients don't usually fall into this category. The Web came into prominence after people became concerned about Internet security, so both Netscape and Microsoft have built proxy support into their browsers from the start. Don't worry about client incompatibility when you're working with the Web.

The other major disadvantage is this: working with proxies could take time away from your other tasks. In general, no one proxy server can cover all your proxying needs. Different services might require different kinds of proxy requests or mechanisms, so you might have to install separate proxy servers for each service you offer. This can be a real pain, so you might find yourself restricting proxy access to certain services. Avoid this tendency if possible, as an incompletely proxied site might have unexpected security softness where you least expect it. You also might find your servers must be reconfigured to take proxies into account. This is certainly the case with Apache, although the solution is quite easy (see the section "The mod_proxy Module," later in this chapter). Regardless of the time it takes, though, setting up and maintaining proxies is an excellent way to increase the security on your site and to make your job easier.

CHOOSING AND COMPILING A PROXY PACKAGE

Once you decide to install proxy software on your network, you need to decide which proxy server to use. Several options exist and the choice depends on your operating system and the kinds of things you want or need the proxy server to do. You might also need to choose a package that will work with your existing services, your router software, or the various security applications you might already be running. Even though many things must be taken into account when you select a proxy package, several good choices and packages are also available to you for a variety of prices, and with different arrays of features and capabilities.

NOTE: When selecting a package, you need to decide whether you want a proxy package designed to work specifically with HTTP or whether you want a more generic proxy server. If you're interested primarily in proxying for Web requests, get a dedicated HTTP proxy server. A dedicated HTTP proxy server can parse headers more quickly and keep the connection between client, proxy server, and Apache as transparent as possible. If you need the proxy server to provide assistance to all the different services you run, get a general proxy server package instead.

For your first proxy package, unless you already have a commercial vendor who understands your security needs and is prepared to give you a good deal on a good package, consider SOCKS. The *SOCKS* proxy package is the most widely used standard on the Internet and has been proposed to the Internet Engineering Task Force (IETF) as a formal protocol. Plus, the basic SOCKS package is free in both the cost and Free Software senses. This is a generic proxy server, so it may not be as efficient in dealing with HTTP requests as a dedicated HTTP proxy server, but you can use SOCKS for all the Internet services you run and for your regular data stream between the Internet and your local network.

TIP: You can also find many commercial implementations of SOCKS or versions that have non-Free components. Let your personal convictions determine which version you end up with. The protocol is solid no matter how you get it.

Learn more about SOCKS, download a basic package, or find further documentation at **http://www.socks.nec.com**. Get a SOCKS5 version because it handles both TCP and UDP data transfer protocols, can do basic user authentication, has multiple logs, and will do its own domain name resolution without involving an external DNS server. Note, many SOCKS versions must run on a Unix machine, though any Unix variant will do. You might already have SOCKS on the CD-ROM if you recently installed a Unix operating system, but check to see that it's version 5. If you aren't running Unix, you might have to purchase commercial SOCKS software to use this proxying method.

CAUTION: You can only use the NEC site's free download of SOCKS on a noncommercial network. If you're running a corporate site, you must purchase a commercial version. SOCKS Reference, the free version, is for academic and personal use only.

CONFIGURING A SOCKS PROXY

When you download a copy of SOCKS, you get several programs in the download. Obviously, you get a proxy server and the required software libraries, so the server can install properly, but you also get some software that makes working with SOCKS easier. For example, you get SOCKS-friendly versions of FTP and other Internet programs that don't normally support proxy servers. You also get SOCKS-friendly wrappers for the critical utilities `ping` and `traceroute`, so you can continue to manage your network, even with the proxy server in place.

Install SOCKS as you would any other source code program (see Chapter 3, "Installing Apache," for general hints and instructions). Be sure to read the README and INSTALL files that accompany the download because you need to make specific configurations for your network. In particular, you need to enable SOCKS support for utilities like `ping` and `traceroute`. When the package finishes installing, you need to edit the `socks5.conf` file to set local configurations for authentication, interfaces, proxy information, and permit/deny settings. The file is reasonably well commented and has its own manual page.

TIP: You can read the man page for SOCKS configuration on the Web at **http://www.socks.nec.com/man/socks5.conf.5.html**.

When you finish editing the configuration file, restart the SOCKS server. It runs as an independent daemon process, so there's relatively little you must do to administer it. Simply keep an eye on logs and on the process until you know what it looks like when it's running normally.

THE MOD_PROXY MODULE

After installing and configuring a proxy server on your network, you need to alert Apache that a proxy is in use. If you don't configure proxy support into the Apache server, it might find answering requests quite difficult. In the same way Apache handles other functions, you can configure proxy support through a module, rather obviously named mod_proxy.

NOTE: At this time, mod_proxy is limited to Apache 1.3.* installations. The module has been moved out of the main module set for Apache 2.0.

mod_proxy can be used as a stand-alone proxy server or it can be compiled to work directly with SOCKS. If you already have SOCKS installed, go ahead and use mod_proxy in conjunction with it because the combination works well. The good thing about mod_proxy is that it also caches frequently requested Web files, so the server can provide particular files without having to make special trips to get the data. Caches are both a security precaution and an excellent way to speed response and system performance.

The mod_proxy module isn't part of the Apache 1.3.* core module set, but should be contained within your Apache download with the other extension and optional modules. Install mod_proxy as you would any other Apache module. (See Chapter 5, "Apache Modules," for more information on installing and configuring modules.) You need to make extensive changes to the configuration file for the proxy to work efficiently and safeguard your data. Learn more about the various configuration settings and directives at **http://httpd.apache.org/docs/mod/mod_proxy.html**.

NOTE: mod_proxy is currently being revised to meet the new Apache 2.0 code requirements. When it's available again, you can download it and compile it as you would any other module. Keep checking **http://www.apache.org/docs-2.0/mod/mod_proxy.html** for more information.

SUMMARY

Every network administrator should be concerned about security. The best way to run a safe system is to build a security regime that includes both hardware and software components, as well as to establish good security-minded habits. Two parts of a strong security system are well-configured firewalls and proxy servers. A firewall is a machine that sits between the Internet and the internal network. It can be a single box running firewall software, a specialized router, or a combination of computers and routers. These machines direct incoming and outgoing data to the appropriate destinations. Some firewalls also do basic user authentication and most can perform packet filtering, in which the data streaming through the firewall is analyzed and accepted or rejected based on what it contains. Firewalls can be used for varying levels of security and can also be placed internally to lock down certain segments of the network more tightly than others.

Proxies, like firewalls, deal with traffic as it enters and leaves the network. Proxy server software can be installed directly onto the firewall machine, if desired. A proxy server operates as a receptionist. As information comes in, the proxy determines where it should go and sends a request to the appropriate server for that information, but the original request goes no further than the proxy. Likewise, when the requested information returns, the proxy sends a copy to the external request process, but doesn't allow the internal network to contact the external network directly. Proxies can be configured to work with a variety of Internet services and are an excellent way to share a single IP number across a multiple-computer internal network.

PART VI

Appendices

APPENDIX A

Internet Resources

No matter how comprehensive any technical book tries to be, it's inevitable that some material will be outdated or changed by the time the book hits the store shelves. While I've tried to give you as much information as possible in the preceding chapters, you'll probably find yourself in search of the most recent news or information as you pursue your work with Apache. Luckily, multiple resources exist for you to investigate to give you some of the information you seek.

TIP: If you're searching for the next level of Apache knowledge, check out the next book in Osborne/McGraw-Hill's Apache series: *Administering Apache*, by Mark Allan Arnold, Clint Miller, James Sheetz, and Jeff D. Almeida. This book is written for the Apache administrator who's moved beyond the basics and is interested in the nuts and bolts of more specialized topics, such as e-commerce and scripting.

Although this is probably glaringly obvious, the best place to find Apache information is on the Internet, and especially on the Web. People who work with Apache are likely to use it to provide Web pages full of information to the Apache community. You can also find interesting conversations and helpful tips in other segments of the Internet, however, such as newsgroups or mailing lists. You can find Apache help at whatever level you need, from urgent beginner questions (though most of those questions should be answered in this book) to arcane developer queries.

NOTE: No matter what kind of question you need to ask, be sure you review what's available before you ask it. Most groups have lists of Frequently Asked Questions (FAQs) or other similar documents. These documents exist to keep conversation at an interesting level. Imagine how boring it must be to read "Where can I get Linux packages of Apache?" over and over again. If the group doesn't have a FAQ, it may have a searchable message archive. Do your homework before you jump in with a question already answered elsewhere. If you begin on the wrong foot, it takes a long time to rehabilitate your online reputation.

The remainder of this chapter provides contact information for these Apache resources. In some cases, you need programs that give you access to particular kinds of information, whether it's an e-mail program or a newsreader. Using individual programs for each of these tasks is best. While programs like Netscape or Microsoft Outlook are advertised as multiple-use programs, you'll find they're best at one kind of thing and not so good at others. Netscape, while a great Web browser, isn't the best e-mail or news program; and Outlook is a fabulous scheduler, but not the best Internet application. Do some investigation to find a stand alone product that works for you.

WEB SITES

Clearly, the Apache project's own Web pages are the best place to start looking for help with the server. Other unofficial sites are equally helpful, however, and they can give you a number of good ideas for configuring your own site. Keeping an eye on technology news is important because you can learn about the latest killer apps or new security patches.

Apache-Related Sites

Whether official or not, many good sites are related to Apache. You can learn how to install and run the server, configure the server for your particular needs, or make it as secure as possible. The following are some Apache Web pages. Follow the good links provided by each of these sites to find even more Web information.

▼ http://www.apache.org

Of course, this is the place to start. Home of the Apache Software Foundation, **www.apache.org** is the best place to find the latest downloads and documentation. A great set of external links to Apache-related information exists, as well as links to the latest Apache news. This isn't a site for technical support or instant response, but it's where you can learn the most about Apache, the Apache Foundation (make a tax-deductible contribution!), and the latest software.

▼ http://nav.webring.yahoo.com/hub?ring=apachesupport&id=7&hub

Yes, it's a nasty-looking URL. You can get the same result, though, by going to **www.apache.org** and clicking Apache Support WebRing. This ring contains quite a few sites providing Apache support and information. At press time, 16 sites were on the ring, including some sites listed in this appendix.

▼ http://modules.apache.org

Although it's part of the Apache site previously listed, this URL takes you directly to the module registry. All developers are encouraged to list their modules or patches in the directory, which is searchable. This is the best place to find the code you need that isn't part of the official distribution, but that can make your administrative life easier.

▼ http://www.irt.org/articles/js180/index.htm

Throughout the book, you've seen various suggestions on customizing your Apache installation, so that does precisely what you want it to do. At this site, you can find another introduction to Apache customization, focusing on Apache modules as the best tool for a unique installation. You can also find handy tips and tricks to get Apache tuned just right for you.

▼ http://www.w3c.org

This is the Web home of the World Wide Web Consortium, familiarly known as W3C. This group develops the HTML standards that drive the Web. You can learn about new standards, proposed developments, and other initiatives that may change the way you run your site. It's in the best interest of every Web administrator to be familiar with the W3C and their work.

▼ http://www.apacheweek.com

Apache Week is a commercial weekly magazine that provides information both for Apache administrators and for those working on the code itself. You can find information about gatherings, new releases of Apache-related software, and useful resources. The site also contains book reviews, feature-length articles, and a set of job postings.

Specific Project Sites

▼ http://www.apache-ssl.org

Secure data transfer is on the mind of almost every Web administrator. The people of the Apache-SSL project are working to integrate Apache's power and flexibility with Secure Socket Layer technology, which allows critical private data—like credit card numbers—to be transferred securely over the Internet. Anyone involved with e-commerce or other sensitive data should be interested in the work being done here.

▼ http://perl.apache.org

The Apache/Perl Integration Project focuses its energy on the mod_perl module, covered extensively in Chapter 12, "Dealing with Innovation (mod_perl case study)." Here, you can find the latest news and downloads, as well as references to mod_perl in the media and information about conferences. You can also find lists of sites using mod_perl, job postings, and other useful information.

▼ http://jakarta.apache.org

If you prefer Java to Perl, check out the *Jakarta Project*, which absorbed the Apache/Java community in 2000. This project works with the integration of Java into the Apache distribution. For those most comfortable working on the Java platform, a lot of good information and useful software is here, as well as servlets and other critical programs.

▼ http://gui.apache.org

As you probably already noticed, Apache requires you to work with text files. For some administrators, especially those coming from a Windows NT background, the lack of a graphical interface is annoying. The Apache GUI-Dev Project is working toward usable GUIs for administrators. Its aim is to support all workable solutions, rather than to create a single monolithic GUI option. At press time, the majority of projects listed here were Linux based, though the list may have changed by the time you read this.

Technology News

Many sites offer technologically oriented news. Some of them, like IDG.net (**http://www.idg.net**) or ZDNet (**http://www.zdnet.com/zdnn/**) are large corporate sites that offer a mix of press releases and articles written on various topics. The equivalent in other journalism sectors would be a large daily newspaper, or CNN Headline News. Other technology news sites are different from traditional journalism. They encourage discussion among readers, and provide both verified stories and rumors. The closest equivalent in print journalism would be a local free weekly with an emphasis on discovering the "truth."

The four sites listed in this section are of the second type. They are run by folks who wanted more information than that provided by traditional news sources and who wanted to create a community around these news items. If you're faint of heart or don't have much time, reading the headlines on these sites should give you an insight into the hot topics. If you have some time and you like to argue, look into the discussion boards and consider participating. Be aware, though, these news communities are aggressive and vocal (not always in polite language, either), and the community posts aren't guaranteed to be factual.

▼ **http://www.anandtech.com**

With an emphasis on hardware news and issues, AnandTech provides downloads, headlines, reviews, and other information necessary for most computer users. The site is especially useful for chip and component information, but has excellent insights into hardware of all sorts. The forums are active and vocal, providing an additional insight into whatever chunk of silicon you might want to buy the next time you're in the store.

▼ **http://www.arstechnica.com/**

The name *arstechnica* means The Technical Arts, and the administrators of this site bill it as the PC Enthusiast's Resource. You can find stories about hardware and software, operating systems and games, and new technologies and old favorites. The emphasis is on news the power user can put into play immediately and on giving readers the information they need to make good choices.

▼ **http://www.sharkyextreme.com**

SharkyExtreme is one of the most comprehensive PC enthusiast news sites on the Web. No matter what you need to know, you can probably find it here. Games, hardware reviews (CPUs, video cards, and monitors get their own sections), software reviews, editorials and articles, price guides, PC system information, and tons of other original content or links to Web resources fill the site.

▼ **http://www.slashdot.org**

Slashdot has the reputation of being a Linux news site, but it's much more than that. The site posts links to stories about a wide variety of technical topics, security, online legal rights, and other topics of interest (including space exploration, penguins, and Japanese animation). This site is an eclectic mix supported by the well-known Slashdot community, which is never afraid to say what it thinks. At least check the headlines if you don't want to participate in the discussion.

Security News

Web administrators must be vigilant about security. There's no excuse for being lax and the penalty for ignoring security issues can be huge. In Part VI: Security and Apache, you learned the basics of Apache security and how to control access to your site. More than any other topic involved with Apache administration, however, security news changes rapidly. If your network connects to the Internet at any point, you should keep an eye on general technology news sites and, more specifically, on security-related sites. If a new virus or method of attack occurs, you can learn about it quickly and apply the relevant patches before your site is compromised.

▼ **http://www.cert.org**

The Computer Emergency Response Team (CERT) is the big granddaddy of security sites. The CERT organization is the central authority for security alerts, identifying security risks like viruses and worms, and finding exploitable bugs in software. If you have users who like to spread virus rumors, you can check the truth at the CERT site before you panic or let your users whip themselves into a frenzy.

▼ **http://www.alw.nih.gov/Security/Docs/network-security.html**

If you're interested in the best way to structure a network so security risks are minimized, look at this page produced by the United States National Institutes of Health (NIH). This provides a good overview of networking (specifically, Unix networks) and shows some good methods to reduce the likelihood of unauthorized entry or attack. The focus here is on firewalls and gateways. While this isn't a specifically Apache-oriented site, a secure Web server on an insecure network isn't secure at all.

NEWSGROUPS

While an entire USENET hierarchy is devoted to Web issues (`comp.infosystems.www.*`), there isn't a specific Apache group there. Of course, because Apache is so dominant, a good chunk of server-related discussion happens to be about Apache. Check through these groups for your particular platform. If you can't find the information you need in that group, you may be able to find it in the miscellaneous group.

NOTE: The `comp.*` hierarchy is especially sensitive to issues of netiquette. Make sure you read any relevant FAQs before you post to these groups and you read a good chunk of the back messages on your news server. In the "olden days" (a few years ago), newcomers were expected to read quietly for several weeks before posting. Those old tenets still hold true in some corners of USENET. Don't jump in to ask a question before you figure out whether it's been asked—and answered—many times before.

▼ **comp.infosystems.www.servers.mac**

Issues specific to MacOS are covered in this group. The group is low-traffic, perhaps because Apache is now integrated into MacOS X and little need occurs for non-Apache server discussion. If you have a Mac-specific question, however, this is probably the best place to start investigating it.

▼ **comp.infosystems.www.servers.misc**

If you have a question or issue that hasn't been addressed in the more specific groups, you can bring it up here. As the miscellaneous group of the server's subhierarchy, anything not on topic in the other subhierarchy groups is on topic here.

▼ **comp.infosystems.www.servers.ms-windows**

The vast majority of traffic in this group is Apache related, both on the NT platform and on personal Windows platforms. Although IIS discussion exists, most of that appears to take place on Microsoft's own Web forums, so this newsgroup is a relatively safe place to discuss Apache/Windows issues without getting sidetracked into an Apache versus IIS religious war. This is a busy group with a good mix between newbie questions and old-hand information.

▼ **comp.infosystems.www.servers.unix**

The true traffic load in this subhierarchy is carried by the Unix servers newsgroup. You can find discussions about Unix-only networks (ranging from Linux to Solaris and through every distribution and variant in between) and about heterogeneous networks. If you're following this book's recommendation and running Apache on a Unix-based machine—even if your network is otherwise exclusively NT—you can find kindred souls here who can answer your questions about NT-domain authentication issues and other problems deriving from the NT-Unix interface.

▼ **comp.infosystems.www.authoring.cgi**

If you're working with CGI scripts, you might find this group a welcome resource. This focuses on the writing of CGI, not its administration, though you can find information on that as well. Note, this is a moderated group, which means all posts must be approved before they appear on the group. This results in a lower-traffic group with a higher "signal:noise" ratio, meaning more on-topic posts and less fluff. The drawback is this: posts might take a while to show up, but when they do, they're usually of better quality.

USENET Archives

Much of USENET history is lost; more precisely, it was never saved. In 1995, however, DejaNews began archiving messages posted to USENET newsgroups (and several other hierarchies as well). The archive was initially greeted with concern and suspicion, but over the years, it became a valuable resource for newbies and those wanting to see what they'd said in the past. As with most dot-coms, once the archive became popular, Deja tried to figure out how it could earn a profit on this database. Unfortunately, this didn't work. People used Deja for USENET research and not for advertising access or comparative shopping.

In early 2001, Deja sold the complete USENET archive and the Deja and DejaNews names to Google, a search engine company. Google plans to provide a new interface to search the archive and promises to be an ethical dataholder, well aware of the importance of the archive to the entire USENET community. You can find the USENET archive at **http://groups.google.com**. At press time, the entire 500 million post archive is available for search. The search capability isn't yet 100 percent functional, however, so you might need to search using several different keywords to find appropriate posts.

Why should you care about Deja, Google, or USENET archives? Quite simply, because no better resource exists for computer-related information. The development community has used USENET as one of its core communication modes for more than a decade and, if you care to, you can read those conversations from 1995 forward. Reading through the archive can show you what questions keep recurring, who the participants are, and what the growth process of any particular project looks like. The most famous example is probably Linux, the germ of which was a post to `comp.os.minix` in 1991 (**http://theory.ms.ornl.gov/~xgz/linus_announce**), but you can find early development discussion of most Open Source and Free Software projects as well, including Apache.

MAILING LISTS

A number of mailing lists exist for Apache administrators and developers. In this section, you can find lists operated by the Apache project. While other lists are out there, you have the best chance of finding help on the Apache lists. In addition, you're more likely to find and talk to someone who helped code the part you're having trouble with if you participate in an Apache mailing list.

TIP: Only a few of the Apache lists are described here. You can find the full list at **http://www.apache.org/foundation/mailinglists.html**. If you're interested in particular Apache projects, like the Jakarta Project or the work being done with graphical user interfaces, see the previous project Web sites listed. You can find information on the project mailing lists on those sites, as well as archives or other useful information.

Subscribing to Apache Mailing Lists

The Apache project uses the `ezmlm` mailing list software for all its lists. You can subscribe to any of the following lists by sending an empty message (no .signature file) to the subscription address noted, which usually takes the form *listname*-**subscribe@apache.org**. Send messages to the list at *listname*@**apache.org** and unsubscribe by sending an empty message to *listname*-**unsubscribe@apache.org**. You can get a list of handy commands by sending an empty message to *listname*-**help@apache.org**, which might be good information to save.

Some of the Apache lists are moderated and used only for announcements, while others are high-traffic and extremely technical. The mod_perl lists tend to be the highest in traffic, just as Perl people tend to be vocal in general. Most of the lists have archived past messages available on the Web and the `ezmlm` software lets you retrieve series of past messages by message number (learn how in the help document previously described).

▼ **announce@apache.org**

This is a low-traffic list, consisting only of official announcements sent by the Apache Foundation. Signing up for this one is a good idea. You won't get much mail, but the mail you do get will contain important information about the project.

▼ **apache-docs@apache.org**

For those interested in Apache documentation, see the apache-docs list. Here you can find discussion of both existing Apache documentation and documentation that ought to exist, but doesn't yet. Notices of changes to existing documentation are automatically posted to this list as well.

▼ **modperl@apache.org**

This is the main discussion list for mod_perl development and use, which is extremely high-traffic and quite technical. Have a good handle on Perl before you jump into this one, though you learn more about mod_perl from discussion on this list than from any other resource.

▼ **new-httpd@apache.org**

If you're interested in what's going into the next version of Apache, this list may be of interest. This is a development list, so it's high-traffic and highly technical. If you can keep up with it, though, it sheds some interesting light on how a project this large is coded and developed.

GETTING INVOLVED WITH THE APACHE COMMUNITY

As with almost all Open Source software projects, the Apache server is the product of a large and vigorous community. You can join this community in several ways, and contribute your skills and time. Perhaps the simplest way to participate is to report bugs when you encounter them. Be sure to note exactly what you did to generate the bug, and then check over previous bug reports to see whether you're duplicating an earlier report. Bug information can be found at the main Apache Web site.

TIP: In addition to donating your time and expertise, you can help the project by donating money. Although the Apache Foundation is a nonprofit organization, it hasn't yet been recognized as a 501(c)(3) corporation by the Internal Revenue Service. This means, while you can donate as much money or equipment as you like, it isn't currently deductible on your United States income tax return as a charitable donation. Ask your accountant for more information.

The following are the current Apache-related projects and their Web sites, where you can find more information about getting involved with their work:

▼   HTTP Server
  http://httpd.apache.org

■   Apache XML Project
  http://xml.apache.org

■   Jakarta Project (Server-Side Java)
  http://jakarta.apache.org

■   Apache/Perl Integration Project
  http://perl.apache.org

■   PHP Project
  http://php.apache.org

▲   Apache/Tcl Project
  http://tcl.apache.org

RELATED RESOURCES

In this section, you can find resources for the various topics covered in this book not directly related to the core Apache program. For example, you can find links here for the topics covered in Part IV: Beyond the Basics. Even though those topics are integral to running Apache at most sites, they aren't part of the most basic Apache installation. Most of these links are introductory, but you should be able to find a good set of resources on each of these pages to learn more.

Heterogeneous Networks

In Chapter 6, "Running A Heterogeneous Network," software was introduced that can be used to network multiple machines running different operating systems. Such software is easy to manage once installed and isn't that tricky to install correctly. Samba is for Windows users, while `netatalk` is for Macintosh users. Those readers running multiple Unix-derived operating systems also have networking issues, which can be solved with some of the information on these sites.

▼ **http://www.samba.org**

This is the home site of the Samba project. You can find downloads, documentation, news stories, and archives at this well-organized site. They provide good links to further sources of help if you have a problem with Samba that you can't solve with the information directly on the site.

▼ **http://www.umich.edu/~rsug/netatalk/**

`netatalk` is the program Macintosh administrators use in place of Samba. This program uses the AppleTalk protocol to manage data flowing between a Unix machine and a Macintosh machine. Here you can find software downloads; links to other `netatalk` sites; and a spare, but useful, FAQ.

▼ **http://www.ee.siue.edu/~bnoble/classes/ece577/links.html**

Although not a site directly about heterogeneous networks, Brad Noble's class materials comprise a great set of documents about network administration in general. You can find sections on administration, security, scripting, and a super set of network administration links. If you're new to networking, this is a great resource.

Virtual Domain Hosting

Finding noncommercial information about virtual domains on the Web is nearly impossible. Running the term through a search engine turns up hundreds of sites trying to sell you their virtual domain service. Luckily, a few pages contain helpful information, and you can always use the material in Chapter 23, "Virtual Domain Hosting," to set up virtual domains on your own server.

▼ **http://cybernut.com/guides/virtual.html**

This site gives a good introduction to virtual domains and how they work. It offers specific information for pre-2.0 Apache, as well as WU-FTP and `sendmail`, two popular packages for standard Internet functions. The page is targeted at people using the FreeBSD Unix variant, but it should be applicable across most Unix-derived operating systems.

E-commerce

As explained in Chapter 24, "E-commerce," contracting your e-commerce needs out to a company that does nothing else is best. The security risks are high, and these programs require an excellent grasp of PHP and MySQL. Even if you do contract these services to someone else, however, it's vital for you to understand how e-commerce software works and how it will interact with your own site.

▼ **http://www.ecommercetimes.com**

The *E-Commerce Times* is an online newspaper that covers stories related to e-commerce in some way. You can find stories about hardware and software, as well as business items about companies that happen to use e-commerce solutions. This isn't a technical site, but it's useful if you like to keep an eye on the industry.

▼ **http://ecommerce.ncsu.edu/**

North Carolina State University offers a self-paced, noncredit class covering basic e-commerce topics, as part of its e-commerce resource site. This is a good and nonbiased site that tells you what you need to know without slanting toward one e-commerce solution over another. Get the information you need here before you go out and find a provider to handle your online sales.

▼ **http://php.resourceindex.com**

The PHP Resources site is a great collection of information about *PHP*, the language used most commonly in writing e-commerce applications. While you needn't be a PHP guru if you're going to contract out your e-commerce needs (as recommended in Chapter 24, "E-commerce"), it's always good to have an idea of the technologies being used on any pages you have some responsibility for.

▼ **http://www.ftc.gov/bcp/menu-internet.htm**

Not that your site would ever run afoul of the United States Federal Trade Commission, right? Here's the FTC's page about e-commerce and its darker side. Learn what to avoid and what the FTC considers good e-commerce business practices, before you hear the knock on the server room door.

Web Page Design

While Web page design is outside the scope of this book, you'll certainly have to deal with design issues if you're administering a site. Part IV: Beyond the Basics introduces a number of page design technologies and explains how they affect your Apache site. These links show you how these technologies work and give you information you can share with your users as they begin to design the pages to be served by your Apache machine.

MIME

▼ http://www.hunnysoft.com/mime/

This is a basic site, but it provides links to the most important information about MIME encoding. You can find links to all the relevant Requests for Comments (RFCs), documents that define a particular technology and how it's to be used on the Internet. You can also find a link to the FAQ for `comp.mail.mime`.

▼ comp.mail.mime

This Usenet newsgroup is focused specifically on MIME queries and discussion. Other text-encoding topics pop up here occasionally, but the vast bulk of the group's traffic is devoted to MIME itself.

Server-Side Includes

▼ http://www.apacheweek.com/features/ssi

Apache Week offers a nice introduction to server-side includes (SSIs). The article explains how SSIs work and why you should consider using them on your site. Hands-on examples aren't provided (for that, you need a tutorial like the next resource in this section), but this is a great way to show your boss or other interested parties what this technology does.

▼ http://hoohoo.ncsa.uiuc.edu/docs/tutorials/includes.html

This tutorial teaches you the basic concepts behind SSIs and walks you through the construction of a small example. This is clear and easy to follow, giving you the tools you need to administer SSIs whether or not you write them yourself.

Image Maps

The more sophisticated the site you administer, the more likely your Web designers are going to use image maps as a navigational tool. These are reasonably easy to create and make an attractive site. Be sure any image maps you host are clearly labeled, so viewers without a graphical browser can still navigate through your pages.

▼ http://hoohoo.ncsa.uiuc.edu/docs/tutorials/imagemapping.html

This is a straightforward and clear introduction to image maps, how they work, and how to build them. NCSA is one of the best sources for accurate information. You can be assured that using its instructions will make your maps work properly.

▼ http://www.ihip.com

If you want something a little more personal to assist you in learning about image maps, consider the tutorial presented by the Imagemap Help Page. The tutorial walks you through a basic image map project and also offers a list of Not So Frequently Asked Questions, which deal with some of the unusual aspects of this page design technique.

Cascading Style Sheets

▼   **http://www.hwg.org/resources/faqs/cssFAQ.html**

The HTML Writers Guild has put together a useful resource for people interested in using cascading style sheets (CSS) in their Web designs. Here, you can find a FAQ partially written by Hakon Lie and Bert Bos, the inventors of CSS, as well as page examples and links to other CSS resources.

▼   **http://jigsaw.w3.org/css-validator/**

Once you or your designers have put together pages with CSS, download this useful tool from the W3C. The Validator checks your pages and alerts you if potential problems or errors exist in the way the style sheets have been coded. This is a valuable resource.

Scripting

Most Apache administrators end up using scripting languages to simplify and automate Apache administrative tasks. In addition, Web page designers are moving toward using more scripts in their pages, to serve unique or dynamic page content to viewers. Administrators should at least be familiar with how these languages work, if not confident in their own scripting skills.

NOTE: It's easy to learn the basics of Perl or CGI, though mastery takes time and patience. If you have the opportunity, learning from a mentor is often faster and easier than learning from a book or the Web. However, you can combine a good book with the more current information found on the Internet to get a good grasp on scripting for Apache.

▼   **http://www.cgi-resources.com**

Like the PHP Resources site previously listed under" E-commerce," this site is an excellent collection of links related to CGI programming. You can find documentation and tutorials here if you want to learn CGI yourself, or you can download one of thousands of prewritten CGI scripts for your own use. (Note, scripts aren't guaranteed. Testing them on a separate system is best, before you commit your own resources and uptime to a script of unknown origin.)

▼   **http://www.perl.org**

Any search for Perl information on the Web should start here, at the Perl Mongers' site. The *Perl Mongers* are an advocacy group devoted to spreading the good news of Perl to the programming world. On this site, they provide documentation, downloads of new and older versions, bug fixes, and other useful information. You can even buy a T-shirt or other Perl-themed stuff!

APPENDIX B

Using a Unix Text Editor

Throughout this book, you've been encouraged to run Apache on a Unix or Unix-derived operating system. Although many advantages exist to using Unix for Apache—advantages that outweigh the few irritants of the Unix OS—using Unix does mean you have to change some habits if you're more familiar with another operating system like Windows or MacOS. One of the major issues for many people is the way in which text is handled under Unix.

Unlike Windows or MacOS, Unix has relied for years on text-mode editors, as opposed to What You See Is What You Get (WYSIWYG) graphical text editors and processors. Even Notepad, the basic Windows text editor, is menu-driven and works more like a word processor than most Unix text editors. Unix text editors have a steeper learning curve than mouse-driven word processors, but you make up the time spent learning with faster work once you figure out how the program works.

In this appendix, I cover three Unix text editors: vi, Emacs, and pico. These editors are text based and keyboard driven. The programs are also presented in the order in

Text Editor or Word Processor?

What's the difference between a text editor and a word processor? Text editors focus on the words you're writing. The text isn't displayed in any particular format on the screen and the menus (if they exist) don't offer a wide array of formatting options. Word processors, however, offer a variety of visual effects ranging from font style to text placement on the finished page. With a word processor, you can see a replica of the finished document on the screen as you work. Although word processors are vastly useful and have become the software of choice for people who work with text, they're certainly overkill for the routine editing tasks required of system administrators. When I discuss editing files in this book, I assume you're going to use a text editor. Text editors permit quick and dirty editing, and, because configuration files and scripts never call for visual flash or formatting, a text editor is the best choice.

Which editor you choose is up to you. If you're familiar with Unix already or if you learn new programs easily, I suggest the old standards of vi or Emacs. However, the slightly more attractive pico, which is becoming more popular, is the editor I use on a regular basis. All three editors are described and explained in this appendix.

Regardless of the editor you choose, don't opt for a word processor like Corel's WordPerfect for Linux or Sun's StarOffice suite. Not only do these programs place an excessive overhead on your system resources, they also take up a big chunk of disk space you could devote to Web files or other resources. At least two of the editors described in this appendix are installed by default with almost every Unix-derived distribution and incur no additional overhead, and the other is free of charge. You pay both for WordPerfect and StarOffice, whether in buying the CD-ROMs or in system resources. Plus, the formatting automatically applied by word processors may actually cause problems with Apache if you use word-processed configuration scripts. Stay safe and use a regular text editor to work with Apache.

which they were developed. Reading through this chapter can give you an idea of historical developments in Unix text programming and show the influence of graphical operating systems on traditional Unix tasks. Just because vi is the oldest program discussed in this appendix, however, doesn't mean it's the least useful. Thousands upon thousands of Unix users still rely on vi for their daily text manipulation needs, and the same is true of Emacs, pico, and most other text editors.

> **TIP:**   Before you pick the editor you plan to use regularly, give all three a try. Many people find pico the easiest program to learn early in their Unix careers. Emacs and vi require more time and devotion to learn, but they reward you with more robust programs that are more popular among programmers and system administrators. There's no reason to pick one over the other, however, except for choosing the program you like best. Don't fight your text editor because someone told you Editor X was the best for Apache administration, even if you hate it and can't remember how to move from screen to screen. Instead, choose another editor and get to work.

vi

The vi text editor was a real advance when it was first introduced because it was the first Unix text editor to work in full-screen mode. Earlier text editors, like ed, worked on single lines, which made working on a multiline document quite difficult and time-consuming. With vi, you can see a full screen of your document at one time, making it easier to move through the file and work on one line while looking at the data in another. Because of this feature, vi is far easier to use than any of its predecessor line editors.

That ease of use doesn't necessarily translate to using the editor itself, though. vi can be quite confusing to the new user. It uses an arcane set of commands and has two modes: Command mode and Insert mode. If you don't keep a careful eye on the mode you're using, you can grow increasingly frustrated as you attempt to enter or format text without your keystrokes registering. People sometimes say vi devotees are so fanatical because learning how to use the editor took them so long!

That said, if vi is so awful, why is it included in this book? Well, it's not all that bad. Yes, it requires some attention; but once you get the basics memorized, you can sail through a document. The main reason vi is here, though, is it's the most widely provided text editor in the Unix world. vi is included in almost every Unix and Unix-derived distribution, whether as vi itself or as one of its clones: vim or vile. In addition, vi is usually the only text editor found on *rescue diskettes*, single disks of basic programs you can use to restore a crashed system that won't reboot on its own.

> **CAUTION:**   If only because vi is usually found on rescue diskettes, you do need to know the basics of the editor. A real problem occurs if you need a rescue diskette, and then realize you can't use the only editor available to you to fix your broken machine! This is especially critical for those readers who are running major Web installations that are time sensitive and carry lots of traffic. Learn the vi basics or at least keep a handy vi reference nearby. You'll be happy you did when the crisis hits.

vi's Modes

Open the `vi` editor by issuing the command `vi` at a system prompt. When the editor first opens, it's in Command mode. The Command mode setting means `vi` interprets every keystroke as a command to the editor, not as actual text meant to be placed in the file. This is one reason `vi` can seem so confusing—people reasonably expect that, when they open an editor and begin typing, they're working on their document rather than issuing commands to the editor itself. If you do begin typing before switching out of Command mode, you'll probably get some error messages. Ignore them.

To switch out of Command mode and into Insert mode, type the single character **i**. A cursor block appears at the beginning of the first line, indicating you changed modes. Whenever you see the cursor, you can enter new text or edit existing text.

NOTE: To open an existing file in `vi`, issue the command **vi filename** instead of simply typing **vi**.

Move around the document with the arrow keys on your keyboard. The BACKSPACE key removes the character to the left of the cursor, while the DELETE key removes the character directly above the cursor.

Once you've entered some text, you need to switch to Command mode again so you can work with the file as a whole. To return to Command mode, simply press the ESCAPE key (usually labeled ESC and at the upper-left corner of your keyboard). Command mode provides a number of file management and editing options. Table B-1 contains many of these keystroke commands.

Category	Command	Action
Cursor Movement	h	Moves the cursor one character to the left.
	j	Moves the cursor one character down.
	k	Moves the cursor one character up.
	l	Moves the cursor one character to the right.
	0	Moves the cursor to the beginning of the current line.
	$	Moves the cursor to the end of the current line.
	n$	Moves the cursor to the end of the nth line below the current line (counting the current line as 1).

Table B-1.   Working with `vi`'s Command Mode

Category	Command	Action
	w	Moves the cursor to the beginning of the next word.
	*n*w	Moves the cursor to the beginning of the word located *n* words to the right of the current word.
	*n*G	Moves the cursor to the beginning of line *n*.
	n |	Moves the cursor to the beginning of column *n*.
	G	Moves the cursor to the last line of the file.
	CTRL + u	Moves the cursor back one-half page (shows on screen as ^U).
	CTRL + b	Moves the cursor back one page (shows on screen as ^B).
	CTRL + d	Moves the cursor forward one-half page (shows onscreen as ^D).
	CTRL + f	Moves the cursor forward one page (shows onscreen as ^F).
Line Movement	n+	Moves the cursor down *n* lines.
	n–	Moves the cursor up *n* lines.
Deletion	*x*	Deletes the character covered by the cursor.
	dd	Deletes the current line.
	D	Deletes all characters from the cursor position to the end of the line.
	:D	Deletes the current line (same as dd).
	:D$	Deletes all characters from the cursor position to the end of the line (same as D).
	ESC u	Undoes the last command (pressed in sequence, not simultaneously).
	:U	Undoes the last deletion.
Text Pattern Matching	/*pattern*	vi searches for the next occurrence of the text string *pattern*.
	?*pattern*	vi searches backward for the most recent occurrence of the text string *pattern*.
	:s/*pattern1*/ *pattern2*	vi replaces the next occurrence the of text string *pattern1* with the text string *pattern2*.
	:s/*pattern1*/ *pattern2*/g	vi replaces all occurrences of the text string *pattern1* with the text string *pattern2*.

Table B-1. Working with vi's Command Mode *(continued)*

TIP: Not sure if you're in Command or Insert mode? First, check for the cursor. You can also ensure you're in Command mode by pressing the ESC key more than once.

NOTE: A *text string* is any series of characters. They can be letters, symbols, or numbers. The editor doesn't discriminate between nonsensical strings of characters and strings of characters that are readable. To vi, a word is any character or set of characters with a space on each side.

Saving and Exiting

Once you make the required edits to the file you're working on, you need to save and exit the file before you can move on to other work at the command prompt. Getting out of vi is one of the more unintuitive commands I've ever experienced in a Unix program, and it—combined with the mode issue—frustrates a significant number of people, who then promptly turn to other editors. If you like vi well enough to use it routinely, you might want to jot down the save and exit commands, and stick them somewhere near the computer until you have the sequences memorized.

You must be in Command mode to save or exit a file in vi. Tap the ESC key to get into the proper mode. To save the file, issue the command :w. To quit the editor, issue the command :q. Table B-2 shows the various save and quit commands.

vi Configuration

If you decide you like vi well enough to use it as your standard Unix text editor, you'll probably want to configure the way it works on your system so it feels most comfortable to you. vi is configured through a file called .exrc, which can be found in your home directory (user directory, not root directory). Open the .exrc file in the vi editor by issuing the command

```
vi .exrc
```

at the system prompt. The file sets the parameters under which vi operates every time you open it.

A sample .exrc file might look like this:

```
set noautoindent
set directory /textfiles
set ignorecase
set wrapmargin=80
```

In this sample, vi has been set to start each line at the far-left margin, to keep the text buffer (unsaved data) in the /textfiles directory, to ignore uppercase or lowercase when doing pattern matching, and to wrap each line to the next when 80 characters have been reached.

Command	Action
:w	Saves the file (writes it to the disk).
:q	Quits the `vi` editor.
:wq	Saves the open file, and then exits `vi`.
:q!	Quits the `vi` editor without saving the open file (use with caution).
ZZ	Saves the open file. and then exits `vi` (same as `:wq`).

Table B-2.   `vi` Save and Exit Commands

TIP: Consult the `vi` documentation (type **man vi** at a system prompt to view the manual page already installed on your machine or check out a `vi` page on the Web) for a complete list of the various parameters possible in an `.exrc` file. You can spend a lot of time tinkering with `vi` if you want to, though you can push a text-mode editor only so far.

Abbreviations and Macros

Interested in speeding up `vi`? You might want to give its abbreviation and macro features a try. These functions can save you a number of keystrokes, each one shaving a tiny bit off your overall time spent entering text. The abbreviation function lets you type a short text string, which `vi` then changes to a preentered, longer text string. For example, you might type the abbreviation apa in a document, having already informed `vi` that the apa abbreviation means the text string Apache Web server. The macro function lets you map a keystroke combination to a particular set of commands. Abbreviations are created in Command mode and used in Insert mode, while macros are created in Insert mode and used in either Command or Insert mode.

Abbreviations

To create a new abbreviation, move into Command mode by pressing the ESC key. Figure out an easily remembered abbreviation (try to keep this under five or six characters, or you run the risk of making the abbreviation as complicated as the actual text). Issue the command

```
:abbr abbreviation fulltext
```

as in

```
:abbr apa Apache Web server
```

Now, whenever you're in Insert mode and type the text string apa, `vi` automatically replaces the apa string with Apache Web server.

Note the inherent problem with this tool, though. If you use an actual word or common acronym as your abbreviation, you can run into real problems. Imagine you issued the abbreviation command

```
:abbr window Microsoft Windows operating system
:abbr moon 'Moon Pie' marshmallow sandwich cookies
```

Makes sense at first, doesn't it? But imagine what will happen when you write the sentence "Jean looked out the window and noticed that the moon was shining brightly." Good old `vi` will do exactly what you instructed it to do, resulting in this sentence:

```
Jean looked out the Microsoft Windows operating system and noticed that the 'Moon
Pie' marshmallow sandwich cookies was shining brightly.
```

Be careful about the abbreviations you use.

Abbreviations are stored in the `.exrc` file described in the previous section. A good idea is to review the abbreviations in `.exrc` regularly. Most abbreviations are useful for one or two major projects. When you move on to the next thing and no longer need to write about Moon Pies, delete the abbreviation. Shorter configuration files work faster.

Macros

Like abbreviations, macros can save you time. *Macros* are most useful for people who routinely issue commands in a series or who use the shell functions of `vi` to check on other processes without leaving the editor. To create a macro, use the map command, as in

```
:map <Ctrl>+y :wq
```

This command would map the `:wq` command (save the open file and exit `vi`) to the CTRL + y key combination. Thus, you could simply press CTRL + y to save and exit, rather than shifting into Command mode and issuing the command.

Of course, using a macro to replace a single command is pretty pointless. If you format your `vi` documents a lot, though, they can be quite useful. Macros, like abbreviations, are stored in the `.exrc` file. Review the file and delete unused macros on a regular basis to speed `vi`, and keep your configuration file clean and readable.

GNU EMACS

For those who are new to Unix, GNU Emacs might be enough to send you away again. This is a dense and complicated program that is usable as a rough operating system. GNU Emacs has an esoteric command structure, a peculiar method of interpreting entered text, and a bogglingly large demand on system disk space and memory. With all these drawbacks, why bring GNU Emacs into the discussion at all?

NOTE: Why GNU Emacs? It's the proper name of the program, which was developed by the GNU Project discussed in Chapter 1, "History and Background of Apache." It's usually called either GNU Emacs, its real name, or `emacs`, the command that invokes the editor. If you choose to use the term Emacs as a proper name, be sure to include the GNU component of the name.

Well, one reason is GNU Emacs is nearly as popular an editor as `vi`. It's amazingly useful for programmers, has a built-in mail reader and news reader, uses a native macro scripting language, and even offers psychiatric help! You're not going to get that array of features from any other text editor and probably not from any other program in existence on the Unix platform.

The downside is that learning this program takes a while. GNU Emacs is definitely not for beginners unless you're the sort of person who's never dismayed by a daunting task. If you're interested and you like a good challenge, though, give `emacs` a try. You might find this behemoth is your cup of tea.

Invoke GNU Emacs by typing **emacs** at the system prompt. If you want to open a particular file in the editor, issue the command as

```
emacs filename
```

instead. The editor then opens, looking like the screen shown in Figure B-1, with several sections. If you want to see multiple views of the same file, you can separate the screen into several windows.

NOTE: All text editors work with *buffers*, or text that's been entered, but not yet saved to disk. GNU Emacs makes this process explicit and has a number of functions that are used only with various buffers. If you want to work with several versions of the same buffer at once, you can do that. You can also have multiple documents open in one `emacs` session, each with its own window. GNU Emacs is the most complex of the Unix text editors and has many functions similar to those of a word processor.

GNU Emacs Commands

GNU Emacs handles commands differently from the other editors discussed in this chapter. Because of the way in which it was written, `emacs` treats every single entered character as a command to the editor. No Insert mode exists, as with `vi`. In `emacs`, everything is Command mode. Thus, if you type the letters ABC in GNU Emacs, you're actually sending a command to the editor to insert the letters *A, B,* and *C* into the buffer; you don't place those letters in the buffer yourself. The concept becomes more important as you work with `emacs`.

Most `emacs` commands use *metakeys*, like the CTRL and ALT keys, in keystroke combinations with other keys.

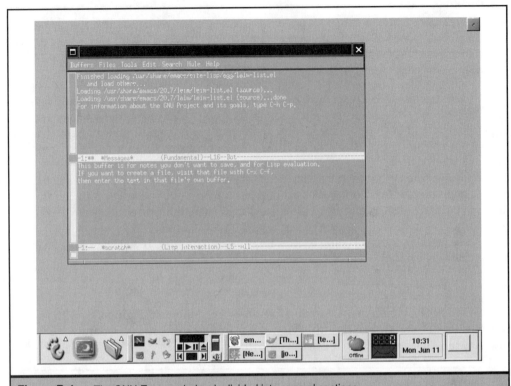

Figure B-1. The GNU Emacs window is divided into several sections.

CAUTION: GNU Emacs defines a particular key as "the metakey": for those on PCs, this is the ALT key; but if you're using a terminal window or are logged in across a network, you may need to use the ESC key instead. Those using Unix, but who have a "Windows keyboard" with Windows-specific keys might need to use the key with the Windows logo. Experiment to see what key works for you.

Over the years, `emacs` documentation has adopted a particular method of writing these keystroke combinations:

▼ C-x This combination means press the CTRL key and type the letter *x* simultaneously. So, C-d would mean the keystroke combination CTRL + d.

■ M-x This combination means press the metakey and type the letter *x* simultaneously. So, M-d means the keystroke combination ALT + d on a PC, or ESC + d if the ALT key doesn't produce the desired result.

▲ C-M-x This combination means press both the metakey and the CTRL key and type the letter *x* simultaneously. Thus, C-M-d means the keystroke combination CTRL + ALT + d, or CTRL + ESC + d, if the ALT key doesn't produce the desired result.

Table B-3 contains a list of the most important GNU Emacs commands.

Category	Keystroke Combination	Function
Cursor Movement	C-b	Moves the cursor back one character.
	C-f	Moves the cursor forward one character.
	C-a	Moves the cursor to the beginning of the current line.
	C-e	Moves the cursor to the end of the current line.
	M-b	Moves the cursor back one word.
	M-f	Moves cursor forward one word.
	M-a	Moves the cursor to the beginning of the current sentence.
	M-e	Moves the cursor to the end of the current sentence.
	M- -	Moves the cursor to the beginning of the current paragraph.
	M-"	Moves the cursor to the end of the current paragraph.
	C-v	Moves the cursor to the next screen of the document.
	M-v	Moves the cursor to the previous screen of the document.
	M-<	Moves the cursor to the beginning of the buffer.
	M->	Moves the cursor to the end of the buffer.
Window Commands	C-x 0	Closes the current window.
	C-x 1	Closes all windows except the current window.
	C-M-v	Moves the cursor in the nonactive window to the next screen of the document.
	M-x shrink-window	Shrinks the current window vertically.
	C-x ^	Grows the current window vertically.
	C-x -	Shrinks the current window horizontally.
	C-x "	Grows the current window horizontally.
	C-x 4 b	Selects the full buffer in the other window.

Table B-3.   GNU Emacs Keystroke Combinations

Category	Keystroke Combination	Function
	C-x 4 C-o	Displays the buffer in the other window.
	C-x 4 f	Finds a file in the other window and opens it.
Help Commands	C-h a	Requests a keyword, and then shows all commands containing that word.
	C-h k	Requests a keystroke, and then shows the command bound to that key.
	C-h i	Opens the hypertext documentation reader.
	C-h p	Starts a browser window showing the help files by subject.
	C-h t	Opens a tutorial program.
Search and Replace Commands	C-s	Prompts for a text string to be found (only searches forward of the current cursor position).
	C-r	Prompts for a text string to be found (only searches backward from the current cursor position).
	M-%	Prompts for the string to be found and the string that replaces it. Press the Spacebar to perform the replacement; press DELETE to skip the replacement; press ENTER or ESC to stop the search-and-replace process; press . to make the replacement, and then end the search; and press ! to replace all matches in the current buffer.
Save and Exit Commands	C-x C-s	Save a file without exiting.
	C-x s	Save multiple buffers at once without exiting.
	C-x C-c	Exit GNU Emacs.

Table B-3. GNU Emacs Keystroke Combinations *(continued)*

The GNU Emacs Screen

As you saw in Figure B-1, the GNU Emacs screen is divided into two major parts. The cursor appears in the text entry area, where your buffer also appears. At the bottom of the screen, a line, called the *mode line,* appears in reversed color. On this line, you can see various information about the active buffer. The file's name, where you are in the file, and other data about the document changes as you work on the file.

Below the mode line is the *minibuffer.* When you issue commands at the keyboard, they appear in the minibuffer. This is also the place where messages from the editor are displayed. Use the minibuffer to keep an eye on what you're doing and the keys you're pressing. This is especially useful if you make errors repeatedly as you try to issue emacs commands.

Working in GNU Emacs

To open a file in GNU Emacs, if you didn't do so when you invoked the program, issue the command

```
C-x C-f
```

Along the bottom of the emacs screen, you see the prompt

```
Find file: ~/
```

Type the name of the file if it's in your home directory. If the filename is in another directory, you must provide the full pathname of the file.

You can move around the file with the arrow keys, and use BACKSPACE and DELETE to remove characters. You can also use the cursor movement commands shown in Table B-3. To open a second buffer, issue the C-x C-f command again and open a new file. The command

```
C-x b
```

switches you between the open buffers, so you can work on both of them at the same time. Close a buffer by issuing the C-x k command. You'll be asked which buffer to close and, if the data in that buffer hasn't yet been saved, whether you want to save changes to the file.

As you can see, GNU Emacs is a complicated program, and this short introduction hasn't even scratched its surface. If you're interested in pursuing emacs further, I strongly recommend you go through all the tutorials in the program (accessed by the command C-h t). You can learn a lot about emacs from these tutorials and more from the lengthy help files that accompany the editor. While GNU Emacs requires some commitment to learn, you can benefit by knowing the most complex and fully featured text editor available for Unix.

PICO

If vi and GNU Emacs have you baffled, consider the pico editor. The pico editor has a reputation of being somewhat frivolous and not as hard core as vi or emacs, but this is its beauty. The pico editor is easy to learn and doesn't come with a slew of difficult commands or functions that get in the way of generating and editing text files. In fact, there's relatively little to say about `pico`. Once you open a `pico` session and begin working, you see how intuitive and straightforward an editor it is.

> **NOTE:** Serious programmers probably won't like `pico`. If you're a serious Unix programmer, though, you already have a favorite text editor and are, in all likelihood, not reading this chapter. For those new to working with text under Unix, `pico` is an excellent choice for a first (or a permanent) text editor.

Open `pico` by typing **pico** at a system prompt. As with the other editors described already in this chapter, if you want to open a specific file in `pico`, issue the command

`pico` *filename*

where *filename* is the particular file's name instead. `pico` doesn't have multiple modes. Once the screen opens, as shown in Figure B-2, you can begin working right away.

Although `pico` doesn't differentiate between Text Entry mode and Command mode, it does reserve the CTRL key for commands. Thus, any command you issue to `pico` is given as a keystroke combination. The `pico` window always has a band at the bottom of the screen, which shows the most commonly used keystroke combinations. Refer to that

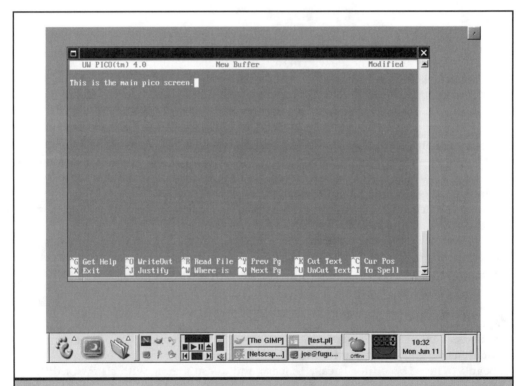

Figure B-2.   The `pico` editor contains both an area for text and a short list of commands.

band or press CTRL + o to see further options. The options shown are context sensitive and change depending on what you're doing.

> **NOTE:** The context-sensitivity of `pico`'s commands is more obvious in Pine, the popular mail and news reader for which the `pico` editor was developed by a team at the University of Washington. If you don't have a favorite Unix mail reader yet, give Pine a try.

To exit `pico`, press CTRL + X. You are then asked whether you want to save the unsaved data in the text buffer. If this is the first time the file has been saved, you need to enter a filename. Table B-4 shows the various control key combinations `pico` uses.

Keystroke Combination	Function
CTRL + a	Moves the cursor to the beginning of the current line.
CTRL + e	Moves the cursor to the end of the current line.
CTRL + f	Moves the cursor forward one character.
CTRL + b	Moves the cursor backward one character.
CTRL + n	Moves the cursor to the next line.
CTRL + p	Moves the cursor to the previous line.
CTRL + v	Moves the cursor forward one page.
CTRL + y	Moves the cursor backward one page.
CTRL + k	Kills (deletes) all the current line of text.
CTRL + u	Undoes the last deletion.
CTRL + j	Justifies the text, distributing it more evenly along each line in the current paragraph.
CTRL + w	Searches for a specific text string (`pico` prompts for the desired string).
CTRL + r	Inserts the entire contents of a specified file at the cursor position.
CTRL + o	Saves the contents of the current file to another specified file (can be used as a Save option).
CTRL + x	Exits `pico` (with prompt to save the current file).
CTRL + g	Opens the detailed help documents.
CTRL + t	Runs a spelling check if you have the `ispell` Unix spelling check program installed.

Table B-4. `pico` Keystroke Combinations

SUMMARY

When you work with Unix programs like Apache, you need to edit various text files to configure and operate the software. The easiest way to do this is to use a Unix text editor. A number of text editors are available, but three of the most popular are the full-screen editors vi, GNU Emacs, and pico.

Each of these editors is managed with keystroke commands: pico has the fewest, while GNU Emacs has a vast array of commands and functions. Depending on your tolerance for learning new programs, you can select the editor with which you feel the most comfortable. Regardless of the editor you choose, though, spend a bit of time learning the vi editor, which is often the only editor available on rescue disks, and you might be required to use it in a crisis situation whether or not you like it.

APPENDIX C

Glossary

A

Affiliate Program

A program offered by some commercial Web sites, such as **Amazon.com**. In an affiliate program, one agrees to place a link to the commercial site on one's own site. In return, a small percentage of the cost of goods ordered through that link is rebated to the individual. Some Acceptable Use Policies ban affiliate program links on their sites.

ALT Text

An HTML tag that provides a text label for graphical image files. Nongraphical browsers and browsers designed for disabled accessibility use the ALT text instead of the visual image. Supplying ALT text for any images served from your site is important.

Anonymous FTP

A method of obtaining files using File Transfer Protocol (FTP). With anonymous FTP, visitors are required to log into the site, but may send the word "anonymous" as the login name. A valid e-mail address is usually required as the password.

B

Beta Release

Software that hasn't been fully tested. Beta software is released to the program's community, so it can be installed and tested on a wide range of machines and operating systems. Beta software is always experimental and should never be relied on for critical or commercial installations.

See also *Stable Release.*

Binaries

Binaries are files that are readable by machines, but not necessarily by humans. Most binaries are executable files, which means they can be run as programs. With many programs, you have the option of downloading precompiled binary files that are already partially configured for a particular operating system.

See also *Source Code.*

Browser

A browser is the user end of the Web equation. Browsers are software that receive HTML-encoded documents from a Web server and process those files so they can be seen on the user's monitor as they were designed. The two most popular browsers are Netscape's Navigator and Microsoft's Internet Explorer, though other browsers have small, but vocal, communities of support.

Buffer

A designated holding space that contains data either waiting to be run through a specified program or data output from that program. Buffers smooth out the response speed of a program so the end user is neither idle nor overwhelmed with the data flow.

Buffer Overflow

A security risk in which the buffer is fed more data than it can handle, causing the program to crash. In Web terms, this is most often a problem with CGI scripts where the buffer is a hard-coded amount of space, such as 1,024 bytes. If you write your own CGI scripts, consider defining the buffer dynamically so it expands and contracts, according to the amount of data currently held in the buffer.

C

Character Set

The complete set of characters for a particular language. For example, a French-language character set includes the carets, right and left accents, and other lexical marks used for writing in French. A German-language character set includes umlauts, and a Spanish-language character set includes tildes. If you serve more than one language on your site, you might need to install additional character sets so the documents in the other languages are sent correctly.

Character String

Any string of letters and/or numbers. A character string needn't be readable or sensible; it merely needs to have a space on either side of it. "w3UIOE89z" is as valid a character string as "mydogis9."

CGI

The Common Gateway Interface (CGI) is a programming convention that translates certain types of requests for the server and translates certain files for the requesting browser. These files are in formats that make sense to the originating software, but not the receiving program, such as database records. In practice, most Web CGI scripts are programs designed to provide a more personalized interface with the site. They can also be used to build forms and interactive features, and work with various kinds of databases.

Cleartext

Data that's stored in readable text. Passwords stored in cleartext, for example, are a security risk. Most operating systems automatically encrypt sensitive data like passwords, but some programs may store this data in cleartext. If you run a program for which this is the case, consider switching to an encrypting version of the program to add extra security to your site.

Client

See *Client-Server Architecture.*

Client-Server Architecture

A form of interaction between computers. Client-server architecture is the basis for the Internet. Individual users run programs, or clients, that connect to other programs or servers. The client program requests a particular piece of data and the server program provides it to the client. The Web uses client-server architecture, as does FTP, e-mail, and USENET news.

Command Line Interface

Interaction with the shell environment that's text-only. Most Unix shells work in command-line mode. If you use a graphical desktop interface that provides a visual overlay, such as KDE or Gnome, you still have the option of opening a terminal window that provides command-line interaction with your machine.

NOTE: This book assumes you're using a command line interface, and all examples are tailored to that assumption. Appendix D, "Common Unix Commands," contains a number of functions and programs that are started at the command line.

Command Shell

See *Shell Environment.*

Command Syntax

The way in which a given command must be issued. Each command has its own unique syntax, but Unix commands usually take the syntax

```
command options
```

When commands are introduced in this book, useful flags or options are often included in the introduction. Appendix D, "Common Unix Commands," contains many tables providing the most common options for the commands listed there. You can also find additional flags or options by consulting the manual page for the command you want to use.

Comments

Lines in a program intended for human eyes, not for the computer or compiler. Good programs contain comments that explain the program's function to its users. Configuration scripts are often heavily commented.

By convention, comments in Unix scripts and programs are noted with the hashmark character #. The hashmark can be placed either at the beginning of a line, which is then completely ignored when the script is run, or in the middle of a line. Anything after the hashmark will be ignored, but material before the hashmark will be executed as part of the script.

Compliant HTML

HTML that's constructed according to the latest HTML standard. Compliant HTML doesn't use outdated tags or extensions that aren't contained in the current standard. Some Web design packages generate compliant code, while others don't. Noncompliant HTML can cause problems on the user end, because it might not display correctly in the latest browsers. In fact, browsers are available that only display compliant HTML, such as the Opera browser. Noncompliant HTML can also cause problems for adaptive Web browsers or wireless Web items like cellular phones or handheld computers.

Compile

When used as a noun, a compile is a program that's been run through a compiler and is ready to be run. If you're installing software that's written in a compiled programming language, you'll compile it first, and then install the program.

Compiler

A program that translates a given program into machine-readable instructions for the operating system or hardware. Compiled programming languages include both the popular languages C and C++. Once a program is written in C, it must be compiled before the program can actually be run.

See also *Interpreter*.

Configuration File

A file that contains all settings for a given program. When the program starts, it reads the configuration file, and enables the appropriate settings and functions. Apache's configuration file is called httpd.conf. In the documentation subdirectory, the sample file for Unix machines is called httpd-std.conf and it's called httpd-win.conf for Windows machines. Many programs have more than one configuration file. Apache modules, for example, each have their own configuration files.

Cookies

Small bits of data transferred as an HTTP header. Cookies can be used to track visits to your site, enabling a previous visitor to bypass authentication, or as a method of collecting information about your visitors. While cookies themselves are benign, many people fear them and think sites using cookies are automatically attempting to violate their privacy. Cookies are immensely useful to Web administrators, but you should make it clear to your visitors that you use cookies, so they can choose to visit your site with full knowledge.

Cracker

Someone who enters a computer network without authorization or legitimate reason. Crackers generally crack sites "because they're there," rather than for a particular reason. They might also steal information that can be sold, however, such as credit card numbers or password files.

See also *Hacker* and *Script Kiddie*.

D

Daemon

A program that does all the work of a particular server. Daemons handle incoming and outgoing requests, and they work automatically without requiring human input. Most servers run daemons, and Apache does as well.

Data Types

A classification system that defines different kinds of files depending on the data contained in the file and the intended purpose of the file. For example, GIF graphical image files are one type, HTML documents another, and database files yet another type.

Database

A method of organizing individual data units, usually with multiple fields. Databases may be flat, storing data in a plain text file, or relational, using a cell-based storage method, where each data unit has a unique address within the file.

Device

Any piece of hardware, although not the CPU or motherboard, managed by the operating system. Devices may be disk drives, other storage hardware, or input devices like tablets or mouses. Devices are individually controlled under Unix and can be mounted or unmounted as needed.

Disk Partition

A segment of a complete hard disk, divided through software commands. Partitions function as separate hard drives, although they reside on the same physical disk. Different operating systems use different terms for a disk partition, including *slice, volume,* and *partition.*

E

Environment Variable

An individual variable that controls some aspect of the shell environment. Typical environment variables include the default text editor and various directory paths. Environment variables are available to all programs running on the server and may affect how those programs appear to the end user or are administered.

Export

How information is transferred across the network. Complete file systems can be exported through NFS. Individual environment variables can also be exported if their values are needed in other programs or environments.

F

File Transfer Protocol

File Transfer Protocol (FTP) is the basic method by which files are transferred across networks like the Internet. FTP is efficient because little extraneous code is applied to the files as they are sent between machines. Running an FTP server, as well as a Web server, is a good idea if you plan to provide files for visitors to download.

File System

The entire contents of a particular machine, partition, or directory. Includes the directory structure itself. File systems can be exported or mounted remotely.

Firewall

A machine that controls information going into and out of a particular network. Firewalls are used as security precautions and may pass or reject particular data after comparing it to a known set of parameters.

Flag

An option for a particular command. Flags might cause the command to include additional functions as it operates, or they might force particular behavior. Most Unix commands don't require the use of flags, but almost all have flags available if you want to use them. You can find a complete list of flags in the command's manual page.

Flat Database

See *Database*.

Free Software

Software released under a license that requires free and unrestricted distribution of the source code. Free Software is a term most closely associated with Richard Stallman, one of the early proponents of open source code distributions, and the Free Software Foundation.

Front End

A user interface for a particular program. Front ends may be graphical or simply easier to use than managing the program directly. apachectl is a front end to httpd, the Apache daemon.

G

Gateway

A machine through which all traffic into and out of a local network must pass. While gateway machines may also contain firewall or proxy software, a gateway in and of itself isn't a security precaution. A gateway may be used to split a single incoming Internet connection across the network.

Graphical User Interface

A program that translates the basic text interface on a Unix machine into a graphical display. Graphical User Interfaces (GUIs) usually permit the use of a mouse and may offer graphical versions of traditional administrative tools. While GUIs are an option under Unix, they are integral parts of the Windows and MacOS operating systems.

H

Hacker

A person who enjoys working on computer software. Hackers created much of the software used on the Internet today. They like to take programs apart to see how they're coded, and often put the programs back together in a more efficient manner. Hackers are benign, but the media has seized on the term to represent those who make illegal entries into computer networks, who are properly called "crackers."

See also *Cracker*.

Handler

A program designed to handle a particular file type. For example, the Adobe Acrobat software, which creates print-quality images of individual file pages, requires the Adobe Acrobat Reader as the handler that interprets `*.pdf` files. Handlers are usually invoked automatically when a file of the designated type is opened or transferred over the network.

Hashmark

The # character, used to denote comments in scripts, configuration files, and programs.

See also *Comments*.

Heterogeneous Network

A network that includes machines running more than one operating system. Such networks need to run special software that translates data into formats understandable by each operating system. The most common heterogeneous networks run some mix of Unix and Windows machines.

See also *Homogeneous Network*.

Hit

An individual connection to your Web site. Site traffic is usually expressed in hit count. Hits are usually counted as connections, rather than requests, because a given user may make more than one request on your site, but counts as only one unique user.

Homogeneous Network

A network in which all machines are running the same operating system. Homogeneous networks tend to be administrative rather than user-oriented, though networks that run Windows NT are often homogeneous because user machines on that network will probably run Windows 98 or another personal Windows variant.

See also *Heterogeneous Network*.

HTML

Hyper Text Markup Language. The coding language used to format a document's structure so that it can be viewed properly by a Web browser.

HTTP

Hypertext Transfer Protocol (HTTP) is the standard that defines how data is sent across a network between a Web server and a Web browser. HTTP offers a number of headers that can be used to carry different bits of identifying data, which can provide information about your visitors and site use.

I

Image Maps

Graphical files used as navigational tools on a site. Image maps have embedded spots that serve as links to other files on the site. Apache must be configured to handle image mapping correctly. Image maps should always be accompanied by textual navigation links.

Initialization Scripts

Scripts that run automatically at bootup. These scripts contain basic configuration information for the operating system. They also contain a list of programs that are started automatically. Under Linux, each runlevel has its own init scripts, so different runlevels can contain different suites of environment settings and programs.

Interpreter

A program that transforms code written in a scripting language, like Perl or Python, into machine-readable instructions.

See also *Compiler*.

Intrusion Detection

Identifying the presence or tracks of crackers. May require software assistance or advanced security mechanisms, depending on the sophistication of the crackers.

IP Number

The unique identifying number given to each computer with a presence on the Internet. These numbers are divided into three classes, as set out in the Internet Protocol: Class *A*, *B*, and *C* networks. The networks define how the IP number is assigned.

ISAPI

The API, or programming instructions, for CGI programs that run on Microsoft's Internet Information Server (the Microsoft Web server). ISAPI native functions aren't usable on Apache, so you might need to configure an ISAPI-enabling module if you need to use such software with Apache.

L

Libraries

See *Software Libraries.*

Load Average

See *System Load.*

Load Balancing

The act of distributing Web traffic across a number of servers in a cluster. Loads are balanced to make the best use of hardware and bandwidth. A number of programs exist to assist you in balancing loads across a cluster, as well as an Apache module designed for the task.

Lockfile

A file created by Apache when it crashes for whatever reason. You must remove the lockfile before Apache can be restarted. This is a precaution against running two httpd server processes at the same time until the error that crashed the first process has been fixed.

Log Scrubbers

Tools used by crackers to erase signs of their presence on a system. Log scrubbers are the technological equivalent of mopping yourself out of a room, so no footprints mark the wet floor.

Logs

Files created by the server, which document particular types of activity or information. Apache's basic logs record server errors and individual browser requests to the site, but different programs record different data in their logs. You can also configure custom logs on Apache that will log whatever information you think is necessary or useful.

M

Macro

A shortcut. Macros are keystroke combinations that are mapped to longer expressions or character strings. The macro can be used instead of typing the same data over and over. Most word processors and some text editors enable you to define your own macros, which can be particularly useful in some programming scenarios.

Makefile

A file generated during installation of source code. The Makefile is usually created by the `configure` utility and contains information about the components of your machine, both hardware and software. Makefiles are then fed to the `make` utility, which directs the compiler to prepare the appropriately configured code before installation.

Manual Page

A document that describes the function of a given Unix command. Man pages are installed when a new program is installed on the machine. You can access a given program's man page by issuing the command

```
man command
```

Manual pages usually contain a full list of any options or flags the command can take. While sometimes highly technical, man pages are the best place to look when you have a question about a particular command.

Metaheaders

HTTP headers that aren't visible to the browser when either sending a request to a Web server or receiving the requested data. Metaheaders may contain identifying information, such as the IP number of the requesting computer, or confirmation that a cookie exists. HTTP headers can also be configured to carry other metadata.

Metacharacter

A programming technique, usually found in shell programming, but also used in some text editors. Metacharacters are regular text characters used to represent a particular system operation instead of their literal meaning. The best-known example is the $ character, which is used to denote a variable.

Metakey

The ESC, ALT , and CTRL keys. These keys are used only in combination with other letter and number keys to achieve a particular response, which differs according to the program in which the metakey is required. The text editor GNU Emacs uses metakeys for all program commands.

MIME

The Multimedia E-Mail Extensions (MIME) standard. The MIME standard describes how different types of data are to be transferred across networks. Apache has built-in MIME support, sending different file types with the appropriate handlers.

Mirror Site

A complete copy of a given Web site, running at a different location. Mirror sites are used to ensure redundancy of information, so the data on the site is available whether or not the original site is down. Mirror sites also speed download times because downloads are faster from machines physically close to the requesting site.

Modularity

A programming concept that assigns particular functions to individual modules. The modules need to be compiled into the basic server for that function to work. Because administrators don't have to compile the modules for functions they don't use, a modular program runs faster and more efficiently. Apache is an excellent example of a modular program.

N

Network File System (NFS)

A method of sharing directories across a network, removing the need to duplicate data on each machine on the network. With NFS, you can mount directories remotely, so they appear to exist on the local machine, but are actually located on a remote computer. NFS has some security risks, but no workable replacement exists for its function on a Unix network.

O

Open Source

Software that includes its source code as part of the distribution. Most Open Source software requires you to pass the source code along if you alter or distribute the program after you get it. The term was developed to avoid some of the confusion inherent in the term "Free Software" and is generally thought to have more of a business orientation.

See also *Free Software* and *Source Code*.

Operating System

The software that interprets your commands into instructions your computer's hardware can understand. Operating systems have their own functions and programs, as well. Some are primarily text-based (Unix, DOS), while others have a tightly integrated graphical interface (Windows, MacOS). The operating system you run determines the kind of software you can use. Software generally isn't interchangeable between operating system platforms.

P

Package Management Tool

A front end to regular program installation. Package management tools are primarily found in Linux distributions, but can also be found on other Unix variants. These tools are usually graphical and enable an administrator to set certain parameters before installing software on the machine.

Packages

Sets of programs that are downloaded together, all of which are required to install a given program successfully. Packages are often preconfigured for a particular operating system, and can be handled with a package management tool. Other packages contain only unconfigured source code, but may include documentation, ancillary programs, or other useful material.

Partition

See *Disk Partition.*

Patch

A small piece of code intended to fix a known problem in a software release. Patches are often released soon after a new version of the program has become available, and fix issues that didn't show up in preliminary testing. A second version of the new release usually incorporates all known patches.

Path

The location of a particular file, expressed using the file system. That is, the file /usr/logs/access_log is located in the /logs subdirectory of the /usr directory, which is itself a subdirectory of the main, or /, directory.

Performance Tuning

The act of streamlining your Apache server's configuration, so it runs more efficiently and makes better use of system resources. If you receive more than one hit per second on your site, or you put out more than 10 Mbps of data, you should tune your Apache server. Those with less traffic might also see gains when Apache is tuned.

Permissions

Codes that determine who has access to a particular file. Three levels of permission exist: user, local, and global. Three types of permission also exist: read, write, and execute. You can set permissions on a user-by-user basis or create user groups and assign permissions to the group. Note, a file must have at least global read permission before it can be seen on the Web.

Pipe

Either the | character or a method that uses the | character to pass information from one process to another, where it's used as input for yet another process. Under Apache, often used for log management.

Port Scanning

A method of detecting vulnerabilities on target computers or networks. Used by those seeking illicit access to a network, so the network's resources can be used for further exploration across the Internet, or to obtain valuable data from that machine itself.

Process

A unique call on the computer's processor. Each process is assigned an identification number. Some processes are started by individual users, but many are started automatically by various programs and daemons running on the machine.

Process Identification Number (PID)

A unique identifier. Every process running on a Unix machine is assigned a unique process identification number. This number can be used to manage the process through the various options of the `kill` command.

Protocol

The standard method for handling some specified kind of information on a network. Protocols are used to ensure that different programs for the same function will produce output readable by the other software. All protocols currently in effect for Internet-related data are stored by the Internet Engineering Task Force at **http://www.ietf.org/rfc.html**.

Proxy

A machine that stands between a local network and an external network. Proxies are security mechanisms that disguise the actual origin of a request from within the network, passing it out (like on to the Internet), as if it stemmed from the proxy machine itself. Proxies are used to shield internal networks' identifying information from external machines.

Q

Quota

A specified amount of disk space that can be used by a given user. The quota can be enforced with software, which usually provides for both a soft quota (warning the user has exceeded the allotted disk space) and a hard quota (the user can no longer write to the disk). Administrators with a large number of users often need to enforce quotas, so the disk is shared equitably.

R

README File

A file contained in most Unix installation packages. The README file contains the latest communications from the programmers to the end user, and items in the README file may replace information contained in printed or online documentation. Always follow the directions in the README file.

Regular Expressions

A programming construct that uses text phrases to match literal text strings. Regular expressions often use metacharacters, and are used to save time and space in program code. Apache doesn't use regular expressions in routine administration, but they are used frequently when programming modules.

Relational Database

See *Database*.

Rescue Kit

A bare-bones set of programs, which can be used to start a Unix computer that failed for some reason. Rescue kits often fit on single floppy disks. You can use the rescue kit to boot the system and make changes so the system boots normally.

RFC

A Request for Comments (RFC) is how the Internet programming community defines rules for participation on the Internet. RFCs define almost every aspect of Internet communication, including many parts of Web traffic.

Root

The supreme user on a given Unix machine. The person who has access to the root account can perform any action anywhere on the machine, including individual user accounts. Many programs are restricted to root, so users can't change the way in which the system is formatted or managed.

See also *Superuser*.

Runlevels

A method unique to System V Unix variants. Runlevels are used to define different suites of programs that are started automatically at bootup or started directly from init. Six runlevels exist by default, some of which have traditional uses: runlevel 1 is single user and runlevel 6 is reboot, for example. See your Unix-variant documentation to learn what runlevels are defined on your machine.

S

Scalability

The capability to maintain a particular level of function as input volume increases. For example, Apache is considered scalable because it's equally efficient with a high volume of hits as with a low traffic stream. Apache is also distributable across several machines, each serving Web requests. Scalability is generally considered a measure of reliability, as well as one of power.

Script Kiddie

A slang term referring to people who download destructive or invasive scripts and run them against target sites. These people frequently don't have the programming skills to write their own scripts and must run those of others. Script kiddies tend to be adolescent males, thus, the "kiddie" part of the term.

Scripting Language

A programming language that isn't compiled. Perl and Python are two popular scripting languages. Rather than compiling programs before they can be run, you run scripted languages through an interpreter. Scripts can be interpreted on-the-fly, rather than needing to be compiled before the function can be invoked.

Server

See *Client-Server Architecture*.

Server Room

A special room with extra air-conditioning equipment and a locked door. Usually found in corporations with large numbers of machines on the network or in server clusters, server rooms provide both atmospheric regulation and additional security.

Shadow Passwords

A method of increasing password protection. Passwords under a shadow scheme are encrypted and stored in a nonstandard location, rather than in the traditional location of /etc/passwd. The practice is usually found on Linux machines, though it has been ported to other Unix variants.

Shell Environment

The "look and feel" of a shell. The shell environment can be manipulated by setting various environment variables to create the optimal user environment. Environment variables differ from shell to shell but, generally, include preferences for text editors, screen colors, font size, and other user information.

    See also *Shell* and *Variable*.

Shell Prompt

The location where commands are entered. Depending on the shell you select, the prompt might contain your user name, directory location, or other information. The prompt is usually followed by a cursor to indicate the text entry location.

Slice

See *Disk Partition.*

Software Libraries

A collection of system functions. Libraries are a convenience for both programmers and users. When the programmer writes a new piece of code, she uses the functions contained in a particular library or set of libraries. For the user to install and use the program successfully, the proper libraries must be available on the local machine.

Source Code

The programming that comprises an individual program or command. Source code cannot be run directly, but must be interpreted or compiled before the program can be run, depending on the language used to write the code.

Spam

A trademark of the Hormel Corporation. Spam is also a slang term for unsolicited e-mail, usually commercial in nature. Many Internet service providers bar users from sending unsolicited bulk e-mail, and the most persistent offenders may be barred from their provider. Offending providers can also be blacklisted, so traffic originating from that site won't be transferred through the Internet. If you gather e-mail addresses from your visitors, don't use those addresses to send e-mail unless the visitor explicitly permits you to do so.

Stable Release

A software release that's been certified reasonably free from bugs. Stable releases can be run on critical or commercial sites with little worry. Most stable releases started out as beta releases, and then were labeled stable after a period of bug tracking and redevelopment.

See also *Beta Release.*

Standard

A document that defines all aspects of a particular protocol. For example, the HTTP standard defines how information is transferred on the Web, while the HTML standard defines how that information is displayed on the end user's browser. When you have the option to adhere to a standard or to deviate from one, always choose standard-compliant options. Nonstandard code can break servers or clients and might result in your program not working correctly.

Stickiness

A measure of how long your visitors stay at your site before leaving for another Web location. The stickier your site, the better. Sticky sites can command higher advertising rates and tend to have a loyal user base.

Style Sheets

HTML documents that define the page's appearance on a visitor's browser. While many of the same functions can be handled through regular HTML tags, style sheets offer a greater chance that the visitor's browser won't change visual elements. Style sheets might affect one page or be applied across an entire site with additional style sheets added for particular sections of the site. In the latter case, these are called *cascading style sheets.*

Superuser

The root account. A person who has access to the root account has the ability to assume superuser powers. Many administrative programs require one assume superuser powers before being able to issue commands or run the program. Apache is one such program.

See also *Root*.

Symbolic Links

A file that doesn't actually contain data. Rather, the file acts as a link to another file elsewhere on the network. You can use symbolic links on your Web sites, but you must configure Apache to follow them. Apache can deal with symbolic links at a number of security levels; but the more security you require, the slower Apache runs.

System Administrator

The person who has ultimate authority for a particular computer or network. System administrators perform all routine administrative tasks, as well as managing users. Some systems may have multiple administrators, but one person usually has supreme authority.

System Load

The amount of work your computer's CPU is doing. System load is expressed in decimals. Most machines operate with a load less than one, meaning the CPU is handling system calls as fast as the calls can be generated by software. A load of 1.0 means the CPU has reached capacity. If the load is higher than 1.0, system calls are waiting for other calls to be completed and machine response is slower than normal.

T

Tarball

An archive file created with the Unix `tar` archiving program. Tarballs can be compressed with the `gzip` utility, if necessary.

Text Editor

A program used to create text documents. Text editors offer a small number of commands and generally don't offer many formatting features. They're an essential part of administering a Unix system, because text editors don't attach a large amount of extra code to the files they create.

See also *WYSIWYG*.

Text String

See *Character String*.

Time Stamp

An identification found on every file on a Unix system. The time stamp shows the last time the file was accessed. Update a file's time stamp with the `touch` command.

U

User Groups

An administrative tool that permits users on your machine to be sorted into various groups. Each group can be given a particular set of file permissions or access capabilities. An individual user may be part of a number of user groups, each with a different set of permissions. User groups are an effective way to restrict access to your Web server.

V

Variable

A word that takes a particular value. Variables can be found in almost every component of an operating system, and shell environments use variables to define the preferred settings. Apache uses variables in its configuration files to determine the various settings used on the server.

Verbose Mode

An option with many Unix shell programs. When a program is run in verbose mode, it prints messages to the screen while it's running or after it has finished. The data in these messages can provide additional insight in case of an error or give you a better understanding of how the program works.

Virtual Host

A way for an individual domain to have an Internet presence without running its own servers. You can configure Apache to provide virtual hosts for other domains besides your own. Many companies provide virtual hosting, offering a range of services for a range of monthly or yearly prices.

Volume

See *Disk Partition*.

W

Warez

A slang term for traded software. The implication with the "warez" term is that the software is being traded free, in violation of the End User License Agreement accepted by the initial purchaser. Free and Open Source software isn't considered "warez," because it's released under an open distribution license.

WYSIWYG

An acronym for What You See Is What You Get. A WYSIWYG text processor displays the document much as it will appear when it's printed, including page formatting and font. Most Unix text editors are plain text mode, not showing or offering much in the way of display or page layout. Word processors, like the one in Sun's StarOffice or Corel WordPerfect, are usually WYSIWYG editors.

See also *Text Editor*.

X

XML

Extended Markup Language, a new coding method. Where HTML defines Web page elements in terms of their appearance on the page, XML defines elements by the kind of data being represented. XML can be used in conjunction with HTML and is expected to become as critical to Web page design as HTML.

APPENDIX D

Common Unix Commands

W hile this is by no means an exhaustive list of Unix commands, the commands contained in this appendix are a useful subset. You can find commands here for routine administrative tasks, as well as commands more specific to file management and Apache administration. Each entry defines the command and provides some of the most common options and flags. Note that most commands shown here have additional options and a more extensive syntax. If you're interested in learning more about a given command, consult the command's manual page.

TIP: View a command's manual page—usually installed by default on Unix systems—by issuing the command man *command* at a system prompt, where *command* is the command name.

Entries use these conventions:

▼ Any word or character string within square brackets, such as [*item*], isn't required to issue the command.

■ Any word or character string within angle brackets, such as <*item*>, must be replaced with an actual filename or program name. Delete the angle brackets once an existing file or program name has been entered.

▲ Any words or character strings that appear within curly brackets and are separated with the pipe character—as in {A | B}—are discrete choices, but you must choose one of the options. However, if the pipe character appears within square brackets—as in [A | B]—you can choose one of the options or not choose any. Options separated by the pipe are always mutually exclusive.

adduser

The adduser command is used to create a single new user account. It can be found on most Unix systems (in addition to any graphical user administration tools that may also be included with a particular Unix variant). adduser takes the syntax

adduser [options] *username*

Table D-1 shows some common adduser options.

Option	Function
-c	Include a comment when creating the account.
-d	Specify a particular path for the user's home directory.
-e	Specify an expiration date for the account.

Table D-1.   Options for the adduser Command

Option	Function
-M	Create the user name without creating a user home account.
-s	Set the user's default shell environment if he doesn't want to use the default shell.

Table D-1.   Options for the `adduser` Command *(continued)*

apropos

The `apropos` command is used to locate a specified manual page on the computer. This command searches the database of manual pages installed on your system only; so if you're looking for information on a command that you haven't installed or for which you declined to install the manual pages, `apropos` won't be able to find the relevant file. `apropos` takes the syntax

```
apropos <keyword>
```

at

Use the `at` command to schedule a single command to be executed at a later time. For example, although you may want to restart the Apache server after you leave work for the day, you don't want to make this a routine event. `at` takes the syntax

```
at [options] <time>
```

`at` is an interactive command. If you decline to use an option with the command, rather issuing the command as

```
at <time>
```

using a 24-hour clock for the time at which you want the command to execute, `at` will show the prompt `at>`. Enter the shell command you want to have executed at the time you specified.

cat

Use the `cat` command to print the contents of a particular file to the standard output device, usually the monitor screen. `cat` takes the syntax

```
cat [options] <file(s)>
```

Two of the most commonly used option flags for cat are used to format the output:

▼ -n causes cat to number the lines of output

▲ -s causes cat to combine consecutive blank lines into a single blank line

TIP: If you have several short files that you want to combine into a single file, use cat. Issue the command cat <*filename1*> <*filename2*> <*filename3*> >> <*newfilename*>.

cd

The cd command is used to change directories within the Unix file system. cd takes the syntax

```
cd [directory]
```

Issuing cd without a directory merely changes your current directory to your home directory.

chmod

The chmod command is used to change individual file permissions. chmod takes the syntax

```
chmod [u|g|a] {+|-} {r and/or w and/or x} <filename>
```

NOTE: You can only use chmod to change a file's permissions if you're the file's owner or if you logged in as root.

Table D-2 contains the various options used with chmod.

Option	Function
u	Grants the specified permissions only to the owner of the file
g	Grants the specified permissions to all members of the owner's groups
a	Grants the specified permissions to all users, including those outside the local network
+	Adds a new permission to the specified file
-	Removes an existing permission from the specified file
r	Assigns read permission to the file, granting read-only access

Table D-2. Options Used with the chmod Command

Option	Function
w	Assigns write permission to the file, granting both read and edit capability
x	Assigns execute permission to the file, granting the capability to run the file if it's an executable binary (includes read and write permissions)

Table D-2.   Options Used with the `chmod` Command *(continued)*

NOTE: If you don't specify a level of permission when you issue the `chmod` command, `chmod` assumes you intend to grant global permissions. Be sure to specify the level if you don't want worldwide visitors working with or viewing the file.

Here are some common `chmod` commands:

```
chmod a+r <filename>
```

This command places read permission on the named file for all global users.

```
chmod g+rw <filename>
```

This command places read and write permissions on the named file for all members of the file owner's group(s).

```
chmod a-x <filename>
```

This command removes execute permission on the specified file for all global users. Note, at least the file's owner should be able to execute the file, so follow this command with one that reestablishes execute permissions for the owner.

chown

The `chown` command is used to transfer the ownership of a specified file. `chown` uses the syntax

```
chown <user> <filename>
```

NOTE: To issue `chown` commands, you must either be the current owner of the file or be logged in as root.

cp

The cp command is used to copy a specified file to a new location. cp takes the syntax

```
cp <filename1> <filename2>
```

where *filename1* is the file to be copied and *filename2* is the name of the destination file.

date

The date command sets the current system time and date or prints it to the screen. date uses the syntax

```
date [options]
```

If no options are issued with the command, date simply prints the current system date and time to the monitor screen.

To set the date with this command, you must be logged in as root. Issue the command

```
date -s
```

and set the system time. Use two-digit numbers for the date, as in 12-01-01. Set time using the 24-hour clock and the format MMDDhhmm[[CC]YY].ss. Therefore, to set the date to 15 seconds after 11:15 A.M., January 15, 1989, you would issue the command

```
date -s 0115111589.15
```

dd

The dd command is another method used to copy a file. dd merely transfers the file data as is—without formatting—from the original location to the new location. Because no formatting is involved, dd is often used to copy files from a removable disk to a hard disk. dd uses the syntax

```
dd if=<originalfilename> of=<newlocation>
```

The variable in the of= field should be the device name of the disk or storage device to which you're transferring the file, *not* a new filename.

diff

The diff command is used to compare the contents of two named files. If differences exist between the files, they'll be printed to the screen. diff takes the syntax

```
diff <filename1> <filename2>
```

diff works by comparing individual characters between the two files. When the two files are radically different (not versions of the same file), the diff output is lengthy and the program will take a long time to finish.

du

The du command is used to measure disk space use. This command can be used to see the disk use of a given user or to see the size of a particular file or directory. du uses the syntax

```
du [options] <file or directory name>
```

Several common options exist for du, which are shown in Table D-3.

exportfs

The exportfs command is used to export a network file system to another drive across the Network File System (NFS).

TIP: Learn more about NFS in Chapter 4, "Running a Heterogeneous Network."

exportfs takes the syntax

```
exportfs [options]
```

Option	Function
-b	Prints the size of the specified directory or file, expressed in bytes
-c	Prints a complete directory listing, including size of each directory, and a grand total of disk space used by this file system
-h	Prints the size of the specified directory or file, expressed in kilobytes or megabytes (depending on the size of the item)
-k	Prints the size of the specified directory or file, expressed in kilobytes
-m	Prints the size of the specified directory or file, expressed in megabytes
-S	Counts only the size of top-level directories, ignoring subdirectories
-s	Prints only the total size of the directory in which the command is issued, including all subdirectories

Table D-3.   Options for the du Command

Option	Function
-a	Exports all file systems listed in the /etc/exports file
-r	Exports all file systems previously exported in this session again
-u	"Unexports" the specified file systems, making them no longer available to other drives on the network

Table D-4. Options for the exportfs Command

A few common options exist for exportfs, shown in Table D-4.

fsck

The fsck command is used to check a file system's integrity. This command is a routine part of system administration for most Unix machines and can provide important information about your various file systems before a problem occurs. fsck uses the syntax

```
fsck [options] <filesystem>
```

A number of options exist for fsck. Some of the most common choices are shown in Table D-5.

Option	Function
-t	Specifies the file system type
-A	Checks all file systems listed in the /etc/fstab file
-N	Does a "dry run," printing the systems that would be checked without actually performing the check
-R	Skips the root file system when the −A option is used
-V	Enables verbose mode
-a	Makes any necessary repairs while the file system is being checked
-r	Makes repairs, but only after prompting for approval and receiving input

Table D-5. Options for the fsck Command

NOTE: You cannot use `fsck` on a file system that's currently mounted and usable. You can use it on unmounted file systems or on those that are mounted "read-only." If you use the `–R` option, you can check the root file system with `fsck`, even though root must always be mounted "read-write" so the machine can continue to operate.

grep

Use the `grep` command to find a specified character string in a given file. `grep` can be used to find numbers or characters, or a mixture of both. `grep` takes the syntax

```
grep [options] <string> [filename]
```

Consult the manual page for `grep` on your system to see what options are enabled in your installation. A vast array of `grep` options exist and many administrators choose not to enable every single choice.

TIP: `grep` is pronounced *grep*, not *gee-rep*.

groups

Use the `groups` command to display all groups to which a given user belongs. `groups` takes the syntax

```
groups [<username>]
```

If you issue this command without a user name specified, `groups` will report your personal group memberships. Specify another user's name to see the groups to which that user belongs.

gzip and gunzip

The `gzip` command is used to compress a file or set of files. The `gunzip` command is used to restore those compressed files to their original size. Both commands use the same syntax:

```
gzip <filename>
gunzip <filename>
```

head and tail

The `head` command is used to view the first lines of a specified file. The `tail` command is used to view the last few lines of a specified file. Both commands take the same syntax:

```
head <filename>
tail <filename>
```

init

On Linux installations, the init command is used to invoke the init daemon, called initd. This is usually used to change the *run level* (the array of programs started at boot). init takes the syntax

```
init <run level>
```

where *<run level>* is 0, 1, 2, 3, 4, 5, 6, or *s*. Table D-6 shows the common uses for Linux run levels.

kill

The kill command sends a defined signal to an active process and takes the syntax

```
kill [-s <signal>] <processID>
```

Although kill is usually used with the signal flag –9 to stop the specified process, a number of signals can be used as arguments. You can see a complete list of these kill signals by issuing the command

```
kill -l
```

at a system prompt. If no kill signal is specified, SIGTERM (signal 15) is used by default.

Run Level	Common Function
0	Shutdown
1	Single-user mode
2	Locally defined set of programs
3	Locally defined set of programs
4	Locally defined set of programs
5	Locally defined set of programs
6	Reboot
s	Single-user mode

Table D-6. Common Linux Run Level Functions

less

The less command enables you to view a given file in screen-sized segments, so a lengthy file can be read without printing to paper. less takes the syntax

```
less <filename>
```

Tap the Spacebar to move to the next section and use the *b* key to see the previous section.

locate

The locate command determines the directory path to a specified program located somewhere on the hard drive. locate also reports any directories or files that have names containing the character string being searched. This command takes the syntax

```
locate <filename>
```

ls

The ls command is used to generate output listing the contents of a specified directory. ls uses the syntax

```
ls [options] [directory name]
```

If no directory name is provided, ls lists the contents of the directory in which it was invoked. Several frequently used options exist for ls, which are shown in Table D-7.

Option	Function
-l	Prints contents in long format, providing additional data about file characteristics and size
-a	Prints all files in the directory, including hidden files whose filenames begin with a dot
-i	Prints all files showing their disk index number, or *inode*
-R	Prints directory contents for the current directory and all its subdirectories
-t	Prints directory contents sorted by timestamp

Table D-7.   Options for the ls Command

ln

Use the `ln` command to create a link to a specified file. The link you create can be either a hard link or a symbolic link, though hard links are the default setting. `ln` uses the syntax

```
ln [options] <linked-to-file> <name of link>
```

Several options exist for `ln`, shown in Table D-8.

logout

The `logout` command ends a user session and is issued as a single-word command at the system prompt:

```
logout
```

make

The `make` command is part of the source code installation process, as described in Chapter 3, "Installing Apache." `make` is a *front end*, or user interface, to the C language compiler installed on your machine. `make` takes the syntax

```
make [options]
```

No standard options exist for `make` because the options change for each package installed. Consult the documentation included with the downloaded package, including the INSTALL and README files, and read through the `Makefile` generated in the configuration step before you run `make`.

man

The `man` command is used to view the manual page, or documentation, for a named command or program. `man` takes the syntax

```
man [options] <command or program name>
```

Option	Function
-s	Causes `ln` to generate a symbolic link
-b	Generates a backup copy of the linked file, as well as creating the link
-v	Turns on verbose output, which prints the name

Table D-8.   Options for the `ln` Command

Option	Function
-p	Defines the file viewer to use when displaying the manual page. The default option is less.
-a	Locates all manual pages that contain the specified character string in *<name>* in the manual page title.
-h	Prints a help message and exits.
-K	Locates all manual pages that contain the specified character string in *<name>* in the text, as well as in the title.

Table D-9.   Options for the man Command

A few common options exist for man, which are shown in Table D-9.

mkdir

The mkdir command is used to create a new directory with the specified directory name. mkdir takes the syntax

```
mkdir <directoryname>
```

more

The more command shows a specified file in screen-size segments. more takes the syntax

```
more <filename>
```

Tap the Spacebar to move forward one screen in the file. Note, you cannot move backward in a file viewed with more. If you need to move forward and backward in the file, use the less command instead.

mount

The mount command, as its name implies, is used to mount a specified file system across the network using NFS. Once the file system is mounted, the remote data is usable on the local machine. mount takes the syntax

```
mount -t <filesystem type> <device> <mount point>
```

where the *<filesystem type>* defines the kind of file system you're mounting (ext2, iso9660, or other Unix types), the *<device>* defines the directory path of the file system to be mounted, and the *<mount point>* defines the local empty directory where the remote file system will be mounted.

mv

The mv command moves the named file to a new specified location. mv takes the syntax

```
mv <oldfilename> <newfilename>
```

The variable *<oldfilename>* specifies the original file, while *<newfilename>* specifies the new location. If *<newfilename>* is a filename in the same directory, the original file is simply renamed. If *<newfilename>* is a directory path, the original file is moved to the new directory, retaining its original name.

CAUTION: If you specify an existing file as *<newfilename>*, the existing data is then overwritten and lost.

netstat

The netstat command is used to view the status of various network functions. netstat takes the syntax

```
netstat [options]
```

If no option is given, netstat reports on all open network sockets. The -e option reports the user ID of each socket user, while the -r option shows the complete routing table. Output from netstat is printed to the screen.

passwd

The passwd command is used to change the login password. It can be issued by root to change the password or user identification for any specified user. If issued by an individual user, the passwd command can be used only to change that user's password or identification. passwd takes the syntax

```
passwd [<user>]
```

ping

The ping command sends tiny packets of data to a named remote machine to test the network connection. ping reports the number of packets sent and the time taken for the packets to return to the originating machine. ping takes the syntax

```
ping [options] <remote machine>
```

Two major options are used with ping, as shown in Table D-10.

Option	Function
-c	Sets the total number of data packets that will be sent. If this option is not used, ping will continue to send packets until you stop the program by pressing CTRL-C.
-i	Sets the number of seconds to delay between each packet; the default is one second.

Table D-10.   Options for the ping Command

ps

The ps command is used to generate a list of all running processes. The list includes the amount of time the process has existed and the amount of CPU cycles the process is consuming. ps takes the syntax

```
ps [options]
```

Several options for ps are shown in Table D-11.

pwd

The pwd command is simple. It prints the full pathname of the directory in which the command was issued. Simply type **pwd** at the command prompt to see the directory path and where you're located in the file system. pwd is useful when you've been working in deeply nested subdirectories and you need to remember the complete directory path to move or copy a file.

Option	Function
-a	Prints all processes running on the machine, whether yours or someone else's
-x	Includes all background processes started by other programs (such as Apache's spawned child processes)
-u	Prints all processes sorted by the user ID of the user who started them

Table D-11.   Options for the ps Command

rm

The `rm` command is used to remove specified files from the machine permanently. `rm` takes the syntax

```
rm [options] <filename>
```

A number of options are used with `rm`. Some of the more common `rm` options are shown in Table D-12.

CAUTION: Use `rm` conservatively. For example, if you combine options and issue the command `rm -rf *.*` as root, you'll delete EVERY SINGLE FILE ON THE MACHINE, including operating system data, rendering the machine essentially useless. If you issue that command in your user directory, you'll delete everything there, including your personal files and all configurations. Never issue an `rm` command unless you are completely sure of what you're about to delete.

rmdir

The `rmdir` command is used to delete a named directory. `rmdir` takes the syntax

```
rmdir <directory name>
```

If you issue the `rmdir` command and name a directory that isn't empty, `rmdir` will print an error message and exit. Be sure to clean everything out of the directory before you try to delete it, including hidden files.

route

The `route` command is used to see a snapshot of the IP routing table or to change data in the table. `route` takes the syntax

```
route [options] <target>
```

Option	Function
`-I`	Enables interactive mode, requiring you to confirm each file to be deleted. Use this flag to keep files from being deleted inadvertently.
`-r`	Enables recursive mode, which deletes all subdirectories of the current directory and the files they contain, as well as the files in the current directory.
`-f`	Enables force mode, causing `rm` to ignore all warnings it issues to itself.

Table D-12.   Options for the `rm` Command

Option	Function
-v	Enables verbose mode (more extensive comments as the program executes).
-n	Shows IP addresses instead of host names.
add	Adds an additional route to the table.
del	Deletes an existing route from the table.
-net	The target is a network.
-host	The target is a host (single machine).
netmask	The netmask number to be used if the target is a network.
default	The default route to be used if no other route can be matched.
gw	Routes packets through a gateway (either an interface or a distinct host). If gateway is a host, usually used along with the default option.

Table D-13.   Options for the route Command

Several common options exist for route, which are shown in Table D-13.

rsync

The rsync command synchronizes named files or directories across a network, as with directories mounted remotely via NFS. rsync uses the syntax

rsync [options] *<source> <destination>*

A number of options exist for rsync. Some of the more popular choices are shown in Table D-14.

Option	Function
-e	Defines the method of transporting data, either rsh or ssh (rsh is the default, but ssh is more secure)
-a	Enables archive mode, preserving all original file attributes
-r	Enables recursive mode, copying files in all subdirectories as well

Table D-14.   Options for the rsync Command

Option	Function
-u	Enables update mode, copying files only if the source file's timestamp is later than the destination file's timestamp
-R	Uses relative pathnames instead of absolute paths
-v	Enables verbose mode
-b	Enables backup mode, creating backups of old files before they're overwritten
-n	"Dry run," where rsync prints a list of what would have been synced, but doesn't actually synchronize the data
-z	Compresses data before sending over the network (especially useful for slow network connections)
--delete	Removes any files on the receiving file system that don't exist on the sending file system

Table D-14. Options for the `rsync` Command *(continued)*

shutdown

The `shutdown` command is used to stop all processes and shut down the machine. `shutdown` takes the syntax

```
shutdown [options] <time> [<warning message>]
```

`shutdown` takes several arguments:

▼ *<time>*   Set the time until the machine shuts down. Options are now, +*m* (where *m* is the number of minutes before shutdown), and *<hh>:<mm>* (using a 24-hour clock to define the time at which the machine will shut down).

▲ *<warning message>*   The string in this argument are sent to all users, printing to their monitor screens, to alert them of the coming shutdown.

You can use several options with `shutdown`. The two most frequently used options are –h, or halt, which causes `shutdown` to stop the system immediately, and –r, which causes the machine to reboot instead of powering down.

TIP: The most common `shutdown` command is `shutdown –h now`.

sort

The sort command, as its name implies, sorts entries in a specified file. Each entry must be on its own line. sort uses either a numeric or an alphabetical sort, depending on the data in the file. The output is printed to the screen. sort takes the syntax

```
sort <filename>
```

ssh

The ssh command is used to open a secure shell, which is an excellent (and far more secure) alternative to rsh, rcp, rlogin, and other similar remote-shell commands. ssh takes the syntax

```
ssh [-l <login name>] [hostname] [command]
```

ssh uses a strong encryption strategy to protect login sessions or commands run remotely. Although most people use ssh as a Telnet replacement, it is far more sophisticated. See the excellent documentation available at a variety of Web sites to learn more about this critical program.

su

Use the su command to change between different user identities. This command is mostly an administrative tool, used to access the root account or to switch between user accounts created for different system functions. su takes the syntax

```
su [-] [<username>]
```

If you use the – character when issuing the command, your environment variables will be changed to those associated with the new user account. However, if you don't use the – character, you'll maintain your own environment variables, regardless of settings in the new account.

TIP: You can use su to issue root commands without having to log into the root account. This is a security precaution. To do so, issue commands with the syntax su –c <command>. You are then prompted for the root password.

tar

The tar command either creates or unpacks an archive file. Files created with tar are usually called *tarballs*. tar takes one of two syntaxes:

```
tar [options] <filename1> <filename2>...<filenameN>
```

or

```
tar [options] <directoryname1> <directoryname2>...<directorynameN>
```

Unlike most other flags to Unix commands, `tar` options don't use the hyphen. If you use a hyphen, the command will fail. Table D-15 shows some common `tar` options.

top

The `top` command generates a table of active processes on the machine. It can be configured to show a variety of different data sets. `top` takes the syntax

```
top [options]
```

Common options for `top` are shown in Table D-16.

TIP: `top` also has a number of interactive commands available. Type **h** while `top` is running to see a list and description of what's available.

touch

The `touch` command updates the timestamp on a named file. It can also be used to create an empty file with no formatting. `touch` takes the syntax

```
touch <filename>
```

If the filename shown in the command doesn't belong to an existing file, `touch` will create a new file with that name.

Option	Function
c	Creates a compressed archive from the named files
x	Extracts all files from the named archive
f	Compresses a single specified file
z	Uncompresses the single specified file using the gunzip protocol
v	Enables verbose output

Table D-15.   Options for the `tar` Command

Option	Function
d	Defines the interval between table updates.
p	Displays only the process name with the specified process identification number(PID). You can issue the command with the p option up to 20 times to create a custom process table.
q	Refreshes top without delay. Caution: this option can overwhelm your CPU and cause other processes on the machine to slow noticeably.
i	Causes top to ignore idle or zombie processes.

Table D-16.   Options for the top Command

traceroute

The traceroute command is used to determine the route packets use to travel from one host to another. This is frequently used to test network configuration or to determine the cause for slow or nonexistent Internet communication. traceroute takes the syntax

```
traceroute [options] <remote machine>
```

If you use the –n option, traceroute displays IP numbers for each machine in the route, rather than host names. Use the –w option to set the maximum number of seconds traceroute will wait for response before timing out.

ulimit

The ulimit command is used to control system resource availability to any processes started by the shell. You can use ulimit to ensure that runaway processes won't take over the majority of your CPU cycles and cause other work on the machine to slow down. ulimit takes the syntax

```
ulimit [options [limit]]
```

Some common options for ulimit are shown in Table D-17.

Option	Function
-S	Sets a soft limit, which generates a warning if an individual process goes over the limit
-H	Sets a hard limit, which doesn't permit an individual process to exceed the limit
-a	Prints all existing limits to the screen
-c	Sets the maximum size permitted for core files
-d	Sets the maximum size permitted for an individual process's data segment
-t	Sets the maximum number of seconds an individual process can use of CPU time
-f	Sets the maximum number of files an individual shell process can generate
-p	Sets the pipe buffer size
-n	Sets the maximum number of open file descriptors permitted
-u	Sets the maximum number of user processes permitted at any given time
-v	Sets the size of virtual memory

Table D-17. Options for the `ulimit` Command

umask

The `umask` command sets default permissions for newly created files. Use `umask` to create a permissions template for files created on this machine at a later time. `umask` uses the syntax

```
umask [-S] [<mode>]
```

If you use the `-S` option, `umask` prints the current file permissions mode to the screen.

NOTE: The mode, or permissions set, can be expressed either as an octal number or by using the symbolic characters frequently used with `chmod`.

umount

The `umount` command unmounts a file system on a Unix machine. `umount` takes the syntax

```
umount [options] <filesystem>
```

The *<filesystem>* component may be a device name or a directory name, as long as it identifies a currently mounted file system.

You can also use umount to umount every file system currently listed in the /etc/mtab file at once by using the –a flag, as in

```
umount -a
```

userdel

The userdel command deletes a specified user's account. On some Unix systems, this program may be called deluser. userdel takes the syntax

```
userdel [-r] <username>
```

The –r flag is the most commonly used option for userdel. It causes userdel to remove all the files contained in the user's home directory, as well as to delete the account itself.

NOTE: You must be root to issue this command.

w

The w command is used to generate a list of all users currently logged into the machine. w takes the syntax

```
w [options]
```

Some of the common options for w are shown in Table D-18.

wc

The wc command is used to determine the number of words in a specified file, where a word is defined as a character string with a space on each side. wc uses the syntax

```
wc [options] <filename>
```

Option	Function
-h	Prints only the user names, not extra header information
-s	Prints output in shortened format
<username>	Prints information about only the specified user

Table D-18. Options for the w Command

Option	Function
-c	Counts the bytes, or individual characters, in the file rather than the words
-l	Counts the file's lines rather than the words
-L	Prints the length of the file's longest line

Table D-19.   Options for the wc Command

Table D-19 contains some common options for wc .

whereis

The whereis command is used to locate a file or program on the hard drive. whereis takes the syntax

```
whereis [options] <filename>
```

Table D-20 shows some common options for whereis.

which

The which command is used to locate a given program on the machine. which takes the syntax

```
which [options] <programname>
```

Use the –a flag, as in

```
which -a <programname>
```

to find all matching filenames in all directories specified as part of the PATH environment variable.

Option	Function
-b	Searches only for executable binaries with the specified filename
-m	Searches only for manual pages with the given filename
-s	Searches only for source code packages with the given filename

Table D-20.   Options for the whereis Command

APPENDIX E

Apache Configuration Files

To configure your Apache installation, you need to edit the file `/etc/apache/docs/conf/httpd-std.conf`. This large and lengthy file contains all the settings that determine how your core Apache server will work; some modules may have their own configuration files as well, but the overall behavior of Apache is based on the choices you make in `httpd-std.conf`. In earlier versions of Apache, configuration was done with several files contained in the `/etc/apache/docs/conf` directory, but current versions use the single `httpd-std.conf` file to configure the entire server. Though raising the level of complexity in the file, using one file for all configuration cuts down on the chance for error or oversight.

NOTE: Depending on your Unix variant of choice, you may need to look for this file in `/etc/httpd/httpd-std.conf` instead. A few Unix-derived operating systems use the `/etc/httpd` directory to house Apache and its files rather than the default `/etc/apache` directory.

In this appendix, we include the entire `httpd.conf` file without additional commentary. You'll also find the full text of `httpd-win.conf`, the file used to configure Apache on Windows systems, and `highperformance-std.conf`, a generic file that tweaks Apache for optimal performance. When you're deep in the guts of this file, it can be hard to move from section to section without losing the spot where you were working—a problem that can sometimes have devastating effects if you don't return to finish the job! Many people find reading lengthy files easier if the files are printed out, rather than reading them on the screen. You can also use the printed version to make notes and flag specific items before you go in and open `httpd-std.conf`; it's good to develop the habit of visiting your configuration files rarely, as it's easy to mess something up if you approach configuration with a cavalier attitude.

TIP: If you're going to keep the old `httpd.conf` file around, rename it so that Apache doesn't get confused by having both the old file and the new file. Rename a file on Unix by issuing the command `mv /etc/apache/docs/conf/httpd.conf /etc/apache/docs/conf/httpd.conf.old`. This renames the file `httpd.conf.old`, making it easier to find.

Once you install the new configuration file and have finished editing it, make a backup copy for safety. Issue the command `cp /etc/apache/docs/conf/httpd-std.conf /etc/apache/docs/conf/httpd-std.conf.bak` to create a duplicate file with the `*.bak` extension, a traditional indicator that the file is a backup version.

TIP: To learn more about working with `httpd-std.conf` and configuring your Apache installation, refer to Chapter 8, "Apache Configuration Files."

HTTPD-STD.CONF

```
#
# Based upon the NCSA server configuration files originally by Rob McCool.
#
# This is the main Apache server configuration file.  It contains the
# configuration directives that give the server its instructions.
# See <URL:http://www.apache.org/docs/> for detailed information about
# the directives.
#
# Do NOT simply read the instructions in here without understanding
# what they do.  They're here only as hints or reminders.  If you are unsure
# consult the online docs. You have been warned.
#
# The configuration directives are grouped into three basic sections:
#  1. Directives that control the operation of the Apache server process as a
#     whole (the 'global environment').
#  2. Directives that define the parameters of the 'main' or 'default' server,
#     which responds to requests that aren't handled by a virtual host.
#     These directives also provide default values for the settings
#     of all virtual hosts.
#  3. Settings for virtual hosts, which allow Web requests to be sent to
#     different IP addresses or hostnames and have them handled by the
#     same Apache server process.
#
# Configuration and logfile names: If the filenames you specify for many
# of the server's control files begin with "/" (or "drive:/" for Win32), the
# server will use that explicit path.  If the filenames do *not* begin
# with "/", the value of ServerRoot is prepended -- so "logs/foo.log"
# with ServerRoot set to "/usr/local/apache" will be interpreted by the
# server as "/usr/local/apache/logs/foo.log".
#


### Section 1: Global Environment
#
# The directives in this section affect the overall operation of Apache,
# such as the number of concurrent requests it can handle or where it
# can find its configuration files.
#


#
# ServerRoot: The top of the directory tree under which the server's
# configuration, error, and log files are kept.
#
```

```
# NOTE!  If you intend to place this on an NFS (or otherwise network)
# mounted filesystem then please read the LockFile documentation
# (available at <URL:http://www.apache.org/docs/mod/core.html#lockfile>);
# you will save yourself a lot of trouble.
#
# Do NOT add a slash at the end of the directory path.
#
ServerRoot "@@ServerRoot@@"


#
# The LockFile directive sets the path to the lockfile used when Apache
# is compiled with either USE_FCNTL_SERIALIZED_ACCEPT or
# USE_FLOCK_SERIALIZED_ACCEPT. This directive should normally be left at
# its default value. The main reason for changing it is if the logs
# directory is NFS mounted, since the lockfile MUST BE STORED ON A LOCAL
# DISK. The PID of the main server process is automatically appended to
# the filename.
#
#LockFile logs/accept.lock


#
# PidFile: The file in which the server should record its process
# identification number when it starts.
#
PidFile logs/httpd.pid


#
# ScoreBoardFile: File used to store internal server process information.
# Not all architectures require this.  But if yours does (you'll know because
# this file will be  created when you run Apache) then you *must* ensure that
# no two invocations of Apache share the same scoreboard file.
#
<IfModule !perchild.c>
ScoreBoardFile logs/apache_runtime_status
</IfModule>


#
# Timeout: The number of seconds before receives and sends time out.
#
Timeout 300


#
# KeepAlive: Whether or not to allow persistent connections (more than
# one request per connection). Set to "Off" to deactivate.
#
KeepAlive On


#
# MaxKeepAliveRequests: The maximum number of requests to allow
```

```
# during a persistent connection. Set to 0 to allow an unlimited amount.
# We recommend you leave this number high, for maximum performance.
#
MaxKeepAliveRequests 100


#
# KeepAliveTimeout: Number of seconds to wait for the next request from the
# same client on the same connection.
#
KeepAliveTimeout 15


##
## Server-Pool Size Regulation (MPM specific)
##


# prefork MPM
# StartServers ......... number of server processes to start
# MinSpareServers ...... minimum number of server processes which are kept spare
# MaxSpareServers ...... maximum number of server processes which are kept spare
# MaxClients ........... maximum number of server processes allowed to start
# MaxRequestsPerChild .. maximum number of requests a server process serves
<IfModule prefork.c>
StartServers          5
MinSpareServers       5
MaxSpareServers      10
MaxClients           20
MaxRequestsPerChild   0
</IfModule>


# pthread MPM
# StartServers ......... initial  number of server processes to start
# MaxClients ........... maximum  number of server processes allowed to start
# MinSpareThreads ...... minimum  number of worker threads which are kept spare
# MaxSpareThreads ...... maximum  number of worker threads which are kept spare
# ThreadsPerChild ...... constant number of worker threads in each server process
# MaxRequestsPerChild .. maximum  number of requests a server process serves
<IfModule threaded.c>
StartServers          3
MaxClients            8
MinSpareThreads       5
MaxSpareThreads      10
ThreadsPerChild      25
MaxRequestsPerChild   0
</IfModule>


# perchild MPM
# NumServers ........... constant number of server processes
# StartThreads ......... initial  number of worker threads in each server process
# MinSpareThreads ...... minimum  number of worker threads which are kept spare
```

```
# MaxSpareThreads ...... maximum  number of worker threads which are kept spare
# MaxThreadsPerChild ... maximum  number of worker threads in each server process
# MaxRequestsPerChild .. maximum  number of connections per server process (then
#  it dies)
<IfModule perchild.c>
NumServers              5
StartThreads            5
MinSpareThreads         5
MaxSpareThreads        10
MaxThreadsPerChild     20
MaxRequestsPerChild     0
</IfModule>


#
# Listen: Allows you to bind Apache to specific IP addresses and/or
# ports, in addition to the default. See also the <VirtualHost>
# directive.
#
#Listen 3000
#Listen 12.34.56.78:80


#
# BindAddress: You can support virtual hosts with this option. This directive
# is used to tell the server which IP address to listen to. It can either
# contain "*", an IP address, or a fully qualified Internet domain name.
# See also the <VirtualHost> and Listen directives.
#
#BindAddress *


#
# Dynamic Shared Object (DSO) Support
#
# To be able to use the functionality of a module which was built as a DSO you
# have to place corresponding `LoadModule' lines at this location so the
# directives contained in it are actually available _before_ they are used.
# Please read the file README.DSO in the Apache 1.3 distribution for more
# details about the DSO mechanism and run `httpd -l' for the list of already
# built-in (statically linked and thus always available) modules in your httpd
# binary.
#
# Note: The order is which modules are loaded is important.  Don't change
# the order below without expert advice.
#
# Example:
# LoadModule foo_module modules/mod_foo.so


### Section 2: 'Main' server configuration
#
# The directives in this section set up the values used by the 'main'
```

```
# server, which responds to any requests that aren't handled by a
# <VirtualHost> definition.  These values also provide defaults for
# any <VirtualHost> containers you may define later in the file.

# All of these directives may appear inside <VirtualHost> containers,
# in which case these default settings will be overridden for the
# virtual host being defined.
#

#
# If your ServerType directive (set earlier in the 'Global Environment'
# section) is set to "inetd", the next few directives don't have any
# effect since their settings are defined by the inetd configuration.
# Skip ahead to the ServerAdmin directive.
#

#
# Port: The port to which the standalone server listens. For
# ports < 1023, you will need httpd to be run as root initially.
#
Port @@Port@@

#
# If you wish httpd to run as a different user or group, you must run
# httpd as root initially and it will switch.
#
# User/Group: The name (or #number) of the user/group to run httpd as.
#  . On SCO (ODT 3) use "User nouser" and "Group nogroup".
#  . On HPUX you may not be able to use shared memory as nobody, and the
#    suggested workaround is to create a user www and use that user.
#  NOTE that some kernels refuse to setgid(Group) or semctl(IPC_SET)
#  when the value of (unsigned)Group is above 60000;
#  don't use Group #-1 on these systems!
#
User nobody
Group #-1

#
# ServerAdmin: Your address, where problems with the server should be
# e-mailed.  This address appears on some server-generated pages, such
# as error documents.
#
ServerAdmin you@your.address
#
# ServerName allows you to set a host name which is sent back to clients for
# your server if it's different than the one the program would get (i.e., use
# "www" instead of the host's real name).
#
# Note: You cannot just invent host names and hope they work. The name you
```

```
# define here must be a valid DNS name for your host. If you don't understand
# this, ask your network administrator.
# If your host doesn't have a registered DNS name, enter its IP address here.
# You will have to access it by its address (e.g., http://123.45.67.89/)
# anyway, and this will make redirections work in a sensible way.
#
#ServerName new.host.name

# DocumentRoot: The directory out of which you will serve your
# documents. By default, all requests are taken from this directory, but
# symbolic links and aliases may be used to point to other locations.
#
DocumentRoot "@@ServerRoot@@/htdocs"

#
# Each directory to which Apache has access, can be configured with respect
# to which services and features are allowed and/or disabled in that
# directory (and its subdirectories).
#
# First, we configure the "default" to be a very restrictive set of
# permissions.
#
<Directory />
    Options FollowSymLinks
    AllowOverride None
</Directory>

#
# Note that from this point forward you must specifically allow
# particular features to be enabled - so if something's not working as
# you might expect, make sure that you have specifically enabled it
# below.
#


#
# This should be changed to whatever you set DocumentRoot to.
#
<Directory "@@ServerRoot@@/htdocs">

#
# This may also be "None", "All", or any combination of "Indexes",
# "Includes", "FollowSymLinks", "ExecCGI", or "MultiViews".
#
# Note that "MultiViews" must be named *explicitly* --- "Options All"
# doesn't give it to you.
#
    Options Indexes FollowSymLinks MultiViews

#
```

```
# This controls which options the .htaccess files in directories can
# override. Can also be "All", or any combination of "Options", "FileInfo",
# "AuthConfig", and "Limit"
#
    AllowOverride None


#
# Controls who can get stuff from this server.
#
    Order allow,deny
    Allow from all
</Directory>


#
# UserDir: The name of the directory which is appended onto a user's home
# directory if a ~user request is received.
#
UserDir public_html


#
# Control access to UserDir directories.  The following is an example
# for a site where these directories are restricted to read-only.
#
#<Directory /home/*/public_html>
#    AllowOverride FileInfo AuthConfig Limit
#    Options MultiViews Indexes SymLinksIfOwnerMatch IncludesNoExec
#    <Limit GET POST OPTIONS PROPFIND>
#        Order allow,deny
#        Allow from all
#    </Limit>
#    <LimitExcept GET POST OPTIONS PROPFIND>
#        Order deny,allow
#        Deny from all
#    </LimitExcept>
#</Directory>


#
# DirectoryIndex: Name of the file or files to use as a pre-written HTML
# directory index.  Separate multiple entries with spaces.
#
DirectoryIndex index.html


#
# AccessFileName: The name of the file to look for in each directory
# for access control information.
#
AccessFileName .htaccess


#
```

```
# The following lines prevent .htaccess files from being viewed by
# Web clients.  Since .htaccess files often contain authorization
# information, access is disallowed for security reasons.  Comment
# these lines out if you want Web visitors to see the contents of
# .htaccess files.  If you change the AccessFileName directive above,
# be sure to make the corresponding changes here.
#
# Also, folks tend to use names such as .htpasswd for password
# files, so this will protect those as well.
#
<Files ~ "^\.ht">
    Order allow,deny
    Deny from all
</Files>


#
# CacheNegotiatedDocs: By default, Apache sends "Pragma: no-cache" with each
# document that was negotiated on the basis of content. This asks proxy
# servers not to cache the document. Uncommenting the following line disables
# this behavior, and proxies will be allowed to cache the documents.
#
#CacheNegotiatedDocs


#
# UseCanonicalName:  (new for 1.3)  With this setting turned on, whenever
# Apache needs to construct a self-referencing URL (a URL that refers back
# to the server the response is coming from) it will use ServerName and
# Port to form a "canonical" name.  With this setting off, Apache will
# use the hostname:port that the client supplied, when possible.  This
# also affects SERVER_NAME and SERVER_PORT in CGI scripts.
#
UseCanonicalName On


#
# TypesConfig describes where the mime.types file (or equivalent) is
# to be found.
#
TypesConfig conf/mime.types


#
# DefaultType is the default MIME type the server will use for a document
# if it cannot otherwise determine one, such as from filename extensions.
# If your server contains mostly text or HTML documents, "text/plain" is
# a good value.  If most of your content is binary, such as applications
# or images, you may want to use "application/octet-stream" instead to
# keep browsers from trying to display binary files as though they are
# text.
#
DefaultType text/plain
```

```
#
# The mod_mime_magic module allows the server to use various hints from the
# contents of the file itself to determine its type.  The MIMEMagicFile
# directive tells the module where the hint definitions are located.
# mod_mime_magic is not part of the default server (you have to add
# it yourself with a LoadModule [see the DSO paragraph in the 'Global
# Environment' section], or recompile the server and include mod_mime_magic
# as part of the configuration), so it's enclosed in an <IfModule> container.
# This means that the MIMEMagicFile directive will only be processed if the
# module is part of the server.
#
<IfModule mod_mime_magic.c>
    MIMEMagicFile conf/magic
</IfModule>


#
# HostnameLookups: Log the names of clients or just their IP addresses
# e.g., www.apache.org (on) or 204.62.129.132 (off).
# The default is off because it'd be overall better for the net if people
# had to knowingly turn this feature on, since enabling it means that
# each client request will result in AT LEAST one lookup request to the
# nameserver.
#
HostnameLookups Off


#
# ErrorLog: The location of the error log file.
# If you do not specify an ErrorLog directive within a <VirtualHost>
# container, error messages relating to that virtual host will be
# logged here.  If you *do* define an error logfile for a <VirtualHost>
# container, that host's errors will be logged there and not here.
#
ErrorLog logs/error_log


#
# LogLevel: Control the number of messages logged to the error_log
# Possible values include: debug, info, notice, warn, error, crit,
# alert, emerg.
#
LogLevel warn


#
# The following directives define some format nicknames for use with
# a CustomLog directive (see below).
#
LogFormat "%h %l %u %t \"%r\" %>s %b \"%{Referer}i\" \"%{User-Agent}i\"" combined
LogFormat "%h %l %u %t \"%r\" %>s %b" common
LogFormat "%{Referer}i -> %U" referer
LogFormat "%{User-agent}i" agent
```

```
#
# The location and format of the access logfile (Common Logfile Format).
# If you do not define any access logfiles within a <VirtualHost>
# container, they will be logged here.  Contrariwise, if you *do*
# define per-<VirtualHost> access logfiles, transactions will be
# logged therein and *not* in this file.
#
CustomLog logs/access_log common

#
# If you would like to have agent and referrer logfiles, uncomment the
# following directives.
#
#CustomLog logs/referer_log referer
#CustomLog logs/agent_log agent

#
# If you prefer a single logfile with access, agent, and referrer information
# (Combined Logfile Format) you can use the following directive.
#
#CustomLog logs/access_log combined
#
# Optionally add a line containing the server version and virtual host
# name to server-generated pages (error documents, FTP directory listings,
# mod_status and mod_info output etc., but not CGI generated documents).
# Set to "EMail" to also include a mailto: link to the ServerAdmin.
# Set to one of:  On | Off | Email
#
ServerSignature On

#
# Aliases: Add here as many aliases as you need (with no limit). The format is
# Alias fakename realname
#
# Note that if you include a trailing / on fakename then the server will
# require it to be present in the URL.  So "/icons" isn't aliased in this
# example, only "/icons/"..
#
Alias /icons/ "@@ServerRoot@@/icons/"

<Directory "@@ServerRoot@@/icons">
    Options Indexes MultiView
    AllowOverride None
    Order allow,deny
    Allow from all
</Directory>

#
# ScriptAlias: This controls which directories contain server scripts.
```

```
# ScriptAliases are essentially the same as Aliases, except that
# documents in the realname directory are treated as applications and
# run by the server when requested rather than as documents sent to the client.
# The same rules about trailing "/" apply to ScriptAlias directives as to
# Alias.
#
ScriptAlias /cgi-bin/ "@@ServerRoot@@/cgi-bin/"

<IfModule mod_cgid.c>
#
# Additional to mod_cgid.c settings, mod_cgid has Scriptsock <path>
# for setting UNIX socket for communicating with cgid.
#
#Scriptsock             logs/cgisock
</IfModule>

#
# "@@ServerRoot@@/cgi-bin" should be changed to whatever your ScriptAliased
# CGI directory exists, if you have that configured.
#
<Directory "@@ServerRoot@@/cgi-bin">
    AllowOverride None
    Options None
    Order allow,deny
    Allow from all
</Directory>

#
# Redirect allows you to tell clients about documents which used to exist in
# your server's namespace, but do not anymore. This allows you to tell the
# clients where to look for the relocated document.
# Format: Redirect old-URI new-URL
#

#
# Directives controlling the display of server-generated directory listings.
#

# FancyIndexing is whether you want fancy directory indexing or standard.
# VersionSort is whether files containing version numbers should be
# compared in the natural way, so that `apache-1.3.9.tar' is placed before
# `apache-1.3.12.tar'.
IndexOptions FancyIndexing VersionSort

#
# AddIcon* directives tell the server which icon to show for different
# files or filename extensions.  These are only displayed for
# FancyIndexed directories.
#
```

```
AddIconByEncoding (CMP,/icons/compressed.gif) x-compress x-gzip

AddIconByType (TXT,/icons/text.gif) text/*
AddIconByType (IMG,/icons/image2.gif) image/*
AddIconByType (SND,/icons/sound2.gif) audio/*
AddIconByType (VID,/icons/movie.gif) video/*

AddIcon /icons/binary.gif .bin .exe
AddIcon /icons/binhex.gif .hqx
AddIcon /icons/tar.gif .tar
AddIcon /icons/world2.gif .wrl .wrl.gz .vrml .vrm .iv
AddIcon /icons/compressed.gif .Z .z .tgz .gz .zip
AddIcon /icons/a.gif .ps .ai .eps
AddIcon /icons/layout.gif .html .shtml .htm .pdf
AddIcon /icons/text.gif .txt
AddIcon /icons/c.gif .c
AddIcon /icons/p.gif .pl .py
AddIcon /icons/f.gif .for
AddIcon /icons/dvi.gif .dvi
AddIcon /icons/uuencoded.gif .uu
AddIcon /icons/script.gif .conf .sh .shar .csh .ksh .tcl
AddIcon /icons/tex.gif .tex
AddIcon /icons/bomb.gif core

AddIcon /icons/back.gif ..
AddIcon /icons/hand.right.gif README
AddIcon /icons/folder.gif ^^DIRECTORY^^
AddIcon /icons/blank.gif ^^BLANKICON^^

#
# DefaultIcon is which icon to show for files which do not have an icon
# explicitly set.
#
DefaultIcon /icons/unknown.gif

#
# AddDescription allows you to place a short description after a file in
# server-generated indexes.  These are only displayed for FancyIndexed
# directories.
# Format: AddDescription "description" filename
#
#AddDescription "GZIP compressed document" .gz
#AddDescription "tar archive" .tar
#AddDescription "GZIP compressed tar archive" .tgz

#
# ReadmeName is the name of the README file the server will look for by
# default, and append to directory listings.
#
```

```
# HeaderName is the name of a file which should be prepended to
# directory indexes.
#
# The server will first look for name.html and include it if found.
# If name.html doesn't exist, the server will then look for name.txt
# and include it as plaintext if found.
#
ReadmeName README
HeaderName HEADER


#
# IndexIgnore is a set of filenames which directory indexing should ignore
# and not include in the listing.  Shell-style wildcarding is permitted.
#
IndexIgnore .??* *~ *# HEADER* README* RCS CVS *,v *,t


#
# AddEncoding allows you to have certain browsers (Mosaic/X 2.1+) uncompress
# information on the fly. Note: Not all browsers support this.
# Despite the name similarity, the following Add* directives have nothing
# to do with the FancyIndexing customization directives above.
#
AddEncoding x-compress Z
AddEncoding x-gzip gz tgz


#
# DefaultLanguage and AddLanguage allows you to specify the language of
# a document. You can then use content negotiation to give a browser a
# file in a language the user can understand.
#
# Specify a default language. This means that all data
# going out without a specific language tag (see below) will
# be marked with this one. You probably do NOT want to set
# this unless you are sure it is correct for all cases.
#
# * It is generally better to not mark a page as
# * being a certain language than marking it with the wrong
# * language!
#
# DefaultLanguage nl
#
# Note 1: The suffix does not have to be the same as the language
# keyword --- those with documents in Polish (whose net-standard
# language code is pl) may wish to use "AddLanguage pl .po" to
# avoid the ambiguity with the common suffix for perl scripts.
#
# Note 2: The example entries below illustrate that in
# some cases the two character 'Language' abbreviation is not
# identical to the two character 'Country' code for its country,
```

```
# E.g. 'Danmark/dk' versus 'Danish/da'.
#
# Note 3: In the case of 'ltz' we violate the RFC by using a three char
# specifier. There is 'work in progress' to fix this and get
# the reference data for rfc1766 cleaned up.
#
# Danish (da) - Dutch (nl) - English (en) - Estonian (et)
# French (fr) - German (de) - Greek-Modern (el)
# Italian (it) - Norwegian (no) - Korean (kr)
# Portugese (pt) - Luxembourgeois* (ltz)
# Spanish (es) - Swedish (sv) - Catalan (ca) - Czech(cz)
# Polish (pl) - Brazilian Portuguese (pt-br) - Japanese (ja)
# Russian (ru)
#
AddLanguage da .dk
AddLanguage nl .nl
AddLanguage en .en
AddLanguage et .et
AddLanguage fr .fr
AddLanguage de .de
AddLanguage el .el
AddLanguage it .it
AddLanguage ja .ja
AddLanguage pl .po
AddLanguage kr .kr
AddLanguage pt .pt
AddLanguage no .no
AddLanguage pt-br .pt-br
AddLanguage ltz .ltz
AddLanguage ca .ca
AddLanguage es .es
AddLanguage sv .se
AddLanguage cz .cz
AddLanguage ru .ru
AddLanguage tw .tw
AddLanguage zh-tw .tw


# LanguagePriority allows you to give precedence to some languages
# in case of a tie during content negotiation.
#
# Just list the languages in decreasing order of preference. We have
# more or less alphabetized them here. You probably want to change this.
#
LanguagePriority en da nl et fr de el it ja kr no pl pt pt-br ltz ca es sv tw


# Specify a default charset for all pages sent out. This is
# always a good idea and opens the door for future internationalisation
# of your web site, should you ever want it. Specifying it as
```

```
# a default does little harm; as the standard dictates that a page
# is in iso-8859-1 (latin1) unless specified otherwise i.e. you
# are merely stating the obvious. There are also some security
# reasons in browsers, related to javascript and URL parsing
# which encourage you to always set a default char set.
#
AddDefaultCharset ISO-8859-1


#
# Commonly used filename extensions to character sets. You probably
# want to avoid clashes with the language extensions, unless you
# are good at carefully testing your setup after each change.
# See ftp://ftp.isi.edu/in-notes/iana/assignments/character-sets for
# the official list of charset names and their respective RFCs
#
AddCharset ISO-8859-1   .iso8859-1   .latin1
AddCharset ISO-8859-2   .iso8859-2   .latin2 .cen
AddCharset ISO-8859-3   .iso8859-3   .latin3
AddCharset ISO-8859-4   .iso8859-4   .latin4
AddCharset ISO-8859-5   .iso8859-5   .latin5 .cyr .iso-ru
AddCharset ISO-8859-6   .iso8859-6   .latin6 .arb
AddCharset ISO-8859-7   .iso8859-7   .latin7 .grk
AddCharset ISO-8859-8   .iso8859-8   .latin8 .heb
AddCharset ISO-8859-9   .iso8859-9   .latin9 .trk
AddCharset ISO-2022-JP .iso2022-jp .jis
AddCharset ISO-2022-KR .iso2022-kr .kis
AddCharset ISO-2022-CN .iso2022-cn .cis
AddCharset Big5         .Big5        .big5
# For russian, more than one charset is used (depends on client, mostly):
AddCharset WINDOWS-1251 .cp-1251    .win-1251
AddCharset CP866         .cp866
AddCharset KOI8-r        .koi8-r .koi8-ru
AddCharset KOI8-ru       .koi8-uk .ua
AddCharset ISO-10646-UCS-2 .ucs2
AddCharset ISO-10646-UCS-4 .ucs4
AddCharset UTF-8         .utf8


# The set below does not map to a specific (iso) standard
# but works on a fairly wide range of browsers. Note that
# capitalization actually matters (it should not, but it
# does for some browsers).
#
# See ftp://ftp.isi.edu/in-notes/iana/assignments/character-sets
# for a list of sorts. But browsers support few.
#
AddCharset GB2312         .gb2312 .gb
AddCharset utf-7          .utf7
AddCharset utf-8          .utf8
AddCharset big5           .big5 .b5
```

```
AddCharset EUC-TW       .euc-tw
AddCharset EUC-JP       .euc-jp
AddCharset EUC-KR       .euc-kr
AddCharset shift_jis    .sjis

# AddType allows you to tweak mime.types without actually editing it, or to
# make certain files to be certain types.
#
# For example, the PHP3 module (not part of the Apache distribution - see
# http://www.php.net) will typically use:
#
#AddType application/x-httpd-php3 .php3
#AddType application/x-httpd-php3-source .phps

AddType application/x-tar .tgz

#
# AddHandler allows you to map certain file extensions to "handlers",
# actions unrelated to filetype. These can be either built into the server
# or added with the Action command (see below)
#
# If you want to use server side includes, or CGI outside
# ScriptAliased directories, uncomment the following lines.
#
# To use CGI scripts:
#
#AddHandler cgi-script .cgi

#
# To use server-parsed HTML files
#
#<FilesMatch "\.shtml(\..+)?$">
#    SetOutputFilter INCLUDES
#</FilesMatch>

#
# Uncomment the following line to enable Apache's send-asis HTTP file
# feature
#
#AddHandler send-as-is asis

#
# If you wish to use server-parsed imagemap files, use
#
#AddHandler imap-file map

#
# To enable type maps, you might want to use
#
```

```
#AddHandler type-map var

#
# Action lets you define media types that will execute a script whenever
# a matching file is called. This eliminates the need for repeated URL
# pathnames for oft-used CGI file processors.
# Format: Action media/type /cgi-script/location
# Format: Action handler-name /cgi-script/location
#

#
# MetaDir: specifies the name of the directory in which Apache can find
# meta information files. These files contain additional HTTP headers
# to include when sending the document
#
#MetaDir .web

#
# MetaSuffix: specifies the file name suffix for the file containing the
# meta information.
#
#MetaSuffix .meta

#
# Customizable error response (Apache style)
#   these come in three flavors
#
#     1) plain text
#ErrorDocument 500 "The server made a boo boo."
#
#     2) local redirects
#ErrorDocument 404 /missing.html
#   to redirect to local URL /missing.html
#ErrorDocument 404 "/cgi-bin/missing_handlder.pl"
#     i.e. any string which starts with a '/' and has
#     no spaces.
#   N.B.: You can redirect to a script or a document using server-side-includes.
#
#     3) external redirects
#ErrorDocument 402 http://some.other_server.com/subscription_info.html
#     i.e. any string whichis a valid  URL.
#   N.B.: Many of the environment variables associated with the original
#   request will *not* be available to such a script.
#
#     4) borderline case
#ErrorDocument 402 "http://some.other_server.com/info.html is the place to look"
#     treated as case '1' as it has spaces and thus is not a valid URL
#
# The following directives modify normal HTTP response behavior.
```

```
# The first directive disables keepalive for Netscape 2.x and browsers that
# spoof it. There are known problems with these browser implementations.
# The second directive is for Microsoft Internet Explorer 4.0b2
# which has a broken HTTP/1.1 implementation and does not properly
# support keepalive when it is used on 301 or 302 (redirect) responses.
#
BrowserMatch "Mozilla/2" nokeepalive
BrowserMatch "MSIE 4\.0b2;" nokeepalive downgrade-1.0 force-response-1.0


#
# The following directive disables HTTP/1.1 responses to browsers which
# are in violation of the HTTP/1.0 spec by not being able to grok a
# basic 1.1 response.
#
BrowserMatch "RealPlayer 4\.0" force-response-1.0
BrowserMatch "Java/1\.0" force-response-1.0
BrowserMatch "JDK/1\.0" force-response-1.0


#
# Allow server status reports, with the URL of http://servername/server-status
# Change the ".your_domain.com" to match your domain to enable.
#
#<Location /server-status>
#    SetHandler server-status
#    Order deny,allow
#    Deny from all
#    Allow from .your_domain.com
#</Location>


#
# Allow remote server configuration reports, with the URL of
#  http://servername/server-info (requires that mod_info.c be loaded).
# Change the ".your_domain.com" to match your domain to enable.
#
#<Location /server-info>
#    SetHandler server-info
#    Order deny,allow
#    Deny from all
#    Allow from .your_domain.com
#</Location>


#
# There have been reports of people trying to abuse an old bug from pre-1.1
# days.  This bug involved a CGI script distributed as a part of Apache.
# By uncommenting these lines you can redirect these attacks to a logging
# script on phf.apache.org.  Or, you can record them yourself, using the script
# support/phf_abuse_log.cgi.
#
#<Location /cgi-bin/phf*>
```

```
#     Deny from all
#     ErrorDocument 403 http://phf.apache.org/phf_abuse_log.cgi
#</Location>


#
# Proxy Server directives. Uncomment the following lines to
# enable the proxy server:
#
#<IfModule mod_proxy.c>
#ProxyRequests On
#
#<Directory proxy:*>
#    Order deny,allow
#    Deny from all
#    Allow from .your_domain.com
#</Directory>


#
# Enable/disable the handling of HTTP/1.1 "Via:" headers.
# ("Full" adds the server version; "Block" removes all outgoing Via: headers)
# Set to one of: Off | On | Full | Block
#
#ProxyVia On


#
# To enable the cache as well, edit and uncomment the following lines:
# (no cacheing without CacheRoot)
#
#CacheRoot "@@ServerRoot@@/proxy"
#CacheSize 5
#CacheGcInterval 4
#CacheMaxExpire 24
#CacheLastModifiedFactor 0.1
#CacheDefaultExpire 1
#NoCache a_domain.com another_domain.edu joes.garage_sale.com

#</IfModule>
# End of proxy directives.

### Section 3: Virtual Hosts
#
# VirtualHost: If you want to maintain multiple domains/hostnames on your
# machine you can setup VirtualHost containers for them. Most configurations
# use only name-based virtual hosts so the server doesn't need to worry about
# IP addresses. This is indicated by the asterisks in the directives below.
#
# Please see the documentation at <URL:http://www.apache.org/docs/vhosts/>
# for further details before you try to setup virtual hosts.
#
```

```
# You may use the command line option '-S' to verify your virtual host
# configuration.

#
# Use name-based virtual hosting.
#
#NameVirtualHost *

#
# VirtualHost example:
# Almost any Apache directive may go into a VirtualHost container.
# The first VirtualHost section is used for requests without a known
# server name.
#
#<VirtualHost *>
#     ServerAdmin webmaster@dummy-host.example.com
#     DocumentRoot /www/docs/dummy-host.example.com
#     ServerName dummy-host.example.com
#     ErrorLog logs/dummy-host.example.com-error_log
#     CustomLog logs/dummy-host.example.com-access_log common
#</VirtualHost>
```

HTTPD-WIN.CONF

```
#
# Based upon the NCSA server configuration files originally by Rob McCool.
#
# This is the main Apache server configuration file.  It contains the
# configuration directives that give the server its instructions.
# See <URL:http://www.apache.org/docs/> for detailed information about
# the directives.
#
# Do NOT simply read the instructions in here without understanding
# what they do.  They're here only as hints or reminders.  If you are unsure
# consult the online docs. You have been warned.
#
# The configuration directives are grouped into three basic sections:
#  1. Directives that control the operation of the Apache server process as a
#     whole (the 'global environment').
#  2. Directives that define the parameters of the 'main' or 'default' server,
#     which responds to requests that aren't handled by a virtual host.
#     These directives also provide default values for the settings
#     of all virtual hosts.
#  3. Settings for virtual hosts, which allow Web requests to be sent to
#     different IP addresses or hostnames and have them handled by the
#     same Apache server process.
#
```

```
# Configuration and logfile names: If the filenames you specify for many
# of the server's control files begin with "/" (or "drive:/" for Win32), the
# server will use that explicit path.  If the filenames do *not* begin
# with "/", the value of ServerRoot is prepended -- so "logs/foo.log"
# with ServerRoot set to "/usr/local/apache" will be interpreted by the
# server as "/usr/local/apache/logs/foo.log".
#
# NOTE: Where filenames are specified, you must use forward slashes
# instead of backslashes (e.g., "c:/apache" instead of "c:\apache").
# If a drive letter is omitted, the drive on which Apache.exe is located
# will be used by default.  It is recommended that you always supply
# an explicit drive letter in absolute paths, however, to avoid
# confusion.
#

### Section 1: Global Environment
#
# The directives in this section affect the overall operation of Apache,
# such as the number of concurrent requests it can handle or where it
# can find its configuration files.
#

#
# ServerRoot: The top of the directory tree under which the server's
# configuration, error, and log files are kept.
#
# Do NOT add a slash at the end of the directory path.
#
ServerRoot "@@ServerRoot@@"
#
# PidFile: The file in which the server should record its process
# identification number when it starts.
#
PidFile logs/httpd.pid

#
# ScoreBoardFile: File used to store internal server process information.
# Not all architectures require this.  But if yours does (you'll know because
# this file will be  created when you run Apache) then you *must* ensure that
# no two invocations of Apache share the same scoreboard file.
#
#ScoreBoardFile logs/apache_status

#
# Timeout: The number of seconds before receives and sends time out.
#
Timeout 300

#
```

```
# KeepAlive: Whether or not to allow persistent connections (more than
# one request per connection). Set to "Off" to deactivate.
#
KeepAlive On

#
# MaxKeepAliveRequests: The maximum number of requests to allow
# during a persistent connection. Set to 0 to allow an unlimited amount.
# We reccomend you leave this number high, for maximum performance.
#
MaxKeepAliveRequests 100

#
# KeepAliveTimeout: Number of seconds to wait for the next request from the
# same client on the same connection.
#
KeepAliveTimeout 15

#
# Apache on Win32 always creates one child process to handle requests.  If it
# dies, another child process is created automatically.  Within the child
# process multiple threads handle incoming requests.  The next two
# directives control the behaviour of the threads and processes.
#

#
# MaxRequestsPerChild: the number of requests each child process is
# allowed to process before the child dies.  The child will exit so
# as to avoid problems after prolonged use when Apache (and maybe the
# libraries it uses) leak memory or other resources.  On most systems, this
# isn't really needed, but a few (such as Solaris) do have notable leaks
# in the libraries.  For Win32, set this value to zero (unlimited)
# unless advised otherwise.
#
MaxRequestsPerChild 0

#
# Number of concurrent threads (i.e., requests) the server will allow.
# Set this value according to the responsiveness of the server (more
# requests active at once means they're all handled more slowly) and
# the amount of system resources you'll allow the server to consume.
#
ThreadsPerChild 250

#

# Listen: Allows you to bind Apache to specific IP addresses and/or
# ports, in addition to the default. See also the <VirtualHost>
# directive.
```

```
#
#Listen 3000
#Listen 12.34.56.78:80


#
# BindAddress: You can support virtual hosts with this option. This directive
# is used to tell the server which IP address to listen to. It can either
# contain "*", an IP address, or a fully qualified Internet domain name.
# See also the <VirtualHost> and Listen directives.
#
#BindAddress *


#
# Dynamic Shared Object (DSO) Support
#
# To be able to use the functionality of a module which was built as a DSO you
# have to place corresponding `LoadModule' lines at this location so the
# directives contained in it are actually available _before_ they are used.
# Please read the file README.DSO in the Apache 1.3 distribution for more
# details about the DSO mechanism and run `apache -l' for the list of already
# built-in (statically linked and thus always available) modules in your Apache
# binary.
#
# Note: The order in which modules are loaded is important.  Don't change
# the order below without expert advice.
#
#LoadModule auth_anon_module modules/mod_auth_anon.so
#LoadModule auth_dbm_module modules/mod_auth_dbm.so
#LoadModule auth_digest_module modules/mod_auth_digest.so
#LoadModule cern_meta_module modules/mod_cern_meta.so
#LoadModule dav_module modules/mod_dav.so
#LoadModule dav_fs_module modules/mod_dav_fs.so
#LoadModule expires_module modules/mod_expires.so
#LoadModule file_cache_module modules/mod_file_cache.so
#LoadModule headers_module modules/mod_headers.so
#LoadModule info_module modules/mod_info.so
#LoadModule proxy_module modules/mod_proxy.so
#LoadModule rewrite_module modules/mod_rewrite.so
#LoadModule speling_module modules/mod_speling.so
#LoadModule status_module modules/mod_status.so
#LoadModule usertrack_module modules/mod_usertrack.so


### Section 2: 'Main' server configuration
#
# The directives in this section set up the values used by the 'main'
# server, which responds to any requests that aren't handled by a
# <VirtualHost> definition.  These values also provide defaults for
# any <VirtualHost> containers you may define later in the file.
#
```

```
# All of these directives may appear inside <VirtualHost> containers,
# in which case these default settings will be overridden for the
# virtual host being defined.
#


#
# If your ServerType directive (set earlier in the 'Global Environment'
# section) is set to "inetd", the next few directives don't have any
# effect since their settings are defined by the inetd configuration.
# Skip ahead to the ServerAdmin directive.
#


#
# Port: The port to which the standalone server listens.
#
Port 80


#
# ServerAdmin: Your address, where problems with the server should be
# e-mailed.  This address appears on some server-generated pages, such
# as error documents.  e.g. admin@your-domain.com
#
#ServerAdmin @@ServerAdmin@@


#
# ServerName allows you to set a host name which is sent back to clients for
# your server if it's different than the one the program would get (i.e., use
# "www" instead of the host's real name).
#
# 127.0.0.1 is the TCP/IP local loop-back address. Your machine
# always knows itself by this address. If you machine is connected to
# a network, you should change this to be your machine's name
#
# Note: You cannot just invent host names and hope they work. The name you
# define here must be a valid DNS name for your host. If you don't understand
# this, ask your network administrator.
# If your host doesn't have a registered DNS name, enter its IP address here
# You will have to access it by its address (e.g., http://123.45.67.89/)
# anyway, and this will make redirections work in a sensible way.
#
#ServerName @@ServerName@@
#
# DocumentRoot: The directory out of which you will serve your
# documents. By default, all requests are taken from this directory, but
# symbolic links and aliases may be used to point to other locations.
#
DocumentRoot "@@ServerRoot@@/htdocs"


#
```

```
# Each directory to which Apache has access, can be configured with respect
# to which services and features are allowed and/or disabled in that
# directory (and its subdirectories).
#
# First, we configure the "default" to be a very restrictive set of
# permissions.
#
<Directory />
    Options FollowSymLinks
    AllowOverride None
</Directory>
#
# Note that from this point forward you must specifically allow
# particular features to be enabled - so if something's not working as
# you might expect, make sure that you have specifically enabled it
# below.
#


#
# This should be changed to whatever you set DocumentRoot to.
#
<Directory "@@ServerRoot@@/htdocs">

#
# This may also be "None", "All", or any combination of "Indexes",
# "Includes", "FollowSymLinks", "ExecCGI", or "MultiViews".
#
# Note that "MultiViews" must be named *explicitly* --- "Options All"
# doesn't give it to you.
#
    Options Indexes FollowSymLinks MultiViews

#
# This controls which options the .htaccess files in directories can
# override. Can also be "All", or any combination of "Options", "FileInfo",
# "AuthConfig", and "Limit"
#
    AllowOverride None

#
# Controls who can get stuff from this server.
#
    Order allow,deny
    Allow from all
</Directory>

#
# UserDir: The name of the directory which is appended onto a user's home
# directory if a ~user request is received.
```

```
#
# Under Win32, we do not currently try to determine the home directory of
# a Windows login, so a format such as that below needs to be used.  See
# the UserDir documentation for details.
UserDir "@@ServerRoot@@/users/"


#
# DirectoryIndex: Name of the file or files to use as a pre-written HTML
# directory index.  Separate multiple entries with spaces.
#
DirectoryIndex index.html


#
# AccessFileName: The name of the file to look for in each directory"
# for access control information.
#
AccessFileName .htaccess


#
# The following lines prevent .htaccess files from being viewed by
# Web clients.  Since .htaccess files often contain authorization
# information, access is disallowed for security reasons.  Comment
# these lines out if you want Web visitors to see the contents of
# .htaccess files.  If you change the AccessFileName directive above,
# be sure to make the corresponding changes here.
#
<Files .htaccess>
    Order allow,deny
    Deny from all
</Files>


#
# CacheNegotiatedDocs: By default, Apache sends "Pragma: no-cache" with each
# document that was negotiated on the basis of content. This asks proxy
# servers not to cache the document. Uncommenting the following line disables
# this behavior, and proxies will be allowed to cache the documents.
#
#CacheNegotiatedDocs


#
# UseCanonicalName:  (new for 1.3)  With this setting turned on, whenever
# Apache needs to construct a self-referencing URL (a URL that refers back
# to the server the response is coming from) it will use ServerName and
# Port to form a "canonical" name.  With this setting off, Apache will
# use the hostname:port that the client supplied, when possible.  This
# also affects SERVER_NAME and SERVER_PORT in CGI scripts.
#
UseCanonicalName On
```

```
#
# TypesConfig describes where the mime.types file (or equivalent) is
# to be found.
#
TypesConfig conf/mime.types


#
# DefaultType is the default MIME type the server will use for a document
# if it cannot otherwise determine one, such as from filename extensions.
# If your server contains mostly text or HTML documents, "text/plain" is
# a good value.  If most of your content is binary, such as applications
# or images, you may want to use "application/octet-stream" instead to
# keep browsers from trying to display binary files as though they are
# text
#
DefaultType text/plain


#
# The mod_mime_magic module allows the server to use various hints from the
# contents of the file itself to determine its type.  The MIMEMagicFile
# directive tells the module where the hint definitions are located
# mod_mime_magic is not part of the default server (you have to add
# it yourself with a LoadModule [see the DSO paragraph in the 'Global
# Environment' section], or recompile the server and include mod_mime_magic
# as part of the configuration), so it's enclosed in an <IfModule> container.
# This means that the MIMEMagicFile directive will only be processed if the
# module is part of the server.
#
<IfModule mod_mime_magic.c>
    MIMEMagicFile conf/magic
</IfModule>


#
# HostnameLookups: Log the names of clients or just their IP addresses
# e.g., www.apache.org (on) or 204.62.129.132 (off).
# The default is off because it'd be overall better for the net if people
# had to knowingly turn this feature on, since enabling it means that
# each client request will result in AT LEAST one lookup request to the
# nameserver.
#
HostnameLookups Off


#
# ErrorLog: The location of the error log file.
# If you do not specify an ErrorLog directive within a <VirtualHost>
# container, error messages relating to that virtual host will be
# logged here.  If you *do* define an error logfile for a <VirtualHost>
# container, that host's errors will be logged there and not here.
#
```

```
ErrorLog logs/error.log

#
# LogLevel: Control the number of messages logged to the error.log.
# Possible values include: debug, info, notice, warn, error, crit,
# alert, emerg.
#
LogLevel warn

#
# The following directives define some format nicknames for use with
# a CustomLog directive (see below).
#
LogFormat "%h %l %u %t \"%r\" %>s %b \"%{Referer}i\" \"%{User-Agent}i\"" combined
LogFormat "%h %l %u %t \"%r\" %>s %b" common
LogFormat "%{Referer}i -> %U" referer
LogFormat "%{User-agent}i" agent

#
# The location and format of the access logfile (Common Logfile Format).
# If you do not define any access logfiles within a <VirtualHost>
# container, they will be logged here.  Contrariwise, if you *do*
# define per-<VirtualHost> access logfiles, transactions will be
# logged therein and *not* in this file.
#
CustomLog logs/access.log common

#
# If you would like to have agent and referrer logfiles, uncomment the
# following directives.
#
#CustomLog logs/referer.log referer
#CustomLog logs/agent.log agent

#
# If you prefer a single logfile with access, agent, and referrer information
# (Combined Logfile Format) you can use the following directive.
#
#CustomLog logs/access.log combined

#
# Optionally add a line containing the server version and virtual host
# name to server-generated pages (error documents, FTP directory listings,
# mod_status and mod_info output etc., but not CGI generated documents).
# Set to "EMail" to also include a mailto: link to the ServerAdmin.
# Set to one of:  On | Off | Email
#
ServerSignature On
```

```
#
# Aliases: Add here as many aliases as you need (with no limit). The format is
# Alias fakename realname
#
# Note that if you include a trailing / on fakename then the server will
# require it to be present in the URL.  So "/icons" isn't aliased in this
# example, only "/icons/"..
#
Alias /icons/ "@@ServerRoot@@/icons/"


#
# ScriptAlias: This controls which directories contain server scripts.
# ScriptAliases are essentially the same as Aliases, except that
# documents in the realname directory are treated as applications and
# run by the server when requested rather than as documents sent to the client.
# The same rules about trailing "/" apply to ScriptAlias directives as to
# Alias.
#
ScriptAlias /cgi-bin/ "@@ServerRoot@@/cgi-bin/"


#
# "@@ServerRoot@@/cgi-bin" should be changed to whatever your ScriptAliased
# CGI directory exists, if you have that configured.
#
<Directory "@@ServerRoot@@/cgi-bin">
    AllowOverride None
    Options None
</Directory>


#
# Redirect allows you to tell clients about documents which used to exist in
# your server's namespace, but do not anymore. This allows you to tell the
# clients where to look for the relocated document.
# Format: Redirect old-URI new-URL
#


#
# Directives controlling the display of server-generated directory listings.
#


#
# FancyIndexing is whether you want fancy directory indexing or standard
#
IndexOptions FancyIndexing


#
# AddIcon* directives tell the server which icon to show for different
# files or filename extensions.  These are only displayed for
# FancyIndexed directories.
```

```
#
AddIconByEncoding (CMP,/icons/compressed.gif) x-compress x-gzip

AddIconByType (TXT,/icons/text.gif) text/*
AddIconByType (IMG,/icons/image2.gif) image/*
AddIconByType (SND,/icons/sound2.gif) audio/*
AddIconByType (VID,/icons/movie.gif) video/*

AddIcon /icons/binary.gif .bin .exe
AddIcon /icons/binhex.gif .hqx
AddIcon /icons/tar.gif .tar
AddIcon /icons/world2.gif .wrl .wrl.gz .vrml .vrm .iv
AddIcon /icons/compressed.gif .Z .z .tgz .gz .zip
AddIcon /icons/a.gif .ps .ai .eps
AddIcon /icons/layout.gif .html .shtml .htm .pdf
AddIcon /icons/text.gif .txt
AddIcon /icons/c.gif .c
AddIcon /icons/p.gif .pl .py
AddIcon /icons/f.gif .for
AddIcon /icons/dvi.gif .dvi
AddIcon /icons/uuencoded.gif .uu
AddIcon /icons/script.gif .conf .sh .shar .csh .ksh .tcl
AddIcon /icons/tex.gif .tex
AddIcon /icons/bomb.gif core

AddIcon /icons/back.gif ..
AddIcon /icons/hand.right.gif README
AddIcon /icons/folder.gif ^^DIRECTORY^^
AddIcon /icons/blank.gif ^^BLANKICON^^

#
# DefaultIcon is which icon to show for files which do not have an icon
# explicitly set.
#
DefaultIcon /icons/unknown.gif

#
# AddDescription allows you to place a short description after a file in
# server-generated indexes.  These are only displayed for FancyIndexed
# directories.
# Format: AddDescription "description" filename
#
#AddDescription "GZIP compressed document" .gz
#AddDescription "tar archive" .tar
#AddDescription "GZIP compressed tar archive" .tgz

#
# ReadmeName is the name of the README file the server will look for by
# default, and append to directory listings.
```

```
#
# HeaderName is the name of a file which should be prepended to
# directory indexes.
#
# The server will first look for name.html and include it if found.
# If name.html doesn't exist, the server will then look for name.txt
# and include it as plaintext if found.
#
ReadmeName README
HeaderName HEADER


#
# IndexIgnore is a set of filenames which directory indexing should ignore
# and not include in the listing.  Shell-style wildcarding is permitted.
#
IndexIgnore .??* *~ *# HEADER* README* RCS CVS *,v *,t


#
# AddEncoding allows you to have certain browsers (Mosaic/X 2.1+) uncompress
# information on the fly. Note: Not all browsers support this.
# Despite the name similarity, the following Add* directives have nothing
# to do with the FancyIndexing customisation directives above.
#
AddEncoding x-compress Z
AddEncoding x-gzip gz tgz


#
# AddLanguage allows you to specify the language of a document. You can
# then use content negotiation to give a browser a file in a language
# it can understand
#
# Note 1: The suffix does not have to be the same as the language
# keyword --- those with documents in Polish (whose net-standard
# language code is pl) may wish to use "AddLanguage pl .po" to
# avoid the ambiguity with the common suffix for perl scripts.
#
# Note 2: The example entries below illustrate that in quite
# some cases the two character 'Language' abbreviation is not
# identical to the two character 'Country' code for its country,
# E.g. 'Danmark/dk' versus 'Danish/da'.
#
# Note 3: In the case of 'ltz' we violate the RFC by using a three char
# specifier. But there is 'work in progress' to fix this and get
# the reference data for rfc1766 cleaned up.
#
# Danish (da) - Dutch (nl) - English (en) - Estonian (et)
# French (fr) - German (de) - Greek-Modern (el)
# Italian (it) - Norwegian (no) - Korean (kr)
# Portugese (pt) - Luxembourgeois* (ltz)
```

```
# Spanish (es) - Swedish (sv) - Catalan (ca) - Czech(cz)
# Polish (pl) - Brazilian Portuguese (pt-br) - Japanese (ja)
# Russian (ru)
#
AddLanguage da .dk
AddLanguage nl .nl
AddLanguage en .en
AddLanguage et .et
AddLanguage fr .fr
AddLanguage de .de
AddLanguage el .el
AddLanguage it .it
AddLanguage ja .ja
AddLanguage pl .po
AddLanguage kr .kr
AddLanguage pt .pt
AddLanguage no .no
AddLanguage pt-br .pt-br
AddLanguage ltz .ltz
AddLanguage ca .ca
AddLanguage es .es
AddLanguage sv .se
AddLanguage cz .cz
AddLanguage ru .ru
AddLanguage tw .tw
AddLanguage zh-tw .tw


# LanguagePriority allows you to give precedence to some languages
# in case of a tie during content negotiation.
#
# Just list the languages in decreasing order of preference. We have
# more or less alphabetized them here. You probably want to change this.
#
LanguagePriority en da nl et fr de el it ja kr no pl pt pt-br ru ltz ca es sv tw

# Specify a default charset for all pages sent out. This is
# always a good idea and opens the door for future internationalisation
# of your web site, should you ever want it. Specifying it as
# a default does little harm; as the standard dictates that a page
# is in iso-8859-1 (latin1) unless specified otherwise i.e. you
# are merely stating the obvious. There are also some security
# reasons in browsers, related to javascript and URL parsing
# which encourage you to always set a default char set.
#
AddDefaultCharset ISO-8859-1


#
# Commonly used filename extensions to character sets. You probably
# want to avoid clashes with the language extensions, unless you
```

```
# are good at carefully testing your setup after each change.
# See ftp://ftp.isi.edu/in-notes/iana/assignments/character-sets for
# the official list of charset names and their respective RFCs
#
AddCharset ISO-8859-1   .iso8859-1 .latin1
AddCharset ISO-8859-2   .iso8859-2 .latin2 .cen
AddCharset ISO-8859-3   .iso8859-3 .latin3
AddCharset ISO-8859-4   .iso8859-4 .latin4
AddCharset ISO-8859-5   .iso8859-5 .latin5 .cyr .iso-ru
AddCharset ISO-8859-6   .iso8859-6 .latin6 .arb
AddCharset ISO-8859-7   .iso8859-7 .latin7 .grk
AddCharset ISO-8859-8   .iso8859-8 .latin8 .heb
AddCharset ISO-8859-9   .iso8859-9 .latin9 .trk
AddCharset ISO-2022-JP .iso2022-jp .jis
AddCharset ISO-2022-KR .iso2022-kr .kis
AddCharset ISO-2022-CN .iso2022-cn .cis
AddCharset Big5         .Big5      .big5
# For russian, more than one charset is used (depends on client, mostly):
AddCharset WINDOWS-1251 .cp-1251    .win-1251
AddCharset CP866        .cp866
AddCharset KOI8-r       .koi8-r .koi8-ru
AddCharset KOI8-ru      .koi8-uk .ua
AddCharset ISO-10646-UCS-2 .ucs2
AddCharset ISO-10646-UCS-4 .ucs4
AddCharset UTF-8        .utf8

# The set below does not map to a specific (iso) standard
# but works on a fairly wide range of browsers. Note that
# capitalization actually matters (it should not, but it
# does for some browsers).
#
# See ftp://ftp.isi.edu/in-notes/iana/assignments/character-sets
# for a list of sorts. But browsers support few.
#
AddCharset GB2312       .gb2312 .gb
AddCharset utf-7        .utf7
AddCharset utf-8        .utf8
AddCharset big5         .big5 .b5
AddCharset EUC-TW       .euc-tw
AddCharset EUC-JP       .euc-jp
AddCharset EUC-KR       .euc-kr
AddCharset shift_jis    .sjis


#
# AddType allows you to tweak mime.types without actually editing it, or to
# make certain files to be certain types.
#
# For example, the PHP3 module (not part of the Apache distribution)
# will typically use:
```

```
#
#AddType application/x-httpd-php3 .phtml
#AddType application/x-httpd-php3-source .phps
AddType application/x-tar .tgz

#
# AddHandler allows you to map certain file extensions to "handlers",
# actions unrelated to filetype. These can be either built into the server
# or added with the Action command (see below)
#
# If you want to use server side includes, or CGI outside
# ScriptAliased directories, uncomment the following lines.
#
# To use CGI scripts:
#
#AddHandler cgi-script .cgi

#
# To use server-parsed HTML files
#
#AddType text/html .shtml
#AddHandler server-parsed .shtml

#
# Uncomment the following line to enable Apache's send-asis HTTP file
# feature
#
#AddHandler send-as-is asis

#
# If you wish to use server-parsed imagemap files, use
#
#AddHandler imap-file map

#
# To enable type maps, you might want to use
#
#AddHandler type-map var

#
# Action lets you define media types that will execute a script whenever
# a matching file is called. This eliminates the need for repeated URL
# pathnames for oft-used CGI file processors.
# Format: Action media/type /cgi-script/location
# Format: Action handler-name /cgi-script/location
#

#
# MetaDir: specifies the name of the directory in which Apache can find
```

```
# meta information files. These files contain additional HTTP headers
# to include when sending the document
#
#MetaDir .web


#
# MetaSuffix: specifies the file name suffix for the file containing the
# meta information.
#
#MetaSuffix .meta


#
# Customizable error response (Apache style)
#   these come in three flavors
#
#     1) plain text
#ErrorDocument 500 "The server made a boo boo."
#
#     2) local redirects
#ErrorDocument 404 /missing.html
# to redirect to local URL /missing.html
#ErrorDocument 404 "/cgi-bin/missing_handlder.pl"
#     i.e. any string which starts with a '/' and has
#     no spaces.
#  N.B.: You can redirect to a script or a document using server-side-includes.
#
#     3) external redirects
#ErrorDocument 402 http://some.other_server.com/subscription_info.html
#     i.e. any string whichis a valid  URL.
#  N.B.: Many of the environment variables associated with the original
#  request will *not* be available to such a script.
#
#     4) borderline case
#ErrorDocument 402 "http://some.other_server.com/info.html is the place to look"
#     treated as case '1' as it has spaces and thus is not a valid URL
#
# The following directives disable keepalives and HTTP header flushes.
# The first directive disables it for Netscape 2.x and browsers which
# spoof it. There are known problems with these.
# The second directive is for Microsoft Internet Explorer 4.0b2
# which has a broken HTTP/1.1 implementation and does not properly
# support keepalive when it is used on 301 or 302 (redirect) responses.
#
BrowserMatch "Mozilla/2" nokeepalive
BrowserMatch "MSIE 4\.0b2;" nokeepalive downgrade-1.0 force-response-1.0


# The following directive disables HTTP/1.1 responses to browsers which
# are in violation of the HTTP/1.0 spec by not being able to grok a
# basic 1.1 response.
```

```
#
BrowserMatch "RealPlayer 4\.0" force-response-1.0
BrowserMatch "Java/1\.0" force-response-1.0
BrowserMatch "JDK/1\.0" force-response-1.0


#
# Allow server status reports, with the URL of http://servername/server-status
# Change the ".@@DomainName@@" to match your domain to enable.
#
#<Location /server-status>
#    SetHandler server-status
#    Order deny,allow
#    Deny from all
#    Allow from .@@DomainName@@
#</Location>


#
# Allow remote server configuration reports, with the URL of
#   http://servername/server-info (requires that mod_info.c be loaded).
# Change the ".your_domain.com" to match your domain to enable.
#
#<Location /server-info>
#    SetHandler server-info
#    Order deny,allow
#    Deny from all
#    Allow from .@@DomainName@@
#</Location>


# There have been reports of people trying to abuse an old bug from pre-1.1
# days.  This bug involved a CGI script distributed as a part of Apache.
# By uncommenting these lines you can redirect these attacks to a logging
# script on phf.apache.org.  Or, you can record them yourself, using the script
# support/phf_abuse_log.cgi.
#
#<Location /cgi-bin/phf*>
#    Deny from all
#    ErrorDocument 403 http://phf.apache.org/phf_abuse_log.cgi
#</Location>


#
# Proxy Server directives. Uncomment the following line to
# enable the proxy server:
#
#ProxyRequests On


#
# Enable/disable the handling of HTTP/1.1 "Via:" headers.
```

```
# ("Full" adds the server version; "Block" removes all outgoing Via: headers)
# Set to one of: Off | On | Full | Block
#
#ProxyVia On


#
# To enable the cache as well, edit and uncomment the following lines:
# (no cacheing without CacheRoot)
#
#CacheRoot "@@ServerRoot@@/proxy"
#CacheSize 5
#CacheGcInterval 4
#CacheMaxExpire 24
#CacheLastModifiedFactor 0.1
#CacheDefaultExpire 1
#NoCache a_domain.com another_domain.edu joes.garage_sale.com


### Section 3: Virtual Hosts
#
# VirtualHost: If you want to maintain multiple domains/hostnames on your
# machine you can setup VirtualHost containers for them. Most configurations
# use only name-based virtual hosts so the server doesn't need to worry about
# IP addresses. This is indicated by the asterisks in the directives below.
#
# Please see the documentation at <URL:http://www.apache.org/docs/vhosts/>
# for further details before you try to setup virtual hosts.
#
# You may use the command line option '-S' to verify your virtual host
# configuration.


#
# Use name-based virtual hosting.
#
#NameVirtualHost *


#
# VirtualHost example:
# Almost any Apache directive may go into a VirtualHost container.
# The first VirtualHost section is used for requests without a known
# server name.
#
#<VirtualHost *>
#     ServerAdmin webmaster@dummy-host.example.com
#     DocumentRoot /www/docs/dummy-host.example.com
#     ServerName dummy-host.example.com
#     ErrorLog logs/dummy-host.example.com-error_log
#     CustomLog logs/dummy-host.example.com-access_log common
#</VirtualHost>
```

HIGHPERFORMANCE-STD.CONF

```
# Ha, you're reading this config file looking for the easy way out!
# "how do I make my apache server go really really fast??"
# Well you could start by reading the htdocs/manual/misc/perf-tuning.html
# page.  But, we'll give you a head start.
#
# This config file is small, it is probably not what you'd expect on a
# full featured internet webserver with multiple users.  But it's
# probably a good starting point for any folks interested in testing
# performance.
#
# To run this config you'll need to use something like:
#     httpd -f @@ServerRoot@@/conf/highperformance.conf

Port 80
ServerRoot @@ServerRoot@@
DocumentRoot @@ServerRoot@@/htdocs

User  nobody
# If you're not on Linux, you'll probably need to change Group
Group nobody

<IfModule prefork.c>
MaxClients        8
StartServers      5
MinSpareServers   5
MaxSpareServers 10
</IfModule>

<IfModule threaded.c>
MaxClients        8
StartServers      3
MinSpareThreads   5
MaxSpareThreads 10
ThreadsPerChild 25
</IfModule>

# Assume no memory leaks at all
MaxRequestsPerChild 0

# it's always nice to know the server has started
ErrorLog logs/error_log

# Some benchmarks require logging, which is a good requirement.  Uncomment
# this if you need logging.
#TransferLog logs/access_log
```

```
<Directory />
    # The server can be made to avoid following symbolic links,
    # to make security simpler. However, this takes extra CPU time,
    # so we will just let it follow symlinks.
    Options FollowSymLinks

    # Don't check for .htaccess files in each directory - they slow
    # things down
    AllowOverride None

    # If this was a real internet server you'd probably want to
    # uncomment these:
    #order deny,allow
    #deny from all
</Directory>

# If this was a real internet server you'd probably want to uncomment this:
#<Directory "@@ServerRoot@@/htdocs">
#    order allow,deny
#    allow from all
#</Directory>

# OK that's enough hints.  Read the documentation if you want more.
```

Index

B

D

I

O

P

T

▼ U

X

INTERNATIONAL CONTACT INFORMATION

AUSTRALIA
McGraw-Hill Book Company Australia Pty. Ltd.
TEL +61-2-9417-9899
FAX +61-2-9417-5687
http://www.mcgraw-hill.com.au
books-it_sydney@mcgraw-hill.com

CANADA
McGraw-Hill Ryerson Ltd.
TEL +905-430-5000
FAX +905-430-5020
http://www.mcgrawhill.ca

GREECE, MIDDLE EAST,
NORTHERN AFRICA
McGraw-Hill Hellas
TEL +30-1-656-0990-3-4
FAX +30-1-654-5525

MEXICO (Also serving Latin America)
McGraw-Hill Interamericana Editores S.A. de C.V.
TEL +525-117-1583
FAX +525-117-1589
http://www.mcgraw-hill.com.mx
fernando_castellanos@mcgraw-hill.com

SINGAPORE (Serving Asia)
McGraw-Hill Book Company
TEL +65-863-1580
FAX +65-862-3354
http://www.mcgraw-hill.com.sg
mghasia@mcgraw-hill.com

SOUTH AFRICA
McGraw-Hill South Africa
TEL +27-11-622-7512
FAX +27-11-622-9045
robyn_swanepoel@mcgraw-hill.com

UNITED KINGDOM & EUROPE
(Excluding Southern Europe)
McGraw-Hill Education Europe
TEL +44-1-628-502500
FAX +44-1-628-770224
http://www.mcgraw-hill.co.uk
computing_neurope@mcgraw-hill.com

ALL OTHER INQUIRIES Contact:
Osborne/McGraw-Hill
TEL +1-510-549-6600
FAX +1-510-883-7600
http://www.osborne.com
omg_international@mcgraw-hill.com